PREFACE: MARXIST CLARITY IN TIMES OF CONFUSION AND DESPAIR

There is no doubt that we are currently living in politically confusing times. Nihilism and despair reign throughout American society, with no shortage of reactionary and irrationalist trends seductively posing as opposition to the hegemonic liberal order that provides no solutions to the problems facing humanity. Instead, it promises us more war and global conflict, while the dispossessed majority of the world struggles to survive under conditions of economic insecurity. There is, of course, also reason to be optimistic — socialist ideas still spread among the youth, and the labor movement is slowly gaining ground in new industries. The possibility of a rebirth of mass socialist politics remains, even if much of its potential is squandered. Still, our historical moment offers few easy answers for those of us looking for alternatives to the present state of things.

The current political landscape is the product of a chaotic series of events that began to unfold in 2020. First was the defeat of Bernie Sanders at the hand of the Democratic National Convention, and his acquiescence to the Biden administration saw the US left almost overnight without a sense of direction or purpose. The cozy and grandfatherly Vermont Senator — who had filled progressive-minded people of the nation with hope for, if not a break from capitalism, at least a functional healthcare system — was no longer a force of insurgency against the elites who ran the DNC. This disorientation came in sync with an even greater historical force, the global COVID-19 Pandemic, an event that filled the American people with fear and paranoia. Anti-police demonstrations blew up in the heat of the pandemic, then fizzled out, partly due to the NGO-ification of dissent as well as the failure of the radical left to cohere any kind of program for an alternative to the prevailing regime. Then, the center of political gravity became focused on a tumultuous presidential election between Joe Biden and Donald Trump.

The tumult of the election peaked on January 6th, 2021, with what was ultimately a pathetic and poorly-planned attempted putsch on the part of an insurgent MAGA movement. By then, the energy of populist opposition was in the hands of the irrationalist right. Right wing demagogues like Tucker Carlson framed themselves as the enemies of the the ambiguously defined "elite." Meanwhile, Sanders and his allies in the Squad seemed dedicated to proving themselves the most loyal opposition that national unifier Biden could possibly have.

Then came the war in Ukraine. Putin launching his invasion of Ukraine led to a wave of war fever amongst American liberals and much of the left. The argument went that Putin had to be resisted in the name of anti-fascism; in this case, that meant the US military-industrial-complex was now a great force of anti-fascist armed struggle. The left scrambled to develop a coherent response to the war, which was in essence the intensification of a conflict stretching back to the US-backed regime change operation of 2014.

Meanwhile, the far right positioned itself as the most prominent voice of opposition to US intervention, framing the weaponization of Ukraine against Russia as "World War Woke" — a clash of civilizations between Russia, a strong Christian nation helmed by a conservative patriarch, and Ukraine, a country that was simultaneously a den of both Nazis and LGBT feminists which stood for the World Economic Forum and the "Great Reset." At the same time, the American right intensified the cul-

FIGHT THE CONSTITUTION

FIGHT THE CONSTITUTION

For a Democratic Socialist Republic

Selected Writings from the Marxist Unity Group

COSMONAUT PRESS

Published by Cosmonaut Press.
Cosmonaut Press is an imprint of Cosmonaut, Inc.

ISBN: 978-1-953273-07-9

Interior Design: Tobias Houlgate
Cover Design: Amanda Levi

CONTENTS

ture war it had always been brewing with attacks on sexual minorities and racial justice education; basically anything vaguely defined as "woke." As I write this in Florida, Governor Ron DeSantis and the Republican-dominated state legislature have passed laws that politicize the simple act of going to the bathroom in a blatant attempt to target the transgender community, a favorite scapegoat of the new right.

The response of the Democrats to these attacks on liberty and free speech by the new right is predictable — protect the system at any cost. And of course, the system will ultimately remain as strong as ever, partly thanks to how despicable the right wing opposition is. While the war in Ukraine does create division, the war drive over China has bipartisan support, giving both parties a common project to unite over. All the contradictions of the global capitalist system point towards conflict with China, a conflict with the potential for economic dislocation that the Ukraine war will look like a mere preview of. Hope for stability, for a return to normal, is a dead letter. The United States and the world is entering a phase of conflict and crisis, and the current state of political confusion of the left will only intensify absent a Marxist intervention that can provide clarity and strategic direction.

The reader presented here hopes to be *a part* of such an intervention in these confusing times, an attempt to lay out what a possible strategy for a disoriented left would look like. Cosmonaut Magazine was founded in 2018 by myself and a group of individuals influenced by works like Mike Macnair's *Revolutionary Strategy* and Lars Lih's *Lenin Rediscovered*[1] (among many others) as well as our own experience organizing in the US left. I myself was a member of the Industrial Workers of the World for some time, and my own negative experiences with various Leninist sects (as well as the dead-end vague populism of Occupy)

1 Audiobooks of these works can be found on the Cosmonaut website: https://cosmonautmag.com/category/audio-books/

left me susceptible to the infamous "infantile disorder" of Left Communism. I eventually founded a small sect known as the Communist League of Tampa, which was essentially a glorified reading group that did occasional propaganda work at strikes and demonstrations. Eventually it fell apart, yet the rise of the Sanders campaign and the DSA produced new political opportunities which I was initially hostile to. I caved in and joined DSA anyway, as my own studies of history and Marxism (as well as frustration with the political aimlessness and nihilism of the milieu I was part of) led me away from my ultra-leftism. In retrospect I can confidently say this was the correct move.

In working to found Cosmonaut, myself and my colleagues sought to create a space where Marxism could thrive and develop to address the existing challenges of the modern era. We were not in as politically tumultuous a time as we are now, but the Trump presidency nonetheless was an environment that called for the serious political thinking that Cosmonaut sought to cultivate. We believed that Marxism was ultimately a project of *scientific socialism,* which meant that we would take questions of both natural and social science seriously. Cosmonaut would be unapologetically *Marxist.* As Lenin famously said: "The Marxist doctrine is omnipotent because it is true. It is comprehensive and harmonious, and provides men with an integral world outlook irreconcilable with any form of superstition, reaction, or defense of bourgeois oppression."

Yet we would not let our confidence in Marxism lead us into a thick-skulled dogmatism, where we would simply preach our truth and expect the masses to follow our lead when economic crisis (or rapture, if you will) came. We believed not in starting another sectarian group, but in engaging the existing left in dialogue and debate. This meant a degree of pluralism, or a willingness to publish opinions we disagreed with. We did not want to create a stereotypical sect rag. Cosmonaut was to be a space where real dialogue and debate about Marxist theory and political strategy could occur, even if it meant sometimes entertaining the occasional crank. If it inspired interesting discussion, why not?

Our willingness to engage in principled debate with the left and our devotion to a truly scientific socialism were also joined by a belief in democratic-republicanism and partyism. The democratic strain of Marxist thought, something that was key to the writings and political work of Marx, Engels, and Lenin, had been obscured by years of Cold War history. Reviving Marxism would mean reviving the radical republican tradition that Marx himself came out of. Democracy is not simply an instrument for achieving socialism, but is itself part of the content of socialism. Socialism must free humanity, not merely from the arbitrary whims of the market, but also the arbitrary domination of kings, oligarchs, bureaucrats, technocrats, patriarchs and militarists. This is, of course, a tall order — our studies of twentieth century socialism, another important part of Cosmonaut, show us the immense difficulty of overcoming all the muck of class society and its attendant tyrannies. Changing the world is hard stuff, and requires clear-headed political realism rather than empty political sloganeering. Yet, "this is hard" is never a justified excuse for a revolutionary.

Cosmonaut's partyism followed from this democratic-republicanism. The United States today, contrary to its pretensions, is not a democracy. Any project for socialism in the US will have to come to terms with this and wage a struggle to overcome the anti-democratic constitution that holds the capitalist class in power. And the only means of doing this, based on the scientific analysis of Marxism, is by uniting the proletariat and its allies around a program for a democratic-republic of the Paris Commune type. In other words, we need a political party; so, party building would be the guiding telos of our intellectual activity in Cosmonaut. Yet contrary to the habits of much of the Marxist left, by party building we did not mean the construction of a sectarian grouping based around adherence towards a particular theorist — a downgrade to the traditions of utopian socialism. Rather, what was needed was a party in the tradition of the Chartists, whose unity was built around a *People's Charter* that expressed the common aims of the movement in programmatic demands. What we needed, in other words, was a mass party, organized around *programmatic unity* rather than *theoretical unity.*

After all, Marxist theory is important and will always guide us. But it is also a *living* body of work, full of internal contradictions and ambiguities. Debates over the correct understanding of Marxist theory will never end, and if this *were* to happen, it would forfeit any claim to a scientific understanding of the world. Such debates have enlivened the space of the Cosmonaut webpage and sharpened our understanding of the world. Yet in the end, it is politics, the project of universal emancipation and the abolition of class society, that unites us above all else. No two individuals have complete agreement on all the details of Marxist theory unless they are in a dogmatic sect guided by a lone theory guru, so to demand that a party have strict unity on questions of Marxist theory can only result in exactly that — with endless splits and fracturing whenever disagreements arise.

Guided by these principles and united by various debates within the milieu we created around Cosmonaut, a number of us came together to organize a political intervention. We were DSA members that were frustrated by the shape of the organization. Tailing the Democratic Party was the norm, and without Sanders to give everyone a common goal, we were in the midst of internal struggle over where to go next. Yet we also saw political opportunity and potential in DSA despite this. In many ways, the absence of Sanders was a liberation of sorts, and an opportunity for something new to provide a direction for the organization that the majority of politically active socialists in the country were coalescing in. Marxist Center, the organization that sought to provide a "left" alternative to DSA, was ultimately going nowhere and would soon collapse. It only made sense to make an organized political intervention in DSA and put our ideas to the test. Hence was born the Marxist Unity Slate:a series of resolutions and amendments that our small group was putting forward at the 2021 Convention.

Using Cosmonaut as a platform, with an existing readership and audience in DSA, we were able to attract support for our resolutions and find allies around the country for our agenda. While our most important agenda items (the *most* important being around programmatic unity) failed at the Convention in 2021, we had made an initial political intervention and found potential allies in the organization. We were also able to have influence on the drafting of the National Platform that was accepted at the Convention, in part because of the prestige we had attained through our articles on the question of the minimum-maximum program. Our debut as a slate at convention created the ground for forming a proper mass-membership caucus, something we planned to do but wanted to be careful and patient about. After all, many of us had been part of earlier attempts to form left wing caucuses in DSA like Refoundation that simply ended up producing a grab-bag of incoherent politics.

Thus Marxist Unity Group would be birthed with a specific strategic vision; our members would be educated in the key texts of classic Marxism that defined our politics. These politics were defined by our Seven Points of Unity, which are reproduced in this manuscript. They represent a broad sketch of what our politics actually mean *in practice* in the specific context of the DSA and the United States broadly. While they were a collaborative effort of several founding members, I would like to credit Ben Grove especially for his key role in articulating a vision of socialist politics that is rooted in the political realities of the current USA. Following these Seven Points of Unity are immediate practical tasks that the Marxist Unity Group has taken up and the Perspectives document that was voted on at our first mass-membership-based convention (where a leading central committee was elected to replace the small group that made up the original Marxist Unity Slate). These aforementioned documents all represent the basic political vision that the Marxist Unity Group pursues, regardless of whatever differences we have regarding how to best do this.

The first series of articles we present puts our focus on winning the battle of democracy in the United States front-and-center. Ben Grove's agitational pamphlet "Fight the Constitution, Demand a New Republic" centers a national political struggle for regime change, making a clear case that the US Constitution is an undemocratic obstacle to social progress that must be taken down entirely — not chipped away at through reform after reform. JR Murray's "Whose Democracy?: An Introduction to Oligarchy in the United States" goes into further detail about exactly why the United States is not a democracy, and like "Fight the Constitution...." can serve as an agitational pamphlet of sorts.

Continuing the theme of democracy and the state are two pieces of a more theoretical type. Gil Schaeffer's "Lenin and the "Class Point of View" is a polemic with Chris Maisano of Jacobin Magazine. Schaeffer gives Maisano credit where credit is due, but finds Maisano's perspective weakened by various inconsistencies and reformist illusions about the United States. In polemicizing with Maisano and other interlocutors like Tim Horras (of the now-defunct Marxist Center) and Tatiana Cozzarelli (of the Trotskyist publication Left Voice), Schaeffer outlines Lenin's approach to the struggle for democracy as a *counterpoint*, providing a bit of personal biography to tell the story of how he came to his understanding of Lenin. For this reason, it serves as a proper example of MUG's "Lenin as democrat" reading of revolutionary history, influenced by historians such as Lars Lih and Neil Harding. Following this is "Making State Theory Revolutionary," a short article by myself on debates in

Marxist state theory and their shortcomings, as well as how a focus on democratic-republicanism can help bring a revolutionary focus back into the often overly-abstract and academic field of Marxist state theory.

Closing out the first section is Luke Pickrell's "Marxism and the Democratic Republic," a piece that serves as a perfect summary of the Marxist Unity Group's position on the democratic republic as well as its own position in Marxist thought. As Pickrell demonstrates in his essay, Republican thought was a key part of Marx's own development as a political actor and philosopher, raising themes from freedom from dependence and domination. This continued in the Marxism of the Second International, but was de-emphasized by later generations of Marxists. In reversing this deemphasis and centering the question of the Democratic-Republic in Marxism, Pickrell shows the way forward for a modern renewal of Marxism in the United States that centers the question of our political regime and its structure.

Section II focuses on the question of partyism and our approach to a political program. It opens with one of the first articles I wrote for Cosmonaut in 2018, "From Workers' Party to Workers' Republic," where I lay out my vision of what a mass party should look like based on the lessons of the First, Second, and Third Internationals. Next are two pieces that outline what has become MUG's basic understanding of the party program, "Why Have a Political Program?" by Parker McQueeney and my own "The Revolutionary Minimum-Maximum Program". McQueeney's is another article from the earliest days of Cosmonaut, showing the beginning of our polemical efforts to bring serious programmatic thinking to the left. "The Revolutionary Minimum-Maximum Program" laser-focuses on Marx and Guesde's *Programme of the Parti Ouvrier,* making the case that this document serves as key for understanding Marx's political thought and can serve as a model for future political programs despite its age. Both articles unapologetically make the case for the minimum-maximum program as the path forward for the left, in contraposition to the Trotskyist approach of the Transitional Program.

After these articles establishing the model of the minimum-maximum program are two polemics against autonomist and spontaneist approaches to Marxism. Cliff Connolly's "Create a Mass Party!" polemicizes with arguments put forward by the organization CounterPower, while my own article "Without a Party We Have Nothing" is a response to Taylor B's "Beginnings of Politics: DSA and the Uprising," also published in Cosmonaut. Cliff's article engages with the historical examples put forward by CounterPower, demonstrating the faulty premises that their arguments for a vague "Party of Autonomy" rest on. My own article tries to match Taylors B's level of abstraction, making a more philosophical argument for the necessity of partyism to the emergence of revolutionary subjectivity in opposition to arguments influenced by Sylvain Lazarus which amount to a reliance on spontaneism through ruptural "events."

Finishing the section on party and program are Myra Janis's "Building the Mass Party" as well as her "Socialism with American Characteristics," co-authored with Luke Pickrell. "Building the Mass Party" represents some of the early thinking of Cosmonaut around practical strategy for building a mass party in the United States, describing an "anti-entryist" approach to electoral politics and the Democratic Party that is worth revisiting regarding debates around the correct approach to electoral races today. "Socialism with American Characteristics" is a more recent article that takes the CPUSA to task for its loyalty to the existing institutions of the US government, particularly the Constitution, as well as its tailing of the Democratic Party. Janis and Pickrell argue that the roots of this flawed strategy can be found in the earlier days of the Party with their Popular Front strategy, and make the case that this strategy must be rejected by the Marxist left if it is to ever build an effective oppositional force to the existing social order.

Section III gives the reader an idea of MUG's own approach to electoral strategy. Jack Lundquist's "When We Fight, We Win! For an Agitational Socialist Electoral Strategy" is a direct intervention in DSA debates around electoral strategy, particularly in New York City, where DSA members comprise several elected officials. Using the example of the 2022 budget and the failure of DSA electeds to use the budget as an opportunity to agitate against the capitalists interests in the Democratic Party, Lundquist stresses an electoral strategy that puts agitation against the ruling class front-and-center. My own "Debating Electoral Strategy in the Comintern, 1920: The Bulgarian Situation" focuses instead on a historical example, looking at how Bulgarian Communists argued against abstentionist approaches in the Comintern and put a revolutionary electoral strategy into practice in their own country.

Most important in Section III is Ben Grove's "A Twelve-Step Program for Democrat Addiction," which acts as a "pre-MUG" manifesto of sorts. Making an appeal for political independence to the DSA rank-and-file in the wake of the victory of Joe Biden, Grove lays out how this political independence is not merely an abstract fantasy but a practical political possibility — in fact, a *necessity* if the socialist movement is going to progress toward victory. Its optimistic vision is still of great relevance to DSA, which as a whole is undecided on both the possibility and practicality of political independence. The "Twelve-Step Program" also makes the case for why DSA is the best area of development for the US left, which I believe still holds to this day.

The final section, Section IV, addresses Labor and Unions. The question of how DSA should relate to the labor movement is heavily contested among our ranks, as well as the ranks of MUG itself. Questions of day-to-day tactics are something we are decidedly non-dogmatic on, with our Immediate Tasks stating: "We do not have dogmatic attachments to any singular model of organizing, and we are eager to learn and grow alongside our comrades." The articles in this section aim to give the reader a sample of the thinking within MUG regarding the labor movement and how socialists relate to it. Marisa Miale's "The Worker and the Hydra" pushes against simplistic ideas of class consciousness organically developing towards communism through confrontations with employers on the shop floor, and instead argues that labor strategy must be incorporated into a broader revolutionary political strategy if it is to advance beyond economism. Two articles by Anton Johannsen are next. "Communists and the Unions in the Twenty-First Century" puts forward a vision of a communist union strategy that focuses on the democratization and politicization of unions while campaigning against repressive labor laws like Taft-Hartley. His next piece, "Of Course Labor Law Advances the Class Struggle" further focuses on the issue of labor law, challenging the IWW-affiliated blog Organizing.Work on their myopic and economistic perspective. Johannsen's articles point to struggles of labor law as a potential avenue for the politicization of the labor movement against the existing state regime.

Closing the collection is a historical piece, Veronica Darby's "Trust the Bridge That Carried Us Over: The Failure of Operation Dixie 1946-53." Operation Dixie was a failed post-war CIO campaign to organize the South, with the textile industry being a key target. Darby explores how Communist Party members were able to develop a more successful labor strategy than other unionists for organizing in a Southern landscape defined by the Jim Crow racial regime. Ultimately anti-communist campaigns would still see the CIO purged of many of its best organizers, and Operation Dixie would leave the American South the union-hostile hellscape it still is today. Learning from the failure of Operation Dixie and the mix of failures and successes of the classic CPUSA will be essential for the revitalization of a militant labor movement; one that will not only organize workers at the point of production but join the battle for democracy under the red banner of socialism.

These articles can help provide a sense of political clarity in these dangerous and confusing times. There are no magic bullets here — merely potential paths forward, none of which are the path of least resistance. Yet the path of least resistance is not an option — it is acquiescence to the prevailing order and failure to actually build an oppositional movement that legitimately challenges the institutions of the system we hope to overcome. With these articles, I hope that the reader can be convinced that genuinely anti-systemic politics today are possible, and that it is feasible to pursue revolutionary ends through pragmatic means. If you need no convincing of this, then I hope our interventions have helped you clarify your own revolutionary efforts. Either way, you are welcome to join the conversation at Cosmonaut Magazine by writing to us.[2]

—Donald Parkinson
Editor-in-Chief of Cosmonaut Magazine

---

2 Write to us at cosmonautmagazine@gmail.com

INTRODUCTORY MATERIALS

About Marxist Unity Group

Marxist Unity Group is an organization committed to political struggle within the Democratic Socialists of America. This makes us a DSA faction, and we aim to be a constructive one. Our words 'Marxist Unity' are aspirational: we hope to rally the thousands of Marxists in DSA around a shared vision for our movement's future.

Our faction is based on seven points of unity that we hope DSA will eventually embrace. These principles of struggle are far-reaching, and they all serve one fundamental goal — one unspoken dream that we will wear on our chest. It is a dream now quietly shared by millions of people in this country: the dream of a socialist revolution in the United States.

MARXIST UNITY GROUP'S SEVEN POINTS OF UNITY

1. Political independence. We want DSA to free itself from the Democratic Party and all other capitalist influences.

Marxist Unity Group strives to transform DSA into an independent socialist party. Independence means establishing a distinct public profile for DSA with our own platform, branding, and rhetoric. It also means building our own institutions and our own party discipline in the halls of power. We would stand with unwavering confidence in our cause, never watering down our socialist vision or subordinating our interests to those of a capitalist party.

Together, we would cultivate a popular mandate for revolution by running militant socialist candidates for public office — while simultaneously organizing grassroots institutions of working class power. We would create party-affiliated media, community services, mutual aid, and defensive organizations. Within the labor movement, we would fight the existing labor bureaucracy, build militant and democratic unions, and strive to win these unions to socialist politics. As we nurture a vast ecosystem of socialist-allied institutions, our socialist party will simultaneously become a mass movement: a party-movement.

Marxist Unity Group calls for immediate steps towards political independence. We become a party by acting like one. For us, the 'break' with the Democratic Party is a continuous process that must begin in earnest *right now*. This will require courage and faith in our ability to succeed as an independent movement, but we believe that the socialist movement is worthy of that faith. We support a transition towards independent campaigns wherever ballot access laws make this readily achievable — even if this causes a temporary decrease in our number of electoral victories. Building a distinct socialist constituency is the paramount task of our political era, and independent campaigns help us cultivate loyalty that is completely disconnected from loyalty to the Democratic Party.

2. Programmatic unity. We want DSA's platform to guide its political work.

To achieve political independence, we must learn to act with greater unity and determination. We want a disciplined, self-reliant organization that is run democratically by its rank-and-file members. Members will be free to publicly voice disagreement with any majority decision, as long as they can accept the decision as legitimate and assist with its implementation. This is the true meaning of democratic centralism.

Now that DSA has an official platform, we want to give it legs to stand on. Ultimately, we would like to make 'platform acceptance' the basis of DSA membership. Acceptance does not mean agreeing with everything in the platform. It simply means being willing to fight for the platform as an expression of the movement's democratically-elaborated aims. Members would have the right to organize for specific changes to the platform at conventions. This approach is called *programmatic unity*: unity based on common struggle for essential political goals, rather than on dogmatic purity or vague slogans that obscure our true objectives.

We view the distinction between a 'minimum' and 'maximum' program as essential. The minimum program refers to the party's comprehensive platform: the policies that it will immediately implement upon taking power to cement working-class political rule and place society on the path of a socialist transition out of capitalism. The maximum program refers to the results of this process: a world free of the market, borders, classes, and all other oppressive structures that exist under capitalism — in a word, communism. We want DSA to arm itself with both elements of a minimum-maximum program. Centering programmatic politics will restore the sense of unity and purpose that socialists enjoyed during the Sanders campaigns. However, our program will have much more ambitious aims, and instead of belonging to a single candidate, it will be developed democratically by the entire socialist movement.

3. Electoral discipline. We want socialist electoral candidates to represent the socialist movement.

Discipline and cohesion are another foundation of our political independence. If DSA candidates are truly dedicated to socialist politics, they should run together on a common DSA platform. Even if some are elected on a Democratic ballot line, they should form their own legislative caucuses, vote as a bloc, and refuse to join the Democratic Party caucus. They should also campaign for other socialists, refuse to endorse non-socialists, and only take the wage of a typical union worker. With these assertive political tactics, our candidates will rise as 'tribunes of the people': organized representatives of the socialist movement. DSA members have already implemented some elements of this approach in the New York state legislature, but we would like to formalize and universalize it.

Horse-trading and spineless compromise have failed to truly advance socialist politics. We will always embrace the struggle for reforms, but we want socialists to conduct that struggle out in the open and win concessions by acting as an intransigent opposition. Instead of cutting backroom deals as a junior coalition partner, socialist electeds can use their platform to raise the expectations of the working class and mobilize it to force concessions from the capitalists.

4. Nationwide struggle. We want socialists to treat US politics as a nationwide struggle for power.

As socialists in the United States, we live in a reactionary political culture that encourages us to think small. Americans are taught to believe that all problems should be solved locally, and socialists often accept this logic by confining themselves to isolated local campaigns, assuming that this is where 'real change happens.' Yet despite our backward federal system, the United States is not an alliance of city-states or a network of 20,000 police departments. It is a colossal empire propped up by the most powerful military on Earth. Even local police are armed, trained, and integrated by the federal government. If we ignore national politics, we will become blind to the true nature of our oppressors. We will obscure their nationwide abuse of the working class, not to mention their imperialist crimes in every corner of the world. Local organizing is an indispensable foundation of our movement, but it will be infinitely more effective when it is connected to a nationwide, pan-American, and global vision for working class revolution.

Marxist Unity Group supports efforts to lift DSA chapters out of parochialism by hiring more staff and integrating locals into larger state-level organizations. It is also why we want DSA to run an organized slate of socialist candidates to contest the House of Representatives. By conducting principled agitation in the halls of Congress, socialists can deliver a common message to every corner of the country. While we use the federal government as a bully pulpit, our candidates could also use their public profiles to support state and municipal organizing efforts. Federal, state, and local struggles — strikes, electoral campaigns, and mass demonstrations — will all be fused together in one grand movement that demands nothing less than a working-class, socialist revolution.

5. Fight the Imperial Police State. We want socialists to challenge the repressive structures of the capitalist state.

US socialists have a duty to stand firm against militarism and police tyranny. With every tool available to us, we must erode the political, cultural, and physical hegemony of the US police state. It is not enough for socialist legislators to rhetorically criticize excessive military spending. They should force a genuine public confrontation over the matter by refusing to vote for the military budget. Police, national security, and intelligence budgets must receive the same unrelenting opposition. As socialist legislators denounce the violence of the Pentagon and CIA, they could also expose the connections between police and military brutality.

To credibly challenge repressive capitalist institutions, socialists will need to develop and champion an alternative model of public safety. Marxist Unity Group believes that a people's army will be essential for the defense of working class interests. The precursors of this institution will emerge under capitalism as the working class develops organs of self-defense. After the socialist revolution, it will consolidate into a permanent institution that embodies working-class sovereignty and the population's right to bear arms. The capitalist armed forces will be abolished in their current form, and their defense capacity will be integrated into the people's army through a sovereign democratic process. Service and training will be universal, with diligent control of weapons and rigorous accountability for all members. Members will have strong democratic rights and union representation. Conscientious objectors will be offered alternative service options. Working under the direct control of the elected legislature, the people's army will carry out public projects and provide genuine public safety.

6. Fight the Constitution. We want socialists to fight to overthrow the Constitution.

Marxist Unity opposes a constitution that was written by a 'holy alliance' of capitalists and slavers to make the United States a perpetual oligarchy. There can be no question of submitting to a political order that exists to divide and conquer the working class, that slices up the government and divorces it from the will of the people — that is set in stone and almost impossible to amend. Black people cannot be free under a constitution written by slaveholders; indigenous people cannot win sovereignty under a constitution designed to facilitate their elimination; women cannot be free under a constitution written before they had the right to vote, and working people cannot be free under a constitution that enshrines private property. No one can be truly free if they are forced to bow to a reactionary constitution written by the dead. We want socialist leaders to erode the popular legitimacy of the US Constitution through combative political agitation: never bowing to the old order, and always acknowledging the need for a working class revolution in the United States.

The socialist revolution will not base its legitimacy on the laws of the slaveholder constitution. We will base it on a democratic majority mandate for socialism. This majority may be expressed by the popular vote of an election, but it does not have to take that form if the state represses our ability to contest elections. We stand for the right of the working class to take power by any means necessary. To win a socialist republic, millions of working people must be mobilized in their workplaces, at the ballot box, and in the street. We recognize that the capitalist class relies on the minoritarian rule of the US Constitution, and they will not give it up peacefully. The working class will need armed self-defense to protect itself from the inevitable violence of reaction. We also recognize that we must fight for the democratic rights of enlisted US soldiers. To complete a successful revolution, we must win a decisive section of the military rank and file over to our side.

7. Demand a New Republic. We want to win a democratic socialist republic in North America.

We fight the Constitution to win a democratic socialist republic in North America. Forged in revolution, this continental republic

29

will strive for the global liberation of all working and oppressed people. We desire the widest possible geographic scope for such a state so that it can most effectively carry out this mission, but we also recognize the principle of national self-determination. All indigenous and colonized peoples must win sovereignty, including those living within the current borders of the United States. No oppressed nation will be incorporated into the socialist republic against its will.

Alongside ecological and economic crises, the minoritarian and sclerotic constitutional order will contribute to massive political crises in the coming decades. This period of crisis will provide our class with an opportunity to topple the old order and convene a revolutionary Popular Assembly: a majoritarian constitutional convention elected by all the people. Under the democratic leadership of a victorious socialist party, the Popular Assembly will proceed to construct the socialist order. It will dismantle the slaveholder constitution and write the founding documents of the new republic.

Immediately upon taking power, socialists will implement a sweeping minimum program to cement working class political rule. We will need to destroy every institution that denies the people an authentic popular democracy, abolishing the Senate, the Electoral College, the Supreme Court, and the independent presidency. We will implement direct, universal, and equal suffrage. Supreme power will rest in the hands of a popular, unicameral assembly elected by proportional representation. Delegates will be recallable at any time and will receive no more than a skilled worker's wage. All parties that accept the laws of the new revolutionary order will be free to operate. Local organs of government will have a wide degree of autonomy. Unrestricted freedom of speech will be guaranteed to all. To make good on the unfulfilled promise of Reconstruction, our republic will launch social programs of targeted wealth redistribution, striving to eliminate all racial inequalities. The socialist republic will put political power and economic resources into the hands of all racially oppressed and colonized people.

Our broader economic program will include unimpeded labor and union rights, a massive reduction in working hours, and a truly universal welfare state that provides for all citizens from cradle to grave. We will create programs to reduce the power of bureaucrats and teach administrative skills to all workers. Worker self-management will be encouraged to the greatest extent achievable in every industry. Large industry will be placed under collective ownership early on, and we will progressively socialize the rest of the economy as we build our capacity for democratic economic planning. We will pursue crash course programs to address the ecological crisis and establish resilient forms of production, distribution, and habitation. Climate refugees will be welcomed into our republic as we embrace open borders and universal citizenship for all long-term residents.

With the shackles of the old order broken, the working class will finally have the power to remake society on egalitarian lines. In cooperation with the global socialist movement, we will move closer with every passing year to a fully liberated classless society: communism. Communism abolishes money, class distinctions, racial discrimination, patriarchy, national boundaries, oppressive gender roles, the mental/manual division of labor, and all other forms of social oppression. It is a society truly based on the principle "from each according to their ability, to each according to their need," where humanity collectively plans its economic activities through a free association of labor. Communism brings freedom to both society and the individual and will be the true beginning of human history.

Our Immediate Tasks

We want Marxist Unity Group to be outward-facing and inclusive. Our application process is open to any DSA member who broadly supports our vision and is ready to work with us in a disciplined manner. We also seek close communication with other DSA caucuses so that we can collaborate on common objectives. Marxist Unity Group will back any initiative that builds the strength and confidence of the socialist movement, no matter who proposes it. Our members are organizing to achieve several immediate aims:

First, we want to build a coalition of all DSA factions that are ready to actively fight for independence from the Democratic Party and pursue a socialist party-movement. These tasks have received empty lip service for far too long. It is time to make them real.

We will also pursue a new model of electoral politics that takes electoral discipline seriously — forging socialist representatives into disciplined blocs that are accountable to DSA and its democratically-adopted platform. Working across the country, we will help locals develop this model and promote resolutions based on it. We will support efforts to increase coordination between locals, building up the strong party structures that can make socialist electoral work infinitely more ambitious and nationally integrated. Our motto will always be quality over quantity in electoral work, and Marxist clarity over empty opportunism.

In our chapters' economic, social, and community organizing, we will strive to make an effective contribution. We will also strive to infuse these activities with a socialist spirit, pursuing the merger of socialist politics with the day-to-day struggles of the working class. We do not have dogmatic attachments to any singular model of organizing, and we are eager to learn and grow alongside our comrades.

Finally, Marxist Unity Group will pursue a rigorous political education, for both our members and DSA as a whole. We must seriously investigate US and global capitalist society, the history of the workers' movement, and what it would take to achieve a socialist revolution in the United States. Marxist theory is vital for the success of any socialist movement. It provides the movement with a scientific understanding of society and the political principles needed to transform it. We hope to promote the importance of Marxist theory by expanding educational infrastructure and member engagement, creating a rich and non-dogmatic intellectual culture.

Our faction is influenced by the best historical lessons of the entire global socialist movement, from the Communards in Paris to the experience of Allende's Popular Unity government in Chile. We are particularly inspired by the Marxism of the Second International, and above all by those that kept its revolutionary spirit alive in the face of political capitulation: Lenin and the Bolsheviks. The Marxists of the Second International grappled with historical tasks not unlike the ones we face today. After a long era of historical defeat for the socialist movement, they confronted antiquated political regimes and worked to merge socialism with the workers' movement. Despite countless obstacles, they built mass worker parties from the ground up and challenged the power of the capitalist class. It was only on this foundation that working class parties were able to pose the question of taking state power in the subsequent period. Marxist Unity Group seeks to creatively apply Marxist politics to the contemporary United States — never trying to reenact the past, but always learning from it.

PERSPECTIVES OF MARXIST UNITY GROUP
2022

Presented below is a summary of the overall perspectives of Marxist Unity Group in the year 2022, as decided and voted on at our founding congress.

The triumph of neoliberal capitalism over bureaucratic socialism in 1989-1991 ushered in a global period of reaction with unique features. In other historic periods of reaction and counter-revolution in which the forces of the ruling class gained the upper hand, the consequence was harsh, explicit, and violent repression of the forces of the proletariat, especially its political arm in the form of socialist and communist parties. However, in this special period, the main feature has not been overt repression of the socialist and communist movements, but their wholesale dismissal as an irrelevant fringe with no significant role in political life. Communist politics no longer carry the same weight in working class existence as they did even in a bureaucratized and diminished fashion during most of the twentieth century.

The onset of this political climate is related to an earlier and deeper capitulation of much of the left to nationalism, reformism, and bureaucratic statism. Other sections fell into fragmentation, with a constellation of sects tailing the spontaneity of the street or strike action du jour, or either the liberal or conservative nationalist wing of the bourgeoisie. However, one source of hope in this period of reaction is that the breakdown of the twentieth century left has opened up a new moment of intellectual reflection in Marxism which allows for a reworking of the whole history of the workers' movement at a distance from the debates of the previous century. This reworking provides the clarity necessary for the development of a political strategy adequate to the task of proletarian emancipation. This is a broad process that has impacted the entire Marxist milieu, but in the United States the magazine *Cosmonaut* has dedicated itself to this purpose.

This is a highly promising process, but it is occurring within a rump isolated and divided Marxist left. The class consciousness of the proletariat in the United States and other imperialist countries remains low overall due to the string of political and economic defeats it has suffered. Nevertheless, there are some signals that conditions are ripe for it to rise again.

What's left of Marxism forms one contingent of a new political left that has emerged since the 2008 financial crisis shattered the illusions of many that 1989-91 constituted the end of history and that neoliberal capitalism had proven itself to be the only possible future mode of organization for human society. In the United States, this reanimated left has progressed in stages from the disorganized street protests of Occupy Wall Street, to the attempt at political intervention through the two Bernie Sanders campaigns for the Presidency, to the current iteration of the Democratic Socialists of America (DSA) — its most advanced form at present. The two major waves of the Black Lives Matter movement in 2014-15 and 2020 also contributed to the development of nascent revolutionary consciousness in this period.

From a Partyist perspective — as a common organization with a relatively democratic political culture, DSA represents a step above the movement that formed around Bernie Sanders as an individual presidential candidate. Its explosive growth and repudiation of the Harringtonite legacy in the form of its exit from the scab Socialist International, its support for the

Boycott, Divestment, and Sanctions movement against Israel, and other examples leave its future undetermined. Many of the left-wing organizations have escaped their isolation by regrouping within DSA.

The trade union movement in the United States and most of the world is weak. Union density is closer to the early twentieth century than any time in the post-1945 era of capital-labor compromise, which formed part of US imperialism's containment strategy aimed at curtailing the influence of the USSR. We live in the aftermath of the subsequent roll-back strategy executed to break this compromise after it had outlived its utility for the capitalist class. The labor bureaucracy in what's left of the trade unions doesn't stand for the organization of the class for itself, but primarily for its own privileged position as mediators between the companies and their unions. The US labor movement's leadership is unflinchingly tied to the capitalist Democratic Party despite this party's repeated betrayals and loyalty to finance capital.

However, gains are at present being made by young workers forming unions at major private sector workplaces such as Starbucks, Amazon, Trader Joe's, and others. There is promise of multiple large-scale strikes in already unionized parts of the transportation and logistics industries in the near future.

DSA has been successful in building a presence in the left-wing and 'reform' elements of the US labor movement, but avoids pursuing a higher merger of socialism and the workers' movement by fighting for its socialist political program within the unions in order to transform them into schools of communism, instead limiting itself to reform agitation. Socialists should openly fight on capping bureaucrat salaries at the average wage, instituting a right to recall officers, and welding the fractured labor movement together to fight for all workers employed and unemployed. The Democratic Socialist Labor Commission should seek to play the role of the Trade Union Educational

League built by the Workers (Communist) Party of America in the 1920s, whose mission was to develop labor organizations into organs of militant struggle against capitalism, expose the reactionary labor bureaucrats, and educate the workers to militant unionism, including by creating a worker-orientated publication that is explicitly socialist. The publication would provide agitation and propaganda as a forum for socialist labor organizers to study militant union strategy and democratic union reforms.

What is needed to qualitatively alter the position of the working class movement, to give coherence to these budding developments, is the forging of a genuine mass Communist Party. Such a party would unite the advanced section of the class around a program for working class rule through a democratic republic (opposed to the present undemocratic liberal-constitutional regime) as a means of achieving socialism and structure an effective unity in action for all communists, while its press would be open to debate the important strategic and tactical questions that face our class.

Achieving such a party will require uniting the Marxists in DSA around programmatic communist politics and pulling in the scattered left groups — all of whose independent efforts to form a direct link to the masses result in their common frustration.

One conception of the path forward for socialists that has purchase in DSA is the necessity of forming a (bourgeois) Labor Party or an equivalent "new mass organization." This sort of party is meant to capture the political base of Bernie Sanders and the "Squad" without being programmatically committed to socialism or a break with the constitutional order through which the capitalist class rules. An organization like this would not fulfill the essential purpose of a working class political party to represent the interests of the class on questions of high politics and constitutional issues and to present a comprehensive and desirable alternative to capitalist class rule in the form of working class leadership of the society.

The argument for this organization is a combination of economism — by drawing the Bernie base into struggle for 'bread and butter' economic demands they can be led by the nose into supporting socialism — and a supposition that the only sort of party worth building is a party that could be an immediate party of government — since Bernie is the most popular politician in the United States and wins presidential matchup polls he could create a new party with as much support as the established bourgeois parties. Of course, such a party in government would behave exactly as its British equivalent has every time it has captured Number 10. A working class party without a clear minimum program for the dictatorship of the proletariat, which seeks to be an immediate party of government is doomed to demonstrate its safety for the capitalist class. In this way the logic of Corbyn's insistence that he could lead Labour into government concluded with Starmer's purge of left-wingers and anti-Zionists. A genuine Communist Party would seek to act as a principled party of opposition until it was able to win a majority for its program of radical democracy in a political crisis. However, it would be sectarian to oppose the formation of a bourgeois Labor Party if there were organic elements of the class moving in that direction, and socialists should seek full affiliation to it in that event in order to fight for the adoption of socialist politics.

A major defect of DSA at present is its lack of control over its elected politicians by the membership as a whole and its relationship to the Democratic Party. There are many flaws with DSA's national political platform but also much in it of great merit. Unfortunately, DSA's coalitionist approach to the Democratic Party makes discussion of the platform's merits and flaws moot, since it is not DSA's platform but the limits of what is acceptable to the Democratic leadership that determines what DSA candidates can campaign on.

Relatedly, in spite of the bold stance DSA has taken as an organization in total opposition to the United States' alliance with Israel, its client apartheid state in the Middle East, and to US arms shipments and proxy war in Ukraine, DSA members in Congress are free to signal that they are "safe" for US imperialism by voting in its interests. Thus, late last year DSA's National Political Committee congratulated itself on preserving its relationship with Representative Jamaal Bowman of New York after members called for him to be disciplined for voting in favor of billions of dollars of funding for Israel's 'iron dome.' Bowman repaid their leniency by announcing afterward that he would gladly vote the same way again, and DSA's reputation as an opponent of Zionist oppression of Palestinians has suffered. Likewise, every DSA member in Congress has shamefully sided with militarism in voting for tens of billions of dollars in arms shipments for the US proxy war in Ukraine.

The United States/NATO's proxy war in Ukraine represents the continuation of a decades-long project of attempting to encircle Russia and eliminate it as a military threat. The United States courted Ukraine with illusory West European standards of living and the allure of NATO membership to entice it into the imperialist geopolitical camp. It stoked the far-right Ukrainian nationalist movement, which imposed chauvinist language and nationality policies on the Russian ethnic and language minority. All of this was in the service of completing the process of the subordination of the Russian economy to US interests that began with the 'shock therapy' applied after the collapse of the USSR. In a wider perspective, the aim is to deprive China, the main threat to US global domination, of an important ally. Those on the left who back arms shipments and line up behind the American proxy are social-imperialists. They mask practical support for their own government's interests in seductive phraseology. Those who support the Russian invasion of Ukraine are similarly deluded but far less prominent. Communists ought to stand against arms shipments, against the existence of NATO, against the presence of Russian troops, and for the right of self-determination of both the Ukrainian nation and the Russian speakers of the Donbass — with an understanding that the main enemy lies at home.

We are witnessing an overall escalation of the rivalry between China and the United States, particularly with the emergence of a "New Cold War" mentality in sections of the US ruling class. This has manifested itself in protectionist economic policies around intellectual property and signals from the United States that it is willing to challenge the long-standing "One China" policy in relation to Taiwan, which formed the basis of US-China detente starting in 1972. As in the case of Ukraine, there are those on the left who cover for the interests of US imperialism in relation to Taiwan, casting the question as one of national self-determination rather than Cold War political division.

In domestic US politics, as in other English-speaking countries, there is an "official" anti-racism, anti-sexism, and pro-LGBT ideology with backing from elements of the capitalist class and the state, particularly in the Democratic Party and the institutions of the bourgeois academy. These ideologies are ultimately pro-capitalist and individualist. They reject the revolutionary and progressive role of the working class and emphasize a fragmentary politics of representation and state recognition within an imperial project over the role of unity through struggle in pursuit of collective emancipation and the liberation of the Global South. There has also spawned a pseudo-radical and easily co-optable variant of identity politics, which sheds the overt pro-capitalism but is bound at the hip to the state through the same politics of recognition.

This does not mean that the oppression of women, Black Americans and other people of color, Indigenous people, or gay and transgender people has ended in US society. In fact, there has been a right-wing reaction to the real gains these groups have made over the past half-century, stoked by an insecurity related to the relative decline of US imperialism and the decline of the welfare state and mobilized in support of the racism that kills at home and abroad. Especially in Republican controlled states, there is a renewed campaign against gay and transgender rights, abortion rights, any sort of progressive education, and for greater arbitrary power for the police to carry out racist terror.

The inability of both official and radical identity politics to counter this reactionary tide and advance the freedom and sovereignty of all the oppressed and exploited increases the urgency of developing a Marxist approach to Black, Indigenous, women's, and LGBT emancipation. We recognize the working class as the vanguard and tribune of the oppressed while emphasizing the vitality and validity of these struggles for self-determination. We recognize the historical role these movements have had in shaping and steering collective struggle and their future role in building an oppositional unifying Communist Party.

The Supreme Court's decision in Dobbs v. Jackson Women's Health Organization is an acute expression of the reactionary agenda. The decision reverses the 1973 Roe v Wade decision that established the right to choose to have an abortion as a constitutionally protected privacy right nationwide and allows the bans or extreme restrictions on abortion contained in the laws of 22 states to come into effect, with more likely to follow soon. This is a grave attack on the freedom of working class women and others capable of becoming pregnant in the United States.

The Dobbs decision is an outgrowth of our undemocratic constitutional order, particularly the institution of Supreme Court judicial review and the federalist system, which allows for reactionary anti-abortion state fiefdoms. As a whole, the United States Constitution was designed to be a block on democratic representation with the Senate, Judiciary, and Presidency, not to mention the world-historic massive military-police state bureaucracy that has grown since World War II. There is an objective tendency toward constitutional breakdown that will continue to empower the most reactionary minority of the population. Without propagandizing our vision of high politics on constitutional questions for a democratic republic, constitutional crises will break to the far-right with no countervailing narratives to compete. A left that refuses to articulate a vision outside of the reactionary liberal-constitutional framework is doomed to tail the failed politics of liberalism.

The national political platform adopted by DSA in 2021 contains rudiments of a radical democratic program for working class rule, but also has serious shortcomings when compared to the programs of classical Marxism. There is a contradiction between a section named 'Deepening and Strengthening Democracy' and its description calling the US "no democracy at all." Rather, we should frame this as 'winning the battle for democracy.' By this we mean the combination of all government powers into the hands of the people's representatives: this should include the abolition of the elected monarchy of the Presidency, the end of judicial review, and the replacement of Congress with a single, truly democratic, directly elected, proportional, recallable, and accountable assembly, with delegates to be paid the average wage of a skilled worker. The section dealing with militarism should also be explicit about the goal of replacing the standing professional armed forces and police with a democratic militia system.

Despite many issues with DSA, it is the most promising organization on the American left in over a generation. While the culture of the organization is under-experienced and under-educated in Marxism compared to the twentieth-century sects, there is also a genuine tendency, though not absolute, of openness and commitment to democratic decision-making over bureaucratic control which makes the fight for Marxist politics possible, particularly in its tolerance of factions. A truly independent and revolutionary mass socialist party-movement is necessary for the seizure of power by the working class and the real flourishing of the human species, but history shows that this can only be built by uniting the existing 'raw material' of the small socialist sects and circles and fighting for Marxist politics within a formal party organization.

Since 2020 saw the failure of the second Sanders campaign and the onset of COVID-19, DSA lacks unity on a coherent strategy. Future presidential elections offer a unique opportunity to back a socialist presidential campaign and present hundreds of millions of people with socialist propaganda and agitation. Squandering the opportunity would be a mistake.

It would also be a mistake to sow illusions in a left or 'workers' government' without fundamentally altering the constitutional regime and bureaucratic state apparatus. Marxist support for a left presidential campaign should be given 'without illusions' in both the idea of a 'liberal workers' government' in general and the specific policy compromises a left candidate would undoubtedly make with US imperialism, petty-bourgeois radicalism, and constitutional cretinism.

The role of Marxist Unity Group is to work with all elements who can be united on the US left around programmatic Marxist politics. Specifically, this means moving away from the strategy of building ambiguous relationships with national, state, and municipal politicians who use the plausible-deniability of the term 'democratic socialism' to act as loyal Democrats, even if 'left-progressive' ones.

Instead, a majority must be built inside DSA to implement a strategy of putting forward campaigns for representatives to act as people's tribunes and build disciplined blocs of DSA fractions in legislatures accountable to DSA's platform and elected leadership rather than the Democratic caucus whip and their donors. DSA members must build unity not on least common denominator politics, nor develop a sectarian unity around theoretical lines, but rather unity around its political platform and its 'final goals.' It must build towards a merger with the existing elements of working class organizations and develop the class as the vanguard fighter for democracy.

SECTION I
DEMOCRACY AND THE STATE

FIGHT THE CONSTITUTION! DEMAND A NEW REPUBLIC!

Ben Grove
March 25, 2021

Ben Grove proposes a radical New Union Act to throw the antiquated US Constitution into the dustbin of history.

It's October 1917 in Petrograd. The Bolsheviks have given marching orders to an insurrectionary mob. It descends on the Winter Palace, the center of state power in Russia. The defenders melt away, barely even putting up a fight. The Provisional Government has fallen.

What do the revolutionaries do? They are sweatshop workers and peasant soldiers — hungry, ravaged by war, and now surrounded by unimaginable luxury. Do they trash the building? Steal things? Brutalize security?

The looting begins, but then a nameless voice cries out: 'Comrades! Don't touch anything! Don't take anything! This is the property of the People!' The mob picks up on the call and repeats it, echoing across the palace: "Revolutionary discipline! Property of the people!" [1]

Everything is put back in place. Just for good measure, a committee spontaneously organizes to prevent further looting. [2]

1 "The Bolsheviks Storm the Winter Palace, 1917," EyeWitness to History, 2006, www.eyewitnesstohistory.com.
2 Ibid.

Here in America, we've historically had our own law-abiding insurrectionists. Take old John Brown for an example. Before he launched his daring raid on Harpers Ferry, he held a convention with dozens of supporters to adopt a Provisional Constitution. This fascinating document opens with a sharp legal justification for war on slavery. It lays out basic rules of engagement and sets up institutions to govern everyone taking part in Brown's revolt.[3]

The Provisional Constitution displays many signs of Brown's Calvinist faith. It bans all "profane swearing," "filthy conversation," and "unlawful intercourse of the sexes." Yet it also gives women the right to vote and bear arms, requires every citizen to work, and promises common ownership of all confiscated slaveholder property. There is no Senate in Brown's political system, only a simple unicameral House of Representatives. The Electoral College is also abandoned — instead, the people directly elect the President and the Supreme Court.[4]

The paintings make John Brown look like a wild insurrectionary tornado. Yet he and the Bolshevik mob understood something that the modern left often forgets: revolutionaries are *lawmakers*. They demolish the old order, but they also establish a new one.

Brown also understood[5] that America's established Constitution is riddled with aristocratic features. The gilded gentry who wrote it in 1787 made atrocious concessions to their slaveholder constituency. The Fugitive Slave Clause required that escaped slaves be "delivered up" to their masters, no matter what state in the Union they fled to. Meanwhile, the Three-Fifths Clause allowed Southern states to count 60% of their slave populations for representation purposes, using their human chattel to inflate their power in the federal government.

---

3 Robert L. Tsai. "John Brown's Constitution," Boston College Law Review, 2010, pp 187-204, https://www.bc.edu/content/dam/files/schools/law/bclawreview/pdf/51_1/04_tsai.pdf.

4 Ibid.

5 Ibid p 158.

The Electoral College builds on this sinister project. As James Madison himself explained, the convoluted system proved necessary "on the score of the Negroes." With their massive nonvoting slave populations, slave states would have been disadvantaged under a national popular vote. By instead having statewide slates of electors choose the president, the plantation overlords dodged this democratic threat, propelling their allies into the White House for nearly seventy years. Lincoln broke that cycle in 1860, but to this day the Electoral College leaves Black Southerners almost voiceless in presidential elections. Under the winner-take-all system, their strong support for Democratic presidential candidates typically counts for nothing, with white majorities handing all of their states' electors to the Republican ticket.

The Framers of the Constitution adopted the Electoral College not only to appease slaveholders, but also to throttle popular democracy. They viewed the people as "unruly steeds," unfit for self-government. That is why only one branch of the government, the House of Representatives, is elected directly.[6] The Senate is a thoroughly elitist body, just as the Framers intended.[7] Its members serve staggered, six-year terms, with two-thirds left in place after each election cycle. Every state gets two senators, despite population trends that make this arrangement more unrepresentative with every passing year. It is essentially affirmative action for conservative white voters.

Political science hacks like to call the Senate "the world's greatest deliberative body." In reality it is the world's greatest obstructionist body, where "grim reapers" like Mitch McConnell can tank desperately-needed reforms on a whim. It approves all cabinet appointments, treaties, and judicial nominations, locking the House out of countless policy decisions. These absurd privileges have allowed the GOP to pack the federal judi-

6 Holton, Woody. Unruly Americans and the Origins of the Constitution. New York: Macmillan, 2007. pp 5-10.
7 Ibid p 251.

ciary with right-wing judges — judges who serve for life, who can strike down any legislation as they see fit.

This rigged system is locked in place by an amendment process so onerous that the Constitution is almost impossible to change. Two-thirds of both houses of Congress followed by three-quarters of the state legislatures must sign off on any change to the Constitution. No other modern country has such a rigid constitutional order.

Both capitalist parties would have us believe that the Constitution is a Heavenly Charter, ordained by Providence to save us from the Tyranny of the Riotous Majority. We know full well that this is Vain and Perfidious Bullshit. The Constitution protects the tyranny of the elite minority, blocking "wicked" left-wing projects like a "rage for paper money ... an abolition of debts ... [or] an equal division of property."[8] By creating a fragmented, convoluted, and geographically vast political system, the Framers made it almost impossible for popular movements to build a majority and decisively win political power. They invented a government that is structurally indifferent to the needs of the many.

James Madison summed up the spirit of the Constitution with an old Latin motto: *divide et impera*[9] — Divide and conquer.

The Wages of Division

Now Madison's machine is sputtering. America's most fanatical "patriots" have stormed the nation's center of constitutional government. No powdered wigs and Latin mottos for that crowd. They had simpler words: "hang Mike Pence!"

Among them were cops, state lawmakers, and real estate brokers. Coddled lapdogs of the Old Order. What drove them to betray the rule of law and form a bloodthirsty lynch mob?

8 Federalist No. 10, https://billofrightsinstitute.org/primary-sources/federalist-no-10.
9 Holton, Woody (2007), p 10.

There were warning signs even before the pandemic. American society is demographically shifting; it is politically gridlocked and rudderless. Quality of life has been stagnant for years. Working-age whites without college degrees feel these changes acutely: they are suffering from staggering levels of chronic pain, addiction, and suicide.

Even the relatively well-off can see the decay and react to it with fear. For centuries the Constitution has catered to the whims of white reactionaries. Now, amid all the chaos, their special status is being challenged. Working class riots tear through the streets, socialists walk in the halls of Congress — and their orange Emperor has fallen. None of these things pose an imminent threat to the Old Order, but Fox News and the growing cesspool of far-right media make them look frightening enough.

MAGA wingnuts may be delusional, but they see something real moving beneath the water. A section of society is *fed up* with Old America. It wants to wipe out the callous conservatism that dominates our culture, and replace it with something very new. For reactionaries, this future is unthinkable. Their interpretation of the Constitution has one underlying spirit: "All power to the true conservative Americans. *All power to myself.*"

Christ said that it is better to maim the body than let your spirit be destroyed in hell. As good Christians, wingnuts were happy to embrace this logic with the Constitution. If "saving America" meant overturning the wishes of the majority, then so be it. After all, the Constitution is against majority rule.

If saving America meant attacking voting rights, then so be it. After all, voting *is not a universal right* under our Constitution.

If saving America meant lynching the vice president, then grab the rope. After all, there is still no federal law against lynching. Efforts by the House to pass one have repeatedly died in the Senate, once in 1922 and again *just last summer.*

Gridlock and division are inevitable in a divide-and-conquer republic. We will find no easy exit. The question for us on the

Left is not how to reverse the country's institutional decay, but how to push through it and come out victorious.

Option One: Accept the Constitution

One option is to climb the dunghill: accept the Constitution and try to attain power within its framework. To implement desperately-needed measures like Medicare for All, labor reform, or the Green New Deal, the Left would simultaneously contest the presidency, the Senate, and the House of Representatives.

This task would require a sweeping electoral supermajority for socialists that is difficult to envision in any country, let alone the United States. Even the Republican anti-slavery victory of 1860 — the closest thing we have ever had to a "political revolution" in America — did not win a clean trifecta. It took only the House and the presidency. Unwilling to share power, the Southern states rebelled, forfeiting their control of the Senate.

Such an outcome is extremely unlikely under modern circumstances. We do not have the clean regional division that sliced the Union in half; we have a partisan divide that spans from coast to coast. Shallow platitudes about "ditching the culture war" will not eliminate that division. If the Left abandons its commitment to egalitarian values such as racial equality and reproductive rights, our existing base will view us as traitors. Reactionaries will also see right through the pandering and dismiss us as two-faced politicians.

If our strategy bows to the slaveholder constitution, we can expect that path to lead us into divided government. Socialists would not be able to pass any legislation without the approval of one of the entrenched capitalist parties. Bernie certainly would have struggled with this reality had he emerged victorious. Ugly compromises would have to be made.

Why does that matter? If the Establishment blocks our policies, couldn't we place the blame on them, "keep building the movement," and fight for a trifecta in the next round? After all, it's not our fault that we have an obstructionist Constitution.

Unfortunately, voters are unlikely to blame these deep structural challenges. They will see yet another progressive politician who won a popular mandate only to "sell out," just like all the others. They will blame the movement that made big promises and failed, not the senators behind the scenes who forced the failure. "Nothing really changes," they sigh — and power swings back to the Right. This is exactly what happened when Barack Obama won the presidency in 2008: a wave of populist excitement was squashed by right-wing obstruction. Hope and change were put on hold, and in 2010 the Democrats received an electoral massacre.

Obama left his supporters completely unprepared. He had no interest in rallying his constituency to insist that the wishes of the majority be respected. But that is exactly what the Left should do: instead of *whining* about the Electoral College or the Senate or the filibuster, we should attack these roadblocks head-on by demanding an accountable democracy.

Option Two: Rig the Constitution

Oh, but *now* Obama *does* have an interest in democracy. In the summer of 2020, just months after his frantic phone calls helped secure Joe Biden's nomination, Obama watched as cities across America descended into chaos. At John Lewis's funeral in early July, he urged lawmakers to build on the congressman's legacy by passing a new Voting Rights Act — and to grant statehood to Puerto Rico and Washington, D.C. If doing that takes eliminating the filibuster, a "Jim Crow relic," to "secure the God-given rights of every American, then that's what we should do."

Clever. Even if he is only making a halfhearted effort to manage social decay, Barack Obama is thinking about institutional reform. If Congress enacted the Obama Program, would it give us an accountable majoritarian democracy?

Not really. A new voting rights act is certainly needed. But what would it do for Black Southerners whose presidential votes get wiped out by the Electoral College, who have almost no representation in the Senate because of the demographic compositions of their states? "You can go anywhere in [South Carolina]," Lindsey Graham croons to his black constituents. "You just need to be conservative, not liberal."

Abolishing the filibuster is a no-brainer, and D.C. residents certainly deserve statehood, as do Puerto Ricans if they so choose. However, even a 52-state Senate would retain a high level of racial bias. In the words of a recent Data for Progress memo, it is an "irredeemable institution," structurally hostile to democracy.[10]

Some pundits have suggested more aggressive solutions. Political scientist David Faris has called for Democrats to "play hardball" against the GOP, not only killing the filibuster and packing the courts, but also dividing California into seven states. This would give Democrats 14 new senators to "fix" their underrepresentation.

What would this fix look like in practice? Faris describes it as a democratizing reform, but the public is unlikely to perceive it this way. Power is not shifted to a unified national people. It is shifted to the lucky Democrats who happen to live in the Seven Californias. Will Democrats in Wyoming, New York, and Mississippi feel liberated? How will the residents of large Republican states react when Faris denies them the same partition treatment?

You'll stare at your television as enraged Texans sack Los Angeles with weaponized bulldozers. "It's so sad that we've come to this," says your grandmother. "I like that Joe, but I never thought partitioning California was a good idea."

---

10 Data for Progress, "The Senate is an Irredeemable Institution," pp2-13. https://www.filesforprogress.org/memos/the-senate-is-an-irredeemable-institution.pdf.

Fun stuff. The point is simple: Faris's "hardball" solutions do not create an accountable democracy. They just slice up the People in a new way that happens to favor Democrats. The Electoral College remains in place (even with the partial modifications that Faris supports). Senators continue to serve staggered terms in gigantic winner-take-all districts. Brett Kavanaugh still sits on the Supreme Court for life. Packing the Senate and the courts is bound to enrage the Right, but these cynical power grabs are unlikely to energize a mass base on our side. It's just more *divide et impera*.

Mass politics is not even on Faris's agenda. His goal is to convince Democratic party operatives to embrace his "hardball" tactics — not a grassroots political movement. Most Democratic leaders, however, are not as clever as Faris and Obama. Just consider Diane Feinstein, who gave Lindsey Graham a hug after he rammed Amy Coney Barrett through Senate confirmation hearings.

The *Harvard Law Review* recently published an anonymous proposal that is far more interesting than Faris's. Titled "Pack the Union," it suggests that Congress grant statehood to every neighborhood in Washington, D.C. for the sole purpose of amending the constitution. Then these 127 new states would ratify constitutional amendments to effectively abolish the Senate, expand the House of Representatives, implement a national popular vote for the president, and create a new majoritarian amendment process.[11]

A brilliant plan! Yet at this point, I think it is fair to say that a line has been crossed. Efforts to "pack the Union" with D.C. microstates are unlikely to be judged solely on their legal merits. It is not really an incremental plan to reform the Constitution. It's just overthrow with extra steps.

---

11 Harvard Law Review, "Pack the Union: A Proposal to Admit New States for the Purpose of Amending the Constitution to Ensure Equal Representation." https://harvardlawreview.org/2020/01/pack-the-union-a-proposal-to-admit-new-states-for-the-purpose-of-amending-the-constitution-to-ensure-equal-representation.

Option Three: Fight the Constitution

So let's do it. Ditch the silly microstates. *Fight the Constitution; Demand a New Republic!*

There are some reforms within the Constitution that socialists can and should demand. The Supreme Court, for example, can be remade with term limits, judge rotation, and jurisdiction stripping. We can fight not just to "pack" it, but to eliminate its godlike power to determine the law.

But to convince our target constituency that these reforms are legitimate, we must attack the entire ideology of Old America. This stodgy, conservative worldview is relentlessly drilled into the American psyche. From kindergarten to our graves, we learn that equal rights is mob rule, that gridlock is better than progress, that the Founders always know best, and so on. Challenging these assumptions means developing an incisive message of our own:

Down with the Old Order. We're sick of this divided republic. It slices up our institutions to make them unaccountable. It lets Mitch McConnell and the Electoral College and nine old men stomp on the needs of the people. It locks the working class majority out of power; it gives us no say in the future of the country.

John Brown fought for a new constitution. Now the Chilean masses are doing the same. Why shouldn't modern Americans give it a try? Women had no say in the writing of the existing Constitution; black people had no say; no one alive today has had a say in the system they live under. We deserve a New Union, a unified democratic republic that answers to the working class majority. A constitution that reflects modern principles of fairness and equality, that guarantees healthcare, education, and economic rights.

The Right says all power to the landlords, to the cops, to the dead Founding Fathers. We say *all power to the living, all power to the people, all power to the New Union!*

But who would take us seriously? Socialists are weak right now. Isn't it too soon to demand something so bold? Too soon? *Look behind you!* Two centuries of sham democracy. Half a million dead from COVID in a system that denies us healthcare, sick leave, basic human dignity. Years of economic turmoil and discontent ahead. Will there ever be an easy time to raise such a transgressive demand? Rip off the band-aid and raise it now.

Demanding a new constitution will alienate many. Yet it may also strike a chord with a growing progressive constituency that is exhausted with endless gridlock and elitist institutions like the Electoral College. Zoomers and Millennials are far more willing to question their country's past than previous generations. When a recent Fox News poll asked voters under 30 for their views on the Founding Fathers, 51% chose "villains" or "it depends."

Leave the technocratic tinkering to Obama. Weak movements *need* strong demands. They shock and capture the imagination; they give meaning to our short-term projects; they forge our supporters into a revolutionary oppositional counterculture.

Back in the 1960s, the Black Panthers demanded a nationwide plebiscite to establish black self-determination in the United States. How many members did they have when they raised that demand? Ten thousand? Twenty thousand?

Two. It was just Huey P. Newton and Bobby Seale sitting in a dining room, drafting a founding document. That audacity — that strategic insanity — won them the respect of millions. For all its shortcomings, they built a nationwide revolutionary organization that captivates the American Left to this day.

Towards a New Union Act?

How could modern socialists convincingly raise the demand for a new constitution? It is hard to imagine introducing the idea door-to-door, persuading one person at a time. Such a shocking idea needs shows of collective support: street parades, rallies, and electoral campaigns.

It is also hard to imagine two-thirds of Congress and *38 separate state legislatures* signing off on a major constitutional amendment. The Constitution does offer an additional path to reform, the Article V "convention of states." Yet for our purposes, this process is equally bankrupt. States, rather than the people as a whole, would be represented in this convention, and its proposals would have to be ratified by an outrageous 38 states, just like the conventional process. Only the most pigheaded conservative demands would be up for debate. Article V conventions are a Koch Brothers scheme, tailor-made for our enemies.

State-by-state amendment is hopeless. The path is grown-over with weeds and thorns, and we will achieve nothing if we try to crawl through it. But there is an alternative approach: instead of crawling, we could point out the absurdity of the system and demand that the federal government clear a new path to constitutional reform. If it refuses to open the door and stand aside, the Old Order will have to be swept away by extraordinary means.

Let's get imaginative. Let's imagine that America's fledgling socialist movement continues its tentative growth. Let's imagine that the Democratic Socialists of America learns some new tricks. Even if it doesn't immediately adopt its own ballot line, it starts recruiting all of its electoral candidates from within its ranks. It runs them in unified slates and has them vote as an independent bloc, against both capitalist parties.

Suppose that it places a special emphasis on running candidates for the House of Representatives. During those electoral campaigns, and on the House floor, these fiery socialist agitators could demand that Congress pass a *New Union Act*.

What would this New Union Act do?

It could open with something along these lines: "An Act of Congress and the Sovereign People. Not subject to judicial review."

It could acknowledge that the federal government has failed to establish justice, promote the general welfare, or secure the blessings of liberty as promised in the Preamble of the Constitution. It would also acknowledge that the federal government has systematically violated the universal human rights established under the Declaration of Independence. It has subjected the people to spiraling inequality, a climate apocalypse, vicious police brutality, and unrelenting racial oppression.

Therefore, the people of the United States have a right to alter or abolish the Constitution as they see fit, by a simple majoritarian mechanism. Even under ordinary circumstances, a free society has every right to do this, as the Framers themselves acknowledged.

The Act would grant instant amnesty and citizenship to all long-term residents of the United States. It would also facilitate self-determination for all oppressed, indigenous, and colonized peoples in the US — from Puerto Rico to Standing Rock. When we bury the old order's constitution, we will bury the Empire with it.

Alongside this decolonization process, the Act would organize a nationwide election for a National Assembly. This Assembly would be empowered to propose constitutional reforms and place them on the ballot for ratification by the people, by a simple electoral majority.

This election would be conducted by the federal government, not the states. The US Postal Service and other federal agencies would be reorganized to manage the process. Voting could be carried out by universal mail-in ballot, with proportional representation in the Assembly to guarantee multiparty democracy.

Meanwhile, the federal government would fund thousands of small-scale conventions so that all citizens could participate in the reform process. Volunteers and repurposed federal employees would be sent to canvass across the country, inviting citizens to get involved. Online and electronic options would be offered free of charge to anyone unable to attend physical meetings. Employers would be required to give their workers paid time off to take part in the conventions. The conventions would collaborate directly with the Assembly and be empowered to call a new national election at any time.

At the end of the process, the Assembly would place its proposals on the ballot for final ratification. Before voting, citizens would be asked to affirm that they have read the proposals and contributed in some way to the convention process. They would also promise to respect the outcome of the referendum no matter the results, as equal citizens of the Union.

And of course, we would be quite clear about what socialists would advocate throughout this assembly process. We will propose that the new republic be as radically democratic as the process that created it. Abolish the presidency, abolish the Senate, abolish the judiciary as we currently know it. All power to an expanded, improved House of Representatives.

"We demand that Congress initiate this process," our leaders would declare. "But *one way or another*, the working people of this country must clear the path to a new republic."

Objections Answered

This is the kind of solution that socialist leaders should advance. The New Union Act is incisive and principled; it does not pack, partition, or gerrymander. Instead, it calls for the working class to unite in struggle for a decisive break with the past. It encourages a new form of polarization, not just over flags and statues, but between those who support the Old Order and those who do not. At the same time, it advances a new era of universal citizenship, based on mutual obligations and respect.

The demand also transforms those who raise it. In a country consumed by greed and amorality, it ignites a nationwide struggle for freedom. It lifts the American Left out of petty localism and onto a grand fighting arena that spans from coast to coast.

"But we'll never win," some might protest. "It's a beautiful dream, but even if the House got on board, the Senate and Supreme Court would strike it down in a heartbeat."

Yes, the barriers are profound. We can't win a new republic next week or next year. But we can wear the demand on our chests as we struggle to organize the working class, block by block, store by store, and district by district. And as we grow, as the conditions around us continue to deteriorate, perhaps what is impossible right now will start to look more plausible. If we win a majority mandate for the New Union, we will be fully justified as a free people to enact it by any means necessary. Let the Senate and the Supreme Court overrule us: we will appeal to the masses and overturn their decision in the streets.

"But even if you win this National Assembly, the Right could use it too!" others will warn. "What's to stop them from forcing through an abortion ban or a balanced budget amendment?"

Certainly, they could try. In Madison's words, these are improper and wicked projects. But thankfully, the New Union Act would initiate a majoritarian process — and whatever the far right believes, it is not a majority. Most Americans have reasonably progressive sentiments, and even Fox News pollsters know it. Demographic trends are also on our side. Put the People together in a disciplined, well-organized process, and we can encourage their best impulses. The National Assembly will not convene tomorrow morning. Winning it will require many years of struggle that will transform the country in ways we could never predict.

If majority rule serves conservative interests, then why do conservatives oppose it so fervently? Reactionaries have no interest in joining socialists to pursue an egalitarian multiracial democracy. From day one, their goal will be to smash our treasonous conspiracy to "destroy America." At best, they will give us free publicity with their hysterical denunciations.

Then there is a final objection: that the demand I suggest is illegal. It would plunge the country into bloodshed and constitutional crisis. If we raise it, what makes us any better than the MAGA mob?

There's only one honest response to this: we already have bloodshed; we already have crisis, and we already have lawlessness. Warlord cops parade the streets and terrorize working class communities; insurance companies gouge prices, leaving countless patients to rot and die; the President of the United States incites a violent mob, attacking the will of the people, and gets off scot-free.

The MAGA mob was driven by selfishness, bigotry, and willful ignorance. They fought to destroy democracy; we will struggle and suffer to expand it. When our time comes, we will not be wearing devil horns. We will not smear our shit in the hallways. Our goal will always be to advance a just, orderly replacement of the US Constitution.

That project will be fraught with challenges. But laws are made for people, and there will be no real healing in this country until the people win a democratic republic that sets them free. There's another Latin principle that sums it up: *Salus populi suprema lex esto* — The health of the people is the supreme law.

In modern practice:

Fight the Constitution! Demand a New Republic!

WHOSE DEMOCRACY?: AN INTRODUCTION TO OLIGARCHY IN THE UNITED STATES

J.R. Murray
June 20, 2019

The United States is a mockery of what democracy is supposed to be. J.R. Murray unpacks the reality of a corrupt system that is designed to empower the rich against the working class majority.

In the eyes of global elites and much of the populations they govern, liberal democracy's defeat of fascism and communism in the twentieth century has left it the only viable political system. Many now assume liberal democracy sits among humanity's crowning achievements — with no greater advocate than the United States. But for all the mythology around the concept, twenty-first century liberal democracy suffers from a crisis of legitimacy. Right-wing populism and its violence exercise power in a growing number of countries with the intention of preventing select populations from taking part in democratic processes. Simultaneously, Marxism, considered defeated and marginal, is seeing a modest resurgence.

Meanwhile, the United States, the wealthiest and most powerful liberal democracy in the world, experiences outrageously high inequality, stagnant wages, an abysmal healthcare system, a housing crisis, routine acts of police violence, and impending ecological catastrophe. The majority of people in the country are suffering with no end in sight. Shouldn't a democratic political system address those problems? If so, then why are they only getting worse?

The fact is that the capitalist class erects such enormous obstacles to actual democracy that most people can't or won't participate in the token democratic processes that do exist. Liberal democracy is, as Lenin once said, "democracy for an insignificant minority, democracy for the rich."

This is an overview of anti-democratic characteristics and institutions of the US political system, the standard-bearer of democracy for the minority.

Voter Suppression

The United States, historically and presently, systematically suppresses votes. Black Americans, enslaved until the mid-19th century and then openly terrorized, segregated, and disenfranchised through the twentieth and twenty-first centuries, did not get the vote until the 1960s due to various legal, illegal, and quasi-legal methods. Additionally, (white) women could not vote until 1920, and up to the mid-nineteenth century, voting was commonly restricted based on property. Today, measures which produce voter disenfranchisement are still in place.

To start, election day is not a national holiday, but a regular workday. Working on election day makes it incredibly difficult to find time to vote. Higher income voters may be able to take time off, but the poorest workers cannot, and with polling places closing between 6pm and 8pm, it is impossible for some to get to the voting booth. Liberals accept early voting as an acceptable solution to the problem but some states enacted laws restricting early voting. For many, the chance to vote remains subject to the whim of employers.

But voter suppression goes deeper than simply making it hard for workers to find the time to vote on election day. Conservatives, in a cynical plot to suppress the votes of the poor, spread the myth of widespread voter fraud and use it to enact repressive voter identification laws in many states. Such laws restrict the types of identification polling stations will accept — work, college, and public assistance IDs are among the types not accepted. Those restrictions disproportionately affect minorities, immigrants, and the poor—populations which may not have the money, transportation, or time required to obtain appropriate identification.

Of course, voter ID laws are an obstacle only for registered voters. In some states, like North Carolina or Florida, state officials purge the roles of registered voters under spurious accusations of voter fraud. Up to 51 million eligible voters in the United States aren't registered to vote, and right-wing lawmakers are attempting to make it more difficult to register. The simple solution is to automatically register everyone to vote, but the political capital to do so is nonexistent.

Only the working class faces myriad obstacles to cast their ballots, and the poorer the worker, the more obstacles appear before them.

Gerrymandering

Gerrymandering is essentially the redrawing of voting districts by a political party to gain an electoral advantage. The party in charge of drawing congressional districts can divide the map any way they want, which often means cutting up known progressive population areas into little pieces and then grouping those pieces with larger conservative districts. This essentially dissolves the left-leaning vote.

In the 2014 midterm election gerrymandering allowed Republicans to retain control of the House, despite being outvoted. In the 2018 midterm elections, Democrats took the House, but by a smaller margin than expected due to gerrymandering. It's clear that the process is both deeply bureaucratic and anti-democratic, but as long as those who benefit are in charge, it will continue.

The Electoral College

Presidential elections are just as bureaucratic and convoluted as legislative ones. On election day it appears that you are casting your vote for president, but really it's more complicated. While drawing up the Constitution, there was a major disagreement centered on whether to have Congress or all land-owning men elect the president. They compromised by creating the Electoral College.

The Electoral College works like this: before the presidential election, a slate of "electors" are nominated by each political party. When you cast your ballot you are not voting for a candidate, but a political party's electors. The Electoral College consists of 538 electors, with 270 forming a majority. All but two states have a "winner takes all" system. For example, the state of New Jersey has 14 elector spots to fill or 14 "electoral votes." If a majority of the population votes for the Democratic Party, then all 14 elector slots go to the Democratic Party electors, who vote for the Democratic candidate at a later date. This occurs in each state until one party has 270 electoral votes. Everyone who voted Republican in New Jersey? Their votes never make it to the Republican candidate. Everyone who voted Democrat in Texas? Their votes are effectively thrown out.

To simplify — each state counts for a certain number of points. New Jersey 14, Utah 3, California 55, etc. Whichever party gains the most votes in California receives 55 points for their candidate. Your vote does not actually count toward your preferred candidate. Instead, it decides which candidate gets the points your state has to offer. This means that the President of the United States is not chosen by popular vote. This has serious consequences. There are presidents who have lost the popular vote but won the election — most recently, Donald Trump and George W. Bush.

The Merger of Capitalists and the State

While it's necessary to examine individual policies that restrict democracy, it's also important to analyze anti-democratic social and economic structures the policies operate within. A simple explanation of capitalism illuminates and contextualizes these structures.

The world can be divided into two broad groups of people: those who own the things necessary for society to function and for people to survive, and those who do not own these things. The first group, the capitalists, owns everything from factories to transportation infrastructure, farmland to real estate, and everything else used to produce our society. The rest of us—the workers—write the code, drive the trucks, stack the shelves, work the call centres, serve the food, pack the packages, and ensure that the things capitalists own operate correctly. It is not a symbiotic relationship, but an exploitative one. The workers own only their labor power, which they sell to a capitalist in exchange for wages. But wages are always less than the profit that workers produce for the capitalist.

One way that the capitalist class maintains this exploitative system is through the state. The state's primary function is as a tool used by one class to suppress another. Under feudalism, it was used to exploit and oppress serfs for the benefit of lords. In modern society, it is used by capitalists to exploit and oppress workers.

We are conscious of this when we speak of "money in politics." US elections, presidential or otherwise, are primarily funded by wealthy individuals and corporations. "Citizens United," the Supreme Court decision allowing corporations to funnel a previously unheard of amount of money into political campaigns via "Super PACs," is the most famous example. But even if Citizens United were repealed the rich would continue to buy our democratic process. Besides individual capitalists bankrolling entire political campaigns, billionaires own the media whose job it is to report on elections, coordinate with and fund influential think-tanks that shape policy, and even draft legislation.

Lobbying by capitalists is particularly detrimental to authentic democracy. Each lobby organizes by industry to convince lawmakers to enact profitable legislation for that industry. Pharmaceutical companies, oil companies, defense manufacturers—every single industry—have powerful lobbyists in Washington. In what amounts to bribery, lobbyists treat members of Congress to expensive dinners, sporting events, and expensive vacations where they plead the case for their industry. During these one-on-one meetings, politicians are often promised jobs as lobbyists if they comply with the industry's demands. The transition from public servant to private lobbyist comes with a pay raise and mostly consists of calling in favors from old friends and colleagues to influence policy. This "revolving door" permeates through all levels of government from high ranking officials to congressional staffers and bureaucrats.

This "revolving door" is a clever metaphor masking a more insidious truth — capitalists and politicians are identical. Legislators, cabinet members, and administration bureaucrats all slide effortlessly between the role of a public official and companies like Goldman Sachs, ExxonMobile, and Lockheed Martin. This is most explicit in the Trump administration, where former CEO of ExxonMobile ran the State Department, and the Environmental Protection Agency is currently run by a former coal lobbyist. And this is not to mention Trump himself, a billionaire real estate developer.

The interchangeability of capitalists and government officials is not unique to the current government, but a fact of every presidential administration. After his stint in government former Attorney General Eric Holder, who chose not to prosecute any of the big banks after the 2008 financial meltdown, rejoined Covington & Burling, a law firm that represents the largest banks on Wall Street. Holder now works alongside Michael Chertoff, Secretary of Homeland Security from 2005–09. Chertoff is the co-founder of the "Chertoff Group," a risk-management and security consulting company that employs former members of the US government including Michael Hayden, former director of the CIA and NSA; a man responsible for Guantanamo Bay, CIA black sites, government surveillance, and countless extra-judicial killings abroad.

The Chertoff Group is far from the only influential business employing former government officials. Lisa Jackson, head of the EPA from 2009-2013 now works for Apple. The former director of the Domestic Policy Council, Melody Barnes, sits on the board of directors for the defense contracting giant Booz Allen Hamilton. Obama's former Deputy Chief of Staff, Mona Sutphen, went on to work for UBS, a global financial services company. She was also a partner for Macro Advisory Partners, whose purpose—which is clear even when coated in sterile language—is to develop strategies for corporate clients to exploit the global poor. Rich Armitage, Deputy Director of the Bush administration's State Department, is a board member for Man-Tech International, a defense and national security company whose other board members include a former CIA official who helped assess intelligence information during the lead up to the Iraq war, the head of an investment management firm, and a retired Lieutenant General. Samuel Bodman, Deputy Secretary of the Department of Commerce from 2001-2004, Deputy Secretary of the Treasury from 2004-2005, and Secretary of Energy from 2005-2009, joined the board of directors for the chemical giant Dupont shortly after leaving the White House.

The list stretches on forever. Every administration official, senator, representative, and congressional staffer comes from or moves onto powerful law firms, lobbying firms, think tanks, NGOs, defense contractors, transnational corporations, or other powerful private institutions.

These are the people socialists refer to as "the ruling class," and they cannot be voted out of power. If a congressman loses an election he merely becomes a lobbyist and gains even more influence. If the term limit of an administration ends, the individual functionaries and bureaucrats join institutions that hold enormous power over the state. No election can rid the state of capitalist interests; no election can force the state to work in the interest of the working class.

Two-Party System, One-Party State

In 1956 W.E.B. Dubois explained his refusal to vote: "I shall not go to the polls. I have not registered. I believe that democracy has so far disappeared in the United States that no 'two evils' exist. There is but one evil party with two names, and it will be elected despite all I can do or say." Dubois's analysis is still applicable. The Democrats and Republicans are factions of the same party—the capitalist party. The division between the two occurs over a difference in strategy, not a difference in goals.

Each party is ultimately beholden to the special interest groups funding them, all of whom wish to maintain capitalism and ensure their industry benefits from its maintenance. A base of committed voters must be catered to, but only within the boundaries set by elites. If possible, all debate is restricted to "culture war" issues that, while important, are debated in a way that refuses to confront capitalism. Additionally, while it is generally true that people suffer more under Republican administrations, people continue to suffer immensely under Democratic ones. Both parties are culpable in creating the conditions for misogyny, racism, poverty, exploitation, and all the ills of capitalism.

Republicans appeal to the economic interests of small business owners and the most backward elements of the working class to cut social programs and attack minority groups, while the Democrats appeal to urban professionals and progressive sections of the working class, to surreptitiously implement policies with similar consequences. Democrats helped lay the groundwork for the Trump administration's worst authoritarian excesses. Some examples include mass deportations, expanding the war on terror, prosecuting whistleblowers, expanding mass surveillance, increasing fracking, and regime change.

Despite not being banned outright, third parties face various anti-democratic measures ensuring their defeat at the polls. During a presidential election, the Electoral College represents the most blatant obstacle to democracy. A candidate, third party or otherwise, can gain 49% of the vote in a state and receive no electoral votes. First past the post voting extends downwards to most congressional and state elections, guaranteeing a loss of representation for everyone who did not vote for the winning candidate. Third party candidates often can't be voted for at all. In the 2016 presidential election cycle, the Libertarian Party was the only alternative party with ballot access in all 50 states. The Green Party gained access in 45. This was possible because they had the money and full-time organizers to petition for ballot access. Explicitly socialist parties do not have the resources to navigate the complexities of gaining access to the ballot.

First past the post voting and ballot access aside, it is still an uphill battle for alternative political parties. Campaign funding reimbursement is only available to parties who receive 5% of the popular vote during federal elections. Any prospect of obtaining it is hindered by poor media coverage and the 15% poll requirement to gain entry into national debates, which are run by an organization completely dominated by the Democratic and Republican parties.

The Executive, the Senate, the Supreme Court

Every US civics textbook explains that the government is built upon a series of "checks and balances." The Executive, Legislative, and Judicial branches of government balance power between themselves and check the power of any branch hoping to gain an advantage over the other two. It is said that these checks and balances are necessary to sustain democracy, and yet, as we have seen, we live in a deeply undemocratic society. The reality is that each branch of government is itself undemocratic, and the most democratic of the three, the legislature, has the most checks restraining it.

The Executive Branch

The Executive branch is a sprawling bureaucracy (headed by a president selected through an undemocratic election process) that gains more power every decade. Each department of the executive branch unfolds into a vast bureaucracy of unaccountable functionaries. The Department of Defense alone encompasses the office of Secretary of Defense, Defense Intelligence Agency, National Security Agency, National Geospatial Intelligence Agency, National Reconnaissance Office, Joint Chiefs of Staff, Department of the Navy, Department of the Army, Department of the Air Force, and accounts for 21% of the federal budget. On election day voters elect one candidate, and that one candidate appoints and oversees this military bureaucracy.

The Executive controls almost all aspects of foreign policy with this endless bureaucracy. The Executive's power in this regard is made clear by the numerous "conflicts" it has initiated over the heads of Congress since the invasion of Vietnam. Congress, allegedly vested with the sole power to declare war, hasn't done so since World War Two. Under Obama, the executive branch improved and formalized its ability to kill anyone around the world at will. Congress was unable to prevent the Trump Administration from tearing up the Iran Nuclear Deal. Now the administration threatens to take military action, likely without approval from Congress. There are no checks or balances on the United States war machine.

Of course, this is simply one section of the sprawling Executive branch. Every section of the branch is similarly large and complex.

These bureaucrats are far removed from any democratic accountability, and as we have seen, often use their positions to make themselves rich and advance the interests of their capitalist friends. Bureaucracy is not inherently undemocratic, and when managing a country of 350 million people some form of it is necessary, but minor checks on Executive bureaucracy do nothing to hold it accountable to voters.

Additionally, the President appoints unelected "czars" to coordinate between different departments. In this way, the Executive unifies its bureaucracy around different issues in an attempt to bypass Congress. Writing for Dissent Magazine, Mark Tushnet explains,

> Presidents appoint czars to deal with new policy problems that cut across regulatory areas, like managing the recent automobile bailout. In a different political environment, presidents might send legislation to Congress. Believing that to be pointless, however, most presidents have decided to appoint czars to pull together everyone who has existing statutory authority in a particular field of policymaking. The czars have no power to develop new regulations, but their prominence and White House credentials give them enormous influence over those who do the regulatory work—and this helps enact presidential policies without congressional oversight.

Ostensibly, it is the purpose of the Legislative and Judicial branches to hold this vast, powerful, bureaucracy accountable, but the Executive has checks on these branches too. Popular legislation passed by Congress can be vetoed by the president, ending the democratic process with a single signature. Additionally, the president nominates which judges sit on the Supreme Court, and no president will nominate a judge keen on limiting executive power.

However, Executive checks on the Legislative and Judicial branches are not the root cause of their ineffectiveness. The two branches are internally dysfunctional and authoritarian on their own.

The Senate

The Legislative branch is the most democratic of the three branches. Unfortunately, this means very little. The Executive branch constantly bypasses Congress, which is evident in the creation of policy czars, the top-down bureaucracy, and the "deep state" that it represents. It is further compromised by the two-party system and the revolving door and is subject to the same voting restrictions and voter suppression detailed above.

Beyond these limits and restrictions, the Legislative branch resists popular demands all on its own. Much of the blame for this falls at the feet of the Senate, the most reactionary, undemocratic, elitist institution of any modern liberal democracy. Its existence is predicated entirely on suppressing the more democratic House of Representatives.

The Senate does not abide by the democratic principle of "one person, one vote." Instead, it practices "one state, one vote." While states send representatives to the House proportionate to their population, the Senate is selected on the premise of equal representation of all states. Wyoming, population 584,000, has the same number of votes in the Senate as New York's almost 20 million people. This is how Senators representing a small minority of the country block the will of the majority. The anti-democratic mechanisms are so blatant that a political party receiving more votes than its opponent won't necessarily gain more Senate seats. Senators representing sparsely populated states effectively hold democracy hostage not only through voting down popular legislation but also through filibustering, which allows 41 Senators representing less than 11% of the population to block legislation from being voted on at all. Any legislation passed by the House can be rejected or altered by the Senate. It has veto powers over executive appointments and treaties. Two-thirds of the Senate is required to pass a constitutional amendment.

The Senate is a powerful minority ruled institution, with members bankrolled by capitalists, acting as a bulwark against popular progressive legislation. As such, it plays an important part in the Right's domination of American politics. Daniel Lazare, writing for Jacobin, explains:

> Over the next decade or so, the white portion of the ten largest states is projected to continue ticking downward, while the opposite will occur in the ten smallest. By 2030, the population ratio between the largest and smallest state is estimated to increase from sixty-five to one to nearly eighty-nine to one. The Senate will be more racist as a consequence, more unrepresentative, and more of a plaything in the hands of the militant right.

As time goes on the Senate will become more dominated by populist white nationalists at the expense of popular working class demands.

The Supreme Court

The Supreme Court is the final interpreter of the US Constitution. It can overturn legislation passed by Congress through the power of judicial review. Each justice is nominated by the Executive Branch and confirmed by the Senate, and every justice serves for life. The House of Representatives has no power in the process of selecting justices.

For a moment, in the twentieth century, liberals viewed the Supreme Court as a vehicle for positive social change. But lasting social change only comes from below. It cannot be handed down from the courts, and so the brief time of progressive rulings inevitably passed. Despite occasional small gains won by the Left, the Supreme Court remains what it was meant to be — a reactionary servant of power guaranteeing the destruction of left-leaning legislation.

The Supreme Court is the greatest threat to legislation born from a mass working-class movement. Popular legislation passed by Congress and signed by the President can be overturned in part or in full by an unelected body of nine people, serving a life term, tasked with upholding and interpreting an outdated and inherently undemocratic document.

If Bernie Sanders is elected in 2020 and manages to shepherd Medicare For All through the House and the Senate, the risk of the Supreme Court ruling the law unconstitutional would remain. If this occurs there would be little recourse. A constitutional amendment is the only way around the Supreme Court, and the requirements are so onerous it took the Civil War to implement recent meaningful amendments.

If all other restrictions on democracy fail the Supreme Court serves as the ultimate negation of popular policy. It is the final backstop against the will of the majority.

A Workers' Republic

Similar to feudal lords who owned the land and the serfs forced to work it, today a few wealthy capitalists own the means of production that wage workers must work. If the serfs were allowed, through a convoluted process stacked against them, to vote for their lords, would we call that democracy? True democracy is only possible when workers have control over their lives, their communities, and the means of production.

Our economy is not a democracy. Workers have no say in how companies are run, how resources are allocated, or how production is arranged. Political democracy is meant to be a consolation for economic dictatorship — at least we are free to pick our leaders. But in the "land of the free" even political democracy eludes us.

The working class is the majority of people in the United States. An average worker spends most of their life producing for society, making society function. And yet the working class has no control over the society that depends on them to survive. What we are living under is the dictatorship of the capitalist class. They control the means of production and use the state to maintain that control. The tyranny of CEO's, Wall Street executives, corrupt politicians, and bureaucrats decide the fate of the majority.

What is needed is a "dictatorship of the working class," i.e., a dictatorship of the majority in the form of a "workers' republic," a true democracy where workers have wrested control of the state from the capitalists, control the means of production, and democratically plan the economy. Democracy, freedom, liberty, equality, the pursuit of happiness are all impossible while the majority of people are ruthlessly exploited and have no control over their lives, where they are denied even the most basic political freedoms promised by liberalism. Humanity's potential cannot be fulfilled without the emancipation of the working class. Until that day comes democracy is a reality only for the ruling elite and remains an illusion for the rest of us.

Lenin and the "Class Point of View": Looking at Chris Maisano's "The Constitution and the Class Struggle"

Gil Shaeffer
March 25, 2021

Gil Schaeffer responds to Chris Maisano's "The Constitution and the Class Struggle" to clarify the meaning of the "class point of view" in Lenin and what it can tell us about the struggle for democracy.

When I first ran across Seth Ackerman's "Burn the Constitution" back in 2011, I thought: wow, here is some writing with the power and incisiveness of I. F. Stone, Malcolm X, Carl Oglesby. I immediately went to the *Jacobin* website, expecting to find a radical democratic publication. It turned out to be something much more tentative and diffuse. Alongside Ackerman's searing indictment of the U. S. political system, there was a mix of articles wrestling with the problems of postmodernism and identity politics in the academy, of the unfulfilled promise of social democracy in Europe, and of what life in a socialist society might look and feel like. Over the next five years, *Jacobin* stuck to this editorial policy of publishing a wide range of views on the left and its history without feeling any pressing need to define a distinctive ideology and strategy of its own. But that changed with Bernie Sanders's 2016 campaign for President. Trying to catch up to and influence the hundreds of thousands of young people drawn to the idea of socialism through Sanders's campaign, *Jacobin* has since put a great deal of effort into articulating its strategy of a "democratic road to socialism." I laid out my criticisms of this strategy and the selective use of Karl Kautsky's writings to justify it in "The Curious Case of the 'Democratic Road to Socialism' That Wasn't There." The aim of this article is the opposite. Its purpose is to pick out what is positive in *Jacobin's* thinking about a democratic road to socialism and carry its logic beyond the scope of that publication.

At the end of "Why Kautsky Was Right (and Why You Should Care)," after presenting his case for a strategy of winning elections within the "capitalist democracy" of the U. S., Eric Blanc tacks on the qualification that the U. S. actually has an "extremely undemocratic political system." Blanc doesn't think that calling the U. S. both democratic and undemocratic at the same time is a problem and patches over this paradox by adding that the strategy of winning elections should also "prompt socialists to focus more on fighting to democratize the political regime." As examples of how this two-pronged strategy of winning elections and democratizing the political regime at the same time might work, Blanc links to two proposals put forward by Jamal Abed-Rabbo[1] and Chris Maisano,[2] respectively. Because Abed-Rabbo's piece only focuses on the particular problem of first-past-the-post electoral systems and does not even mention the problem of disproportionate representation in the Senate or the unaccountable power of the Supreme Court, it doesn't really address the most serious anti-democratic features of the Constitution and can safely be put aside. Maisano's article, on the other hand, does confront the full scope of the Constitution's undemocratic structure and therefore merits closer examination.

1 Jamal Abed-Rabbo, "Ready for (Political) Revolution?" DSA Socialist Forum, Fall, 2018

2 Maisano, Chris. "The Constitution and the Class Struggle," The Call, November 27, 2018. https://socialistcall.com/2018/11/27/the-constitution-and-the-class-struggle/

I'm going to break down Maisano's article into three parts: its solid political and historical core, its weak tactical and agitational recommendations, and the theoretical question about the relationship between democracy and the class struggle suggested in the title.

Like Ackerman, Maisano lists the many ways in which the Constitution violates the basic democratic principle of one person, one equal vote, but Maisano goes further and places the problem of democracy in a larger historical and international context. Urging the DSA to "develop a national political platform that includes a call for the establishment of a truly democratic republic for the first time in our country's history," Maisano emphasizes that the demand for a democratic republic has been at the center of working-class and socialist movements from the start, beginning with the U. S. Workingmen's Party and the Chartists in the 1820s and '30s, continuing in the work of Marx and Engels, and finally becoming the primary political demand of pre-WWI European Social Democracy and the US Socialist Party. He ends with the assertion that the democratic republic is "the framework in which the transition from capitalist oligarchy to democratic socialism will eventually be achieved."

So far, so good. Maisano has outlined the classic Marxist conception of the relationship between winning the battle for democracy and the transition to socialism. The next question is what tactics and forms of political agitation the demand for a democratic republic calls for. Here Maisano abandons any reference to how working-class and socialist movements fought for democracy in the past and shifts to a legalist constitutionally loyal framework, concluding that "Given the egregiously high barriers to calling a constitutional convention or amending the current constitution, a demand for a wholly new constitution would be utopian." Not surprisingly, this statement triggered criticisms that Maisano was giving up the fight for democracy before it had even begun. Tim Horras in particular zeroed in on this statement as proof that "the reformists turn back before even reaching the limited horizon of bourgeois legality."[3]

However, Horras's criticism of Maisano's tactical timidity, unfortunately, did not include a reassertion of the political centrality of the goal of a democratic republic. To be sure, Horras agreed with Maisano that the U. S. political system is undemocratic, but for Horras this lack of democracy is just one more reason to begin to prepare immediately for armed insurrection and socialist revolution. Maisano responded that Horras's insurrectionist strategy would lead only to the left's political isolation. To avoid isolation, Maisano argued[4] that participation in elections should be the primary focus of socialist political activity in "a formal democracy like the U. S." Now, notice the funny thing that has happened in the course of this back and forth: the demand for a democratic republic has dropped out of the picture. What started out as a promise by Maisano to explore the relationship between the Constitution and the class struggle ended up with Maisano falling back into calling the US a democracy and forgetting about the democratic republic. I think Maisano's original promise to discuss the relationship between the Constitution and the class struggle is too important to let go.

It is not clear what moved Maisano to take up the subject of the Constitution in the first place and to urge the DSA to include the demand for a democratic republic in its platform. Although *Jacobin* has continued over the years to publish articles on the Constitution and the history of the working class's struggle for democracy, its main political and theoretical preoccupation has been the failure of post-WWII European social democratic par-

3 Horras, Tim. "Goodbye Revolution?," Regeneration Magazine, April 15, 2019. https://revolutionaryleftradio.libsyn.com/regeneration-goodbye-revolution

4 Maisano, Chris. "Which Way to Socialism?," The Call, May 21, 2019. https://socialistcall.com/2019/05/21/democratic-socialism-revolution-chris-maisano/

ties in genuine parliamentary democracies to continue down the road to socialism. The Bread and Roses caucus of the DSA has codified this Eurocentric focus in its "Socialist Politics: A Reading List," which leans heavily on the work of Miliband and Poulantzas. Maisano raising the problem of the Constitution and the possibility that the U. S. isn't a democracy at all is definitely an outlier in this theoretical scheme. Obviously, something bugged him about the peculiarity of the U. S. political system and he felt the need to write about it. This willingness to question and expand the received categories of prevailing socialist thinking is the positive element in *Jacobin's* strategy of a democratic road to socialism. My aim is to follow Maisano's turn down the road toward a democratic republic to the end.

Maisano himself stops and then veers off this road. He stops in the first article because he thinks the immediate demand for a democratic constitution would be "utopian" and he veers back onto the electoral road in his reply to Horras, reverting to the fairy tale that the U. S. is a democracy, that its electoral system possesses a controlling legitimacy, and that participation in this system is the main way to constitute the working class as a collective political subject. I'm not going to try to get inside Maisano's head to figure out why he veered back or to polemicize too strongly against this electoral road. Rather, I'm mainly going to measure Maisano's political positions against his own references to the history of the struggle for democracy. Let's start with utopian. Utopian means adhering to an ideal that is not humanly realizable. What does Maisano mean when he says that the demand for a wholly new constitution would be utopian? The working-class movements of the past that Maisano references did not think the demand for democracy was utopian, and a good number of countries now have democratic political systems as a result. Maisano is misusing the word and seems to be saying that the demand for a democratic constitution in the US is not *immediately* realizable. But no one would dispute that.

The issue is what demands are for. They are not just for what is immediately realizable; they can also be analytical, educational, and aspirational. The history of Marxism is largely made up of debates about what demands should be included in a political program and how these demands might best be communicated to workers in the hope they will adopt them as their own. Maisano doesn't delve very deeply into this history and drops the subject altogether when he switches over to his dispute with Horras.

Horras is an easy target, a modern-day reincarnation of one of Lenin's left-wing communists. Because capitalism is historically obsolete and ultimately can only maintain itself through armed force, Horras thinks the main job of socialists is to pound away at this truth and to get ready militarily for the final showdown. He forgets Lenin's admonition that what is historically obsolete is not necessarily politically obsolete. Lenin was certainly a believer in Marx's theory of the state when he launched *Iskra*, but that newspaper's purpose was not to repeat Marx's doctrine of the state over and over again and urge immediate military preparedness but to take mass political sentiment as it existed in order to develop it into a political movement demanding that society's laws be made by a democratic assembly of the people. Building the consciousness for such a political movement was his main preparation for the ultimate conquest of power. Luxemburg's approach was the same when German workers rose up to demand suffrage reform in 1910. Horras completely ignores this history of how Marxists went about building mass political movements. Maisano makes a similar criticism of Horras's stunted conception of mass politics and argues that "Political Action Is Key." He is right. The question is what kind of political action.

For Maisano, political action is overwhelmingly electoral action. In his reply to Horras he writes, "elections and participation in representative institutions plays a crucial role in constituting classes as collective political subjects. As Carmen

Sirianni has argued, parliaments 'have been the major national forums for representing class-wide political and economic interests of workers... there was no pristine proletarian public prior to parliament, and the working class did not have a prior existence as a national political class.'"[5] Really? I have no idea what a "pristine proletarian public" is supposed to be, but I do know that the Chartists and the European workers' organizations and parties that led mass campaigns for the right to vote already had a sense of themselves as a national political class in order to demand the vote in the first place. And even after they had won the right to vote but were trapped within systems of unequal representation, the leading expressions of national political class consciousness were centered in the literature, protests, demonstrations, and strikes demanding further suffrage reform and complete democracy. Of course, electoral campaigns and parliamentary oratory also played a role in these movements, but the working class's sense of political legitimacy was invested in the goal of true democratic representation, not in the restricted power and choices of existing unrepresentative parliamentary elections and institutions.

The underlying problem with Maisano's analysis and with the *Jacobin*/Bread and Roses political tendency is that they take as their baseline the world of post-WWII European social democracy. There are two reasons why this model is inadequate for understanding the challenges facing the U. S. left. The obvious one is that the U. S. is still a pre-democratic state in which elections are vastly less representative than in European social democracies. The less obvious one concerns the historical and political origins of Europe's social-democratic institutions themselves. It must be remembered that fascism

5 Sacks, Adam J. "Like Voting Rights? Thank a Socialist," Jacobin, December 21, 2018. https://jacobin.com/2018/12/workers-movement-universal-suffrage-socialism-second-international. Sacks presents a good short history of the development of working-class political consciousness prior to entry into parliament.

crushed the European workers' parties and movements and was only defeated by the Allied armies in WWII. In the western part of Europe, the U. S. then oversaw the construction of parliamentary institutions remarkably more democratic than its own in order to neutralize the appeal of more radical left and Communist political forces; yet these new national governments were enmeshed in a web of super-national Cold War military and economic structures dominated by the U. S., a dominance that continues today. *Jacobin* talks very little about this difficult history, but it is a decisive factor weighing against their position that contemporary European social-democracy is a useful guide for understanding how our own struggle for democratic political institutions is likely to develop.

In arguing that the DSA should include the demand for a democratic republic in its platform, Maisano linked to the 1912 Platform of the U. S. Socialist Party, which called for the abolition of the Senate and the veto power of the President, the removal of the Supreme Court's power to abrogate legislation enacted by Congress, the election of the President by popular vote, and the ability to amend the Constitution by a majority of voters in a majority of the states. Where have these demands been for the last one hundred years? Very roughly, WWI and the Bolshevik Revolution not only split socialists into hostile revolutionary and reformist camps, they also gave rise to the entirely new concepts of soviet vs. parliamentary democracy and one-party rule vs. multi-party elections. For Marxist-Leninists, the old goal of a democratic republic was no longer enough and was summarily dismissed as just another form of bourgeois democracy. On the reformist side, liberal capitalist republics like the U. S., no matter how distorted and unrepresentative their political systems, were increasingly referred to as democracies in contrast to the Soviet dictatorship. The reputation of the U. S. was further enhanced by the contrast between the New Deal and fascism. This democracy/dictatorship dichotomy so dominated political thinking over the last century that even democratic-minded comparative historians such as Barrington Moore, Eric Hobsbawm, Perry Anderson, and Michael Mann were not able to break away from classifying the U. S. as a liberal or social democracy. They couldn't see that we are still in the Age of the Democratic Revolution.

There was a brief revival of democratic language and thinking in the Civil Rights Movement and in the participatory democracy of the New Left, but that gave way by the late 1960s to revolutionary anti-imperialism and Maoism. After twenty years in the doldrums, which included the collapse of the Soviet Union, some new thinking began to emerge in the mid-1990s. On an intellectual level, fundamental critiques of the Constitution's structure started popping up, beginning with Thomas Geoghegan's "The Infernal Senate" (1994), followed by Daniel Lazare's much more comprehensive *The Frozen Republic: How the Constitution Is Paralyzing Democracy* (1996), Robert Dahl's *How Democratic Is the American Constitution?* (2001), and Sanford Levinson's *Our Undemocratic Constitution* (2006). Popular dissatisfaction with the political system grew in parallel. The list of offenses is long: the Democratic Party's failure to reverse conservative policies and pro-corporate economic dogma after twelve years of Republican rule; the Supreme Court's intervention in the 2000 election; the lies and deception of the Iraq war; the failure, again, of the Democrats to come to grips with the economic and health care crises, this time hiding behind the fig leaf of the filibuster; and then the 2016 election and the absurdity of the Electoral College. The response has been Occupy Wall Street, Black Lives Matter, increasing working-class activity, Bernie Sanders, DSA expansion, and the electoral victories of Justice Democrats. Maisano has attempted to pull these historical, intellectual, and political strands together into a coherent ideological and strategic whole. He doesn't get it right, but he does raise the right question: What is the relationship between democracy and the class struggle?

There is no way to answer this question without first pinning down more specifically what we mean by democracy. Maisano and *Jacobin* in general wobble back and forth between defining democracy as universal and equal suffrage or just universal suffrage.[6] The 1912 Platform of the Socialist Party contained no such ambiguity and neither did the programmes of the socialist parties of the Second International. The most comprehensive analysis of this issue by a Marxist was made by none other than Karl Kautsky in his 1905 essay "The Republic and Social Democracy in France."[7] In a comment on my last article, Jacob Richter called this essay "*State and Revolution* before Lenin's pamphlet, minus overheated polemical language." This characterization is accurate because the aim of both was to use Marx's writings on the Paris Commune as the measure of the meaning of democracy and the institutional requirements of a truly democratic republic. The target of Kautsky's critique was the Third French Republic, which had universal and relatively equal voting for the lower house of its legislature but restricted and indirect voting for its Senate and powerful centralized presidency. Engels had called this system "nothing but the Empire established in 1799 without the Emperor," and Kautsky's argument was that social democrats should not take ministerial positions or expect adequate reforms within such a system but should concentrate their agitation and activity on complete democratization. The logic was simple: If the leaders of a bourgeois republic were truly open to meaningful reform, they would remove the electoral barriers preventing reform. Means and ends went together. Without a fully democratic political system,

6 In "Electoral Politics, Class Formation, and Socialist Strategy," Socialist Forum, Spring/Summer 2019, Maisano explicitly adopts universal suffrage as the measure and drops the equal part.
7 Karl Kautsky on Democracy and Republicanism, (Brill: Leiden, The Netherlands, 2020), Edited and translated by Ben Lewis. Paperback out from Haymarket Books, October, 2020. Partial translation at weeklyworker.uk., Issues 863, 866, 867.

it was a "republican superstition" to expect democratic results. When Maisano and the Jacobin/Bread and Roses group choose only universal suffrage rather than universal and equal suffrage as their standard of democracy, they are falling for this republican superstition.

Left-wing politics follow a predictable pattern in political regimes with universal suffrage but unequal representation. Those who are under the influence of the republican superstition elevate the winning of elections over agitation for full democracy. Then, because little or nothing changes, large sections of the population lose patience with politics-as-usual and rise up in protest. Those willing to pursue electoral victory on the lowest possible political basis then typically react by accusing the protesters of undermining the chances for electoral success. The dispute between Luxemburg and Kautsky in 1910 followed this pattern, as did the confrontation at the 1964 Democratic Party National Convention over the seating of the Mississippi Freedom Democrats, and, in our own recent mini replay of this drama, we have Dustin Guastella in *Jacobin* condemning militant protest activity and identity politics for endangering his bread and butter electoral strategy (his final rant coincidentally appearing on the same day as George Floyd's murder).[8] Guastella's remarks may have been unusually crude, but they were still well within *Jacobin's* current ideological framework that distinguishes "anti-electoral movementism" from their strategy of "class struggle elections."[9] Of course, this either/or dichotomy is incomplete and mislead-

8 Dustin Guastella, "Where Do We Go After Last Night's Defeat," Jacobin, 3/11/2020, and "We Need a Class War, Not a Culture War," Jacobin, 5/25/2020.

9 Paul Heideman, 'Mass Politics, Not Movementism, Is the Future of the Left," Jacobin, 4/12/2020. For the concept of "class struggle elections," see Megan Svoboda, "What Are Class Struggle Elections?" The Call, 7/16/2019; Marianela D'Aprile, "Reality Check: We Need Class-Struggle Elections," The Call, 5/8/2020; and Meagan Day and Micah Uetricht, Bigger Than Bernie, (Verso: 2020).

ing because it leaves out *Jacobin's* and Maisano's own historical reminders that the first priority of the class struggle in classical Marxism was the fight for universal and equal suffrage. They seem to forget that in an undemocratic political system there can be such a thing as a movement for electoral democracy.

Just as the meaning of democracy gets whittled down in Maisano's post-Constitution article to fit his electoral strategy, so too does the concept of the class struggle. In his Constitution article, Maisano emphasized the broad political content of the class struggle in traditional socialism. A combination of the Utopian Socialist critique of capitalist property relations and the radical democratic egalitarianism of Tom Paine and the French Revolution, Marx and Engels created a theory of the class struggle that was opposed to exploitation and oppression of every kind, whether economic, political, religious, national, racial, or patriarchal. In the *Jacobin/*Bread and Roses strategy of "class struggle elections," this broad conception of the class struggle gets narrowed down to across the board economic demands such as Medicare for all, raising the minimum wage, and support for unions. Racial, feminist, LGBTQ, and immigration struggles, even when fully justified and deserving of support for moral reasons, fall outside the category of "class" politics in *Jacobin's* formulation.[10] While this position has rightly been called class reductionist, *Jacobin's* critics on this point haven't entirely overcome their own form of reductionism, much as Horras couldn't offer an adequate conception of mass politics to counter Maisano's form of electoralism. Tatiana Cozzarelli's "Class Reductionism Is Real, and It's Coming from the Jacobin Wing

10 Articles on this issue include Melissa Naschek, "The Identity Mistake," *Jacobin*, 8/28/2018; Jeremy Gong and Eric Blanc, "Race, Class, and Socialist Strategy," The Call, 8/30/2018; R.L. Stephens, "Editorial: The Mistaken Universalism," DSA Weekly, 9/4/2018; Jeremy Gong and Eric Blanc, "Class Politics and the Fight Against Oppression," The Call, 7/7/2018; and Chris Maisano, "No, the Racial Justice Protests Are Not at Odds with Class Politics," *Jacobin*, 6/26/2020.

of the DSA" is both a good summary of where this debate now stands and an example of how many self-described revolutionary socialists come up short when formulating an alternative.

Cozzarelli begins by defining class reductionism as "the belief that class causes all oppression and, in turn, that economic changes are enough to resolve all forms of oppression." Eugene Debs's view of race and socialism fits this definition — "There is no Negro question outside the labor question. The real issue... is not social equality but economic freedom. The class struggle is colorless." — but *Jacobin* and Bread and Roses are not reductionists of this kind. They do not deny that there are struggles against particular oppressions that socialists should support and they do not hold that economic changes by themselves will resolve all other forms of oppression. They say that socialists should fight both the class struggle and other oppressions at the same time, though they view their so-called class-wide demands as strategically primary. Cozzarelli recognizes the difference between *Jacobin* and Debs and consequently adjusts her definition of class reductionism. Rather than saying that *Jacobin* reduces race to class, she, like R. L Stephens's critique cited in note 11, says that *Jacobin* shrinks the concept of class to exclude race and other struggles from class. Quoting an often-cited passage from *What Is to Be Done? (WITBD)*, Cozzarelli agrees with Lenin that a real socialist should "react to every manifestation of tyranny and oppression, no matter where it appears, no matter what stratum or class of the people it affects... and produce a single picture of police violence and capitalist exploitation... in order to set forth before all his [sic] socialist convictions and his democratic demands."[11] She then interprets this passage to mean that "fighting against racism is a class-wide demand," that taking "up the demands of the most oppressed sectors of society ... strengthens class consciousness and working-class unity," that "socialists should be able to show that ... socialist revolution

11 Lenin, CW, vol. 5, p. 423. All citations from 4th ed.

89

is the path towards liberation for all oppressed and working-class people," and that it is time for a mass politics not of the *Jacobin* economic electoral type but of socialist revolution.

There is a blind spot in this critique. The passage from Lenin that Cozzarelli quotes comes from the section of *WITBD* titled "The Working Class as Vanguard Fighter for Democracy," and the quotation itself says that socialists should set forth not only their socialist convictions but also their "democratic demands." Cozzarelli doesn't ask why Lenin would call the working class a vanguard fighter for democracy rather than socialism. Nor does she inquire into what he meant by democratic demands or acknowledge that Lenin's primary political goal was the establishment of a democratic republic. This neglect of the difference between democratic and socialist demands is its own form of reductionism and involves viewing and treating non-socialist mass struggles as if they were primarily opportunities for socialists "to show that socialist revolution is the path towards liberation for all oppressed and working-class people." That's a recipe for sectarian socialist preaching, not political leadership. Lenin's approach was different.

I started reading Lenin's agitational writings in late August 1971. After three years in SDS, I had joined the Revolutionary Union in Oakland following the invasion of Cambodia and the national student strike. On August 21, 1971, George Jackson was killed at San Quentin Prison, and I got the job of writing an article for the RU's local monthly newspaper explaining why it was important for the working class to support the struggle that Jackson had waged against the prison industrial complex and for Black liberation. Putting the Black liberation struggle together with an as yet non-existent revolutionary workers' movement in a coherent way was proving difficult, so the RU leader heading up the paper suggested I read "The Drafting of 183 Students into the Army,"[12] a 1901 article by Lenin from *Iskra*, to get some

12 Lenin, CW, vol. 4, pp. 414-19.

ideas. The article, which was a report on the punishments meted out to university students demanding academic and political reforms from Tsarist authorities, read more like something from *I. F. Stone's Weekly* than one of Lenin's dense major polemics; but the bigger surprise came at the end of the article. In the conclusion, Lenin argued that "The workers must come to the aid of the students," that the working class "cannot emancipate itself without emancipating the whole people from despotism, that it is its duty first and foremost to respond to every protest and render every support to that protest," and that any "worker who can look on indifferently while the government sends troops against the student youth is unworthy of the name socialist."

Even though I had read through most of Lenin's major works over the previous year and a half, they were obviously too much to take in all at once. I hadn't picked up at all on the parts of *WITBD* that called for opposing oppression of every kind. In SDS, support for the Panthers and the Black freedom struggle had always relied more on the national liberation rhetoric of Che and the NLF than on Lenin, partly because the Progressive Labor Party's anti-nationalist workerism and bloc voting within SDS had given Lenin a bad name and partly because most discussions of Lenin were still centered on the hoary controversies over organizational centralism and socialist consciousness coming from outside the working class. The *Iskra* article forced me to reconsider what I thought I knew.

Reading back and forth through the first five volumes of the *Collected Works*, particularly the programmatic and agitational articles in volumes 2, 4, and 5, it became obvious that Lenin's advocacy of "socialist" consciousness or "Social-Democratic" consciousness in *WITBD* did not just refer to consciousness of the need for socialism versus the Economist theory of trade union reformism, but also to consciousness of the need for already convinced socialists to support all other classes and groups in conflict with the Tsarist autocracy. On top of this double meaning of socialist consciousness, Lenin also used the terms "democratic" or "all-round political" at times instead of the more general "socialist" or "Social-Democratic" to refer specifically to the democratic content of anti-Tsarist political agitation and consciousness. Thanks to the work of Neil Harding[13] and Lars Lih,[14] most of these terminological ambiguities in Lenin's writings have now been cleared up, but not all. In my last article, I pointed out how Lih substituted the limited goals of freedom of speech and association for Russian Social-Democracy's larger political goal of a democratic republic. In a related narrowing, Lih also blurs what Lenin meant by "class consciousness," the "class struggle," and "the class point of view." Because I think the controversy between Lenin and his critics over the political content of these words is the most important ideological debate in the history of Marxism, we need to go over it in some detail.

During the crucial years 1901-04, both his Economist critics prior to the Second Congress and his Menshevik critics after the Bolshevik-Menshevik split accused Lenin of forgetting "the class point of view" because he placed the all-class democratic struggle against Tsarism ahead of the class struggle between workers and capitalists. Lenin's eventual response to this criticism was that the strategy of the all-class democratic revolution was "the class point of view," but it took him several tries and several months to state this theoretical position clearly. The phrase had first popped up in a letter sent to *Iskra* in late 1901, which Lenin printed and responded to in "A Talk with Defenders of Economism."[15] The authors of the letter differed with *Iskra* both on the empirical evaluation of the readiness of the working class to engage in the political struggle against the autocracy and on the theoretical matter of how to engage in that struggle. They claimed that *Iskra* was seeking allies among other classes to fight

13 Lenin's Political Thought, Vol. 1 (St. Martin's Press: New York, 1977).
14 Lenin Rediscovered, (Haymarket Books: Chicago, 2008).
15 Lenin, CW, vol. 5, pp. 313-20.

the autocracy because it felt that the working-class movement was too weak to challenge the autocracy on its own. It was, they said, this impatience with the low level of working-class activity that led *Iskra* to depart from "the class point of view" and downplay the working class's differences with these other classes. In the authors' opinion, the working class first needed to build up its own strength in the economic struggle against the employer class before it could graduate to the political struggle against the autocracy. It was therefore the fundamental task of Social-Democratic literature to criticize the bourgeois system and explain its class divisions, not to obscure these class antagonisms by seeking allies among other classes.

Of course, Lenin disputed every one of these points. The spontaneous awakening of the workers and other social strata had already outgrown the ability of the Social-Democrats to keep up. This spontaneous upsurge demanded that the Social-Democrats abandon their local insularity and join *Iskra* in forming a nationwide organization to coordinate the struggle against the autocracy. As for abandoning "the class point of view" and neglecting "close, organic contact with the proletarian struggle," *Iskra* was proud of its efforts to rouse political discontent among all strata of the population and never obscured "the class point of view" when doing so. It was Social-Democracy's obligation to lead the democratic struggle against the autocracy, otherwise political leadership would fall into the hands of the bourgeoisie and cripple the working class's ability to shape the future of the country.

The main thing to note about this response is that Lenin did not claim at this point that the democratic struggle against the autocracy was a direct expression of "the class point of view." He was still operating within the framework laid out in his programmatic essay from 1898, "The Tasks of the Russian Social-Democrats," before Economism had emerged as an explicit trend. In "The Tasks," Lenin divided the working-class struggle into two branches, the "socialist (the fight against the capitalist class aimed at destroying the class system and organizing socialist society), and democratic (the fight against absolutism aimed at winning political liberty in Russia and democratizing the political and social system of Russia)."[16] To be sure, Lenin held that both of these struggles were parts of the single overall Social-Democratic class struggle of the proletariat, but his emphasis was on delineating the different characteristics of each. The rhetorical move of the Economists in 1901 was to appropriate the socialist/economic half of this dual class struggle and claim that it alone constituted "the class point of view."[17] Lenin bridled at this attempt by the Economists to seize the high ground in the rhetoric of the class struggle, but he did not yet directly counter it.

Lenin had received the Economists' "Letter" while he was already in the middle of writing *WITBD* and immediately made it the focal point of his critique. As he wrote in the "Preface" to *WITBD*, "A Talk with Defenders of Economism" "was a synopsis, so to speak, of the present pamphlet." The last part of the section in Chapter III titled "The Working Class as Vanguard Fighter for Democracy" (the section from which Cozzarelli draws her quotation) was devoted to responding in more detail to the Economists' letter. However, although there is more detail, Lenin's theoretical framework remained essentially the same. While he added many passages where he argued that "Working-class consciousness cannot be genuine political consciousness unless the workers are trained to respond to *all* cases of tyranny, oppression, violence, and abuse, no matter *what class* is affected," when he came to the "the class point of view" phrase his tactic was to undermine its pretensions rather than to take it over as his own. It was not until the article "Political Agitation and 'The Class Point of View'" that he made the latter move.

16 Lenin, CW, vol. 2, p. 328.
17 Lenin, CW, vol. 5, pp. 337-43.

Although "Political Agitation" appeared in the February 1902 issue of *Iskra* before *WITBD* was published in March, it was written after *WITBD* was completed.[18] My guess is that the time pressure of getting *WITBD* out to the activists in Russia precluded any more modifications, yet Lenin felt there was still a loose end that needed tying up. "Political Agitation" starts off with a review of an incident in which a member of the Russian nobility by the name of Stakhovich gave a speech to a local Zemstvo [landlord] assembly calling for freedom of religion. The pro-autocracy conservative press denounced the speech and reminded the noble that it was only because of the power of the police and the Orthodox Church's theology of absolute obedience to authority that the landlord class could keep its control over the peasantry and continue to eat well and sleep peacefully. Lenin then commented that the state of affairs in Russia must really be in dire straits if even members of the nobility were becoming dissatisfied with the tyranny and incompetence of the priests and the police. Of course, Lenin went on, we know that the conservative press cannot discuss openly why dissatisfaction with the autocracy was reaching even into the ranks of the landlord class, but it was a real mystery why many revolutionaries and socialists seemed to suffer from the same disability: "Thus, the authors of the letter published in No. 12 of *Iskra,* who accuse us of departing from the 'class point of view' for striving in our newspaper to follow all manifestations of liberal discontent and protest, suffer from this complaint." They were like the writer who asked *Iskra* in astonishment: "Good Lord, what is this — a Zemstvo paper?"

Lenin continued:

All these socialists forget that the interests of the autocracy coincide only with certain interests of the propertied classes, and

18 I say this because there is no reference in WITBD to "Political Agitation" even though it covers the same subject matter and because "Political Agitation" takes a different line of attack than WITBD.

only under certain circumstances.... The interests of other bourgeois strata and the more widely understood interests of the entire
bourgeoisie... necessarily give rise to a liberal opposition to the
autocracy.... What the result of these antagonistic tendencies is,
what relative strength of conservative and liberal views, or trends,
among the bourgeoisie obtains at the present moment, cannot be
learned from a couple of general theses, for this depends on all
the special features of the social and political situation at a given
moment. To determine this, one must study the situation in detail and carefully watch all the conflicts with the government, no
matter by what social stratum they are initiated. It is precisely the
'class point of view' that makes it impermissible for a Social-Democrat to remain indifferent to the discontent and the protests of the
'Stakhoviches.'

It is in the last line of the quotation above that Lenin turns the
tables on his critics and introduces for the first time his own conception of "the class point of view." He then proceeds to explain
where this conception comes from:

The reasoning and activity of the above-mentioned socialists
show that they are indifferent to liberalism and thus reveal their
incomprehension of the basic theses of the Communist Manifesto,
the 'Gospel' of international Social-Democracy. Let us recall, for
instance, the words that the bourgeoisie itself provides material for
the political education of the proletariat by its struggle for power,
by the conflicts of various strata and groups within it....

Let us recall also the words that the Communists support every
revolutionary movement against the existing system. Those words
are often interpreted too narrowly, and are not taken to imply support for the liberal opposition. It must not be forgotten, however,
that there are periods when every conflict with the government
arising out of progressive social interests, however small, may under certain conditions (of which our support is one) flare up into
a general conflagration. Suffice it to recall the great social movement which developed in Russia out of the struggle between the
students and the government over academic demands [the drafting of the students], or the conflict that arose in France between
all the progressive elements and the militarists over a trial [the
Dreyfus Affair] in which the verdict had been rendered on the
basis of forged evidence. Hence, it is our bounden duty to explain

to the proletariat every liberal and democratic protest, to widen and support it.... Those who refrain from concerning themselves in this way (whatever their intentions) in actuality leave the liberals in command, place in their hands the political education of the workers, and concede hegemony in the political struggle to elements which, in the final analysis, are leaders of bourgeois democracy.

The class character of the Social-Democratic movement must not be expressed in the restriction of our tasks to the direct and immediate needs of the 'labour movement pure and simple.'... It must lead, not only the economic, but also the political struggle of the proletariat...

It is particularly in regard to the political struggle that the 'class point of view' demands that the proletariat give an impetus to every democratic movement. The political demands of working-class democracy do not differ in principle from those of bourgeois democracy, they differ only in degree. In the struggle for economic emancipation, for the socialist revolution, the proletariat stands on a basis different in principle and it stands alone.... In the struggle for political liberation, however, we have many allies, towards whom we must not remain indifferent. But while our allies in the bourgeois-democratic camp, in struggling for liberal reforms, will always look back..., the proletariat will march forward to the end,... will struggle for the democratic republic, [and] will not forget... that if we want to push someone forward, we must continually keep our hands on that someone's shoulders. The party of the proletariat must learn to catch every liberal just at the moment when he is prepared to move forward an inch, and make him move forward a yard. If he is obdurate, we will go forward without him and over him.

There is a lot packed into this short seven-page manifesto, and we can't expand on all of it here, so I'll just make a few comments before continuing with "the class point of view." First, if anyone thinks that Lenin's emphasis on democratic questions can be dismissed as a peculiarity attributable to living under an absolute monarchy without civil or political rights, think again. The Dreyfus Affair in France, a thoroughly modern bourgeois republic, is one of the two examples he gives of a seemingly minor conflict that flared into a general political conflagration. Lenin thought the Dreyfus Affair was so important as an illustration of why it was necessary to pay attention to even minor political conflicts, he pointed to it again in *"Left-Wing" Communism*[19] as a lesson for doctrinaires. Second, Lenin's statement that there is no difference in principle between bourgeois and proletarian democracy, only a difference in degree, might sound strange to some; but that then is an indication of just how much has been lost in our understanding of the political content of classical Marxism. Third, when Lenin says that the proletariat "cannot emancipate itself without emancipating the whole people from despotism," that should not be taken to mean that the emancipation of the whole people is a byproduct of the proletariat emancipating itself. Rather, as the vanguard fighter for democracy, the proletariat both leads and needs allies in the fight for democracy. Now, back to "the class point of view."

Faced with the undeniable fact that the democratic political struggle against the autocracy was a multi-class struggle but that the economic struggle against the capitalists was a purely working-class struggle, Lenin had to find some standpoint from which he could claim that the democratic struggle represented the true working-class point of view. He did this by appealing to the *Communist Manifesto,* the "Gospel" of International Social-Democracy. Lenin argued that the theory of the working-class movement developed by Marx and Engels constituted the only true working-class point of view. Of course, Lenin was then accused of insulting the workers' intelligence and perverting the meaning of socialism for claiming that socialist political consciousness could only be brought to the workers by bourgeois intellectuals from without. On this issue, I agree with Lih that this accusation was baseless and misguided from the beginning.[20] Lenin and other orthodox Social-Democrats had the same right

19 Lenin, CW, vol. 31, p. 98.
20 Lih, pp. 275, 631-58.

as any other political grouping to claim they represented the interests of the workers. On the flip side, however, neither they nor anyone else possessed any power to make the workers do anything they didn't want to do. Workers have minds of their own and can choose to follow or become Marxists themselves, or not. Marx and Engels believed that the working class was the social force that embodied the potential to end all exploitation and oppression and dedicated their lives to helping realize that potential. Lenin followed in their path and elaborated his own distinctive interpretation of how to go about it in *WITBD* and "Political Agitation and 'The Class Point of View.'" Whether we want to call it "the class point of view" or simply the democratic point of view, I think Lenin's theory of democratic strategy and political agitation is still essential today because it is egalitarian, universal, systematic, and non-reductionist.

That finishes my review of Lenin's theory of "the class point of view." Because Lars Lih also discusses "the class point of view" extensively in *Lenin Rediscovered*, and because it seems that many people's knowledge and impression of Lenin has been shaped or influenced over the past ten years by Lih's work, I think a brief comparison of how our interpretations differ can further clarify the issues at stake.

Lih discusses the "the class point of view" in three places in *Lenin Rediscovered*, but none of these discussions include any mention or analysis of the "Political Agitation" article. As a consequence, Lih leaves out how Lenin turned the tables on his Economist opponents and took over "the class point of view" for his own purposes by basing it directly on the *Communist Manifesto*'s democratic political imperatives. Failing to acknowledge that Lenin put the phrase to this new use, Lih operates throughout *Lenin Rediscovered* with the Economist/Menshevik definition of the term, leading him to say at one point that Lenin's political agitation focused so much on the theme of political freedom "that often it is difficult to remember that the author is a Marxist socialist. Of the twenty-seven articles in the [Iskra] series, only two contribute to the reader's strictly Marxist education." More than just a poor choice of words designed to highlight how different Lenin was from his opponents, Lih here completely muddles the question of what constitutes Marxism. Satisfied with Karl Kautsky's general formula about the merger of socialism and the workers' movement, Lih avoids confronting Lenin's insistence that a more definitive dividing line between real Marxism and lip service Marxism can be drawn based on Marx's and Engels' political writings. With this overview in mind, let's see how Lih's approach plays out in his specific comments on "the class point of view" controversy.

Of Lih's three comments on "the class point of view," the one on the Economists' "Letter" is the most important. The other two, both of which involve a later dispute with the Mensheviks, are variations on the first.[21] Lih's summary of the Economists' "Letter" and mine are the same, except on one point. Lih writes that "The central dispute is empirical [about the strength of the mass movement] rather than theoretical."[22] I find this minimization of the theoretical differences between Lenin and the Economists baffling. Lenin's and the Economists' disagreement over what constituted "the class point of view" was a disagreement over the political content of the class struggle, not just "optimism" or "skepticism" about the strength of the popular movement at a particular point in time. Clear evidence that the

21 Representative articles by Lenin in his dispute with the Mensheviks are "The Zemstvo Campaign and Iskra's Plan," vol. 7, pp. 495-516, and "Working-Class and Bourgeois Democracy," vol. 8, pp. 72-82. Also, the section of the Bolshevik Report to the Amsterdam Congress of the Socialist International in August 1904 that Lih discusses on pages 178-189 as reflecting Lenin's conception of "the class point of view" should be discounted because it wasn't written by Lenin (though he is said to have reviewed it), was written in extreme haste, was not directed at a Russian Social-Democratic audience, and is contradicted not only by the original "Political Agitation" article but also by the two articles cited in this note that were written within months of the Congress.
22 Lih, p. 349.

content of class political consciousness was a distinct issue separate from any estimation of the strength of the mass movement comes from the attitude of one of Lenin's other political opponents, the newspaper *Rabochee delo.*

Rabochee delo was, like *Iskra,* also enthusiastic about the strength of the mass movement in 1901, but that did not then cause it to adopt *Iskra's* politics and Lenin's "class point of view."When faced with this dispute between *Iskra* and *Rabochee delo* over ideology and tactics rather than the dispute over the level of the mass movement, Lih chooses not to take a position on which of the two was more grounded in the works of Marx and Engels. He settles instead for the noncommittal observation that both were principled advocates of Erfurtianism who happened to differ on how "to apply Erfurtianism in the current Russian context."[23] It is here that the weakness of Lih's concept of Erfurtianism comes into play. Lenin's whole point was that general pledges of allegiance to the goal of socialism were insufficient. The struggle for democracy and socialism also required specific tactical plans and a commitment to developing a specific kind of political consciousness, imperatives that Lenin claimed were drawn directly from Marx, Engels, and the *Communist Manifesto.* While Lih refrains from any detailed investigation into whether Lenin's claim was justified, he does make a long comment in a footnote[24] on Lenin's "The Tasks of the Russian Social-Democrats" regarding Kautsky's merger formula that indicates he genuinely does not understand what Lenin was saying. Because his comment is long, I'll put my reply to it in a footnote[25] and end this review of Lih with the conclusion

---

23 Lih, p. 280.

24 Lih, p. 131.

25 Lih, following Kautsky, defines Social-Democracy as the merger of socialism and the worker movement, which means that Social-Democracy is the political movement formed when the workers adopt as their own the doctrine of socialism first developed by Marx and Engels (p. 44). However, as Lih points out, this formula was so broad even "opportunists" could agree with it in words

that Lenin was justified in his claim that his political theory was drawn directly from Marx and Engels and that it is right to say that Lenin's theory of democratic political consciousness and the goal of a democratic republic was and is the "strictly Marxist" position.[26]

I'll end this article where it began, with the beginning of *Jacobin*. The same Issue 2 that contained Ackerman's Constitution article also contained an article by Chris Maisano titled "Letter to the Next Left," a reflection on C. Wright Mills's "Letter to the New Left" from fifty years earlier. Maisano argued that Mills was wrong to think that intellectuals were the new agents of his-

(p. 103). So, when arguments about tactics broke out within the movement, they quickly turned into historical investigations and debates about the true content of Marx's and Engels' doctrine. Lenin's "Tasks" was one such effort to clarify the Marxist position on the relationship between the struggle for socialism and the struggle for democracy. However, there is a problem in "Tasks" in that Lenin used the term "Social-Democracy" as the name both for Social-Democracy as a political movement and for the doctrine of Marxism, which in other places is variously called scientific socialism, proletarian ideology, or just socialism. Lih sees that Lenin is not using the words "Social-Democracy," "socialism," and "merger" ["combination" in CW 4th ed. translation] in the same way as he and Kautsky and concludes that Lenin must be a little bit confused and is really talking about the tactics of working-class leadership of the democratic revolution in Russia and not the doctrine of socialism. Actually, it is Lih who is confused. Lenin is talking about both, saying that the tactics of the working class as the leader in the fight against the autocracy "is very precisely determined by the basic principles of Social-Democracy expounded in the famous Communist Manifesto" (CW, vol. 4, pp. 333-4), which, as the name Social-Democracy clearly expresses, unites both the socialist and democratic tasks of the proletariat into a theory of a single, indivisible class struggle. Socialism and democracy are united at the level of doctrine, the product of the merger of the democratic political struggle of the workers represented by Chartism and the tradition of the French Revolution and the theory of socialism created by the Utopian Socialists.

26 Of course, to decide these issues it is necessary to read Lenin directly. My recommendation is to read Harding's much more direct, concise, and chronological analysis along with Lenin's programmatic and agitational writings in volumes 2, 4, and 5 before reading Lih.

torical change who could take over the leading role traditionally played by the working class in Marxist ideology. Believing in the working class as the leading historic agency for radical change is not a "labor metaphysic," Maisano wrote, "it's a recognition of the enduring realities of life under capitalism." In the next issue, Pam C. Nogales responded to Maisano in "Two Steps Back," arguing that Maisano misunderstood what Mills was trying to say. Mills wasn't saying that intellectuals were a new class that could replace the working class as the central agent of historical change, but that intellectuals had an important role to play in examining the reasons why the working class had ceased to act as a transformative historical force. Nogales was right about Mills. He was asking the Left to reflect on its history and its current condition in order to formulate new perspectives and new theories that might help reconstitute the Left as a political subject. He wasn't dismissing labor as a potential political actor — "Of course we cannot 'write off the working class.' ... Where labor exists as an agency, of course we must work with it" — what he meant by political agency was the traditional Marxist commitment to liberate all of humanity from the terrors of war, colonialism, economic exploitation, and racial oppression. During the Cold War in the U. S. and Great Britain, there was no longer any mass working-class movement actively interested in these goals. Mills was saying that intellectuals should not stand by and wait for the working class to act but should begin on their own the intellectual and political process of reviving the discussion of the traditional Marxist goal of human liberation. His final bit of advice to the New Left at the end of his letter was "Forget Victorian Marxism, except when you need it; and read Lenin again (be careful) — Rosa Luxemburg, too." In this cryptic shorthand, Victorian Marxism stood for the economic interests of the working class while Lenin and Luxemburg represented the universal emancipatory core of Marxism. When Maisano, Ackerman, and *Jacobin* in general explore the history of the struggle for democracy over more than two centuries in the U. S. and Europe, they are acting in the emancipatory tradition of Marx, Engels, Lenin, and Luxemburg. When they settle for the strategy of "class struggle elections," they are falling back into Economism and the labor metaphysic.

MAKING STATE THEORY REVOLUTIONARY

Donald Parkinson
February 1, 2019

Donald Parkinson argues that state theory must move beyond questions of methodology and move into deeper political questions such as the political form of a workers' regime.

Perry Anderson in his *Considerations on Western Marxism* makes the point that it was primarily questions of methodology and not political debate that occupied Marxist intellectuals in Western Europe during the post-war era up until the 1970s. Anderson links this focus on methodology over strategy to the general weakness of the class struggle at that time, with Marxist intellectuals focusing on arcane, although often useful, debates concerning the correct reading of Marx, whether Hegelian, structuralist, Kantian, or existentialist. The debates over state theory in Marxism since the post-war era have been no exception to this trend — they have been primarily fixated on questions of methodology in theorizing the state. But what if we moved beyond questions of methodology, aiming to take Marxist state theory into the field of substantive political questions? In this attempt to do so I will offer a quick overview of the main debates in methodology and then point towards the kind of questions that would concern a more revolutionarily-oriented approach to state theory.

The primary trends in the debates in Marxist state theory are instrumentalism and structuralism. Other schools of thought include the form-analytic school. The instrumentalist school is regarded by Clyde W. Barrow in his *Critical Theories of the State* as the inheritor of "Plain Marxism," continuing the tradition that Lenin began in *State and Revolution.* Instrumentalist state theory was initially conceived by Sweezy and Baran, but was perhaps most effectively articulated by Ralph Miliband, particularly in his book *The State and Capitalist Society.*

Put simply, instrumentalist state theory takes seriously the claim by Engels that the state is "but a committee for managing the common affairs of the ruling class." Instrumentalist state theorists argue that not only is there a ruling class with cohesive group interests but that the state is a means through which the ruling class can express these interests. It is within state institutions that class power is organized; the ruling class is able to have control over these institutions because of its own networks of influence and policy-making through which the power of the ruling class is embedded. To quote Miliband:

> It is these institutions in which 'state power' lies, and is through them that this power is wielded in its different manifestations by the people who occupy the leading positions in each of these institutions.[1]

According to this theory, classes exert their power over state apparatuses through "colonizing" them. This is the process by which the ruling class keeps the state's loyalty, maintaining dominance over state institutions so as to make the state an instrument of the class's rule. This theory thus explains how the ruling class rules through the state and exercises a class dictatorship through the processes of class formation and colonization of the state apparatuses, institutionalizing its rule. By class formation, we mean the process through which a class becomes a consciously organized force that can act in history according to its class interests.

1 Miliband, Ralph. The State and Capitalist Society. United Kingdom: Quartet Books, 1973. pg. 54.

A typical critique of the instrumentalist approach begins by pointing out that it conceptualizes the state as merely an instrument for different classes to pick up and use. Instrumentalists, this critique continues, give undue importance to ideology and the behavior of managers, emphasizing these factors over the importance of social structures over which the managers have no control. This critique was made by Poulantzas (targeting Miliband), who would develop a structuralist theory of the state inspired by Louis Althusser's reading of Marx.[2] Poulantzas's structuralism would develop in the course from his initial critique of Miliband to his final work *State, Power, Socialism*. However, from the beginning what was important for Poulantzas was that the state is understood in terms of social relations and structures rather than actors and that what mattered was not the class loyalties of politicians but the deeper historical logic with which the state was intertwined.

Structuralist state theory did not disagree with Miliband empirically so much as theoretically; its critique was aimed primarily at what it saw as the flawed methodology underlying instrumentalism. Structuralist Marxism itself was a project designed to rid Marxism of its "humanist" aspects, a sort of Marxism that saw the study of abstract social structures as more scientific compared to the Hegelian reading of Marx which focused on alienation and made room for what was seen as a creeping idealism. This could mean a cold and impersonal Marxism that leaves little room for human agency, but it also allows the theorist to look at certain social formations at a "macro" level of abstraction.

This can be useful in the sense of understanding the state as something that exists beyond the will of certain individual actors with unlimited power and determining which state tendencies are beyond human control. For the structuralists, one ought not

2 Nicos Poulantzas, "The Problem of the Capitalist State," New Left Review, Dec 1969, https://newleftreview.org/issues/i58/articles/nicos-poulantzas-the-problem-of-the-capitalist-state

to understand the state as an object but as a social relation, and in particular a class relation. The state can be understood as a set of institutions that, regardless of ideology, is set up to reproduce capitalist social relations because its aim is to reproduce classes. This has been useful for explaining why social-democratic politicians so often bowed down to the capitalist class while in power despite their rhetoric. What mattered was not the dedication of these politicians to pro-worker policies, but the greater social structure in which state actors worked, a structure inherently predisposed to reproducing capitalist relations.

However, through the course of his thinking, Poulantzas would eventually develop his state theory in directions that go against key aspects of Marxist state theory, in particular, the concept of class dictatorship. In *State, Power, Socialism*, Poulantzas mocks Balibar, himself a structuralist Marxist, for maintaining the theory of the dictatorship of the proletariat, apparently a "stupendous dogmatism."[3] For Poulantzas, there is no class which can hold control over the state; rather, the class struggle itself traverses the state, which serves as a locus where class antagonisms are expressed and worked out. The state is not ruled by a capitalist class that can be defined economically but is an institution that serves in the reproduction of all classes and therefore can not be said to be the specific terrain of a ruling class. Instead, there are ruling 'power blocs' which are composed of alliances of fractions of different classes. The political implications of this for Poulantzas were clear: the working class could build power *within* the capitalist state through building class alliances and shoring up hegemony within the state apparatus. This meant that a "democratic road to socialism" was possible *without* a rupture between the bourgeois dictatorship and the proletarian dictatorship, through a protracted struggle to gradually transform the state from the inside backed by movements from below.

3 Poulantzas, Nicos. State, Power, Socialism. London: Verson Books, 2014. pg. 20.

In the end, despite their aim to prove that the state structurally reproduced capitalism regardless of the motives of state actors, the structuralists ended up embracing the reformist politics of Eurocommunism, Poulantzas being one of the key theorists of this attempt to revamp communism with social-democratic and liberal revisionism. Instrumentalist theorists of the state such as Erik Olin Wright have also come to similar political conclusions. Both theoretical schools, despite their methodological quibbles, ended up lending theoretical ammunition to reformists in opposition to the concept of the dictatorship of the proletariat. Despite the aim of both schools of thought to develop Marxist theory, they instead became more like sociologies of the state removed from any kind of revolutionary politics. These debates lost the important focus of class politics, leading to theory that was a mere rationalization of the reformist turn much of the Official Communist movement was already making. Today Poulantzas is used to argue for entryism into the Democratic Party, with the Bernie Sanders campaign being an example of class struggle within the state.[4]

While both instrumentalism and structuralism can lend credence to reformism, as theories of the state we can still learn from both of them, seeing them as ways of looking at the state at different levels of abstraction. The instrumentalist theory shows how the state in action acts as a protection racket for the ruling class and how these factions of the ruling class work to reproduce their class power. On the other hand, the structuralist theorists show the social structures that these state actors are embedded in. While this methodological debate can lead to reformist conclusions on both sides, it can also be used to help us deepen our arguments for a properly Marxist theory of the state. These arguments are not useless, but we must go beyond them. This means putting Marxist state theory back onto the track of explaining the reality of class dictatorship, as Lenin did in *State and Revolution*.

4 Adherents to this argument include Nora Belrose and Adam Proctor.

The fact that Marxist state theory allowed itself to become focused on methodology is a product of Marxist theory becoming divorced from revolutionary politics. This doesn't mean we cannot use the insights of the structuralist Marxist or instrumentalist state theorists in analyzing the state. However, what should be clear is that Marxist state theory needs to focus on the issue of dictatorship, which relates to a number of practical questions. The first is on the nature of smashing the state. What does it mean to smash the bourgeois state? Secondly, there is the question of the character of what comes after the bourgeois state, i.e., the proletarian state, or dictatorship of the proletariat. How do we determine whether a state is a dictatorship of the proletariat or not? What form of state best ensures the rule of the working class?

To begin answering this question, we must begin with the assertion that states are ultimately forms of class dictatorship. What this means is that in a given social formation, the state is a means through which a class ensures and reproduces its position as the ruling class. While the state is contested by multiple classes, as Poulantzas points out, it ultimately reproduces a class system with the state apparatus ensuring that one class comes out on top. To quote the "stupendous dogmatism" of Etienne Balibar:

> State power is always the power of a class. State power, which is produced in the class struggle, can only be the instrument of the ruling class: what Marx and Engels called the dictatorship of the ruling class.[5]

Why the term dictatorship? Balibar paraphrases Lenin defining a dictatorship as "absolute power, standing above any law, either of the bourgeois or the proletariat. State power cannot be shared."[6] Essentially this means that in a given state, the class's rule over this state is non-negotiable, and is ultimately above the

5 Balibar, Etienne. On the Dictatorship of the Proletariat. London: Verso Books, 1976. pg. 66.
6 Ibid.

110

law. If the law becomes a barrier to the rule of the dominant class, the law is ultimately less important, and the state will break with the rule of law if necessary to ensure 'order.' The importance of recognizing this is that legal codes are not neutral forces standing above classes, but means through which class power is expressed.

The necessity of "order" and the maintenance of the rule of law is the normal operation of the bourgeois state. Yet when "order" is threatened, often through the convulsions of class struggle, the state will use extra-legal methods to maintain order. The class dictatorship of the bourgeoisie is mediated through parliaments and courts, yet also will throw such forms of mediation out the window if the establishment of order is threatened. Thus there is a tension in the bourgeois state between its own forms of democracy and the necessity of maintaining a bourgeois dictatorship.

The other important aspect of the theory of class dictatorship is that the state does not share power between classes; the proletariat and bourgeoisie do not have a compromised state where both rule halfway, but rather one class rules over all others. This has clear implications for political practice, in that there must be a rupture in the form of the state in the proletarian revolution, where the bourgeois form of the state is smashed and is replaced by a state of a fundamentally different form that puts power into the hands of the working class. The question remains, however: what form does this state take? Rather than simply assuming the 'class character' of a state as given due to the ideology of the ruling party, we must understand what institutions can actually allow the working class to rule as a class. Here, Charles Bettelheim is useful:

> The basic difference between a proletarian state apparatus and a bourgeois state apparatus is the non-separation of the proletarian state apparatus from the masses, its subordination to the masses, i.e., the disappearance of what Lenin called a "state in the proper sense and its replacement by the proletariat organized as a ruling class.[7]

7 Charles Bettelheim, "Dictatorship of the Proletariat, Social Classes, and Pro-

Key to the proletarian state in this conception is the non-separation of the masses from the state, the state being subordinated to the masses. This entails that there must be a form of democracy that is based in mass collective participation from the proletariat that would allow for the masses to subordinate the state to their interests. This must be a democracy based on collective decision-making in public association rather than the atomized democracy found in the bourgeois state that reduces mass politics to the individuated casting of a vote. The form of the proletarian state is, therefore, a form of the state that in all meaningful ways is more democratic than any capitalist state — democracy is a means through which the masses can take political decision-making into their collective hands. The alternative is the rule of experts, of bureaucracy, unhindered in their rule and increasingly graced with arbitrary power by their social status.

One element of democracy is that it operates through a sort of "political culture," or set of political norms in collective decision making that empower the collective to the greatest possible extent. Therefore a proletarian state must promote certain civic virtues, essentially an ideological apparatus that promotes certain forms of socialization over others, forms that promote collective decision-making in a solidaristic fashion overseeing politics as an instrument for personal success. In fact, one of the key aspects of proletarian democracy is that it is not possible to use politics as a form of career. As in the Paris Commune, the workers representative should be not only recallable but also paid the average working person's wage. Public officials should be elected and transparency should become the norm, as well as freedom of the press and freedom of association. Democracy must not be understood as merely majoritarian decision-making, but rather collective decision-making where everyone has a say. One could call this political culture "workers' republican-

letarian Ideology." Monthly Review, Nov 1971, https://doi.org/10.14452/MR-023-06-1971-10_3

ism," and the state a "workers' republic." Such a state would not overcome the principle of representation — this is not a call for direct democracy — yet it would maximize the means through which representation is truly derived from the "people's will" or, more accurately, the will of the propertyless class.

Another key aspect of the proletarian state is the arming of the people. The smashing of the state at its core is the dissolution of the existing bourgeois state apparatus, the military, national guard, and police. What replaces these institutions is the people's militia, which is run through municipal committees that all citizens can join. The universal arming of the people through such a system is an acid test of whether a state can be said to have a proletarian "class character," whether the working class truly holds power or if power is being taken into the hands of a petty-bourgeois bureaucracy. The working class must *become* the state itself and absorb all arbitrary and alienated bureaucratic powers to the fullest extent while putting those that do exist under democratic control.

This approach toward defining a "workers' state" differs from the Trotskyist method, which judges a workers' state by the dominant property relations. For example, if a state has a nationalized economy but is run by a bureaucratic caste that politically disempowers the working class, it is still a workers' state, albeit a degenerated one. This way of using property relations alone as a metric is ultimately economically reductive to the point where the working class does not have to actually hold power in its own state but merely exist in a nationalized economy compatible with any kind of arbitrary despotism. The workers' state may be degenerated and need a political revolution, but the implicit assumption is that property-form defines a workers' state. Yet would one say that the USSR ceased to be a workers' state during the NEP, where private property was tolerated, and then returned to being one after the collectivization of agriculture under Stalin? Rather than focusing on the property form dominating the economy, the focus should be on the political form of the state.

An argument against this interpretation of the state is that a workers' state could simply be an extremely democratic state with a capitalist economy. But this opens up another avenue of Marxist state theory that could be more vigorously examined: the contradiction between the market and democracy. One could theoretically make an argument that the rule of the market as an impersonal force and authentic democratic rule of the people and their interests over all of society are incompatible; thus the tendency for the capitalist class to limit democracy when necessary and the tendency for the proletariat to fight for democracy more than other classes. One sees this contradiction historically play out in the bourgeois revolutions, where the most militant and radical mobilizations against the old regime came from the small proprietor masses who were in the process of proletarianization. On the other hand, the actual merchant class tended to play a more conservative role in the revolutions, seeing the extreme democracy of the masses as a threat to their property. One sees this dynamic in the history of the United States itself, one famous example being the Constitution itself as being framed for the purposes of curbing excess democracy.[8] A sufficiently empowered proletariat that amasses enough control over society organized as a universal class would simply not be compatible with the rule of the bourgeoisie, as it would be compelled to make "despotic inroads" on property, to use the words of Marx. To quote Jacques Ranciere, referencing a report from the Trilateral Commission on the problems of democracy:

> Democracy, said the report writers, signifies the irresistible growth of demands that put pressure on governments, lead to a decline in authority, and cause individuals and groups to become refractory to the discipline and sacrifices for the common good.[9]

8 For an in-depth look into this, see: Holton, Woody. *Unruly Americans and the Origins of the Constitution*. New York: Macmillan, 2007.

9 Ranciere, Jacques. Hatred of Democracy. London: Verso Books, 2005. pg. 7

We must understand that the dictatorship of the proletariat for Marx is merely a stage in the class struggle, one where the proletariat becomes the most powerful class in society, but still nonetheless within a capitalist society. The point of the dictatorship of the proletariat is that the proletariat is in control of the "general means of coercion" and can now make concrete steps towards the abolition of class society itself. Radical political democracy serves the purposes of allowing the masses to take these concrete steps.

On this occasion, Poulantzas does give us a useful frame of reference, despite his conclusion of class dictatorship not being a viable concept. If we see the form of the state as something which is determined by the concrete class struggle, then it is possible that the strength of the proletariat as a class would impact the form of the state. Yet whether a strong proletariat would mean a more democratic or despotic state is not something that can be predetermined. While a strongly organized proletariat may be able to win significant concessions from the state such as democratic rights, the state could also react to an empowered proletariat by becoming more authoritarian and clamping down on democratic rights. However, even if the proletariat is strongly organized enough within a capitalist state to win certain rights, these rights are mere legalities in the eyes of the bourgeoisie and can be suspended if necessary — hence why even the most democratic state is not a state where the proletariat and bourgeois share power somehow, but rather is always a dictatorship of the bourgeois. In fact, where the proletariat has gained significant democratic rights, one can see the bourgeois state compensate through forms of corruption and voter manipulation. One can say there is essentially a contradiction between political democracy and the market, where political democracy being extended gives more power to the plebian classes and therefore can lead to policies that clash with the market.

In conventional Leninist political terminology, where the Comintern or at least its first four congresses are used as a key reference point for politics, democracy is contrasted to Demo-cratic Centralism. It is my opinion that Democratic Centralism is essentially a redundant term, and is more often than not sim-ply used as a cudgel against democracy in the name of central-ism. Any democratic decision made by a collective, by a majori-ty, has to be enforced on the whole. The part must be subsumed to the whole, and so some form of central authority is needed so that the needs of the whole can be met. Decentralization of power, where autonomy and localism are emphasized over the rule of any central authority and subjugation to authority is a matter of contractual agreements worked out between function-ally autonomous communes, pretends to be an ultra-democratic alternative to democratic systems that rely on some level of cen-tralism. Yet if a locality is truly autonomous and not accountable to a center, then it is not accountable for the needs of the rest of society, a situation which is fundamentally anti-democratic.

The neo-republican theories of Skinner and Pettit, while tainted by social-democratic politics, are a valuable asset to state theory despite coming from a non-Marxist background. For Pettit, freedom can be defined as the absence of domina-tion.[10] We are essentially unfree when we are subject to the will of another. However, when we enter a political community, we essentially subject ourselves to the rule of a state and are subject to the will of the authority of this state. This provides us with a conundrum: how are humans supposed to be free if we live in a society where we are forced to live under the control of gener-alized political authority? The argument of the neo-republicans is that said political authority is not a form of domination if it is an authority that is derived from the said political communi-ty through open and collective deliberation. Furthermore, this political authority must be exercised in a way which is not *ar-bitrary*. The issue of arbitrary authority is a major one for the

10 Pettit, Philip. *On the People's Terms*. Cambridge, UK: Cambrige University Press, 2012. pg. 26.

neo-republicans, as they see republican democracy as a means to limit and perhaps eliminate arbitrary authority, which is an authority that is not legitimated by the norms of the political community and there is a form of domination in operation.

Skinner argues against the notion of freedom as "non-interference," as we can only exist as "free" beings in a community with others, and therefore cannot be free from some interference from the needs of others without being atomized, anti-social beings.[11] Humans are social animals, and so we have no choice but to be subject to the interference of others in a political community. However, what we can be free from is dependence, where we are subjected to the arbitrary will of a social force in order to survive. This can be extended to the dependence of a woman on her husband for financial support, dependence on competition in the free market to survive, and dependence on a state which is free from any kind of democratic control.[12] Therefore freedom is not freedom from the interference and input of others, but freedom from arbitrary forms of domination and dependence.

By looking at modern thinkers of republican theory like Pettit and Skinner, as well as the general ideals of radical republicanism that were common parlance in circles frequented by Marx and Engels, we can learn to develop what was mentioned earlier as a "political culture," a culture not in the sense of an aesthetic but in the sense of a complex of social and institutional norms. Through developing such a culture in the masses, we can develop through concrete struggle the forms of workers' democracy that will define the proletarian state of the future, training the working class to become a class capable of self-governance. Marxist state theory should shift focus from purely methodolog-

11 Quentin Skinner. "A Geneology of Liberty." Youtube, Dec 1, 2016. https://www.youtube.com/watch?v=PjQ-W2-fKUs
12 William Clare Roberts puts Capital in a radical republican context. See: Robert, William Clare. *Marx's Inferno*. Princeton, NJ: Princeton University Press, 2016.

ical issues and instead begin to venture into the practical questions of the proletarian state.

One can ask how one can reconcile the notion of a dictatorship of the proletariat with mass republican democracy. The answer to this is that Marx did not see dictatorship and democracy as mutually exclusive, but instead in a mutually reinforcing relation with one another. For example, in applying the lessons of 1848 in his *1850 Address to the Communist League*, Marx calls for the use of terrorist methods in order to attain democratic demands. Marx sees class dictatorship as a means through which one class suppresses the former ruling class, which in turn allows for the development of new democratic forms that come from undermining the power of this class. For Marx, the Jacobin dictatorship of the French Revolution was inspiring: in order for the bourgeoisie and its allies in the plebeian classes to win a republic that totally undermined the aristocracy's power and put democracy in the hands of the masses, it was necessary to violently suppress the aristocratic class whose interests were contrary to the rise of mass democratic politics. One can understand proletarian dictatorship in a similar way: the capitalist class must be put out of power and politically disenfranchised in order to construct sovereignty based on the power of the workers and organized through democratic association. For Marx, class dictatorship is a means of securing democracy against the power of the former ruling class and is thus not contrary to democratic principles.

Marxist state theory must move beyond mere questions of methodology and into questions of political importance, such as what actually demarcates proletarian states from bourgeois states, the question of what denotes the "class character" of a state beyond mere proclamations, and so on. It means asking what kinds of polities we aim to create, and what kind of political cultures will need to accompany them. Structuralism, instrumentalism, or other approaches from the form-analytic, systems theory, or organizational realist schools can only tell us so much about these questions and have mostly related to best theorizing the capitalist state. In analyzing the state we may use elements of all of these methodologies, but what matters is that our understanding of the state is based in concrete historical analysis and not simply left in the realm of abstraction. Marxist state theory gives us important tools for understanding the capitalist state and its development, providing us with a set of methodologies that look at the state with different levels of abstraction. Yet a theory of the state must also be able to understand the state beyond the capitalist state. This means developing a theory of the state that can understand pre-capitalist states and their continuities with the modern state. Yet more importantly, as partisans of communism, we must also theorize the proletarian state, a question which relates to how we now try to organize a polity of the working class for its historical interests. It is my suggestion that the democratic-republican principles of the milieu that created Marxism carry much to offer us in addressing this question.

Marxism and the Democratic Republic

Luke Pickrell
May 24, 2023

Luke Pickrell emphasizes the centrality of radical democracy to the communist project and reintroduces the construction of the democratic republic as the foundational political goal for socialists today. He emphatically asserts that if socialists are to defeat the tricephalic hydra of capitalist domination, we must aim for the heart — "the source and parent of all the other atrocities" — the US Constitution.

The final point of Marxist Unity Group's Points of Unity calls for a democratic socialist republic in North America.[1] This concept is unheard of for many Marxists today and begs many questions. In this article, I will jump around while remaining connected to the red thread of this demand. First, I'll touch on why the demand for a democratic republic isn't a part of contemporary left discourse. Next, I'll cover a bit of the history of Marx as a democratic republican and the goings-on within the 2nd International after his death. After that, I'll focus on an influential take on Marxism and republicanism found in William Clare Roberts's *Marx's Inferno*,[2] in which Roberts presents Marx's conception of republican freedom as focused on non-domination. Finally, I

1 Marxist Unity Group. 'Points of Unity and Immediate Tasks.' https://www.marxistunity.com/

2 Roberts, William Clare. *Marx's Inferno: The Political Theory of Capital.* Princeton, NJ: Princeton University Press, 2016.

will bring us up to the present, explaining why Marx's republicanism and the demand for a democratic republic are essential and what that demand tasks the left with doing today.

History of a Demand

The demand for a democratic republic is undoubtedly not in the vocabulary of the existing Communist, Maoist, or Trotskyist parties, nor is it a demand consistently championed by either the Democratic Socialists of America or authors published in the popular Jacobin Magazine (though a few articles about the subject have appeared). While Leon Trotsky referred to the democratic republic in his mid-1930s writings on France,[3] the demand disappeared from communist party programs after the Russian Revolution. It remained submerged within a sea of Cold War discourse which split the world between Western 'democracies' on one side and various 'dictatorships' and 'totalitarian' powers on the other, with Marxism[4] and the somewhat problematic 'Leninism'[5] lumped in with the latter. The United States and the Soviet Union were interested in portraying their respective political system as emblematic of democracy. Lost in all of this was what Marxism says about democracy, democratic republicanism, and what the state form of the dictatorship of the proletariat looks like — it wasn't the USSR.

3 Leon Trotsky. 'A program of action for France.' https://www.marxists.org/archive/trotsky/1934/06/paf.htm
4 Richard Hunt's 'The Political ideas of Marx and Engels: Totalitarianism and Social Democracy, 1818-1850' (1974) goes a long way in dispelling the mythical connection between Marxism and totalitarianism. August Nimtz's 'Marx and Engels: Their Contribution to the Democratic Breakthrough' (2000) correctly describes Marx and Engels as political leaders in the mass democratic workers' movements of their time.
5 Neil Harding's "Lenin's Political Thought" (1977) and various works by Hal Draper like "The Myth of 'Lenin's Concept of the Party" (1990), led the way in dispelling the myth of Lenin as an aspiring totalitarian who paved the way for Stalin.

Today, when the left speaks of democracy, it's often in combination with the pejorative 'bourgeois' and scorned as such. Communism is seen as somehow better than or distinct from democracy. Republicanism is also treated as "entirely reducible to petit bourgeois ideology that undermines the working-class struggle, [being] hence unworthy of serious study."[6] As Bruno Leipold points out, the preeminent source of Marx's thought — the *Die Marx-Engels-Gesamtausgabe* (MEGA) — refers to democratic republicans as "mere petty-bourgeois windbags."[7] In their distaste for the existing rule of undemocratic Constitutional law and order that *goes by the name of* democracy, socialists have thrown the baby out with the bathwater.

It's as if everything Marx, Engels, and the 2nd International ever wrote about democracy, the democratic republic, and the state form of the dictatorship of the proletariat went out the window after the Russian Revolution. To a large extent, a particular reading of Lenin's *The State and Revolution*[8] — one that focuses on references to the Soviets and largely ignores what Marx said about the Paris Commune — became the definitive statement on what the workers' state would look like. The story goes: a true Marxist (who dreams of the workers taking state power) envisions workers' councils, not a democratic republic; if you want a democratic republic, you want something called 'bourgeois democracy,' and aha! — you've revealed yourself as a reformist.

Another reason why much of the left rejects the idea of a democratic republic is that they misunderstand the task of the working class once it takes political power. Communism is not realized once the working class comes to power. Instead, the class struggle continues under capitalism, just at a higher level, with the working class controlling the state and finally in a po-

---

6 Leipold, Bruno. "Citizen Marx: The Relationship Between Karl Marx and Republicanism." Ph.D. diss. St. Cross College, 2017. p. 20.

7 Ibid. p. 20 fn. 94.

8 V.I. Lenin. State and Revolution (1917). https://www.marxists.org/archive/lenin/works/1917/staterev/

sition to eliminate private property and commodity production. The revolution is a two-step process. Additionally, some sections of the left exemplify an economistic approach: they think only those demands which workers are already conscious of are appropriate to take up.[9] If the workers aren't currently demanding the abolition of the standing army or the abolition of the senate, then neither should socialists. Finally, some leftists consciously or unconsciously remain trapped in an insurrectionary mode of thinking, which I think is best exemplified in the idea that the working class could take state power now *if only* it had the correct leadership. I'm relatively confident that this comes from a particular interpretation of Trotsky. Capitalism is rotten and is ripe for socialism. Therefore, the fight for democracy distracts from the fight for socialism.

Today, one may not know that Karl Kautsky called democracy the "light and air" of the workers' movement,[10] or that Rosa Luxemburg later exposed Kautsky as a renegade (before Lenin!) over the demand for a democratic republic in 1910. Friedrich Engels critiqued the SPD's Erfurt program for not demanding a democratic republic,[11] and the 1912 program of the Socialist Party of America demanded the abolition of federal courts and the senate, the overturning of national laws only by a vote of the people, and a constitutional convention. "Such measures of relief as we may be able to force from capitalism," declared the SPA's program, "are but a preparation of the workers to seize the whole powers of government, in order that they may thereby lay hold of the whole system of socialized industry and thus

9 Harding, Neil. *Lenin's Revolutionary Thought: Volume One.* Chicago, IL: Haymarket Press, 2019. See chapter 6.
10 Kautsky, Karl. The Social Revolution. Chicago, IL: Charles Kerr & Co, 1903. p. 90.
11 Friedrich Engels. "A Critique of the Draft Social-Democratic Program of 1891." p. 6. https://marxists.architexturez.net/archive/marx/works/1891/06/29.htm

come to their rightful inheritance."[12] In 1892, Engels reiterated: "Marx and I, for forty years, repeated ad nauseam that for us the democratic republic is the only political form in which the struggle between the working class and the capitalist class can first be universalized and then culminate in the decisive victory of the proletariat." And what of Marx himself? His comments on the Paris Commune are the clearest evidence that he imagined working class political power as a democratic republic — not the type of so-called "democratic republic" found in the United States and France.

Only recently — due in part to a reexamination of 2nd International Marxism and challenges to the historiography of the official Communist parties and various Marxologists and Leninologists[13] — is the centrality of democratic republicanism to Marxism re-emerging. Still, the demand for a democratic republic is scarcely heard outside a few individuals in the academy. The Communist Party USA, a century-old splinter from the SPA, advocates for democracy while leaving the US Constitution intact.[14] The Socialist Workers Party also defends the Constitution, claiming that it protects citizens from government abuse and enshrines rural Americans' right to representation in the Senate[15] (this last point might have something to do with the SWP's fixation on a 'workers and farmers alliance'). Still, any interest in reevaluating the past and challenging existing myths is a promising development. Our task is to find what lies buried under layers of history, both actual and invented. Only by drawing the correct lessons from history can we improve our work in the present.

---

12 Socialist Party of America. "Socialist Party Platform of 1912." https://sageamericanhistory.net/progressive/docs/SocialistPlat1912.htm.

13 See, for example, Lewis, Ben. Karl Kautsky on Democracy and Republicanism. Chicago, IL: Haymarket Books, 2020; Lih, Lars. Lenin Rediscovered: What is to be Done? In Context. Chicago, IL: Haymarket Books, 2008.

14 Luke Pickrell and Myra Janis. 'Socialism with American Characteristics.' https://cosmonautmag.com/2023/03/socialism-with-american-characteristics/

15 Author's conversation with members of the SWP in Chicago.

Labor Republicans in the United States

I now turn to the history of Marx's republicanism. Normally, I'd present this history through the lens of work by Bruno Leipold and Richard N. Hunt, who both emphasize the early 1840s and works such as the *Critique of Hegel's Philosophy of Right*, *On the Jewish Question*, and *Critical Notes on the King of Prussia* as examples of Marx's development from republicanism to a re-publican communist synthesis. Leipold uses the phrase "radi-cal republicans" to describe republican thinkers who pushed for democracy at the political and social level but who Marx eventually critiqued for not consistently infringing on the rights of private property or insisting on the political independence of the working class. Instead, I view Marx's republicanism through the work of Alex Gourevitch and Sean Monahan, who discuss the influence of American Workers — labor republicans — on Marx and the earlier European socialists (who were *undemocrat-ic* compared to Marx).

Marx initially thought the French Revolution of 1789 had achieved something akin to human freedom by creating a demo-cratic state.[16] When Marx turned his attention toward the Amer-icas in the 1840s, the United States was a constitutional republic with higher levels of suffrage than anywhere in Europe, and its president was a member of a political party with democracy in its name. But in reading descriptions of the United States by Alexis de Tocqueville, Thomas Hamilton, and Gustave de Beaumont, he quickly learned that political freedom doesn't equate to social freedom.[17] A state can't be democratic, nor a people free, so long as property remains private rather than social.

Traditionally, Republicans had described freedom as the ability to control one's labor. But by the end of the nineteenth

16 Monahan, Sean F (2021). The American Workingmen's Parties, Univer-sal Suffrage, and Marx's Democratic Communism. Modern Intellectual His-tory 18 (2): 379-402. p. 387.
17 Ibid.

century, the condition of permanent wage labor had eliminated any semblance of control over the labor process. These worker-citizens of a nominal republic critiqued their country within the republican tradition. Reviewing what he terms the "labor republican" movement, Alex Gourevitch concludes:

The best chance republicanism had of transcending its aristocratic origins and of developing an egalitarian critique of enslavement and subjection was when someone other than society's dominant elite used republican language to articulate the concerns. This is precisely what happened when nineteenth-century artisans and wage laborers appropriated the inherited concepts of independence and virtue and applied them to labor relations. The attempt to universalize the language of republican liberty, and the conceptual innovations that took place in the process, were their contributions to this political tradition.[18]

These workers understood that the 'freedom' supposedly gained under the republic wasn't living up to its potential in the face of wage labor, in which the worker sold away his body and mind for most of the day. Wage slavery was a popular term to describe the discrepancy between the idea of freedom and the reality of unfreedom, between appearance and substance. "For he, in all countries, is a slave, who must work more for another than that other must work for him," wrote Thomas Skidmore, founder of the Workingmen's Party of New York; "It does not matter how this state of things is brought about; whether the sword of victory hew down the liberty of the captive, and thus compel him to labor for his conqueror, or whether the sword of want extort our consent, as it were, to a voluntary slavery, through a denial to us of the materials of nature..."[19] Knights of Labor leader and 1st International member Terence Powderly likewise explained how wage labor made "slaves of men who proudly, but thoughtlessly, boast

---

18 Gourevitch, Alex (2011). Labor and Republican Liberty. Constellations 18 (3):431-454. p. 441.

19 Quoted in Alex Gourevitch's 'Wage-slavery and Republican Liberty' (2013). https://jacobin.com/2013/02/wage-slavery-and-republican-liberty/

of their freedom — that freedom which they claim came down to us from revolutionary sires as a heritage." Powderly wondered aloud, "...are we the free people that we imagine we are?"[20] Finally, labor leader George McNeil described the American wage-laborer as someone who "assent[s]" but does not "consent," who "submits[s]' but does not "agree."[21]

Contemporary scholars have presented various interpretations of Marx's early republican views and later commitment to communism. Richard Hunt explains that when Marx and Engels began their collaboration in 1845, both agreed that the institutions of government and decision-making in a classless society wouldn't be separate or estranged from the masses; there would be no division between state and civil society.[22] Both young revolutionaries had a profound faith in the proletarian masses to use democracy to realize their interests, and that belief never wavered. Universal suffrage, freedom of the press, and freedom of association would lead to socialism. The trick was in getting those freedoms. Bruno Leipold contends that Marx questioned his initial republicanism after witnessing the bourgeoisie betray the revolutions of 1848 — when "the new French republic sent in the army to ruthlessly crush the insurgent workers who had naively believed that the republic would be theirs"[23] — only to find a communist-republican synthesis after seeing the internal structure of the Paris Commune.[24] In his interpretation of *Das Kapital*, William Clare Roberts calls Marx's republican-communist synthesis a marriage between the "concern for freedom" and a "systematic dissection of capital."[25] More recently, Gil

20 Gourevitch, Alex (2011). p. 438
21 Gourevitch, 'Wage-slavery and Republican Liberty' (2013).
22 Hunt, Richard N. (1974). See chapter 4 on the political development of Engels.
23 Leipold, Bruno (2017) p. 8
24 Ibid. p. 11
25 William Clare Roberts. 'The Value of Capital.' p. 5. https://jacobin.com/2017/03/marxs-inferno-capital-david-harvey-response

Schaeffer has traced the republican thread (though perhaps a *thick rope* would be a more appropriate analogy) throughout Marx's life, writing:

> Of the three sources and component parts of Marxism, English political economy, German philosophy, and French revolutionary republicanism and socialism, Marx and Engels critique and modified all three save for the democratic republic, retaining its principles unchanged from its origin in the French Revolution as the state form of the dictatorship of the proletariat.[26]

At no point did Marx or Engels renounce their commitment to the political rule of the working class as the *first step* toward winning the class struggle and realizing a classless society. At no point did Marx or Engels renounce democracy — the political expression of the majority in the interests of the majority — as how the working class would come to power. Whether or not the ruling class would push back against that expansion of democracy with violence, and whether or not that reaction would necessitate a violent revolution, was another matter. "The first, fundamental condition for the introduction of community of property is the political liberation of the proletariat through a democratic constitution," stated Engels in 1847.[27] One year later, in their *Manifesto of the Communist Party*, Marx and Engels declared that "the first step in the revolution by the working class is to raise the proletariat to the position of the ruling class, to win the battle of democracy."[28]

26 Gil Shaeffer. 'On the Democratic Republic, Working-Class Rule, Dictatorship, and Reconstruction' p. 15 https://cosmonautmag.com/2022/07/on-on-the-democratic-republic-working-class-rule-dictatorship-and-reconstruction/

27 Friedrich Engels. 'Draft of a Communist Confession of Faith.' p. 5 https://www.marxists.org/archive/marx/works/1847/06/09.htm

28 Karl Marx and Friedrich Engels. 'Manifesto of the Communist Party.' p. 26. https://www.marxists.org/archive/marx/works/download/pdf/Manifesto.pdf

The Second International and Republican Superstitions

The French Third Republic was declared in September 1870. Karl Kautsky detailed how the Republic was far *less* democratic than the previous empire of Charles-Louis-Napoléon Bonaparte. The critique from the German Social Democratic Party (SPD)'s leading theorist was so biting that he wrote a lengthy piece explaining why the SPD wasn't secretly monarchist.[29] Despite its name, Kautsky explained, the French Third Republic was just what Engels had called it years before: a monarchy with a president at its head. The modern state, to use a phrase from the pre-communist Marx of 1840, had replaced the monarch with the rule of the people only in a formal — not substantive — manner.

With the republic as its sacred banner, the bourgeoisie won over large sections of the French working class and some socialists like Alexandre Millerand by trumpeting the sanctity of its supposed 'democracy' against the alleged threat of a monarchical and clerical reaction. The bourgeoisie, explained Jeffrey Isaac in a seminal work on Marx's Republicanism, donned the "lion's skin"[30] of republican language to hide its eminently undemocratic nature. The trick was effective: "The word [republic] has a magical effect on the mind of the worker. This fata morgana fills them with hope,"[31] wrote a historian of the time, quoted by Kautsky.

Even in the United States, where the struggle between worker and employer had reached a fever pitch by the end of the century, the working class eventually fell under the sway of "republican superstitions."[32] Kautsky stated:

29 Lewis, Ben. *Karl Kautsky on Democracy and Republicanism.* Chicago, IL: Haymarket Books, 2020.
30 Isaac, J. C. (1990). The Lion's Skin of Politics: Marx on Republicanism. Polity, 22(3), 461–488, p. 472.
31 Lewis, Ben (2020), p. 251.
32 Ibid. p. 163.

The American worker still believes that thanks to his democracy, he is better than workers living under monarchies and that he has no need for socialism, a mere product of European despotism... The main task of our American comrades... [is] to make the worker see reason... [that] just like in a monarchy, democracy has become a tool of class rule, that democracy can only again become a tool to break this class rule when he has overcome its republican superstitions.[33]

The American working class forgot their predecessors' understanding of the difference between form and content. The meaning of democratic republicanism needed rescuing from its bourgeois usurpers. That said, Kautsky's authority on who is or is not under the sway of "republican superstitions" is contested. I think it's a little too easy (and therefore enticing) to point to a group of people and say that they don't understand the undemocratic nature of the state.

Almost a decade before Kautsky's criticism of the French Republic, Engels critiqued the SPD's 1891 Erfurt program for its failure to demand a democratic republic and appreciate the significance of its (albeit necessary) omission from party literature. "If one thing is certain," Engels wrote, "it is that our party and the working class can only come to power under the form of a democratic republic."[34] The Russian Social Democratic Party did what the Germans couldn't (or wouldn't) in putting the demand for a democratic republic in their 1903 party program,[35] and Lenin polemicized against members of his party because they called themselves social democrats but weren't championing the political movement for a democratic repub-

33 Ibid.
34 Friedrich Engels. 'A Critique of the Draft Social Democratic Program of 1891.' https://marxists.architexturez.net/archive/marx/works/1891/06/29.htm
35 Program of the Russian Social Democratic Party, 1903. https://www.marxists.org/history/international/social-democracy/rsdlp/1903/program.htm

lic against the Tsar.[36] "If you were willing to fight for political freedom," explains Lars Lih, "you were Lenin's ally, even if you were hostile to socialism. If you downgraded the goal of political freedom in any way, you were Lenin's foe, even if you were a committed socialist."[37] Famously, Kautsky became Lenin's foe after 1914. But the one-time Pope of Marxism ultimately reneged on his social democratic duty to champion the republic several years earlier during the Prussian suffrage debate in 1910.[38] He thought it possible to bring about working class political rule *without* breaking from the existing state. His reneging opened him up for a forceful retort from Rosa Luxemburg, who insisted on the orthodox social democratic position that the working class could only come to power through the democratic republic. She explained that:

By pushing forward the republican character of Social Democracy we win, above all, one more opportunity to illustrate in a palpable, popular fashion our principled opposition as a class party of the proletariat to the united camp of all bourgeois parties.[39]

Freedom from Domination

Having reviewed some of the history of democratic republicanism in the worker and social movement during and after Marx's time, I now present Marx's republicanism as an interest in eliminating all forces of arbitrary domination. An extension of Marx's

36 V.I. Lenin. What is to be Done? https://www.marxists.org/archive/lenin/works/1901/witbd/

37 Lih, Lars. 2008. P. 9

38 On the party debate regarding the Prussian suffrage campaign of 1910, see chapter seven of Carl Schorske's 'German Social Democracy, 1905-1917.' https://platypus1917.org/wp-content/uploads/German-Social-Democracy-1905%E2%80%931917-The-Development-of-the-Great-Schism-by-Carl-E.-Schorske.pdf

39 Rosa Luxemburg. 'Theory and Practice.' https://www.marxists.org/archive/luxemburg/1910/theory-practice/index.htm

republicanism was his identification of the democratic republic of the Paris Commune as the state form necessary to render the state subservient to society. Marx fought to realize freedom for humanity by eliminating all forms of arbitrary domination, the most significant source of all being the rule of capital. William Clare Roberts identifies three areas where this domination appears in capitalist society: "the *political domination* of the workers affected by the state, the *objective domination* or despotism to which workers are subjected in production, and the *impersonal domination* experienced by all commodity producers."[40]

Marx understood communism as the struggle of the working class for self-determination and self-actualization. This struggle would throw all of existing society into the air and free humanity from bonds of superstition and want. Workers strive for a voice in the decisions impacting their lives to fully engage in all life's meaningful activities. With this desire in mind, it's a fundamental problem for someone with an eye for non-domination that capitalist society presents a vast array of uncontrollable and arbitrary obstacles. Like the sorcerer in *Fantasia* who enchants a broom only to have it sweep with abandon, the working class has no control over the society it reproduces each waking hour. Marx was less concerned with stopping bad things from happening than with society's ability to control its fate collectively. The inner workings of society must be clear and understandable. Marx, for example, preferred direct taxation over indirect taxation because the former "prompts" the person to "control the governing powers imposing the tax."[41] Life is tough, but it's one thing to error or suffer because of decisions one understands and has some control over and another to error or suffer due to arbitrary forces behind one's back.

Marx located the sources of domination in capitalist society not just in the actions of individual capitalists or politicians but

40 Roberts, William Clare (2016). p. 245.
41 Ibid. p. 249.

in the market as a whole — the aggregate of billions of isolated decisions. The purchase of commodities, the ability to sell one's labor power to buy necessities, the decision to hire or fire an employee — all of these events are determined not by personal preferences or individual proclivities but by the logic of the market operating outside of any collective debate or deliberation.[42]

The most obvious example of the market's impersonal domination is the necessity of finding a buyer for one's labor power or risk starvation. One may not want to work, but one must. William Clare Roberts provides another example of how the market overrides individual preferences:

> When your favorite independent bookstore closes down in the face of competition from discount and Internet booksellers, you might moan about how good it was for your town to have such a place, and how unfortunate it is that the shop was not a profitable venture anymore. And yet you might also have done much of your own book buying on the Internet...In each of these cases, something (buying books from the local bookstore, having a unionized and local workforce, refraining from fracking) is not done, not because the agents involved don't think it is worth doing, but because they feel compelled to bow to economic imperatives. We can set aside the question of whether or not these particular judgments about what is worth doing are correct. The bare-bones structure of the intuition is only that there may be some divergence between what is worth doing and what is economically advantageous, and that, when the two come into conflict, people might feel both compelled to follow the economic incentives, and regret forsaking their previous judgment about what is worthwhile.[43]

Society is immensely unfree under capitalism because individuals cannot gather together in the service of collective decision-making and are instead at the whim of impersonal forces. Everyone — the workers who depend on the ups and downs of the market and *must* labor to survive, the capitalists who *must* squeeze surplus value out of their workforce and find the cheap-

42 Ibid. p. 85.
43 Ibid. fn. 118.

est source of labor power — is dominated. Humans made this world, yet it appears as so much quicksilver in each individual's hands. The task of communism is to take back the world we have created by giving the masses democratic control over society. The overarching obstacle in this goal's way is the bureaucratic, undemocratic, alienated bourgeois state.

Roberts writes that "so long as exchange constitutes the social nexus, producers will be dominated by market forces, workers will suffer overwork and despotism in their work, and masses will be excluded from access to the means of subsistence."[44] Yet, the market isn't a God and the events shaping our lives aren't supernatural.[45] Marx explained:

> If the product of labor does not belong to the worker, if it confronts him as an alien power, then this can only be because it belongs to some other man than the worker. If the worker's activity is a torment to him, to another it must give satisfaction and pleasure. Not the gods, not nature, but only man can be this alien power over man.[46]

Human relations define capitalist society, and human relations are a matter of politics. That Marx was, in addition to everything else, a political thinker interested in political projects and political struggles can't be overstated. He recognized domination as surmountable only through a political project injecting democracy into all spheres of human activity and thereby beginning to move towards the complete elimination of private property and a new realm of human relations. It's in the deepening of democracy — the willingness to touch private property and collectivize the means of production — where Marx takes hold

---

44 Ibid. p. 97.
45 William Clare Roberts, interview with Donald Parkinson, Cosmopod, podcast audio, February 15, 2021, https://cosmopod.libsyn.com/republican-ism-and-freedom-in-marx-with-william-clare-roberts
46 Karl Marx. 'Economic and Philosophical Manuscripts: Estranged Labor.' https://www.marxists.org/archive/marx/works/download/pdf/Economic-Philosophic-Manuscripts-1844.pdf

of traditional republicanism as non-domination and stretches it like a rubber band.

The Democratic Republic as Political Solution

Marx was eminently aware that individuals under capitalism are unfree in the sense of being endlessly subjected to arbitrary domination. The political solution to the freedom problem appeared to Marx in the self-activity of the Parisian working class during two months in 1871: the events of the Paris Commune and the creation of a democratic republic in miniature.

During an all-too-brief two months, the Communards made crucial changes to the state: universal (male) suffrage was enacted across Paris; officials were to be revocable and accountable to their constituency; the executive and legislative branches were combined, turning the commune into a "working, not a parliamentary body";[47] the standing army was replaced with a citizens' militia; all records of the Commune's internal activities were publicized; the police were to be under the control of the commune and subject to recall; all judges were to be elected and likewise subject to recall; and finally: every city, village, and town would model the commune with representatives from those communes sent to make decisions in higher bodies. Decision-making would be as local as possible while retaining a degree of centralization. The state was made subordinate to society, democratic rights extended into the workplace, and the division between political and social existence was made a political project. The Communards worked under unfavorable circumstances; their revolt was isolated and lacked an organized party and clear theoretical direction. While they planned (and in some cases carried out) inroads into the arbitrary domination of the existing states, they didn't move against the domination of the commodity market. The personal (direct) domination of the

47 Karl Marx. 'The Civil War in France.' p. 4. https://www.marxists.org/archive/marx/works/1871/civil-war-france/index.htm

bureaucrat over the citizen and the employer over the worker was reduced, but the impersonal (indirect) domination of the market over everyone remained.

The fact that the Communards didn't eliminate capitalism isn't a mark against them. As I've already explained, the revolution is a two-stage process: political and then social. Marx described this process best when he called the Commune "...the political form at last discovered under which to work out the economic emancipation of labor"; it "supplied the Republic with the basis of really democratic institutions."[48] Kautsky stated: "Only when the French state is transformed along the lines of the constitution of the First Republic and the [Paris] Commune that it can become that form of the republic, that form of government, for which the French proletariat has been working [and] fighting..."[49] Lenin, in a piece written to recover orthodox Marxism, offered a provocative take on the transformative power of democracy within the democratic republic. "The [Paris] Commune ... appears to have replaced the smashed state machine 'only' by fuller democracy: abolition of the standing army; all officials to be elected and subject to recall. But this 'only' signifies a gigantic replacement of certain institutions by other institutions of a fundamentally different type. This is exactly a case of "quantity transforming into quality": democracy, introduced as fully and consistently as is at all conceivable, is transformed from bourgeois into proletarian democracy, from the state (a special force for the suppression of a particular class) into something which is no longer the state proper."[50] The purpose of the transitional workers' state, understood by Lenin, is to run society and hold the bureaucrats accountable by subordinating them to the masses.[51]

48 Karl Marx. 'The Civil War in France.' p. 15 https://www.marxists.org/archive/marx/works/1871/civil-war-france/index.htm
49 Lewis, Ben. (2020). p. 269.
50 V.I. Lenin. 'The State and Revolution.' p. 15 https://www.marxists.org/archive/lenin/works/1917/staterev/
51 Mike Macnair. 'Control the Bureaucrats.' https://weeklyworker.co.uk/worker/552/control-the-bureaucrats/

But we shouldn't let the grandeur of the Commune distract us from the fact that Marx was a champion of the democratic republic before 1871. His 'Demands of the Communist Party of Germany' — which called for a united German republic and the universal arming of the people[52] — prefigured the Paris Commune by almost a quarter-century. Even earlier, Marx scrutinized *supposedly* democratic constitutions and made detailed lists pointing out their undemocratic provisions. Marx didn't need the Paris Commune to make him a champion of democracy and an opponent of human bondage in all its personal and impersonal manifestations: whether iron shackles, undemocratic constitutions, or the domination of the market. The Paris Commune *did* provide Marx with a greater appreciation for the speed with which the workers would have to subordinate the armed forces of the state to popular control and deprofessionalize the state bureaucracy.

Tasks for Today

The socialist party embarks on its journey with the immediate goal — the democratic republic — detailed in its minimum program. The party's final goals — communism and freedom — are detailed in the maximum program. The fight to achieve the minimum demands strengthens the working class while making inroads against existing states — such demands as a single legislative assembly elected by proportional representation; the abolition of the independent presidency and the Supreme Court's right of judicial review; the election of judges and other state officials; the expansion of jury trials and state-funded legal services; the unrestricted right of free speech; the abolition of copyright laws and monopolies of knowledge; the immediate dissemination of all state secrets; the abolition of police and standing army in favor of a people's militia characterized by uni-

52 Karl Marx. 'Demands of the Communist Party of Germany.' https://www.marxists.org/archive/marx/works/1848/03/24.htm

versal training and service, with democratic rights for its members; and the immediate convening of a constitutional convention based on universal suffrage. Fully enacted, these demands smash the existing state. The democratic republic, because it is connected to society, remains subordinate to the masses during the transition to communism. With the state subordinate, democracy would begin to penetrate all aspects of political and social life. Having obtained freedom *from* the domination of the rule of the capitalist state, our society could work toward the freedom *to* self-actualize.

Many of the party's minimum demands also appear in its internal organization. Leadership positions are decided based on one person, one vote — not by slate.[53] The party minority has the right to become a majority through debate, forming factions, and publishing opinions. Electeds are accountable to the membership, mandated to serve as tribunes of the people in the political arena, and recallable by a majority vote. Finances and minutes are documented and accessible. Members have the right and duty to express their ideas, especially when they conflict with those of the majority. Ultimately, the party is strong because of its "unity in diversity"[54] of opinions and ideas. Debate strengthens the party by exposing all ideas to the light of day and combining the intellectual power and experience of the entire class. A strong argument can be made that, on the other hand, bureaucratic centralism renders socialist parties inoperable beyond a certain size.

Organized around democratic republican lines, the socialist party can also engage in political spaces (parliaments, Congress, etc.) that would otherwise swallow up a non-partied do-gooder. As Kautsky noted, it's a strong party that allows for a principled engagement in politics, not the engagement in politics that

53 Brian O Cathail. 'The Origins of the Slate System.' https://rupture.ie/articles/the-origins-of-the-slate-system
54 Mike Macnair (2006). p. 91.

makes for a strong party.[55] The RSDLP lived up to this social democratic maxim by remaining in constant opposition to the Tsar (and for a democratic republic) during the Duma period of 1906 to 1917. Crucial sections of the SPD reneged on this maxim by succumbing to parliamentary cretinism, especially in prioritizing Reichstag elections over extra-parliamentary struggles for Prussian suffrage reform in 1910 and voting for war credits with the hope of winning favor after the First World War.

Finally, working within a democratically structured socialist party acclimates the masses to engage in politics, either directly as party representatives or indirectly by keeping officials accountable. This training in political life and the creation of democratic structures is necessary for the present if the future state is to be subservient to the people. The working class must learn to lead, manage, and account for all aspects of society — an eminently political project. The representatives of the party must learn to subordinate themselves to the will of the majority. Learning how to engage in disciplined and principled political bodies is one of the many ways the working class rids itself of the muck of ages. In dereliction of duty, the left all-too-frequently avoids the question of hierarchies and decision-making by dodging the issue entirely; a vague notion of "socialism from below," or what amounts to the complete rejection of politics, is no solution to the problem of accountable leadership and leads to *less* democracy.[56] 'Socialism from below' was a prevalent slogan in the International Socialist Organisation (we even made t-shirts!) The slogan expresses a desire to create distance between 'our socialism' as the democratic rule of the working class, and the various bureaucratic regimes that ruled in the name of socialism during the twentieth century. A friend once joked that given the state of the left, he wouldn't mind some 'socialism from above.'

55 Lewis, Ben (2020). p. 133.
56 Mike Macnair. 'Socialism from below: a delusion.' https://weeklyworker. co.uk/worker/1071/socialism-from-below-a-delusion/

In hindsight, the fact we couldn't imagine a state structure in which leadership is held accountable — that the only alternatives seemed to be between a mass strike (unlikely) or rule by bureaucrats (not socialism) — is telling.

Conclusion

I'll return to the three realms of domination in capitalist society identified by Roberts: "the *political domination* of the workers affected by the state, the *objective domination* or despotism to which workers are subjected in production, and the *impersonal domination* experienced by all commodity producers." Where do we strike this three-headed hydra so that it stops growing new heads? The impersonal domination experienced by all producers won't end once the working class takes state power because capitalism will still exist. Exploring the commodity form is theoretically interesting, but it does not provide a way for socialists to engage the working class. The domination of the working class at the point of production will be a constant source of conflict — sometimes higher, sometimes lower — so long as classes exist. But focusing our attention on labor struggles to the detriment of political struggles — as some critique the Rank and File Strategy for doing — concealed that the struggle of class against class is political.

Only one head remains: the state's political domination of the workers. A massive shift occurs in the class struggle when the working class recognizes the government is a far worse enemy than their employer. At that point, the class moves one step closer to realizing its historic mission of liberating all of humanity because it moves one step closer to contesting state power. To this end, Marxist Unity Group reaffirms the DSA's statement that the USA is "no democracy at all." We emphasize that "in preparation for the Third American Revolution, to be a socialist in this country is to be an enemy of the US Constitution."

I'm not convinced, like I used to be, that simply saying the word "socialism" or responding to each grievance with "the problem is capitalism" is always the best approach, nor is it inherently the most "radical" thing to do. The root problem is capitalism, but starting at the root doesn't necessarily make pulling out the tree any easier (nor is it even possible to start at the root: you must dig). Demanding a democratic republic in the United States is very radical. Challenging the Constitution is semi-sacrilegious. I asked a friend why he thinks leftists are quicker to say 'socialism' than they are 'democracy' or 'democratic republic.' He responded that democracy is more complicated than socialism — it asks more of people, demands more engagement, and a greater understanding of how our incredibly complex political system functions (or doesn't function). Democracy is also hard because it challenges socialists to win *the masses* of people to our ideas. There are no shortcuts to lasting power. If our ideas are correct, we should not be afraid to expose them to the scrutiny of others. Socialists believe their arguments about the necessity of socializing the economy and abolishing the commodity form will have majority support. Only at this point can we start taking the first steps toward communism.

SECTION II
PARTY AND PROGRAM

FROM WORKERS' PARTY TO WORKERS' REPUBLIC

Donald Parkinson
October 17, 2018

Donald Parkinson takes a look at the history of the First, Second, and Third Internationals, arguing for an approach to party-building and political strategy that is informed by the positives and negatives of these experiences.

This piece aims to be an engagement in wider debates occurring in the left on the question of the party and revolutionary strategy, particularly in the US. Calling for a "workers' party" is hardly a unique position in US leftism. What this actually means, however, is a whole other issue, with much of the far-left attached to a strategy of lobbying the Democrats as a sufficient alternative. My aim here will be not to convince those who have failed to comprehend the obvious — that a party and participation in mass politics independent from the Democrats is needed if we want to achieve any radical political goals. In recent leftist history, it was perhaps a controversial point to argue that a new revolutionary workers' party should be the goal of the left, with ideas of "horizontalism" and "changing the world without taking power" having active currency. In the diffused activist left around the time of the Occupy protests, a sort of anarchist common sense that parties and state power were inherently oppressive reigned dominant. Now it is clear to more people that to change the world one must engage in mass politics, and that to do so we must organize around a vision of change, or a program. This necessitates forming a party, an organization of people who collectively share a commitment to a program. Yet what kind of party we are fighting for is a topic of intense debate, regarding both its form as well as general strategic orientation. To develop a genuine communist party, we will need a positive vision of what we are working for. My aim in this piece is to help develop such a positive vision. I will begin with a historical overview of the party question, then critique modern Leninism, articulate what an alternative vision of a party and strategy may look like, consider the question of whether revolution is necessary and what it entails, and speculate on what a future workers' republic that puts the working class into power (and on the path to communism) may look like.

As well as the general assumption of the necessity of a party, my arguments will rest on another general assumption, which is that we need to form a communist party instead of a simple labor party. Some may immediately insist there is no difference, and that communists are never separate from any general party of the working class. However, a party can have a working-class base and only fight for the interests of the national working class within the state as a sort of corporate group with interests that can be balanced with the needs of the whole nation. A labor party that merely fights for legislation within the confines of the nation to benefit the immediate position of said nation's working class is not a party that fights for the actual long-term interests of the working class, which is to globally unite. In fact, such parties, because they are national in character, must help maintain the competitiveness of that nation-state on a global capitalist market. This means the party can only go so far even in benefitting its working-class base. It also serves to divide the working class along national lines. Following these criteria, such Labor Parties can be categorized as 'Bourgeois Labor Parties.' They fight for the interests of labor within the confines of the bourgeois order, even if they at times come in contradiction. In the end, it is the goal of the bureaucracies of 'bourgeois labor parties' to win the loyalty of the rank and file and smooth over these contradictions, often through appeals to nationalism and imperial projects.

Some leftist groups will argue that we must first agitate for such a party, and then form factions within it so communists can do entryism in order to transform the party into a vehicle for revolution. This approach is to be rejected out of hand. Communists should organize the kind of party that we need, which is not a bourgeois labor party that fights for the immediate interests of one national section of the class, but for the long-term interests of the world proletariat. This means a party organized around a program for a worldwide workers' republic and the long-term goal of communism. A communist party cannot merely be a labor party with a red flag, but must directly agitate for communism and internationalism, fight against all forms of oppression, and disdain to conceal its aims. It must not merely sit at the bargaining table as a good faith representative of the class, but act as a party of opposition not beholden to loyalty towards the bourgeois rule of law and constitution. Before going any further into describing the ideal communist party, we shall look at the history of the First, Second and Third Internationals which represented the global communist movement at its height.

From the Communist League to the Comintern

To begin, we shall start with Marx and Engels on the issue of the party and trace the development of Marxist thought through the Second and Third Internationals. Marx and Engels' views on the state and politics changed and developed over time, as they did on issues such as colonialism and historiography. The topic of revolutionary organization was no exception.

Marx wasn't the first Communist and became embedded in an already existing movement of revolutionaries that ranged from radical republican neo-Jacobins, utopian socialists, conspiratorial socialists aiming to follow the tradition of Babeuf, "True Socialists," Chartists, and Proudhonian mutualists. The organization that became the Communist League, the League of the Just, was similar to the secretive societies in the tradition of Babeuf's Conspiracy of Equals and politically dominated by Weitlings "true socialism." Marx and Engels would, of course, renovate the League, infusing it with their materialist conception of history and political strategy oriented around class struggle. Yet the Communist League still retained the shell of a Communist organization rooted in a tradition that existed before Marx and Engels developed a concrete view of the party.

After the experience of the Communist League, Marx focused on his own studies before joining into another party-building venture. Marx, in an 1860 letter to the poet Ferdinand Freiligrath, described the Communist League as only a party in the "ephemeral sense" and compared it to the Blanquist Société de Saisons.[1] From this, it is clear that Marx had developed a critique of the original Communist League and believed its organizational apparatus was suited for an earlier, less mature period of class struggle. A small militant minority acting in a mass uprising, the 1848 revolution, had proven to be insufficient for the needs of the proletariat. This critique of his old organization can be seen as influential to his later political career.

Marx, inspired by his involvement in the First International, would develop his own understanding of the party as a sort of mass workers association united around a minimum program of *working-class independence.* By this Marx did not mean that only waged workers could join the party or that the program would only benefit waged workers, rather, all members were disciplined around a program which expressed the general in-

1 Marik, Soma. *Revolutionary Democracy*. Chicago: Haymarket Books, 2018. p 68.

terests of the working class as opposed to the interests of other classes. For Marx, this entailed the abolition of the wage-system, with which would bring the emancipation of all humanity. It was not a party of the "whole people" as the bourgeois parties would proclaim, but a party of opposition rooted in the combined strength of the organized working class.

The combination of workers across countries culminated into the First International and could be seen as a general united front of different tendencies in the workers' movement. There were public factions that openly debated their views and aimed for political victories through majoritarian democracy. Marx recognized his own tendency was not dominant, facing opposition from followers of Lasalle, Proudhon, Bakunin, and many others. Yet overall, it was no single 'ideology' or school of thought that dominated the International, beyond basic republican virtues. Rather, the party was united around a founding program, and its centralism was based on the party program. This was something the First International worked up to as opposed to a program that was forced on membership. It would be through democratic deliberation that unity would be found, even if Marx had no doubt his views should be implemented by the party (as does any political partisan).

This form of the party would influence the Second International after the First International collapsed over debates between the followers of Marx and Bakunin. Like the First International, the Second International was a federation of national parties with their own programs, bound to rules set at the general congress. Yet the level of centralism was low on the international level. Politically, the Second International was based on a compromise between the Lasallean "state socialists" and orthodox Marxists. The Lasallean current believed in using bourgeois elections to win funding for workers cooperatives and state workshops, endorsing a form of socialism that unlike Marxism directly embraced the capitalist state. In 1881 Karl Kautsky, set to become the leading theorist of Marxist orthodoxy, would condemn the "state socialism" of Lasalleans as "... socialism by the state and for the state. It is socialism by the government and for the government. It is thus socialism by the ruling classes and for the ruling classes."[2] For Marxism to consolidate itself in the Social-Democratic movement its adherents had to win the political struggle against other currents of socialism. This eventually became the case.

In 1891 the largest party in the International, the German SPD, would draft the classic *Erfurt Programme* under the theoretical guidance of Kautsky which symbolized the achievement of Marxist domination over the party. This didn't mean the entire International took up the 'orthodox' Marxist line, as dissident factions still existed. The classic instance is the example of Bernstein's revisionists, who argued against revolution in favor of evolutionary reform to transform the capitalist state into socialism. Bernstein was also pro-colonialist, and while the Second International hardly extended beyond Eurocentrism in practice, in writing it was a majority anti-colonial party. Until 1914, Bernstein's views represented a minority. While anarchists had been successfully removed from the party, the SPD accommodated these revisionist trends. While the Second International represented a continuity with the First International in its diversity of trends, it was relatively more consolidated politically while still retaining sharply divergent factions. The tension with the 'revisionists' in the Second International is illustrated by Rosa Luxemburg's call for the expulsion of the revisionist wing in 1898. This move was unsuccessful, as Kautsky and Bebel defended their right as a minority tendency. The need for greater political unity around the program was seen as overriding these ideological differences, despite Kautsky's intense scrutiny and critique of the revisionist wing.[3]

2 Karl Kautsky, "State Socialism," marxist.org, 1881, https://www.marxists. org/archive/kautsky/1881/state/1-statesoc.htm
3 Steger, Manfred B. *The Quest for Evolutionary Socialism: Eduard Bernstein and Social Democracy.* Cambridge, UK: Cambridge University Press, 1997. p 84.

The general strategy of the Second International laid out by Kautsky in his classic *Road to Power*, can be summarized as a "strategy of attrition" or "revolutionary patience." This strategy was somewhat based on arguments made to Wilhelm Liebknecht by Engels that the party should "not fritter away this daily increasing shock in vanguard skirmishes, but keep it intact until the decisive day."[4] In other words, one must build an army before going into battle. According to Kautsky, the party would grow increasingly large through success in electoral and trade union work, as well as through its "alternative culture," which grew to include party schools, hiking clubs, cycling groups, a rowing club, socialist choirs, women's associations, and mutual aid organizations along with a variety of party publications. Elections would show not only how much success the party had in winning over the general public but would mobilize the working class in political campaigns to develop their class awareness. The party also spearheaded the union movement, helping transform the union movement from guild-like organizations with sectoral interests into a unified trade unionist movement.[5] Overall, as the crisis of capitalism developed, the ranks of the party would grow until the contradictions of capitalism would eventually lead to a moment of crisis where the party could take power and install a workers' republic. The party must be careful not to rush into insurrection or provoke the class enemy into repression; the memory of Bismarck's anti-socialist laws and how they held back class organization was not forgotten. This meant that the party should not simply fight for economic gains but also for democratic rights. These fights were seen to educate the working

4 Frederick Engels, "Introduction to Karl Marx's Class Struggle in France 1848 to 1850," marxist.org, 1895, https://www.marxists.org/archive/marx/works/download/pdf/Class_Struggles_in_France.pdf

5 Steenson, Gary P. *Not One Penny, Not One Man: German Social Democracy 1863-1914.* Pittsburgh, PA: University of Pittsburgh Press, 1981. See chapter 3 for details on the union movement's relation to the SPD.

class in the art of politics and prepare the class to become the body able to govern society. While not all Second International parties maintained this principle, the German SPD refused to enter into electoral alliances in coalition governments with the bourgeois parties or send ministers into the executive government. The proletariat could only take power on its own terms when it had mass support and capitalism was in collapse.

This general strategy still has much merit within it, yet has largely been rejected in whole by revolutionary Marxists in favor of the Third International (or Comintern) model that dismisses the Second International model as entirely reformist. There is a good reason for this — the strategy ultimately failed as the Second International parties developed nationalist tendencies. When the moment of crisis arose in WWI, the majority of parties became partisans of their own nation rather than their class. Internationalism was easy to proclaim, but when the tough moments came it wasn't easy to live by. This, of course, led to the departure of radicals from the Second International and after the Bolshevik Revolution the creation of a Third, Communist International. Social democracy had split into reformist Social-Democrats and proper revolutionary Communists, and the Communist International, or Comintern, aimed to consolidate all revolutionary Communists in a single world party. The Comintern was an attempt to replace the decrepit Second International with a properly revolutionary Marxist organization, initially composed of veterans of the old Second International parties and minorities of newly radicalized workers, often straight out of the trenches. It was formed on the observation that global capitalism had entered a period of 'Wars and Revolution' where capitalism itself was in decline and the revolutionary proletariat ascendent. In a way, the initial Comintern saw itself as a "general staff" of the world proletariat, with each national section acting as a battalion that would be sent into battle in a global civil war against capitalism. Many workers joined the early Comintern parties wanting to immediately deploy to the front of this battle.[6]

The Comintern was founded not only on the assumption that the period of 'wars and revolution' demanded a shift in political strategy, but also that a radical break was needed from all aspects of the Second International. This was based on the correct observation that the politics of the Second International materialized as a right-wing distortion that led to the disaster of 1914. The Third International introduced a more centralized structure and required its parties to purge themselves of reformist influences. The idea was to make it impossible for someone like an Ebert or Schneiderman (SPD leaders who would come into government and have a hand in crushing the Communist Spartakus Uprising) to win leadership over the party. This centralized structure resembled a military chain of command, reflecting the view that parties were soon going to be engaged in armed civil war. It also reflected changes in the Bolshevik Party itself, from a more democratic mass organization to a militarized war party. For many radicalized workers and intellectuals, October had signaled the dying days of capitalism. It was the job of the workers of the world to join in and finish what the Bolsheviks had started. Purging the party was seen as a tool used to strengthen its ranks and maintain purity from the influence of reformists. This policy had appeal due to the treachery of Social-Democracy, which had once again helped the bourgeoisie spill proletarian blood in their role of the suppression of the Spartakusbund as well as its support for Kerensky's provisional government in Russia, which had continued an offensive war in Germany. By its second congress, the Comintern had set up a non-negotiable list of 21 political conditions that its parties had to adhere to. Like any program, these 21 conditions were a

6 See Pierre Broue's *The German Revolution* and its description of the early KPD, or Theodore Draper's *Roots of American Communism* which describes the immediatist politics of the earliest formations of the CPUSA.

way of setting the boundaries of party membership. This created political divisions with the reformist socialists over a variety of issues. Of these, imperialism was key, a wedge that separated authentic communists from social-chauvinists.

The Comintern made a deliberate effort to overcome the Eurocentrism of previous Internationals by attempting to form parties throughout the entire world. Anti-colonialism became a priority, reflected by the Baku Conference where Zinoviev called for revolutionaries in the colonial world to join the world revolution. For these reasons alone, the Third International was an improvement of the Second. Marxists moved towards a truly internationalist universalism which saw the entire world as having agency in the revolutionary process and struggled politically against internal European chauvinism. To quote Zinoviev in his debate with Martov at the Halle Conference (in response to Martov mocking Bolshevik efforts to win over third world revolutionaries at the Baku Conference), "'the Second International was restricted to people with white skin. The Third International does not classify people according to the colour of their skin."[7] Whether or not the Comintern took the correct programmatic approach to anti-colonialism is another important discussion. Though with an increased centralization and a serious attempt to exist at an international scale, the Comintern was more of a proper "world party." This was a vital correction of the Second International's nationalist deviations. While they planned for the proletariat to take power in one country at a time, the Comintern properly aimed to unite the proletariat in a world revolution. What was then unclear was how protracted the struggle for a world revolution would actually be.

While the Second International made rightist deviations, the early Comintern could be said to have made "ultra-left" distortions, in some ways regressing to the Communist League's strat-

7 Lewis, Ben. *Martov and Zinoviev: Head to Head at Halle.* London: November Publishing, 2011. p 137.

egy of a militant minority acting in a semi-spontaneous mass uprising. If the Second International had a "strategy of patience," the Third was plagued with a sort of revolutionary impatience, acting on the assumption of inevitable world revolution and increased faith in the power of a militant revolutionary minority. This was partly due to a desire to break from social democracy in favor of a more insurrectionary politics, a militant working class minority that wanted to fight the class enemy as soon as possible, and a misreading of the Bolshevik Revolution as a takeover by a small party. The break from the tactics of social-democracy had the benefit of allowing for the promotion of more militant tactics like mass strikes and accounted for the possibility of violent clashes with capitalist reaction before the seizure of power. However, this also would lead to a fetishization of direct action and spontaneity. For the most extremist members like Bela Kun, the party was conceived as a "militant minority" that would push the masses into revolutionary action as mass strikes erupted, inevitably throwing the proletariat into struggle against a decaying capitalism. While the Third International had become more willing to break the straightjacket of constitutional legalism, it overestimated both the capacity of the "militant minority" to spring the working class into action by intervening in waves of mass strikes, a process that could lead to the formation of Soviets that could command political authority and be lead by the Comintern parties to communism.

This tactic had a big problem: the majority of the working class was not aligned with the Comintern and still had loyalties to the SPD. The question of leadership of the labor movement had yet to be seriously dealt with, and the hegemony of Social-Democracy was underestimated. In its first four congresses, the Comintern would increasingly come to grips with this fact and tried to develop a strategy of winning the working class over from Social-Democracy. Lenin's *"Left-Wing" Communism: An Infantile Disorder* can be seen as a polemic against tendencies in the Comintern that aimed rush into battle without winning leadership over the labor movement, and an implicit reminder that certain tactics of the Second International were still useful. Many of the "Lefts" Lenin was arguing against, like Herman Gorter and Anton Pannekoek, claimed that the historical situation had changed and that it was now necessary to abstain from elections and break with unions in favor of factory organizations. They saw such tactics as a remnant of an earlier phase of the workers' movement which was made obsolete and even harmful by the tactics of mass strikes, with workers councils being the key forms of proletarian organization. Some "Lefts" were in favor of a minority "vanguard party" that would guide the spontaneous struggle of the workers' councils, while others such as Otto Rühle were against party organization entirely. However, by making these bold statements about tactics and the historical periods they belonged to, the Lefts were incapable of adapting to changing situations. Strong theoretical chops and an ability to see past the opportunism of reformists were not enough without a keen sense of politics. Organizing for revolution requires tactical flexibility: the proletariat must use every tactic possible to win. For Lenin in his rebuttal to the "Lefts," what was important was not tactics, but the animating principle behind them. Lenin argued winning elections and leadership of the unions were not tactics inherently corrupted by the legacy of Social Democracy, but rather tactics that needed to be utilized for revolutionary rather than reformist ends. If they failed to do so, they simply ceded ground to reformists. The left tendency in the Comintern was not simply reflected in the ideas of a few idealist intellectuals lost in abstractions and separate from the class struggle, but also within the rank-and-file itself. There was a strong distrust of Social-Democrats and the union bureaucracy among the rank-and-file and for good reason. This distrust would last through to the rise of Hitler, yet the rank-and-file of both parties also showed a willingness to unite from below.

However, as long as long the as the SPD held hegemony over the German labor movement, the KPD would not be able to take power except via a putsch.

Responding to relative isolation in the broader working class movement and faced with the dominance of Social-Democracy even after the war, Comintern theorists like Bela Kun devised the "theory of the offensive" where the communist "militant minority" would attempt to incite militant conflict with the state, aiming to shake reformist workers out of their Menshevik boots and spring them into militant action against the state itself alongside the communist vanguard. The aim was to as Mao put it, be the spark that lit the prairie fire, to push the working class into action thought the militant vanguard. This strategy manifested itself in the KPD's March Action which failed miserably and simply divided the working class movement even further. The KPD's effort to "go on the offensive" did not see the Social-Democratic workers join Communist workers against the wishes of their leaders, it instead saw KPD and SPD workers fighting each other in the streets and an unleashing of state repression when already under constant threat from right-wing militias. Based on this experience, the idea of a minority or vanguard acting decisively to push the masses into more radical action was shown to be an ineffective strategy. There was no shortcut to winning a revolutionary majority. The March Action would be an astounding failure — hundreds of Communists killed, around 6000 arrested, and 4000 convicted including key party leaders like Heinrich Brandler. Party membership was essentially halved, with hundreds of thousands of workers leaving, slimming the ranks of the party from approximately 400,000 to 180,000.[8]

The failure of the March Action, while not clear to all Communists, was a sign that the Comintern had to develop a united strategy to win mass working-class support. The solution that

8 Florian Wilde, Building a Mass Party: Ernst Meyer and the United Front Policy, sourced from *Weimar Communism as a Mass Movement 1918-1933*, p. 67.

the Comintern arrived at was the United Front, which was first officially suggested by the party leadership in Paul Levi and Karl Radek's *Open Letter*. The united front strategy called on the unity of the entire workers' movement (including all the unions and the Social-Democrats) in campaigns for demands of higher pay, unemployment relief, price controls, emergency expropriations, the disarming of right-wing militias and the arming of the workers, and freedom for political prisoners. The letter also called for the involved organizations to not "conceal the disagreements that divide us" and simply "limit themselves to lipservice for proposed basis for action."[9] This meant unity in campaigns for these reforms, not meaning that parties surrender the right to critique each other and lose their political independence. This letter was published in the KPD party press approximately two months before the failed March Action, and with its disaster leading to the implosion of the party, the united front now seemed to clearly represent a superior strategic approach. By the 4th Congress of the Comintern, the need for winning a working-class majority through the united front tactic was recognized officially by the Comintern's Executive Committee (whose authority was binding on all member parties).[10]

The United Front policy was a call for unity of the workers' organizations for specific struggles, with each organization maintaining its independence and the right to critique each other. The united front policy was applied by various Communist parties differently, as it was received with great skepticism by those who were unwillingly forced to adopt it. Some communists, like the PCI's chief theorist Amadeo Bordiga, argued the united front should only be applied 'from below,' meaning without any official agreements made with the leaders of reformist parties. This was contrasted with a united front 'from above,'

9 Open Letter to German Workers' Organisations, sourced in *To the Masses: Proceedings of the Third Congress of the Communist International, 1921*, 1061-63.
10 On Tactics of the Comintern, sourced in *Toward the United Front: Proceedings of the Fourth Congress of the Communist International, 1922*, p 1157.

which involved making agreements and alliances on the political level rather than merely uniting across party lines in economic struggles. This desire to draw a distinction in order to avoid making deals with the leadership of reformists reflected a real expression of hostility towards uniting with the Social-Democratic parties from the party rank-and-file. Yet this tendency in the rank-and-file was not universal, as workers had already begun to unite across party affiliation on their own before the united front policy was imposed formally. Ultimately, the distinction between united fronts from below or above was less than useful; even if leadership rejected cooperation, this would simply be more evidence that Communists had the interests of the workers at heart in the concrete class struggle. Simply making deals with reformist leaders for joint action was not the same as a political coalition with a capitalist party to make easy electoral gains while sacrificing one's politics.

It also important to distinguish the United Front from the Popular Front policy, which is not a common alliance of workers' organizations, but rather an alliance with the bourgeois state to restore the constitutional order. The Popular Front policy is an explicit call for national unity with the bourgeoisie for a cause that supposedly carries more importance than the class struggle. This policy means a *sacrifice* of class-independence, while the United Front policy aims to allow for common action while *preserving* class-independence. The United Front aimed to give communists an opportunity to push for class struggle against the acceptable bounds of reformists, whereas the Popular Front was a retreat into the bounds of reformism.

An example of the United Front policy being put to the test can be found in the great railway strike in Germany in February 1922. The strike was triggered by cuts and layoffs of workers who were on the state payroll, with no opposition from the SPD despite protest from the conservative railway workers' union. When the strike launched, the SPD ministers in government banned the strike and threatened disciplinary action. In response, the KPD backed the strikers demands and called for the leaders of the Railway Workers Union, the Trade Union Confederation, the UPSD, and the SPD to all unite in defense of the workers' economic needs and their right to strike. While the SPD leadership denied cooperation, locally, SPD workers and Communists were able to cooperate. While the main backer of the strike was the KPD, the strike eventually reached a level of 800,000 workers and became the largest transportation strike in German history. Through their attempts to unite all workers and support the strikers, the KPD was able to come out as a more powerful party with mass support. Zinoviev even praised the actions of the KPD in the German railway strike as a "textbook example of the proper application of the United Front tactic."[11]

Despite this success, the United Front policy was not flawless. One of its more questionable elements was the concept of the 'workers' government' where the Communists would form a halfway-house to the dictatorship of the proletariat through a coalition government with the Social-Democrats. The formation of 'workers' government' was meant to create a crisis that would eventually put power purely in the hands of the Communist Party. This was based on the assumption that the dictatorship of the proletariat could only function with single-party rule, something which grew to become Comintern orthodoxy. This concept was also another 'shortcut' to seizing power without winning mass support, and relied on Social-Democratic votes to boost the parties position of authority. In 1923, the attempt to put the workers' government tactic into practice in Saxony ended in failure and led to an unsuccessful insurrection that would foreclose hope of revolution in Germany for the coming years. Ultimately, the hope of climbing the ladder to power with the help of a 'workers' government' was a chimera; the party had no

11 Florian Wilde, Building a Mass Party: Ernst Meyer an the United front Policy, sourced from *Weimar Communism as a Mass Movement 1918-1933*, p 72.

alternative but to win a relative working class majority and displace Social-Democratic hegemony over the labor movement. This hope for spontaneity to fill in the gaps left by a lack of actual leadership over the class movement was the source of the Comintern's 'ultra-left' distortion, but could also express itself in inconsistent opportunism.

Regardless of the flawed "workers' government" policy, the united front was an overall effective tactic that, when utilized, saw the greatest levels of growth in the Comintern.[12] One can see this as a sort of realization on the part of the Comintern that its initial hope to form parties of civil war against an imminent demise of capitalism was a flaw. Communists were not guaranteed the support of the masses due to historical necessity — they had to fight for political support from the working class. This realization stood in contradiction to the logic behind the "theory of offensive," and would continue to clash with it throughout the history of the Comintern, with the dominance of either approach not always reducible to a certain periodization. For example, it was after the successful merger with the USPD's left wing at the Halle Conference when the KPD went on the suicidal March Action. Inability to unite around a solid strategy meant an approach of consistency and patience wasn't pursued.

The rest of the history of the Comintern is a sad story. In the 'third period, from 1928-33, the parties fully moved away from their tactics of the united front and took up ultra-sectarian positions. This manifested most infamously in Germany with the KPD's unwillingness to form a united front with the SPD against Hitler, leading to one of history's greatest disasters when Hitler came to power without a serious united struggle against him by the working class. This idiotic "ultra-leftism" would then be matched by the equally bankrupt rightism of the Popular Front, where Comintern Parties decided to forgo the

12 Jacoby, Russel. *Stalin, Marxism-Leninism and the Left.* New England: New England Free Press, 1976, pp 51-52.

struggle for socialism in hopes that the colonial powers of the world would back them against fascism due to their "democratic" characteristics. The bourgeois powers only opposed fascism to the extent it threatened the stability of their own empires.

One could judge from this history that the Second and Third Internationals were just shitshows with little redeeming qualities, essentially evidence that the twentieth century was proof of the impossibility of communism. It would be foolish to expect the first attempts at a global communist party to succeed, and despite their ultimate failure, they were the organized expression of the revolutionary working class at its height, with all their flaws and heroism in full display. As communists, we have no choice but to learn from our history. Ignoring the twentieth-century communist movement or simply semantically distancing ourselves from the realities don't make them go away. While the Second International primarily made rightist political errors, the Third International primarily made 'ultra-left' political errors. From this observation, we can come to a sort of center, where the positives and negatives of both Internationals can be learned from. This overall position, of building a mass party around a program for revolution through patiently consolidating the organized forces of the proletariat, could be described as "Centrist Marxism" or "the Marxist Center." While the term 'centrism' is often used by Trotskyists as a term of derision, we use it here in this sense of a strategy that would mean patiently building up the forces of the revolutionary proletariat into democratically organized institutions, rather than trying to build a small "vanguard" or "militant minority" that will either intervene in a spontaneous movement or spark a revolution through armed struggle. It also entails a strong commitment to both Internationalism and democracy, emphasizing Marxism as in continuity with democratic and republican principles that developed in the struggles against aristocracy, monarchism, and clericalism. Flexibility in tactics must be matched with a strong commitment to principles. One could say that the center strategy is a sort of pragmatism for the means of revolution rather than reform.

Beyond "Leninism"

What would it mean for a party to accept the positive and negative lessons of both the Second and Third Internationals? To begin with, it would mean disregarding either as models to copy that we can identify as carrying some invariant "red thread." Both failed, the Second International becoming an ally of the capitalist order and the Third International leaping into the ultra-leftist madness of the Third Period, the opportunistic Popular Front and eventually its full dissolution by Stalin. Today, much of what calls itself the 'revolutionary left' wants to essentially revive Comintern style parties, though perhaps only on a national scale. This attempt at revival, typically referred to as Leninism or Bolshevism, was last attempted in the United States with the New Communist Movement, having little to do with the actual history of Bolshevism before the Comintern. These views and the leftovers of this wave of Leninist party forming have come to represent what is seen as mainstream Leninism in the United States. Their results give us the micro-sects we have today; Workers World Party, Party for Socialism and Liberation, Freedom Road Socialist Organization-Fight Back, as well as countless Trotskyist groups that are all of varying quality in politics. In this particular section, when I refer to Leninists I do not mean the "Leninism of Lenin" which I very much admire, but rather the "Leninist movement" of attempts to form vanguard parties in the mode of the Comintern. What differentiates this mode of Leninism from orthodox Marxism is its embrace of the single monolithic party-state as a model for the dictatorship of the proletariat, the belief in a "party of the new type" that transcends the mass party through selective elitism, centralization around a specific theoretical line, and a militaristic chain of command that is not actually 'democratic' or 'centralist' but rather bureaucratic and autocratic.

Leninists argue the key innovation of their "party of a new type" was democratic centralism. Democratic centralism, most simply defined, is the hardly disagreeable formula of democratic deliberation combined with unity in action. By this definition, democratic centralism was also practiced by the Second International. Any democratic decision making requires centralism because the will of the majority needs to be enforced against the minority. The SPD, for example, voted as a bloc in parliament and had centralism enforced in the party, it was not internally a federalist organization (like other parties in the Second International) despite the wishes of its right.[13] What made the "Leninist party of a new type" different was not democratic centralism. Rather than simple centralism, Comintern parties had a form of 'monolithism' to use the phrase of Fernando Claudin.[14] In other words, Comintern parties emphasized centralism over democracy or often just disregarded democratic norms entirely. While this wasn't absent in the Second International, the Third was born as a sort of militarized civil war organization rather than a political party in the sense of a mass workers association as envisioned by Marx. While this may have been justified at a time when an actual global civil war against capitalism was on the table, this is not the case right now — we are not living in the same era of 'Wars and Revolutions' as the leaders of the Comintern were. When modern Leninists claim the secret of their parties' road to success is 'democratic centralism,' it tends to mean an overly bureaucratized group that puts heavy workloads on individual members to make them more 'disciplined,' and a lack of actual democracy in favor of a more militarized party structure. Factions are forbidden, ideological centralism (rather than pro-

13 Schorske, Carl. *German Social Democracy, 1905-1917.* Harvard, MA: Harvard University Press, 1983.

14 Fernando Claudin's, *The Communist Movement, From Comintern to Cominform Part 1,* pp 103-125, contains a critique of Comintern monolithism.

grammatic centralism) is imposed from above, and groups aim to build an 'elite' cadre that tails existing mass struggles, hoping to bank in on them to recruit members. The Comintern model is simply a recipe for failure in today's conditions, just another guide to building yet another sect that will compete for the latest batch of recruits. How this actually works in practice is exemplified by the state of actually existing contemporary Leninism in the USA.

Take PSL, FRSO-FB and the ISO as case studies. Alongside schemes to take over union bureaucracy, these organizations essentially form front groups that hide affiliation to any kind of communist goals and aim to mobilize students around the latest liberal social justice issues and work in alliance with NGOs to throw rallies of mostly symbolic value. Through these activities, the cadre (or inner group) of the Leninist organization hopes to recruit parts of the liberal activist community in order to grow their base of support and garner more influence in these social movements. The organizations themselves proclaim democratic centralism, but in reality, there is no public debate about party positions allowed between congresses. At the congresses debate, takes place as little as possible and is usually led by an unelected central committee that composed of full-time staffer careerists. By using their "militant minority" tactics to act as the "spark that lights the prairie fire" in popular struggles, the modern Leninists (with some exceptions of course) tend to tail these struggles instead of fight for a class-conscious approach to issues of civil and democratic rights. One tactic often used is to hand out as many of their signs as possible to appear larger in number, when in reality this is often protesting street theater backed by NGOs connected to the Democrats who are simply using leftists as useful idiots for "direct actions" against the Republicans. Usually, the rationale for this activism is to raise consciousness among liberals. Theoretically, by 'riding the wave' of spontaneous activism, the militant minority group will build up enough influence to launch an insurrection. This is a delusional hope. It leads to chronic involvement in activism that takes up time and energy but doesn't build working class institutions that can actually offer concrete gains for working people through collective action. One could describe this general strategy of tailing social movements as 'movementism.'

The critique of movementism has developed in Leninist circles, specifically by Maoists around the theorist J. Moufawad-Paul. He has written that movementism is the "ideological articulation of the default form of opportunism in the capitalist centre" and a product of internalized anti-communism.[15] Yet the Maoist critique of the logic of economism and defeat that fuels movementism has no real alternative to offer beyond a fantasy of "protracted people's war" where a mass movement grows in the process of waging a violent guerrilla struggle against the state. The *actually existing* Maoist alternative to the politics of movementism in the US is no better, mostly consisting of politically substanceless militant posturing and sectarianism. While the Maoists may be correct in their critiques of other Leninists, their alternative seems to entail acting like insurrectionary anarchists with red flags. Nor do they move away from the model of the "militant minority" — they instead double down on it with calls to "put politics in command" and boast about their supposed "military policy."

While modern Leninist groups obviously have no organic or meaningful connection to the Comintern, it is still the reference point to which these organizations orient. Amongst Leninist organizations, the idea of the party as a minority "vanguard" that doesn't rely on majority support is based on a misunderstanding of the Russian Revolution. Like bourgeois scholars, this misunderstanding views the October Revolution as a coup but embrace it, believing it to be evidence that a minority party can

15 http://moufawad-paul.blogspot.com/2012/10/lets-avoid-being-sucked-back-into.html

slip its way into power by being in the right place at the right time. This perspective leaked into the Comintern, despite Lenin's protestations in *Left-Wing Communism*. Instead of critical engagement with the politics elaborated in the text Leninists choose to use it as a guidebook for justifying rank opportunism. The idea of the militant minority channeling the energy of spontaneous mass action is essentially what unites both the early Comintern and today's 'movementism' as well as the Maoist critics of movementism.

It is necessary to go beyond actually existing Leninism. This doesn't mean disputing Lenin or distancing ourselves from his legacy; he was one of the greatest Marxists and revolutionaries of all time and his works and life are marked with political brilliance. Yet today, "Leninism" almost completely distorts or disregards the early Bolshevik party and its relation to the Second International and simply focuses on repeating the Comintern experience. What we need is to move beyond an attempted systemization of the Comintern and Lenin in particular, but rather continue the systemization of Marxism as a whole based on the entire history of class struggle. This is what Lenin did. Lenin didn't see himself as a "Leninist," creating a new stage of Marxism, but as an orthodox Marxist applying a system of thought to his own conditions. This doesn't mean we should reject the most vital contributions of Lenin, for example, his views on revolutionary defeatism and imperialism. What it does mean is that much of what made Lenin great was already in Marx, Engels and even Kautsky. It means, much in the same way that Marx critically learned from the failures of the Communist League in developing his theory of the party, that we must critically learn from the failures of all past Internationals, especially the Second and Third (which historically had the most impact on mass politics).

Negative lessons, as in what *not* to do, are the easiest to pick from our history: we know the end result and can pick out where actors had incorrect judgment. But positive lessons, as in what we *should* do, are harder. The common orthodoxy of "Leninism" is that there are only negative lessons to learn from the experience of the Second International, and to suggest otherwise is to commit to reformism. Yet a mass workers' party with class independence run on democratic lines is still relevant, despite its basic roots in the First and Second International. The strategy of these types of parties, to patiently build up forces through union and electoral struggles, organizing proletarian communities and building a sort of alternative center of power run by the working class — eventually to seize power and become the governing class — seems to make more sense than whatever kind of hope in spontaneous insurrectionism or a general strike that the left has to offer as an alternative. We can accept this strategy while also rejecting the social-chauvinism of the German SPD. We can also accept the advances of the Third International, especially in its aim to build a truly international party resolutely opposed to imperialism and the bourgeois state, willing to use non-legal means if necessary, and closed to nationalist reformists like a Bernstein or Bernie Sanders. We also can reject the bureaucratic, semi-militarized chain of command model taken up by modern Comintern-inspired parties in favor of a robust intra-party democracy, tolerating factions without enforcing rigid ideological centralism. As the First International did, we should aim for programmatic rather than ideological unity. As the experience of the Second International showed, it was necessary to draw the line *somewhere* and not tolerate reactionary views having a platform in the party. The future Communist International must develop programmatic unity through collective activity as a whole, and will probably never wholly have ideological unity. However, there must be basic minimum political standards enforced. Ideally, it is in a strong, clear program that one can develop these standards of principled unity. Yet one cannot make a formal rule that will prevent falling to the monolithism of the

Comintern or opportunism of the Second International — it is also a question of ideological, of political debate.

The forces of the proletariat are weak and divided, it will take a long-haul approach to develop a party that can be a vehicle of independent political action. This doesn't rely on any kind of 'get rich quick' scheme, where the party uses a mass line or transitional demands to attract the working class without actually convincing and winning them over to revolutionary politics. It means actually having to develop the actual organizational strength to put the working class into command of society. One has to essentially build a 'state within a state' which stands in opposition to the bourgeois order and command the loyalty of proletarians in their majority against the capitalist state. We cannot hope that crisis simply accelerates the working class into such misery that it has no choice but to go on mass strikes to form workers councils and then try to insert our militant minority into the movement to guide it on its proper track. Building a real alternative to capitalist rule requires, as Lenin pointed out, a principled core that is able to stay politically *consistent* while utilizing every tactic possible. No space left open in civil society, where we can agitate and educate, should be left unutilized. A class-independent workers' party which does not neglect this fight is a necessity.

What Kind of Party?

What does it mean for a party to be a "class-independent workers' party"? Should the "class party" be a vanguard party or mass party? To answer these questions, we must first look at the more abstract principle of "class interests" to understand what is meant by class independence. A workers' party means, in a more plainly-spoken language, a *proletarian party*. For Marx, the proletariat is generally all those in society "without reserves," meaning they own no property from which to subsist, and are forced to rely on the general fund of wages paid out by the capitalist, property-owning, class. The proletariat is not simply factory workers, but the entire section of society that relies on the wage fund to survive, in many cases they are not even formally employed. The proletariat has no existing property relations of its own to maintain. It performs cooperative labor on a global scale but mediated through the anarchy of the market. The broad proletariat can only liberate itself by cooperating across all its social divisions and collectively ending their separation from the means of production. Yet the bourgeois, propertied class, has interests in the maintenance of property relations that allow them to exist as a class. By nature, these two classes ultimately struggle not only over the needs of workers or the drives of capitalists on a day to day basis, but contest modes of production themselves. Class interests, however, are not derived from the subjective consciousness of individual members of a class, but from an abstract analysis of the capitalist mode of production. Because of the impossibility of liberation through reversion to small commodity production, communism is the only option for the liberation of the proletariat (and besides, self-employment for the entire proletariat via a return to petty commodity production is not a desirable or possible historical outcome). It can be said that the proletariat as a class because it is the class compelled to fight for communism, carries with it the interests of humanity, as communism entails the liberation of humanity as a whole. Yet only those without any real stakes in the capitalist system will never collectively, as a class, fight to abolish it.

When discussing class interests, we mean not only short-term needs like better economic conditions and expanding democratic rights, but the long-term need to overthrow waged labor and establish communism. By class independence we mean that the class interests of the proletariat are independent and exclusive to the proletariat and are antagonistic with the objective interests of all other propertied classes as they exist in capitalism — hence standing opposed to all class rule itself. There is a contradiction

that cannot be resolved through any scheme of 'harmony' between the propertied classes (the bourgeoisie, their bureaucratic
elite, and landlords) and the dispossessed class (the proletariat,
which grows as small proprietors are knocked out of business and
specialized labor becomes de-skilled). Class independence means
organizing around a program of politics that expresses the exclusive interests of the proletariat that differ from other classes — the
need to overthrow the capitalist system, which only the propertyless proletariat has no stake in. It also means not forming electoral blocs with bourgeois parties, or aiming to win support from
the bourgeoisie by changing the class program to de-emphasize
communism or the seizure of state power by the waged class. A
class-independent party and communist party essentially mean
the same thing, if we accept the greater Marxist theory about the
politics of class interests. An independent class program is, therefore, one which expresses not the subjective needs of the workers
at a given moment, but on the overall role of the proletariat in history according to a Marxist analysis. Of course, a program must
be more than simply words, but also express the principles which
animate the day to day activity of the party.

Does a party that makes concessions in its program to small
property owners lose its class independence? This question
raises why it's important to differentiate between a minimum
and maximum program. The minimum program should be a set
of measures that if enacted, will bring the proletariat to power. This should include the creation of a commune state, the
arming of the proletariat, dissolution of the police and military,
nationalization of monopolies, leading to a decisive break with
bourgeois state power. It is *not* the abolition of the bourgeoisie
(and therefore all class distinctions), but of their political rule
initially in a certain region (the larger the better). The proletariat and bourgeoisie are still reproduced as categories, but capitalism exists in a state of decay, the bourgeoisie primarily existing
in small production and the intellectual property of bureaucrats.

Because of their role in social reproduction (often as specialists or producers of vital goods), concessions will have to be made to these classes for the proletariat to hold onto power without social reproduction breaking down. Therefore, a *minimum program* that makes certain economic concessions to small producers such as small business owners is not necessarily incompatible with the interests of the proletariat. Such demands, however, are incompatible with the *maximum program*, which express the final goal of communism. The full development of a socialized sphere of social reproduction will eventually leave small property relations in the dustbin of history, but this requires the long-term transformation of both the forces and relations of production. The small property owners will not immediately be forcibly collectivized by the proletariat in the same way as the largest monopoly capitalists will be. Because small proprietors control small patchworks of the economy, such as parts of agriculture and technology, they will not be easy to collectivize immediately — cooperation with these sectors is necessary to keep society running. They should be urged to form cooperatives and integrate into the socialized sector, but eventually, they will fall out business in competition with the growing socialist sector. The proletariat can't cede too much economic power to small proprietors without risking its own power and having to limit democratic governance. A difficult balance is needed.

The minimum program should not be a set of measures that "complete the bourgeois-democratic revolution" either, as some suggest. There is no "completion" of the bourgeois revolution where all oppressive leftovers of the pre-capitalist order are destroyed, short of the proletarian revolution that transcends the bourgeois revolution altogether, eliminating all forms of class exploitation and oppression, including those that preceded capitalism. It should be a set of measures that change the form of the state such that the proletariat, or the working-class, is now the governing class. Such a society was called a "dictatorship of the proletariat" by Marx, but perhaps a contemporary, more politically viable term could be the "workers' republic." In the minimum program, some aspects may be reforms achievable under capitalism, but if enacted in full it should transform the bourgeois state to a workers' republic; a metamorphosis from the dictatorship of the bourgeoisie to a dictatorship of the proletariat.

A proper minimum program also avoids the pitfalls of economism, not simply focusing on economic demands of the immediate class struggle, but also demands that address the struggle for democratic rights of women and oppressed nationalities as well as the general tyrannical and anti-democratic nature of the state. This means taking up demands for sexual freedom, for freedom from censorship, for the right own firearms, and democracy in all sphere of life. To quote Lenin in 1890, "In waging only the economic struggle, the working class loses its political independence; it becomes the tail of other parties and betrays the great principle: 'the emancipation of the working classes must be conquered by the working class themselves.'"[16] The party must be a school of politics where the workers are trained not to follow orders, but to take politics into their own hands and constitute their class as one that fights for the liberation of all humanity. 'Class independence' should not be interpreted in a narrow economistic sense where the working class strictly fights for things that solely benefit workers. Rather, the working class should pose itself as the most militant and uncompromising force in these democratic struggles, leading them to give as much of a communist perspective as possible.

The workers' party itself should be a prefiguration of the workers' republic, in the sense of its internal governance. This means it should practice a form of democracy distinct from and beyond the democracy of liberalism. This means experimentation, investigating new forms of collective decision making and seeing what

16 Lidke, Vernon T. *The Alternative Culture: Socialist Labor in Imperial Germany.* Oxford, UK: Oxford Universtiy Press, 1985.

works. The party should be economically organized (as all parties are firms) on a cooperative basis with no salaries that allow for careerism. The Central Committee should be directly elected by the membership and recallable. Open debate and tolerance of factions, rather than the imposition of an ideological monolithism are key if the party wishes to demonstrate to the class that communism, not capitalism, is the truly free society.

The party is a workers' party because it is organized in the working class districts, campaigns electorally primarily in these districts, and builds working class organizations of all kinds, such as tenants unions and mutual aid groups, in these communities. The party must present itself as a complete alternative to the existing bourgeois parties but just as serious. The majority of the proletariat does not even vote, as the blog Cold and Dark Stars pointed out, meaning that a working-class party would have to tap into the disappointments of the mass of the population with existing politics while offering a compelling alternative politics that speaks to their deeper sense of human solidarity to build a culture of class struggle. A form of "insurgent electoralism" is needed, one that aims not simply to gradually capture the pre-existing capitalist state machinery for the proletariat, but to use the election campaign as a ruthless propaganda tool against the bourgeois parties, to help delegitimize the bourgeois state, and legitimize communist politics. We won't win simply by acting like professional politicians and pandering to the center, but by being the more dangerous vote in an election.

However, a workers' party is more than just an electoral party, and if it is going to even succeed as an electoral party it needs a base to mobilize in the first place. It requires well-trained cadre and education programs for all members, and it needs to distribute these skills and knowledge amongst the membership as much as possible. By learning to run alternative unions, mutual aid societies, and election campaigns, we learn the skills needed to run society on new political grounds. The party becomes a smaller state within and without the state that grows through a course of the protracted struggle to become the hegemonic force in society and stands as an alternative center of authority to the existing bourgeois state when crisis emerges.

Becoming a "state within the state" would also mean forming what is often called an "alternative culture" by historians of the Second International-era SPD.[17] This would include things ranging from party-run sports teams to free clinics to breakfast programs or hiking clubs. The point of such 'alternative cultures' is not just to draw in wider layers of the working class, but also to develop new forms of socialization contrary to capitalism and meet needs of workers that the capitalist state ignores. One thing that modern-day anarchists get correct is the need to create such an alternative culture within capitalism. However, largely due to self-imposed ideological limitations, anarchist subcultures do not have the working class orientation, level of centralization, institutionalization, and access to resources (as well as cultural barriers) to actually make an alternative culture that is appealing, and instead, create a mostly 'DIY' alternative to charities. A workers' party would bring a level of professionalization and discipline to such activities, as well as incorporating them into a larger political project with democratic accountability to a mass movement, moving beyond the limits of current left 'counterculture.'

We also should never forget the importance of the party school, which is one of the key aspects of the party. The party school should aim to not only educate its members in Marxism, but also in skills related to organization, finance, science, technology, and logistics. The party's educational institutions work to not only raise the class's own class-awareness in history but also their skills in fighting against capitalism and constructing an alternative order. Most importantly, party schools should

17 "Albert Parsons," Spartacus Educational, Sept. 2022, https://spartacus-educational.com/USAparsonsA.htm

not simply be transmission belts for a certain leader's ideology, but also promote free thinking and debate. Marxism should be treated as an open system, a progressive research program in the Lakatosian sense that develops through critical inquiry. The party must, therefore, have an intellectual culture of open debate and collective deliberation, reflected in its own institutions. Though the educational institutions of the party, workers should develop a system superior at creating well-rounded individuals than bourgeois education, creating a model that demonstrates the potentials of the communist alternative.

As for the question of unions, a party should aim to win leadership of the overall union movement as much as possible. However, winning leadership is a means to an end and should strive to push the union movement towards industrial unions that break beyond the divisions of craft and skill. Forming one united union for all workers, both skilled and unskilled, should be the overall aim of the party. This is, of course, a lofty ideal to achieve, something hardly imaginable to happen until after the consolidation of a workers' state. However, communists in the union movement should not simply call for more militant direct action from rank-and-file caucuses, but strive to win union elections and build relations with other unions. Rather than seeking to form a stratum within unions that is merely willing to push strike actions into more militant directions, the aim should be for the party to campaign for democratic reforms in the union and make them schools of socialism, eventually winning them to supporting socialism as a long-term goal. Simply forming caucuses for militant struggle is not enough; workers can engage in militant strikes but still hold reactionary views. Communists must take an active role in education by participating in union politics and holding strong positions against the union bureaucracy's association with the Democratic Party, apoliticism, and general opportunism.

Some have argued that industrial unionism is impossible in the United States because of labor law. This relies on two assumptions — that labor law cannot be challenged by electoral action or simple mass transgression of the law. It is also possible that the existing unions in the United States, in large part, are too conservative to reform. However, the majority of US proletarians aren't unionized, giving a large pool of potential recruits for a new union movement that escapes the straightjacket of the official unions. In a period where old institutions meet their limitations and new ones struggle to find footing in the terrain of modern capitalism, it is hard to say what exactly the general defensive organizations of the working class will look like. The need for such organizations is eternal in capitalism, and the constant dislocations caused in the working class by the brutality of market competition at some point make defensive class organization of some kind a necessity.

What the party does need to avoid in the unions is bureaucratic careerism. Union representatives of the workers' party need to be subject to the party rather than their own career interests, which creates a phenomenon that moves the party's politics to the right. This means the focus of work in the unions needs to be a form of base building as well as education amongst the rank-and-file rather than using opportunistic machinations to climb the ranks of the union.

From Sects to Parties to State Power

How we can build such a party is no easy question. To begin to answer this seriously would require an analysis of the dynamics of the various sects of the left, and thinking of a way to transcend the dynamics of the sect system while moving toward greater programmatic unity. Many argue the best option right now is to work in the DSA; others in the Marxist Center network, and still others in the IWW. What is clear is that serious communists need to start working towards some kind of programmatic unity that could be the basis of a new party. Potentially, we could also derive lessons from the 'united front' tactic of the Comintern on how to unite and consolidate our forces despite the division of the left. Unity in common action can help communists overcome pointless divisions and find their broader programmatic unity.

The road to building such a party will not be simple and will require ideological and political struggles. It is important that these debates be had in good faith and publicly in the press of revolutionary organizations without either anti-intellectualism or obscurantism. Compromises on tactical questions will have to be made. Old historical struggles will have to be put to rest. Dogmatism, faith in holding the one true red thread of the communist tradition, or believing in the one correct interpretation of the "immortal science" (and thus the unlimited authority it grants), should be fought against with open debate and inquiry. Factions will have to be tolerated; people will have to tolerate losing votes without splitting in response. Clear lines of ideological demarcation will be drawn, and political tendencies will grow that reflect the diversity of the proletariat in all its forms. The general strategy of base-building can be seen as a sort of 'bread-and-butter' of party organizing. The general task of building institutions with a proletarian base outside the state and capable of exercising class power is key, and institutions that can exist both within and outside a political party must be created. Building power cannot be done within the bourgeois state. Rather, a workers' party must build power by first building its own independent base, not merely "conquering" the base of another party. Electoral successes are not so much a source of power as much as they merely measure and consolidate existing power.

A workers' party worthy of the communist name must be closely connected to the class struggle. It is not going to arise spontaneously out of the unions and other defensive organizations but will begin through the consolidation of communists who then take an active role in organizing such institutions. A communist party must not simply "intervene" in strikes after they pop off, but be an organizational expression of class power that helps *increase* the number of strikes and class conflict. It must aim to win leadership of the working class's own defensive institutions democratically, not through bureaucratic machinations. The communists must demonstrate their party to be different, not only in name from the bourgeois parties but in practice, fighting as the *vanguard* in the class struggle, not only for economic aims but in the fight for democracy too. A historical example of what this would look like is the way CPUSA was in the vanguard of the struggle for black democratic rights. By demonstrating they are the vanguard in such fights against all forms of capitalist tyranny, the communists can win the support of the proletariat at large by giving expression to and clarifying their class interests. The communists bring to the rest of the proletariat the "good news" that collectively, they can transform the world to eliminate all exploitation and oppression. But to convince them a vision is needed, the purpose of a program is in part to help the public envision the kinds of changes the party is fighting for.

A communist party building mass support socializes humanity in a new way and prepares the class and human solidarity that will be the basis of communism. By representing a better potential world in its organizational form, it gives life to the hopes of a better world that is otherwise suppressed by capitalist society. The rise of such a party is only compatible with the capitalist order to a certain degree; eventually, capitalism will fall into crisis and the party will have enough power to launch a social revolution if it continues with a secular rate of growth (meaning long-term continuous growth over a period of time). This was assumed by SPD theoretician Karl Kautsky who saw the growth of the party's success as inevitable due to the growth of the proletariat. But history proved to be more cunning than this at-first believable situation, as the development of the socialist movement was bifurcated into different competing currents while the labor movement itself never followed a simple secular trend of steady growth. The hopes of Kautsky and many of his early followers proved to be too ideal for the complexity of actual politics. As the party develops and consolidates its positions, it will at times lose or gain members and support while taking necessary principled stands on issues. What matters is that the party lives up to its class independence in deed and not just word and that it does not vacillate to accommodate the interests of the propertied classes in order to win support.

How could a such a party actually win state power? Could it do so peacefully through elections? Even if the party won a majority in an election and came to power on its own, if it began to actually implement a revolutionary program to throw out the old constitutional order, dissolve the military, and arm the people, in all likelihood the bourgeoisie would react to the transgression of their class power and property with a coup or armed revolt. In this case, the only option is to either defend the revolution through the armed working class or concede to the bourgeois military. It is because of this political reality that one cannot promise a "democratic road to socialism" without the eruption of violent civil conflict. The unlikelihood of radical social change happening peaceful and without civil strife, at least in the United States, is well articulated by the American revolutionary socialist Albert Parsons:

> I do not believe that capital will quietly or peaceably permit the economic emancipation of their wage-slaves. It is against all the teachings of history and human nature for men to voluntarily yield up usurped or arbitrary power. The capitalists of the world will for this reason force the workers into armed revolution. Socialists point out this fact and warn the workingmen to prepare for the inevitable.[18]

18 For example see Erik Olin Wright, *How to Think About (and Win) Socialism* and Vivek Chibber's *Our Road to Power*.

In the end, we will have no choice but to "smash" the repressive apparatus of the bourgeois state, meaning in practice the dissolution of the police and military, arming the proletariat, and putting power in the hands of the working class by building a new form of representation fit for workers' rule. Whether or not the party has a mandate for forming a workers' republic shouldn't be decided based solely on having a proper majority in the legislature itself. What matters is building up enough mass support and legitimacy that, when a crisis of political legitimacy most strongly expresses itself, the communist party represents the alternative pole of power with legitimacy from the majority of politically mobilized proletarians.

No matter how much support the communist party has, the transition to socialism can only happen if there is some rupture between the old ruling class and the newly-ruling proletariat which consolidates power against the collapsing regime — in other words, a revolution. In this case, revolution is simply defined as a change in which class governs the state. Such a change will require a radical rupture with previous forms of state and governance, passing political power into the hands of the masses. Since such a rupture would not likely be tolerated by the decadent classes, it is likely going to incite some form of armed struggle. It is exactly the change of power from one class to another that defines a social revolution. The hope for a rupture-less "democratic road to socialism" is merely a road to modernizing the welfare state. Unless there is a change in which class governs — in who shall rule whom — the bourgeoisie will never tolerate a transition to socialism by savvy politicians passing "evolutionary" or "non-reformist reforms" under their nose. A revolution may only be possible once the masses have been convinced that no other means are possible to solve the current crisis, and the only way towards a desirable change in society is through social revolution. The difficulty of this does nothing to negate the historical reality of bourgeois counter-revolution. The hope that a revolutionary rupture can be avoided in favor of 'evolutionary socialism,' favorable among theorists influential in today's DSA, is equally delusional as some immediate apocalyptic transition to communism.[19]

Let us look at a classic historical example. The abolition of slavery in the United States was attempted through gradual legislation when Lincoln's Republican Party won elections on the platform of no longer expanding slave states. This prompted the slave states to form a confederacy and secede, leading to a war that began to reunite the nation but transformed into a revolutionary war to end slavery via military occupation of the south. Karl Marx was fascinated by the US Civil War for its political and strategic implications. It is likely this event influenced his views on how revolution would happen. Essentially, a revolutionary party would exhaust all means possible until either insurrection is the only way forward, or the bourgeoisie still simply launch a 'slaveholders revolt' and force a civil war that itself will call the existence of the bourgeois regime into question. One can look at the October Revolution similarly; the Bolsheviks and their coalition partners won a political victory in the Soviets and used it as a democratic mandate to overthrow the provisional government and form a Soviet Republic. The course of events, where the bourgeoisie went into revolt backed by imperialism via the White Army, forced the Bolsheviks to politically consolidate their regime through civil war. They did this through mobilizing the peasantry via the Red Army until 1922, finally leaving the harsh era of war communism toward the more stable New Economic Policy.

It is a fool's errand to tell the masses that a peaceful road to a workers' republic, essentially a change in class governance, is something that can be promised. Even if it was possible and the government was able to enforce a minimum program without

19 V. I. Lenin, "A Proletarian Militia," marxist.org, 1917, https://www.marxists.org/archive/lenin/works/1917/apr/20b.htm

prompting civil war, it would still require mass civic mobilizations to combat sabotage by the bourgeoisie that would accompany a shake-up of property relations. Those who hope for a "democratic road to socialism" don't desire a new revolutionary state that is backed by the masses. They treat the liberal state as a neutral site of class conflict that the proletariat can transform to its own ends over time, slowly enough to avoid a period of social conflict where a rupture in the class nature of the state will occur. This idea assumes we can sneak a revolution pass the bourgeoisie and ignores problems like capital flight that crash attempts at social-democratic reforms. This can't simply be combated by a hope in pressure from "mass action in the streets." And it ignores that the capitalist class will happily resort to breaking with democratic norms in face of a government that seriously threatens the rule of property if need be, even if socialists have a democratic mandate. In Chile, an attempt was made at an electoral road to socialism through the Popular Unity government that aimed to avoid a rupture with the bourgeois state and the possibility of Civil War. Instead of arming the working class and dissolving the power of the state, Allende's government kept the military in place and hoped for their support. This led to workers being defenseless in the face of Pinochet's counter-revolution against the Popular Unity government that installed a military dictatorship which had devastating consequences.

It would be outside the confines of this article to speculate in detail exactly how a future communist revolution will occur, what chain of historical events will lead to it, how a civil war against reaction will play out, and how such a society will transition to communism. There will no doubt be continuities with previous revolutions, but the communist revolution will also look like no revolution that ever has occurred. It should not aim to merely win a single nation to communism, but an entire continent so as to establish a "beachhead" for the greater world revolution (Latin America would be one example). While making room for the creativity of the masses, one must have plans and institutions that are dedicated to turning questions of revolutionary governance from abstract fantasies to concrete issues to be dealt with. This is ultimately the aim of the party. It must organize the proletariat more effectively than the bourgeoisie, acting as an institution that not only can form plans counter to the rule of the bourgeoisie, but has the means of enacting these plans. Yet the question remains: what is the role of the party *after* the social revolution?

The aim of the party, organized around a minimum program with the goal of establishing a workers' republic, must use some type of political mandate to mobilize the proletariat to smash the bourgeois state and form its own. The party will play a key role in leading the initial revolution, provide necessary coordination across all factions of the proletariat and act as an alternative sovereignty that replaces the capitalist state. As the party establishes this new sovereignty its aim should be to dissolve into different factions within the representative bodies of the workers' republic freely voted on and recallable by the entire public. The legislative and executive bodies must be merged, the government becoming a 'working body' of delegates. This process marks the beginning of the withering away of the state, but it does not mean that a unitary, centralized, and repressive (of the capitalist class interests) state ceases to exist. A representative system should be composed of municipal councils and a central communal council that are accountable to each other. The aim should not be decentralization towards regional autonomy, with various municipalities having their own forms of government or law, but rather coordination and centralization of all bodies around a common plan. The purpose of the party is to take a role in leading the formation of such a government and providing the leadership to give it coherence. It should not aim to establish a Marxist-Leninist-style one-party state, instead of using forms of radical democracy that it has developed in the process of building a working-class movement. This is the only possible way forward to form a workers' republic truly built on the foundation of proletarian mass power and put the world on the road to communism.

From the Workers' Republic to Communism

How the workers' republic will transition into communism is a whole other question, one which requires both a look into earlier attempts at socialism and a dangerous willingness to speculate. We can only say this: in an early workers' republic, the immediate goal will not be the nationalization of all property, even its socialization or collectivization. The primary aim of the workers' republic will be to collectivize political power, putting it into the hands of the working class. Central to this is the transfer of actual armed power into to the hands of workers' militias through the destruction of the old military and police. A key element of any state, despite which class is at its helm is force, and this force is controlled by those who control the arms that back it up. Lenin excellently summarizes the changes necessary in order to make this happen:

> The people need a republic in order to educate the masses in the methods of democracy. We need not only representation along democratic lines, but the building of the entire state administration from the bottom up by the masses themselves, their effective participation in all of life's steps, their active role in the administration. Replacement of the old organs of oppression, the police, the bureaucracy, the standing army, by a universal arming of the people, by a really universal militia, is the only way to guarantee the country a maximum of security against the restoration of the monarchy and to enable it to go forward firmly, systematically and resolutely towards socialism, not by "introducing" it from above, but by raising the vast mass of proletarians and semi-proletarians to the art of state administration, to the use of the whole state power.[20]

20 V. I. Lenin, "'Left-Wing' Childishness," marxist.org, 1918, https://www. marxists.org/archive/lenin/works/1918/may/09.htm

Another goal of the new proletarian regime would be to end the existence of politics as a career. This demand is often echoed by the populist call to "get money out of politics." However, removing money from politics doesn't address the issue of bureaucrats creating fiefdoms of loyalty that shield their self-interests from public accountability. This phenomenon is not due to some flaw in human nature, where "power corrupts all," but rather that bureaucrats use their specialist knowledge to hold a monopoly on decision-making and information in order to elevate themselves above others in status, thus developing interests similar to those of small proprietors. As long as bureaucrats exist due to the social division of labor, they will have these tendencies. What matters is that the workers' republic uses democratic norms to make bureaucrats accountable (such as term limits, pay maximum, public supervision, recallability) as well as programs to simplify the political process and collectivize their skills for the masses to take hold of all aspects of political life.

The primary aim of the workers' regime will be to essentially create and consolidate a new form of the state, rather than immediately destroy capitalism. Despotic inroads on private property will obviously be made, with the key commanding heights of the economy seized and the use of nationalization to fight economic sabotage. Workers will have to seize industries as the bourgeoisie flee, and the new workers' state will make no constitutional sanctities for property rights. Initially, it will primarily be political transformations that occur, as economic transformations will take a longer period of time due to to the necessity of transforming forces and relations of production and to integrate the world economy. Such an approach may be called gradualist, whereas the seizure of power by the proletariat, on the other hand, makes immediate political changes. An immediate nationalization of all means of production and move to state rationing in place of markets will not actually abolish commodity production, but lead to the flourishing of black markets. Voluntaristic attempts to ban markets by fiat have a poor history, often simply being replaced by bureaucratic rationing prone to corruption. Under the initial economy of a workers' republic, one can imagine a "market sector" primarily comprised of small producers, a "cooperative" sector of small producers self-socializing their property, and a "socialized" or planned sector. In fact, many of the initial steps made will not so much be direct negations of capitalism but the rationalization of state-monopolies towards greater efficiency. The existence of a market sector, no matter how small, is nonetheless a sign of the incomplete socialization of the economy; the question is not whether or not to abolish commodity production and have a planned economy, but how.

It is important to understand that nationalization is itself simply a means to socialization. Under a workers' republic, a nationalized factory becomes the property of the state; it is still governed by a capitalist labor process, in many cases with technical division of labor that inherently creates a need for specialists and hierarchy in industry. While an industry can be nationalized, this does mean it has been transformed on a socialist basis or socialized. Key industries, especially those previously in the form of monopolies, can be nationalized and more quickly transformed into socialized industries that operate on a planned, worker-controlled basis, but even then this process requires a transformation of the entire division of labor that may take years (depending on the industry). Steps towards socialization, like workers self-management, should, of course, be actively pursued and implemented when possible. As Lenin points out, nationalization is merely confiscation of property, socialization is a far more difficult task to carry out:

> Yesterday, the main task of the moment was, as determinedly as possible, to nationalise, confiscate, beat down and crush the bourgeoisie, and put down sabotage. Today, only a blind man could fail to see that we have nationalised, confiscated, beaten down and put down more than we have had time to count. The difference

between socialisation and simple confiscation is that confiscation can be carried out by "determination" alone, without the ability to calculate and distribute properly, whereas socialisation cannot be brought about without this ability.[21]

Simply put, the desire nationalize everything immediately after the revolution to wipe out all remnants of capitalism can only be a desire, the socialization of industry is not something that can be achieved by calling upon the inner willpower of the workers. This is because it runs against the limits of material conditions: the stability of the food supply, the provision of basic housing, reliance on skilled forms of specialized labor, and as Lenin points out, the ability to "calculate and distribute." Many initial nationalizations may seize property to turn it into a munitions factory for the needs of civil war. Others may be to replace archaic and environmentally destructive forms of industry. It would be a mistake to nationalize all industries immediately and aim to set everything on an immediate course to socialization, especially since small proprietors will resist by turning to black markets and refuse integration into planned socialist production en masse. Small proprietors will either have to integrate into the planned sector of the economy, or eventually go out of business when faced with competition from the socialist sector.

The form of the state under a workers' republic is the dictatorship of the proletariat, just as the form of the state in any bourgeois republic is, in the end, a dictatorship of the bourgeoisie. The phrase 'dictatorship of the proletariat' implies the existence of the proletariat, which itself implies the existence of capital. Hence, it would be wrong to say that the dictatorship of the proletariat moves beyond capitalism as a mode of production. Rather, the proletariat becomes the most powerful class within capitalism: capitalism is in decay. In the dictatorship of the proletariat, the proletariat has won the class struggle to become

21 Preobrazhensky, Eugene. *The New Economics.* Oxford, UK: Oxford University Press, 1965.

the leading class in society, having defeated the bourgeois state. Yet the class struggle continues on new grounds, now primarily against the petty-bourgeois and bureaucracy, which within them each carry class interests to restore various forms of class society. The proletariat must fight against these elements, not through violent campaigns of expulsion, but by transforming the economic base of society, transcending capitalism and class society itself. A key part of this is breaking down the mental/manual division of labor that at the core of bureaucracy and collectivizing skills held by specialists through mass campaigns combining education and labor. Because the proletariat holds state power it can use the power of centralized administration to take on such a task. The class struggle takes on a different form, becoming more directly about the transformation of social relations between humans.

One suggestion is that the transition will occur through the progressive reduction of labor time through the application of planning rather than primarily through nationalization of the entire economy and the enforcement of a rationing system. For some production, if there is not sufficient abundance, abolishing the commodity form in favor rationing may simply create black markets. Obviously, nationalization and the reduction of work hours aren't mutually exclusive. It is important to note that in transitioning to communism, the focus should be on the process of transforming labor and other productive forces, reducing work hours, and collectivizing skills, rather than the percentage of the economy that has been confiscated by the state. Nationalization should be seen as a means towards achieving these goals, but not an end in itself. As we put the development of productive forces under new social relations via socialized scientific planning, new forces of production will be developed, which in turn develops our freedom beyond the limits of necessity and the ability to transform our environment. The two categories of social relations of production and forces of production can develop in a mutually reinforcing relationship. Developing communism is not a matter of privileging productive forces over relations of production or vice versa, but transforming both in a mutually reinforcing relationship.

In line with Marx, it makes sense to distinguish between a lower and higher phase of communism. The higher phase of communism implies a society where not only production is fully socialized, but distribution, meaning that has free access to goods without a form of money or rationing by the state mediating between humanity and the means of production. This is distinguished from the lower phase of communism, where socialized production is still on the basis of use but goods are distributed to the laborer according to their contribution of labor time (with some form of social insurance provided for those not able to work). The end of production based on exchange-value in favor of the direct production of use-values is a basic property of both the lower and higher phases of communism. Communism entails an end to buying and selling. This is what is meant by saying it is necessary to abolish the value-form. This is well summarized in the *The ABC of Communism* by Bukharin and Preobrazhensky:

> The communist method of production presupposes in addition that production is not for the market, but for use. Under communism, it is no longer the individual manufacturer or the individual peasant who produces; the work of production is effected by the gigantic cooperative as a whole. In consequence of this change, we no longer have commodities, but only products. These products are not exchanged one for another; they are neither bought nor sold. They are simply stored in the communal warehouses, and are subsequently delivered to those who need them. In such conditions, money will no longer be required. 'How can that be?' some of you will ask. 'In that case one person will get too much and another too little. What sense is there in such a method of distribution?' The answer is as follows. At first, doubtless, and perhaps for twenty or thirty years, it will be necessary to have various regulations. Maybe certain products will only be supplied

to those persons who have a special entry in their work-book or on their work-card. Subsequently, when communist society has been consolidated and fully developed, no such regulations will be needed. There will be an ample quantity of all products, our present wounds will long since have been healed, and everyone will be able to get just as much as he needs. 'But will not people find it to their interest to take more than they need?' Certainly not. Today, for example, no one thinks it worth while when he wants one seat in a tram, to take three tickets and keep two places empty. It will be just the same in the case of all products. A person will take from the communal storehouse precisely as much as he needs, no more. No one will have any interest in taking more than he wants in order to sell the surplus to others, since all these others can satisfy their needs whenever they please. Money will then have no value. Our meaning is that at the outset, in the first days of communist society, products will probably be distributed in accordance with the amount of work done by the applicant; at a later stage, however, they will simply be supplied according to the needs of the comrades.

To achieve such a task society will need to greatly develop its productive capacities and rationalize its social organization. Abolition of the value-form does not occur through fiat, repressing it through a "communist dictatorship against value." The aim is instead to change the relations and forces of production to put society on a developmental path toward such an end. It is necessary to not merely negate the value-form and suppress the existence of commodity production in favor of bureaucratic rationing but to transcend the value-form by producing new social relations that allow for a non-alienating and non-exploitative form of social reproduction.

It should also be clear that communism is not a possibility on the national scale, because it requires the full cooperation of the world division of labor. A dictatorship of the proletariat's ability to transcend itself and wither away as a state is reliant on the success of world revolution; as long as the world is capitalist, revolutionaries will have to make economic compromises with capitalism. What matters initially is that politically, power is in the hands of the proletariat. From there, the proletariat begins to take steps to socialism in line with what is materially possible, initially creating an embryonic socialized sector by seizing key industries and planning them, as well as putting them under workers control, and gradually increasing the amount of social product that is freely available to all despite the time spent laboring on said product. As production becomes planned scientifically according to human need, distribution can increasingly be done on a free, communal basis, what exists of the remaining market sector of small producers will fade away. One can think of Preobrazhensky's notion of the law of planning and the law of value, where the law of planning grows with the socialization of industry to displace regulations of goods by the law of value. The process should be done with care, at a pace that prevents major disruptions of social equilibrium. Merging labor with education to produce a surplus of skilled laborers is necessary so that specialists cannot use their knowledge as monopolies to benefit from. It will rather be collectively used to contribute to the general intellect of society.

The new socialist society that develops out of the workers' republic transitioning into communism will be a unique creation evolving from the shell provided by the old capitalist society, a creation of the proletariat taking production and science into its own hands. As more goods become socialized in distribution, the mental/manual division of labor eroded, and the necessary labor hours for all greatly reduced, people will have more free time, not only for leisure but to improve oneself and engage in the kind on non-alienated human flourishing that Marx claimed would become generalized. Such a society free of a repressive state will be a "free association of producers" where all of humanity forms a common, unified community. Yet to get there, one must travail the class struggle, which is ultimately a political struggle: a struggle for power.

WHY HAVE A POLITICAL PROGRAM?

Parker McQueeney
September 3, 2018

Parker McQueeney lays out the case for building a party around a minimum-maximum program.

Every party pursues definite aims, whether it be a party of landowners or capitalists, on the one hand, or a party of workers or peasants, on the other... If it be a party of capitalists and factory owners, it will have its own aims: to procure cheap labour, to keep the workers well in hand, to find customers to toil harder — but, above all, so to arrange matters that the workers will have no tendency to allow their thoughts to turn towards ideas of a new social order; let the workers think that there always have been masters and always will be masters... The programme is for every party a matter of supreme importance. From the programme we can always learn what interests the party represents.
— Nikolai Bukharin and Yevgeni Preobrazhensky
The ABC of Communism, 1920

In the Autumn of 1891, Germany's socialist party — the Social Democratic Party of Germany, or SPD — had only the world to win. Just one year prior, the party's chief prosecutor and pre-eminent tyrant of the European continent, Otto von Bismarck, was forced to resign. The Reichstag refused to renew Bismarck's Anti-Socialist laws, which had shut down dozens of newspapers, trade unions, and socialist meetings. This all happened within the span of a month. It is safe to say that when the party met for its

Congress in Erfurt, they were bolstered in a manner that European socialists had not been since the rise of the Paris Commune twenty years before. The Erfurt Program is notable for a myriad of reasons, not least of which includes the declaration that:

> The German Social Democratic Party ... fights for the abolition of class rule and of classes themselves, for equal rights and equal obligations for all, without distinction of sex or birth... it fights not only the exploitation and oppression of wage earners in society today, but every manner of exploitation and oppression, whether directed against a class, party, sex, or race.[1]

The Erfurt Program asserted, as Marx had, that socialists must fight for democratic rights within bourgeois society. With historical hindsight, it seems clear enough that capitalism cannot be abolished via a socialist party simply winning elections in a bourgeois government. In Bolivarian Venezuela, Mitterand's France, and Tsipras's Greece, the governing socialist parties were able to sit behind the wheel of a liberal democracy, yet none of these countries were able to meaningfully disrupt capitalism. This does not mean that basic bourgeois-democratic rights have no use to even the most revolutionary of socialists; the SPD learned under Bismarck that universal suffrage, the right to free assembly, the ability to form unions, and the abolition of censorship are all helpful to a proletariat undergoing a transformation into a "class-for-itself." Although winning these reforms are not the first step *on* the path to socialism, they *do* clear debris that blocks the entrance. "If all the 10 demands were granted," Friedrich Engels speculated in his critique of the Erfurt Program draft, "we should indeed have more diverse means of achieving our main political aim, but the aim itself would in no [way] have been achieved."[2]

---

1 *Protokoll des Parteitages der Sozialdemokratischen Partei Deutschlands: Abgehalten zu Erfurt vom 14. bis 20. Oktober 1891* [Minutes of the Party Congress of the Social Democratic Party of Germany: Held in Erfurt from October 14–October 20, 1891]. Berlin, 1891, pp. 3–6.

2 Engels. Friedrich. "A Critique of the Draft Social-Democratic Program of 1891," June 1891. https://marxists.architexturez.net/archive/marx/works/1891/06/29.htm

The more lasting legacy the Erfurt Program had on socialist thought was in its popularization of the *minimum* and *maximum program* — though these were abstracted from Karl Marx and Jules Guesde in their program for the French Workers' Party, eleven years prior.[3] Since Erfurt, the program has been the focal point for every party of the class. As Bukharin and Preobrazhensky argue in *The ABC of Communism*, "The programme is for every party a matter of supreme importance. From the programme we can always learn what interests the party represents."[4] Theoretically, the *minimum program*, which was the party's reform platform, would win over a mass base of workers by improving their immediate conditions. When enacted in full, it would give the party the necessary mandate and class power to enable its *maximum program*, or the revolutionary measures required to actually eradicate the dictatorship of capital and begin the process of developing a socialist mode of production. In reality, the SPD — along with the other parties of the Second International — eschewed their maximum programs as they became gradually more entrenched into the bourgeois constitutional order. Whether in the trade union bureaucracy, the universities, or the Reichstag, the Second International's loyalty to the capitalist state and nation eventually led the majority of its parties to abandon internationalism by siding with their respective home countries during the outbreak of World War I. It is a tragedy often lamented on the Left.

Although the term amounts to welfare state liberalism today, the social democrats of Erfurt were largely Marxists. Nevertheless, as a nominally social democratic movement appears to be re-emerging onto American politics for the first time in the life of many of its participants, what can contemporary socialists

3 Marx, Karl, Guesde, Jules. "The Program of the Parti Ouvrier," May 1880. https://www.marxists.org/archive/marx/works/1880/05/parti-ouvrier.htm
4 Bukharin, Nikolai, Preobrazhensky, Yevgeni. *The ABC of Communism.* 1920. https://www.marxists.org/archive/bukharin/works/1920/abc/index.htm

in the United States learn from the original social democrats? In many ways, the US Left is in a similar position that German social democrats found themselves in around the time of the Erfurt Congress. Both had recently come out with some unthinkable — at least to the ruling class — victories after decades of suppression and neither had ever meaningfully seen power. More importantly, the 1891 SPD and the 2018 American Left share a common primary task: the consolidation of workers into a class-for-ourselves, cognizant of our common condition and interests.

What were the minimum demands of the Erfurt Program? The first seven dealt exclusively with securing and expanding democratic-republican rights. Perhaps shockingly, many of their demands would still be progressive gains 127 years later: legal holidays on election days, ending voter suppression, popular militias in place of standing armies, free meals for school children, gender equality in the legal sphere, elected judges, and the end of capital punishment. The first seven demands read:

Universal, equal, and direct suffrage with secret ballot in all elections, for all citizens of the Reich over the age of twenty, without distinction of sex. Proportional representation, and, until this is introduced, legal redistribution of electoral districts after every census. Two-year legislative periods. Holding of elections on a legal holiday. Compensation for elected representatives. Suspension of every restriction on political rights, except in the case of legal incapacity.

Direct legislation by the people through the rights of proposal and rejection. Self-determination and self-government of the people in Reich, state, province, and municipality. Election by the people of magistrates, who are answerable and liable to them. Annual voting of taxes.

Education of all to bear arms. Militia in the place of the standing army. Determination by the popular assembly on questions of war and peace. Settlement of all international disputes by arbitration.

Abolition of all laws that place women at a disadvantage compared with men in matters of public or private law. Abolition of all laws that limit or suppress the free expression of opinion and

195

restrict or suppress the right of association and assembly. Declaration that religion is a private matter. Abolition of all expenditures from public funds for ecclesiastical and religious purposes. Ecclesiastical and religious communities are to be regarded as private associations that regulate their affairs entirely autonomously.

Secularization of schools. Compulsory attendance at the public Volksschule [extended elementary school]. Free education, free educational materials, and free meals in the public Volksschulen, as well as at higher educational institutions for those boys and girls considered qualified for further education by virtue of their abilities.

Free administration of justice and free legal assistance. Administration of the law by judges elected by the people. Appeal in criminal cases. Compensation for individuals unjustly accused, imprisoned, or sentenced. Abolition of capital punishment.

It is important to note that although these were serious, immediate demands, some were not "realistic" nor "winnable." Women's suffrage was not granted in Germany until nearly 30 years after the Erfurt Program was drafted. Replacing the standing army with a militia was perhaps the most radical of all their demands: the Prussian state was highly centralized, and to eradicate the standing army would have amounted to a revolutionary rupture within the state. When drafting a political program, even when demanding reforms, it's important for socialists not to limit our horizons to what bourgeois politicians and their apologists tell us is possible; otherwise, we are liable to again tail their inevitable sprints to the right. Ideally, a socialist program would include measures that, once undertaken, will not only improve the condition of the working class, but begin to dismantle the dictatorship of capital.

The next group of demands were in the economic sphere, and included free healthcare, burial, a progressive tax, a series of labor demands surrounding unions, the work-day, the creation of a department of labor, etc.:

Free medical care, including midwifery and medicines. Free burial.

Graduated income and property tax for defraying all public expenditures, to the extent that they are to be paid for by taxation.

Inheritance tax, graduated according to the size of the inheritance and the degree of kinship. Abolition of all indirect taxes, customs, and other economic measures that sacrifice the interests of the community to those of a privileged few.

Fixing of a normal working day not to exceed eight hours.

Prohibition of gainful employment for children under the age of fourteen.

Prohibition of night work, except in those industries that require night work for inherent technical reasons or for reasons of public welfare.

An uninterrupted rest period of at least thirty-six hours every week for every worker.

Prohibition of the truck system.

Supervision of all industrial establishments, investigation and regulation of working conditions in the cities and the countryside by a Reich labor department, district labor bureaus, and chambers of labor. Rigorous industrial hygiene.

Legal equality of agricultural laborers and domestic servants with industrial workers; abolition of the laws governing domestics.

Safeguarding of the freedom of association.

Takeover by the Reich government of the entire system of workers' insurance, with decisive participation by the workers in its administration.

The reason these demands were *worth fighting for* was two-fold. Most obviously, things like political enfranchisement and universal healthcare alleviate some of the alienation caused by capitalist society. Perhaps more crucially though, these demands were posited by a *working-class institution* with a *working-class awareness*.

What is a working-class institution? Historically, they may mirror republican civic institutions, but *within* the class party. A good example of an institution within the SPD was its party school. Every class party needs political education, recruiting the working masses is a foolish endeavor without internal political clarification and cadre training — not to unquestioningly accept party dogmatism, but to properly apply the historical materialist methodology and critical analysis to the daily struggles of workers. In her piece on the SPD party school for the British left magazine *The Clarion*, Rida Vaquas writes:

> ...the best demonstration of what the Party School could achieve of a project comes not from the words of its teachers, but from the legacies of its students. In a 1911 retrospective of the Party School after 5 years of its existence, Heinrich Schulz recorded the debts students owed their school experience: "A trade union official observes that he learned how to conceive of phenomena in economic life better through his school instruction, another gained a deeper insight into the whole political and trade union life, a third traces back his greater confidence against political and economic opponents to the school." The school, when it succeeded, was a training in how to think, not what to think.[5]

Working class institutions can take forms not only of political education but of what some socialists label "dual power" (though not in the way Lenin used the term). They have taken the form of free health clinics, breakfast programs for school children, housing, and worker cooperatives, or any number of things, but they need to be part of a larger project of working-class political struggle: the class party.

Despite the innovations of the Erfurt Program, the SPD, along with most of the parties from the Second International, voted for war credits in 1914 causing a traumatic rupture in the international socialist movement. There were, however, a few examples of the classical social democratic parties that retained their internationalist class solidarity. One of these was a party that contemporary American socialists can and should study, and it's one of our own ancestors: the Socialist Party of America. The 1912 SPA platform, adopted in May at a congress in Indianapolis, follows a similar format to the Erfurt Program. The 106-year-old document is chillingly relevant. The introduction of its minimum program plainly states its ultimate goal:

5 Rida Vaquas. "What's a Good Political Education? A Debate from the SPD, June 25, 2018. https://theclarionmag.org/2018/06/25/whats-a-good-political-education-a-debate-from-the-spd/

As measures calculated to strengthen the working class in its fight for the realization of its ultimate aim, the co-operative common-wealth, and to increase its power against capitalist oppression, we advocate and pledge ourselves and our elected officers to the following program...

It starts with several paragraphs outlining the broad goals of the Socialist Party — its maximum program — declaring the nation to be "in the absolute control of a plutocracy which exacts an annual tribute of hundreds of millions of dollars from the producers." It declares unilaterally that capitalism is the source of destitution in the working class, that "the legislative representatives of the Republican and Democratic parties remain the faithful servants of the oppressors," and any legislation attempting at balancing the distance between classes "have proved to be utterly futile and ridiculous." It says plainly that

... there will be and can be no remedy and no substantial relief except through Socialism under which industry will be carried on for the common good and every worker receive the full social value of the wealth he creates.

The minimum demands of the 1912 SPA platform constitute a significant improvement compared to the Erfurt Program. Instead of two sections — one political, one economic — the SPA platform includes four sections: collective ownership, unemployment, industrial demands, and political demands. The collective ownership section only reinforces the point that the socialist platform when enacted should create a rupture in the class character of the state:

The collective ownership and democratic management of railroads, wire and wireless telegraphs and telephones, express service, steamboat lines, and all other social means of transportation and communication and of all large scale industries.

The immediate acquirement by the municipalities, the states or the federal government of all grain elevators, stock yards, storage warehouses, and other distributing agencies, in order to reduce the present extortionate cost of living.

The extension of the public domain to include mines, quarries, oil wells, forests and water power.

The further conservation and development of natural resources for the use and benefit of all the people . . .

The collective ownership of land wherever practicable, and in cases where such ownership is impracticable, the appropriation by taxation of the annual rental value of all the land held for speculation and exploitation.

The collective ownership and democratic management of the banking and currency system.

It is clear that the nationalization of the bourgeois state's institutional levers of power; banks, currency, natural resources, land, distribution centers, transportation, and communications, would catalyze the disintegration of capitalist class rule. It's important to note that these were the very first things listed on the platform.

The next section dealt with a universal jobs demand. Unlike the Erfurt Program, here the American socialists remind themselves of who their ultimate enemy is in evoking the maximum program and capitalist class "misrule":

The immediate government relief of the unemployed by the extension of all useful public works. All persons employed on such works to be engaged directly by the government under a work day of not more than eight hours and at not less than the prevailing union wages. The government also to establish employment bureaus; to lend money to states and municipalities without interest for the purpose of carrying on public works, and to take such other measures within its power as will lessen the widespread misery of the workers caused by the misrule of the capitalist class.

This isn't a radical demand in 2018; it's even looking likely that Senator Bernie Sanders will make it a key point in the next presidential campaign, and he is often the first one to admit his positions are not radical. In 1912 however, before the Wagner Act of 1935 was passed, "employees... [did] not possess full freedom of association or actual liberty of contract." The Wagner Act, also known as the National Labor Relations Act, which had legalized strikes and union organizing as well as guaranteed the right to collective bargaining, was severely gutted twelve years later under the Truman administration.

The SPA's industrial demands contain standard labor issues that American socialists had been calling on for years, mostly dealing with workplace safety, reducing work hours, child labor laws, establishing minimum wage, etc. One calls for an establishment of a pension system. A few demands stand out, however, one prefiguring prison abolitionism calling for "the co-operative organization of the industries in the federal penitentiaries for the benefit of the convicts and their dependents." Another calls for "forbidding the interstate transportation of the products of child labor, of convict labor and all uninspected factories and mines." Perhaps their most creative and radical demand was "abolishing the profit system in government work and substituting either the direct hire of labor or the awarding of contracts to co-operative groups of workers." It's hard to imagine events like the Iraq War or the recent human disaster in Puerto Rico happening the way they did without the juicy private contracts (although there is nothing about a worker cooperative that inherently prevents it from taking part in imperial plundering).

The political demands section proposes a broad outline for transforming the state:

> The absolute freedom of press, speech and assemblage.
> The abolition of the monopoly ownership of patents and the substitution of collective ownership, with direct rewards to inventors by premiums or royalties.
> Unrestricted and equal suffrage for men and women.
> The adoption of the initiative, referendum and recall and of proportional representation, nationally as well as locally.
> The abolition of the Senate and of the veto power of the President.
> The election of the President and Vice-President by direct vote of the people.
> The abolition of the power usurped by the Supreme Court of the United States to pass upon the constitutionality of the legis-

201

lation enacted by Congress. National laws to be repealed only by act of Congress or by a referendum vote of the whole people.

Abolition of the present restrictions upon the amendment of the Constitution, so that instrument may be made amendable by a majority of the voters in a majority of the States.

The granting of the right of suffrage in the District of Columbia with representation in Congress and a democratic form of municipal government for purely local affairs.

The extension of democratic government to all United States territory.

The enactment of further measures for the conservation of health. The creation of an independent bureau of health, with such restrictions as will secure full liberty to all schools of practice.

The enactment of further measures for general education and particularly for vocational education in useful pursuits. The Bureau of Education to be made a department.

The separation of the present Bureau of Labor from the Department of Commerce and Labor and its elevation to the rank of a department.

Abolition of an federal districts courts and the United States circuit court of appeals. State courts to have jurisdiction in all cases arising between citizens of several states and foreign corporations. The election of all judges for short terms.

The immediate curbing of the power of the courts to issue injunctions.

The free administration of the law.

The calling of a convention for the revision of the constitution of the US.

Here the Socialist Party lists some serious alterations to the existing governmental structure. They call for the abolition of the Senate with its overrepresentation for people in less populous states, the electoral college, the presidential veto, and judicial review. They demand a process for popular recall of politicians and legislation. They even call for a new constitutional convention. All of these things would be improvements and are predicated on a big enough success of the Socialist Party to implement them (otherwise, a constitutional convention could obviously be disastrous). These demands on their own however do not constitute a rupture with the bourgeois state. It is the political demands *in combination* with their collective ownership demands that do, by first eviscerating the major sources of economic power from their capitalists. These measures would only constitute the beginning of a revolutionary rupture from the capitalist class rule, as the last part of the platform states,

> Such measures of relief as we may be able to force from capitalism are but a preparation of the workers to seize the whole powers of government, in order that they may thereby lay hold of the whole system of socialized industry and thus come to their rightful inheritance.

The socialist magazine Jacobin, which is heavily associated with the Democratic Socialists of America (and its largest chapter in New York City) has seemingly adopted as creed what Andre Gorz named "non-reformist reforms." Gorz believed the dichotomy of the pre-war era between militant revolution or reform no longer existed. Now that armed insurrection was forever a relic of a simpler time, Gorz argued that the only route to socialism was by pushing reform that couldn't be usurped by capital. Like many in his generation, Gorz saw the development of a postwar middle class and concluded that class struggle would forever be muted in the imperialist countries. The logical basis for this assumption can only be one thing: by entering the middle class and becoming propertied homeowners (among other things) first-world workers transitioned into a social category where revolution was no longer in their interests. As the onslaught of austerity and neoliberalism has proven, class struggle is *not* mutable, and to proclaim so is the gravest abandonment of the historical materialist methodology. Today, the question of reform vs. revolution is just as relevant as when Rosa Luxemburg wrote:

> Legislative reform and revolution are not different methods of historic development that can be picked out at the pleasure from the counter of history, just as one chooses hot or cold sausages.

Legislative reform and revolution are different factors in the development of class society. They condition and complement each
other, and are at the same time reciprocally exclusive, as are the
north and south poles, the bourgeoisie and proletariat.[6]

Truly "non-reformist reforms," like those in the SPA platform
of 1912, do not discount the possibility of a class social revolution, they *depend on it*. The current use of the term repeats all the
same mistakes of Bernstein's evolutionary socialism that Rosa
Luxemburg famously polemicized.

The major "non-reformist reforms" today seems to be shaped
around a few key maxims, not dissimilar to some of the demands
from the earlier German and American socialists: "tuition-free
public universities," "Medicare-for all," and more recently,
"abolish ICE." But how did these demands develop? They were
not produced organically by working-class institutions. They
were touted by individuals claiming to be democratic socialists,
running on the Democratic Party ballot line. First by Bernie
Sanders, next through Alexandria Ocasio-Cortez. Immediately
they were taken up by Jacobin and the DSA.

Could socialists temporarily use the Democratic ballot line,
where third party campaigns are untenable until the mass base
for an independent socialist party is built? Perhaps, though this
is a debate for another time. But should this really be how socialist demands are developed? Instead of echoing demands scribed
by politicians, *they* should be echoing *our* demands. And our
demands should be in service to the ascension of the proletariat
as a politically independent class actor, and towards a rupture
with the capitalist nature of the state.

The most prominent socialist group in the US, Democratic
Socialists of America, lacks any real political program. Its chapters are too federated, and the biennial national conventions are
not frequent nor far-reaching enough for it to be a force for class

6 Luxemburg, Rosa. "Reform or Revolution." marxist.org, 1900. https://
www.marxists.org/archive/luxemburg/1900/reform-revolution/

struggle on a wide scale. How can there be "non-reformist reforms" without a class organization with unified goals pushing them? Instead of allowing independent politicians with support from socialists to steer the conversation with demands like "abolish ICE," we should be giving *our* demands to *them*. The Immigrant Justice Working Group of the Central New Jersey DSA provides for us a good example of what twenty-first century socialist demands look like:

- An immediate end to all detentions and deportations, and dismissal of all related charges.
- Abolition of ICE and all other military or quasi-military border forces.
- Unconditional right to asylum to be granted upon request to anyone coming from a country that has been negatively impacted by US military or economic policies, or the policies of US corporations.
- Citizenship and full rights (such as access to entitlement programs) upon request to anyone who has lived or worked in the US for at least six months.

The modern United States is not the Prussian state of 130 years ago, nor are its socialists facing the same conditions they faced in 1912. Demands that socialists make must reflect the realities of contemporary capitalism and its world system: nobody wants to merely recreate the old SPD or SPA. Still, there is no need to reinvent the wheel. Socialists should be making demands that go *beyond* reverting to Bush-era normalcy: they should be pushing demands that the bourgeois parties tell us are impossible, and a political program is the only way to do so. These demands should aim to build class power both in the economic and political spheres. If DSA chapters started internally adopting programs with a little vision, they could eventually map one onto the national organization. DSA needs to become part of an organization with real class power independent of the Democrats, and it will never do that without first adopting formal demands at the national level that differentiates itself as a party divested from the interests of the capitalist class. Without a political program, we have no way of seriously posing an alternative to the established parties of capital, and articulating a vision of society for the democratic class rule of workers.

THE REVOLUTIONARY MINIMUM-MAXIMUM PROGRAM

Donald Parkinson
May 5, 2021

Donald Parkinson explains and defends the format of the minimum-maximum program using the model established in Marx and Guesde's Programme of the Parti Ouvrier.

In this essay, I am going to talk about an important part of Marx that is often ignored: his contribution to the art of political program. There is no lack of literature exploring the theories and philosophical ideas of Marx. Yet we often forget that Marx was not only a political strategist but someone who contributed to existing political movements. The *Communist Manifesto* is probably the most famous of his contributions of this type, written in the midst of the struggles of 1848. However, this was early in Marx's political career. If we want to attain an understanding of his most "mature" political contributions, a key document is the *Programme of the Parti Ouvrier*, co-written with Jules Guesde. This document stands not only as an expression of the political views of the mature Marx, but as a model to base the construction of a minimum-maximum program, which in my opinion is the model that today's socialist movement should orient itself around.

The reason I am focusing on this question is not to perform an exercise in historical archaeology, but to shed light on modern issues regarding the question of political program for today's socialist movement. It is my opinion that the *Programme of the Parti Ouvrier* holds up to this day as a model for political programs, not simply because it was an authentic contribution of the "mature" Marx after his experiences with the First International and the Commune, but also because its minimum-maximum structure is superior to other programmatic methods commonly used by the socialist left today. One such method, which I will examine later on, is the Transitional Programme favored by the Trotskyists at the publication *LeftVoice*, who recently took aim at the minimum-maximum program in a recent critique.

A Political Program for the French Workers

To begin, I will take a close look at the *Programme of the Parti Ouvrier.* The origins of the program can be found in a workers' congress eight years after the fall of the Paris Commune, the French Workers' Congress of 1879, which declared the formation of an independent workers' party and the necessity of collectivizing the means of production. This was a blow to Proudhonian trends that had previously dominated socialism in France and represented the rise of Marxist politics as an organized force in France. The two main figureheads of Marxist (or what would come to be known as Marxist) ideas in France at the time were Paul Lafargue and Jules Guesde. Lafargue was Karl Marx's son-in-law, while Guesde became the leader of the newly formed Federated Socialist Workers' Party. Both sought collaboration with Marx himself in writing the party program in preparation for the national legislative election in 1881.[1]

The process of drafting the program began with Marx drawing up a 101-item questionnaire for working-class readers of the socialist paper *La Revue socialiste.* The aim of the questionnaire was to find information about the living and working conditions

1 Derfler, Leslie. *Paul Lafargue and the Founding of French Marxism, 1842-1882.* Massachusets: Harvard University Press, 1991. pp 184-185.

of the French proletariat that could help inform the drafting of demands. Guesde toured the country to organize local and regional groups, finding that most workers groups were primarily interested in reformist demands for greater social and civil rights. Following the tour, Guesde traveled to London to meet up with Marx and Engels and draft the program itself in May of 1880.[2]

The preamble of the party was written by Marx is one of the most effective yet to-the-point summaries of communist politics ever put to paper. Engels himself called it "a masterpiece of cogent argumentation rarely encountered, clearly and succinctly written for the masses: I myself was astonished by this concise formulation."[3] Marx begins the preamble with a simple summary of the communist thesis: "that the emancipation of the productive class is that of all human beings without distinction of sex or race." Right here is a clear rebuttal of all claims that Marx's communism was only of concern to industrial workers, refuting in one simple phrase that Marxism is mere "worker-ism." The struggle of the proletariat, the productive class under modern capitalism, is seen not as an end in itself or related to particularist interests in class society, but as a means towards the emancipation of universal humanity. And to make it clear, Marx emphasizes the truly universal nature of this humanity by clearly stating that he means humanity without distinction of sex or race. The internationalist and anti-patriarchal character of Marxist politics is thus made clear from the beginning.

The next section states the condition upon which the productive class can be emancipated: that "they are in possession of the means of production." This may sound straightforward from our standpoint, but in Marx's time, it needed to be clarified. This is why the next line of the preamble differentiates between two forms through which the means of production can be under

2 Ibid pp 185-186.
3 Friedrich Engels, "Letter from Engels to Eduard Bernstein," Militant Archives, October 25th, 1881. https://wikirouge.net/texts/en/Letter_to_Eduard_Bernstein,_October_25,_1881

the possession of the producers: the individual and collective. The individual form is a reference to the peasant and artisan, who own their own means of production as individuals. This form of ownership was seen as an ideal to be strived for by the followers of Proudhon, who were dominant in French socialism until this time. Marx's argument is that this form of ownership is increasingly antiquated and irrelevant with the development of capitalism, which itself socializes the means of production within the framework of private ownership and market competition. As a result, the means of production can only be appropriated collectively, by moving beyond the framework of private ownership in favor of social ownership. Capitalist development has proletarianized the laboring population by separating them from the means of production, developed the forms of labor themself to be far more cooperative, and closed off the possibility of restoring small ownership if the current forms of production are to be maintained and improved upon. A return to individual ownership is impossible, making the only possibility for the emancipation of the producers to come in the form of collective appropriation.

From this flows the next section of the preamble, which states the need for the class independence of the proletariat and its need to be organized as a political party: "collective appropriation can arise only from the revolutionary action of the productive class — or proletariat — organized in a distinct political party." In other words, only the proletariat as a class will be compelled through a struggle to take hold of the means of production, as they have no property titles that give them a stake in the maintenance of the system of private appropriation. Therefore, the proletariat must organize its own political party with politics that express its needs as a class and not the needs of the property-holding class. This doesn't entail that only proletarians can be a member of the party or that only proletarians can benefit from the politics put forth. Peasants, intellectuals, professionals, even class traitors of the bourgeoisie can be members of the party. Yet when they enter the party they must leave their particular class interests at the door and fight for the needs of the proletariat, even when they come into contradiction with their own class.

The preamble then states that this class independent party of the proletariat shall pursue its goals by all means necessary. Yet the example given of such means is not armed struggle or a general strike, but universal suffrage, "transformed from the instrument of deception that it has been until now into an instrument of emancipation." It is through mass politics, not the action of militant minorities, that the proletariat must struggle as a class, and this entails contesting elections with the parties of the bourgeoisie. Marx was aware of the limitations of the electoral process and knew that it was used as a legitimation apparatus for the bourgeoisie. Yet he also realized that universal suffrage had massive potential as a tool for the proletariat that could be subverted. The electoral arena must not be left in the sole hands of the bourgeois but must be contested by the workers' party, bringing its politics into the national arena.

The preamble then ends, proclaiming that the *Parti Ouvrier* must enter into elections with a following list of demands. Before exploring these demands, a certain point must be pressed: The preamble of the program can be understood as a *maximum program*. It represents the final goal of the party that will be attained after a period of economic reconstruction and social transformation. It describes the general aim of human emancipation and that this must be achieved through the proletariat and its party coming to power and collectivizing the means of production. In other words, it proclaims the long-term goal of moving beyond capitalism into a communist society.

The demands that follow are both political and economic in character, representing a *minimum program*. These represent immediate changes that the party will fight for before taking power and will collectively institute before taking power. While taking a closer look at these demands, we will see two important things: 1) that these demands taken individually do not entail a break with the capitalist economic system and 2) if instituted *in totality* would entail a break with capitalist rule over the state and the establishment of the political rule of the proletariat. In short, the aim of a minimum program is not to simply create a list of reforms that a party will fight for to gain support and popularity but to provide a roadmap for the proletariat to seize state power entirely in a revolutionary break.

This minimum-maximum format is not unique to the *Programme of the Parti Ouvrier*. As Jack Conrad has pointed out,[4] it can be found in the Communist Manifesto, The Erfurt Programme, and the 1902 Programme of the Russian Social-Democratic Labor Party. The reason for my particular focus on this historical document is that it is a very simple and clear expression of this format that clarifies many confusions about its nature if one gives it a close and attentive reading, particularly of its political demands.

Political and Economic Demands

The first demand in the political section is instructive in that it is focused on the democratic rights of the working class:

> Abolition of all laws over the press, meetings and associations and above all the law against the International Working Men's Association. Removal of the livret, that administrative control over the working class, and of all the articles of the Code establishing the inferiority of the worker in relation to the boss, and of woman in relation to man.

Marx and Guesde here are primarily concerned with political freedom — the light and air of the proletariat, without which it cannot breathe. Considering the history of "actually existing

---

4 Jack Conrad, "Our Republic," Weekly Worker, Nov 23, 2006, https://weeklyworker.co.uk/worker/650/our-republic/

socialism" this may be surprising for some. After all, should the suppression of the bourgeois press not be the focus? Certainly, we should not allow the capitalist monopolies to hold control over the media as they do now. It is also clear that Marx here is most concerned with the press freedom of the working class, as he says the focus should be on laws against the International Working Men's Association. The focus here is on ensuring that the working-class has the capacity to govern, and in Marx's mind this must mean the establishment of a free press where the working-class is able to freely associate. Questions of shutting down the capitalist press were secondary and contingent to the circumstances of revolution.

Mentioned next is the *livret*, essentially a form of bonded labor that existed in France until 1890. The *livret* was essentially a passport one needed in order to change employers. It took the form of a card that listed one's outstanding debts and obligations to former employers, meaning that in order to change employers these debts and obligations must be cleared by one's former employer. Such a system shows the backwardness of French capitalism, not yet able to use the "carrot" of unemployment to control the labor force and instead relying on the "stick" of internal passports. The abolition of the *livret* in the program is then followed by the destruction of all laws of the Napoleonic Code that ensure not only the "inferiority of the worker in relation to the boss" but also those that enforce the inferiority of woman in relation to man. While these demands may not necessitate a break with bourgeois governance, they are nonetheless necessary but not sufficient for such a task.

After discussing press freedom and the *livret,* Marx and Guesde move on to what is essentially an anti-clerical demand, calling for the "Removal of the budget of the religious orders" and the "the return to the nation of the 'goods said to be mortmain, movable and immovable,'" citing the example of the Paris Commune, as well as the "suppression of the public debt." These demands are both inspired by the example of the Commune, and are essentially compatible with a thoroughgoing bourgeois-democratic revolution and not necessarily demands that necessitate a dictatorship of the proletariat. It is the next two demands that best help us understand the nature of the minimum program as not simply reformist demands to rally the workers but rather carry revolutionary content. First is the classic socialist demand for the people's militia: "abolition of standing armies and the general arming of the people." This is then followed by calling for "the commune to be the master of its administration and its police."

What is important by these demands is that they would require a break with the existing state in France, the Third Republic that was denounced by French radicals as "the monarchy without the monarch."[5] Breaking down the standing army and the general arming of the people coupled with the transfer of administration and control of armed force to the commune would have meant a transfer of sovereignty and a rupture in the general form of the state. The reference to the Commune makes this clear, as Marx made it clear that the main lesson of the Commune was that "the working class cannot simply lay hold of the ready-made state machinery, and wield it for its own purposes."[6] These minimum demands, taken as a complete package, are therefore no mere reforms — they are a call for a radical break with the existing state and a transfer of power to the working class in a new democratic republic.

The radical nature of these political demands was lost on Guesde, who saw the planks of the program as mere slogans to rouse the workers into action in the hope that they would take up a truly revolutionary struggle. Marx had no time for such "revolutionary phrasemongering" and emphasized the practical yet *transitional*

5 Bernstein, Samuel. "Jules Guesde, Pioneer of Marxism in France." Science & Society 4, no. 1 (1940): 29.
6 Karl Marx, "The Civil War in France," marxist.org, 2009, https://www.marxists.org/archive/marx/works/1871/civil-war-france/index.htm

nature of these demands. They were meant to provide a practical roadmap for the workers' movement in taking political power, not mere slogans to shout in order to inspire mass strikes that would throw up workers' councils. It was this disagreement with the empty sloganeering of Guesde that inspired the chronically misused statement from Marx that if this was Marxism, "What is certain is that I myself am not a Marxist."[7]

A possible source of confusion as to the revolutionary nature of this program is the nature of the economic demands. They include things such as a reduction in the working day to 8 hours and the working week to no more than 6 days of the week, the responsibility of society for the deaf and disabled, the supervision of apprentices by workers associations, abolition of inheritance above a certain amount, prohibition of immigrant labor being hired at wages below that of French workers, and other demands that are essentially reforms. These demands do not necessitate a break with capitalism as an economic system, whereas the political demands *taken as a whole* do necessitate a break with the capitalist state.

Marx's Two-Stage Revolution

The reasoning behind this is simple. Marx essentially saw revolution as a two-stage process — first, the proletariat is to seize political power and establish the democratic republic, and then afterward within this newly established framework can now take up the tasks of reconstructing society on a communist basis. The seizure of political power by the proletariat does not inevitably lead to the victory of socialism. What is accomplished with the seizure of power is the inauguration of a new phase of the class struggle, where the proletariat holds control over the general means of coercion. Classes still exist, and the capitalist mode of production is still intact. The dictatorship of the proletariat as

7 Friedrich Engels, "Engels to Edward Bernstein in Zurich," History is a Weapon, 1882, http://hiaw.org/defcon6/works/1882/letters/82_11_02.html

a phrase entails the existence of the proletariat, hence the existence of classes. One enters a contradictory situation where the exploited class now holds power over the exploiters. It is only through the victory of communism that this contradiction can be resolved.

When writing on the Paris Commune, Marx argued that a general form of the proletariat in political power had been uncovered by the motion of history. The Commune hardly laid its hands upon the institution of private property. What made it revolutionary was that it radically transformed the form of the state, establishing a radical democracy that allowed the wage-earning class to rise to a position of political supremacy. Measures such as the recall of delegates, the leveling of wages and the people's militia were all meant to politically expropriate the capitalist class. By placing the working class in power, Marx wrote that the Commune "...affords the rational medium through which the class struggle can run through its various phases in the most rational and humane way."[8] This, combined with Engels' comments that the Paris Commune was an example of the Dictatorship of the Proletariat, sets the first steps of a theory of transition as a class struggle itself. A state where the proletariat rules is still a situation where the proletariat exists as a class, and is therefore not a classless society. It is merely the first step towards such a society, and this makes it no less of a rupture with the existing social order.

The Transitional Program as an Alternative

The minimum-maximum program as exemplified by the *Programme of the Parti Ouvrier* is often negatively compared to Trotsky's *The Transitional Program*, originally titled *The Death Agony of Capitalism and the Tasks of the Fourth International* and

8 Quoted in Johnstone, Monty. "The Paris Commune and Marx's Conception of the Dictatorship of the Proletariat." The Massachusetts Review, vol. 12, no. 3, 1971, pp. 447–462.

later reprinted under the title *The Transitional Program and the Struggle for Socialism*. The recent article by Nathaniel Flakin in the Trotksyist publication *Left Voice* is one example of such a negative comparison, taking aim at the approach of myself and comrades in Cosmonaut Magazine and Marxist Unity Slate in DSA. Flakin argues that the minimum-maximum bifurcation was accepted due to the immaturity of capitalism at this era, accepting the common understanding that the demands of the *Programme of the Parti Ouvrier* were meant to be mere day to day reforms, which I hope to have demonstrated as a falsity. Flakin also goes on to claim that the minimum-maximum program was a source of the SPD's own degeneration into supporting World War One as a cause of passivity and reformism, a simplistic historical narrative to say the least.

Flakin's argument is that the minimum-maximum program contains no bridge between minimum demands and maximum demands and is therefore not suitable for an era where capitalism's contradictions have developed to an intensified degree. The crisis of capitalism has intensified so much that there is no time for "several decades in which the socialist movement can win political and economic concessions from the bourgeoisie, and leave the question of socialism to the distant future." Therefore, it is necessary to raise demands that will somehow lead to a revolutionary situation if taken up and pursued by the working class. This idea is rooted in Trotsky's own *Transitional Program*, which begins by stating that the objective criteria for revolution has been fulfilled, leaving only the subjective factor of leadership to be put in place.[9] This leads to an approach where what the

9 Leon Trotsky, "The Transitional Program," marxist.org, 1938, https://www.marxists.org/archive/trotsky/1938/tp/: "All talk to the effect that historical conditions have not yet "ripened" for socialism is the product of ignorance or conscious deception. The objective prerequisites for the proletarian revolution have not only "ripened"; they have begun to get somewhat rotten. Without a socialist revolution, in the next historical period at that, a catastrophe threatens the whole culture of mankind. The turn is now to the proletariat,

workers need is essentially better leaders who will provide better slogans and demands than the reformists and Stalinists who hold back the working-class masses who would otherwise be in a revolutionary situation if not for their misleadership.

Flakin uses the example of housing — rather than demanding public housing from the bourgeois state, a genuine revolutionary party would call on workers to take part in the "occupation of luxury condos and office buildings to house all working-class and poor families" so that "Such occupations can be integrated into a plan to make all housing public, administered by renters and their representatives via direct democracy." What organization will lead such an occupation is left to the imagination — it is almost as if such demands are simply a way to rouse the workers into action with hopes that such a struggle will organically develop into a struggle for socialism itself when they realize that occupations of luxury condos won't be tolerated by the bourgeois police.

What we have here is essentially a strategy of impatience — rather than using the program as a means to unite the working class around a vision of political change, the aim is to provide slogans and tactics that will get the masses into action, hoping it will somehow lead to a "transition" towards a genuine struggle for socialism. How this transition is supposed to happen is unclear — Flakin mentions workers' councils and factory committees, suggesting that perhaps the demands raised by a Trotskyist party will help lead to their formation. Even if this is true, and the workers are roused into action, forming workers' councils through their struggle, the mere existence of councils is not an actual substitute for a working-class majority that desires a regime change while having an actual roadmap for how to achieve it. Mass actions of the class are no substitute for this, and in the end, the transitional program as imagined here can only fall back on spontaneity when pressed on how its demands are transitional toward socialism.

i.e., chiefly to its revolutionary vanguard. The historical crisis of mankind is reduced to the crisis of the revolutionary leadership."

Flakin admits that the version of the minimum-maximum program espoused by Marxist Unity is meant to lead to a break in the class rule of the bourgeoisie. So what's the problem? That there is no explanation of what this transition would look like and an arbitrary division between the minimum and the maximum. Regarding the first objection, the transition that this vision of the Transitional Program espouses between its demands and the direct struggle for socialism is illusory. It presses upon the workers to take militant action in hope that such action will spill over into a revolutionary situation, or at least inspire a mass action that will inspire workers' to produce one at a future date. The hope seems to be that transitional demands will mobilize the workers into action, creating a need for workers councils or soviets which then gives the revolutionary vanguard an opening to guide these councils in the proper direction. Such scenarios are a pipedream at best, at worst they are attempts to trick the working class into making revolution.

The second objection, that if our proposed program is actually revolutionary then a minimum-maximum division is pointless, misses the fact that a socialist revolution is a two-stage process.[10] The minimum demands taken as a whole are meant to establish the power of the working class. Yet as I clarified earlier, this is not the same as the establishment of a socialist economy. It is merely the creation of a political framework that establishes the rule of the working class and opens the possibility of an economic transformation. Class struggle does not end, but merely enters a new stage, where the class struggle takes on the character of the abolition of classes itself through the transformation of the relations of production. The minimum program corresponds to the first stage of this process, the maximum to the second. Unless we believe that revolution itself will be the creation of communist relations of production, a proposal of various ultra-leftists

10 This is masterfully explicated in Karl Kautsky's excellent pamphlet *The Social Revolution* (1902).

such as the obscure French pamphleteer Gilles Dauvé,[11] then the separation of the minimum and maximum is not arbitrary but rather a clarification of the process of revolution itself.

In the end, what the approach of Flakin amounts to is revolutionary phrase-mongering, just with slogans more radical than the ones Guesde was stuck with in the *Programme of the Parti Ouvrier*. The working class doesn't need radicals telling them to occupy luxury condos in hope that they will see the necessity of socialism. What they need is a vision of what kinds of changes are necessary to break with the political rule of the bourgeoisie and a party that can fight for these changes in the arena of mass politics and provide the organizational basis for a new proletarian sovereignty. There is no substitute for building such a party through rousing the workers into mass actions. The modern Trotskyists at *LeftVoice* are certainly not opposed to building a workers' party, but their strawman of "several decades in which the socialist movement can win political and economic concessions from the bourgeoisie" comes off as a dismissal of the years of patient struggle and education that it will take to form such a party that has the legitimacy to govern.

A Minimum-Maximum Program For Today

The minimum-maximum format of Marx and Guesde's *Programme of the Parti Ouvrier* is suited exactly for such a task. It puts the political changes necessary for the working class to hold power front and center, allowing us to build a majority that is aware of what it is fighting for. It promises no shortcuts into power, no false hopes that if the masses are roused into action by radical slogans they will create a potential revolutionary situation. It clarifies that revolution is the establishment of the workers' democratic-republic, opening the path for the economic reconstruction of society on socialist lines, and that the seizure of power by the proletariat is only the beginning of a new stage in the class struggle rather than an immediate leap into communist society. It brings to surface the still relevant battle for democracy and excludes revolutionary phrasemongering and empty calls to action. Clarity and openness must be the hallmark of all our movements agitation and education, and the minimum-maximum format best lives up to these ideals.

The minimum-maximum format however is simply that: a format. We cannot take programmes fossilized in time and cut and paste them onto our own political situation. Political programs need to be based on both the accumulated experience and theory of our historical movement as well as a deep understanding of the current political situation. In developing such a program today, an aspiring socialist movement would have to develop demands that speak to the current needs of workers and their existing struggles. But it would also have to include demands that may not be immediately popular but are "correct" in the sense that they are necessary measures for the working class to take power. The aim of a program should not simply be to give expression to popular demands from the masses but to also inject revolutionary demands into mass politics. Often demands will go into contradiction with prevailing popular consciousness, and this is to be expected, the program should be an educational tool that explains the necessary steps for achieving a genuine socialist transformation.

Let us take up the question of the police as an example. Popular consciousness in the United States today is very much divided on the question of the police; some polls claim 67% of Americans are opposed to abolishing or eliminating the police, while 43% of Americans support transferring funds from police budgets to other social services. To programmatically address this question we cannot fall into the trap of chasing opinion polls, nor can we simply take up slogans from the popular movement without further consideration. A proper Marxist program would clarify the tasks of the proletarian revolution in regards to the question of law enforcement, which has classically meant the abolition of the current armed forces in favor the arming of the working class through the organization of a popular militia. Marxists have taken up this demand because we recognize that if the working class is to genuinely command state power through its own institutions it must smash the repressive bourgeois state apparatus instead of hoping to wield it as an instrument. Simply raising the slogan of police abolition as a transitional demand, hoping that it will mobilize the masses into a collision course with capitalism when they realize the necessity of its abolition to achieve this goal does not provide the clarity that a program needs to provide. Nor does simply calling for the defunding of the police in favor of social services suffice; while it may be more palatable to existing popular opinion, it does not explain the necessary tasks that the working class must perform upon coming to power.

This counts for questions related to the democratization of the state and the constitution. Loyalty to the US Constitution is a fixture in American politics, yet a proper political program in this country would nonetheless call for its abolition and the drafting of an explicitly socialist constitution as the basis of a new democratic republic. It would address the necessity of developmental reparations and self-determination for internal neo-colonies. Its economic section would lay out the basic socialization of the commanding heights of the economy as well the need for radical overhauls in infrastructure and urban planning. It would abolish the current labor law regime and institute a new labor regime based on the initiatives of workers on the shop floor. By refusing to only take up demands that are already popular (such as the people's militia) and therefore winnable in the immediate term, the party is forced to fight for its beliefs among the masses and explain the necessity of revolution rather than mere reform.

By making the minimum part of the program a description

of the basic tasks the working class must perform if it is to take power, our movement is able to insert these basic questions of institutional change into our basic agitation. This will forever be preferable to an approach that simply echoes reformist demands or makes calls for militant action that fall on deaf ears. Our movement can tell the public with an honest and straight face the political and economic transformations that we hope to enact upon coming to power and articulate the long-term goal of human emancipation they are meant to bring us towards. The minimum-maximum program in the spirit of Marx and Guesde's *Programme of the Parti Ouvrier* is not a wishlist for the capitalist state, but a roadmap for building a revolutionary workers' movement that is conscious of what it is fighting for and confident in its political aims. And to make such a program more than a fantasy we must fight for the unity of the Marxist left and bring the good news of socialism to the masses of workers who have yet to be politically activated.

WITHOUT A PARTY, WE HAVE NOTHING

Donald Parkison
November 14, 2020

Donald Parkinson responds to Taylor B's "Beginnings of Politics: DSA and the Uprising," arguing that a workers' party is necessary to advance an emancipatory politics.

The past eight months have been unlike any other. Political strife in the Democratic Primary had already been taking place when the Covid-19 pandemic brought about a massive health crisis coupled with economic dislocation that led to historic levels of unemployment. It was only a matter of time before mass unrest began, with the murder of George Floyd by the police state acting as the spark that set into motion months of protesting and rioting. In these months countless Americans had their first taste of collective political action. The intensity of the wave of struggles for many felt like a rupture with the past. Politics was no longer confined to the plaything of property owners and technocratic experts but something contested by the plebian masses in struggle. This feeling of a decisive break, of a new qualitative situation, is what leads Taylor B to declare the rise of democratic socialism through the Sanders campaign and the mass protests of Black Lives Matter as a "birth of politics," a singular event that in its own processes of social mobilization create new possibilities for a future communist horizon. This feeling of a qualitative break leads him to see these events as singular, as heralding a new creative process that will break from all the old muck of the past and create new forms of organization. It is this approach that leads Taylor B to mistakenly declare that in this singular process, we must instead declare our fidelity to the spontaneous energies of the event, to see where it goes and what it creates rather than trying to impose our own ideas upon it. And the most dangerous of those ideas is the notion of the workers' party, which Taylor B declares to be a force of neutralization in the current conjuncture.

What we find here is a logic of *movementism* and *spontaneism* where the energies unleashed by social movements and mass actions are seen organically leading to a higher form. This is essentially the argument of Rosa Luxemburg's *Mass Strike* — that the workers' movement in struggle will find the solutions to its problems and develop new forms of organization that can apply these solutions. The arguments were taken to a greater extreme by the council communists like Anton Pannekoek, who eventually rejected the party as a force of neutralization much like Taylor B does in *Birth of Politics*. As Mike Macnair has pointed out, these ideas have far more in common with the political approach of the anarchist Mikhail Bakunin than his main rivals of the time in the First International, Karl Marx and Engels. The appeal of spontaneism and movementism is a common and popular reaction to the reality of countless sectarian Leninist groups who claim to be holders of the true wisdom of Marxism that will organize and lead the proletarian revolution. When the inability of these sects to consciously engineer a revolutionary movement from above into existence is clear, the appeal of a solution *from below* is seductive. The masses, uncorrupted by the sectarian dogmas of the failing left, will bring a new sense of energy and vision into play and overcome the forces of the old, bringing the new politics of the genuine social movement to the fore. The failure of the socialist sects to find a solution to the problems that socialists face today makes hope in the purity of social movements and their spontaneous motion almost common sense in the activist left.

The problem with this approach is that it contradicts the very goal of communism itself. Communism, at least in part, can be understood as the conscious planning and democratic control of the producers over society. Capitalism creates forms of domination and control that appear as impersonal forces of the market throwing us around according to the whims of profit. The anarchy of capitalism, or its lack of planning, means that our social and productive processes dominate us (the human species) as an arbitrary force, just as religious fetishizations dominate traditional religious communities as forces beyond their control. It is for this reason that the conscious planning of society in communism is not an incidental feature but a part of its very nature as a social system. The party, an instrument of conscious political vision, is counterposed to the spontaneous *unconscious* energies of the mass movements unleashed by the Bernie campaign and Black Lives Matter. It is no wonder that Taylor B sees Black Lives Matter as containing more potential despite its admitted domination by the petty-bourgeois; while Black Lives Matter is technically a non-profit foundation with its own organizational existence, it's clear that the energy of the movement is in the uncontained moments of rebellion, of street fighting against the cops.

The amount of energy expressed by the masses in the street is nothing to write off, and it is easy to see why so much of the left invests more hope in these moments of unmediated attacks on the state than the sloganeerings of sects selling newspapers. In moments like this, it is tempting to say, as Taylor B does, that the masses in struggle are more politically advanced than the various leftist sectarians. Yet if we understood communism to be a project of humanity talking *conscious* control of its own conditions of existence, then placing hope in the *unconscious* spontaneous energy of mass actions is not sufficient. Yes, we can find levels of organization emerge from the movements of the crowd, with the formation of assemblies, affinity groups, and even new nonprofits as initiatives from activists. It would be a mistake to deny the obvious creativity that arises from mass movements like the ones we saw this summer. Yet it would be an even bigger mistake to declare that this creativity can produce the organization and class consciousness needed to transform the existing class struggle into one that can transcend capitalism.

If we accept that the conscious planning of social-productive processes to meet the needs of the human species is a defining quality of communism, then we should also be willing to apply this principle to communist politics. As partisans of communism who believe that we have a duty to fight for our ideas, it is necessary that we develop an analysis of our situation, determine what is needed to further advance the struggle for communism, develop a plan of action based on this analysis, and put it into practice. We look at the social forces that promulgated these dynamics, but it is necessary to also analyze how our situation fits in a broader historical struggle of the proletariat throughout history. We cannot develop an entirely new form of struggle or organization for any given conjuncture but instead look to our past for insight into how we can best act and develop a strategy that can help us spearhead the class war towards communism. After all, the current conjuncture isn't something simply unfolding before our eyes as passive observers. We can analyze the situation and collectively act in ways informed by our analysis to influence its unfolding.

But who is this 'we' that I speak of? Is it whoever jumps into the crowd with a hope for liberation or a desire to break with the current order? Is it only other leftists? Other Marxists? To ask the strategic question of '*what is to be done?*', there needs to be a collective 'we' that can act as a subject. Otherwise 'we' are simply acting as individuals, an affinity group in the streets, a nonprofit, or a temporary general assembly that will only last as long as people can stay in the streets. Questions like "should we focus on building unions or elections, should we oppose the war, should we form a coalition with this party, should we organize nation-wide demonstrations, should we form an armed struggle?" all only make sense when the 'we' in question is some kind of organized collectivity that already has unified around a certain goal. Otherwise one is simply shouting at the atomized masses hoping they will follow. The 'party' is simply this organized collectivity that allows a 'we' to form and act in a decisive way. This is to say nothing of what a party looks like, which I have said more about in other places. In this instance, I am focusing on and arguing on a more abstract philosophical level about why the party is necessary. This is not the imposition of an abstract historical model completely foreign to the conjuncture as Taylor B claims. The call for a party is instead a call for strategy and the capacity to put it into practice through forming a political subject, a 'we' that can pose and answer questions through collective action.

I do not doubt that Taylor B accepts the need for strategy and an organized political subjectivity that can put it into practice. The problem is that he sees the current political sequence as a singularity that exists in a break with the past so radical that it will herald a completely novel form of political subjectivity, leaving us incapable of learning from the accumulated lessons of the past. There supposedly has been such a radical break in history that these accumulated lessons can only be the "traditions of generations weighing on us like living nightmares." Arguments like this can be found everywhere, from ultra-left proponents of the immediate communization of society like the journal *Endnotes* to left-populists like Laclau and Mouffe. The old forms of worker identification and the corresponding forms of organization such as the party and union were expressions of a historically specific era that is long gone. Today we will see new forms of subjectivity and organizational forms, and those who raise the old forms of a bygone era are simply imposing a nostalgic past onto the present. Or so the argument typically goes. I like to call these types of arguments the 'appeal to novelty.' The version of it that Taylor B cites is an essay by Sylvain Lazarus, "Lenin and the Party, 1902 — November 1917." Its argument is worth summarizing before dissecting, as it gives us a sophisticated version of the 'appeal to novelty' argument. Lazarus begins by saying that the notion of 'the party' is the basis of politics in the twentieth century, which is an innovation marked by Lenin's *What Is To Be Done?* in rupture with the previous conception of politics which centered on the insurrection of the class, exemplified by the Paris Commune and the ideas of Marx. Lenin's development of the thesis explicated in *What Is To Be Done?* is seen as a break from Marx's idea of the class as the revolutionary subject:

> In What Is to Be Done? Lenin broke with the thesis of Marx and Engels in the Communist Manifesto (1848) with regard to the spontaneous character of the appearance of Communists within the modern proletariat. In contrast to the Marxist thesis that can be stated as "Where there are proletarians, there are Communists," Lenin opposed spontaneous consciousness and Social Democratic (that is, revolutionary) consciousness and stretched this opposition to the limit.[1]

This break with Marx is said to comprise a new sequence, the discovery of a truth that marks an era which demonstrates this truth. Yet the sequence comes to an end in 1917, as 'the party' is now something that becomes intertwined with the state. Now one can only speak of the 'state party,' a force of conservatism because of its 'standing over society.' A new sequence begins, and the word becomes 'revolution' rather than 'party.' What this means is unclear beyond the fact that a new form of politics that goes beyond the party. Rather than seeking state power, it seeks its "subversion, its transitory cessation."[2] In his

1 Sylvain Lazarus, "Lenin and the Party, 1902-November 1917," in *Lenin Reloaded*, ed. Sebastian Budgen, Stathis Kouvelakis, and Slavoj Žižek. Durham and London: Duke University Press, 2007. pp. 259-59
2 Ibid. p. 262

rejection of a politics oriented around state power and the party, Lazarus goes so far as to say the signifier of 'revolution' should be rejected as it "is a nonpolitical, historicist notion, reducing the thought of politics, its condition of possibility, to that of an event character in exteriority, and placing this latter in a chain in which 'party' and 'state' also figure...rendered obsolete in 1968, as far as France is concerned."[3]

My first reaction to Lazarus's argument here is that he's making a claim that's impossible to disprove because it's impossible to prove. Looking at history and developing a periodization can be useful. That said, one has to ask whether they are imposing a periodization by coming up with a conclusion and then reading history backward to validate that conclusion. Historical narratives are supposed to be explanatory, and the only thing that Lazarus's narrative explains is why he thinks we need to abandon all the past concepts of Marxist politics and come up with something completely novel. Problems with method aside, the narrative Lazarus paints is simply not true. Lenin was not breaking with the political practice or conceptions of Marx and Engels in *What Is To Be Done?* and wasn't making any kind of original argument. As Lars Lih has pointed out, *What Is To Be Done?* Is an impressive exercise in aggressive *un*originality. Lenin's arguments about the need for class consciousness to be brought from without due to the inadequacy of economic struggles to develop into Social-Democratic politics on their own is simply an application of Karl Kautsky's 'merger formula.' The merger formula postulates that socialist intellectuals such as Marx and Engels developed their applications from a study of history and political economy, while the working class by necessity organized into a labor movement to collectively defend its conditions within capitalism. The socialist intellectuals, consciously dedicated partisans of political conviction, must merge their knowledge with the working-class movement by uniting to form a party dedicated to the cause of socialist revolution that is

3 Ibid. pp. 265-66

armed with a scientific theory of social change. Kautsky based this idea on the very life and work of Marx and Engels themselves, as he shows in his pamphlet *The Historical Accomplishment of Karl Marx*. By heralding Lenin's theory of the party as a radical break from Marx, Lazarus falls into the trappings of Cold War historiography as well the myths that Leninist sects tell themselves about the "party of a new type." What Lazarus is doing is projecting a radical break into history so as to justify that another radical break is necessary. Lenin (supposedly) broke with Marx's view of the class as the subject of revolution with his view of the party in order to successfully seize power in October. Then the party became a source of conservatism through its merging with the state after October, meaning that if we are to truly be working in the spirit of Lenin then another break is necessary, this time with the party itself. Yet the break never really happened in the first place. Marx himself fought to form the workers' party in his own time and struggled within it for programmatic clarity. His own life was an example of the merger formula in practice. Kautsky merely systematized it and Lenin applied it to Russian conditions.

Lazarus's periodization is essentially just an assertion of novelty to the expense of continuity, showing history as a series of sequences where each represents a clean break from the prior where a totally different type of politics is necessitated by history. What exactly changes in terms of socio-economic conditions to produce these sequences and necessitates the accompanying break in political frameworks is left to the imagination. Against this vision of history as pure novelty, we must instead see the continuity in history so as to better assimilate the accumulated past struggles of the proletariat and oppressed, building on the years of trial and error practice passed down to us by our forebearers to produce the institutions and knowledge that exist with us today. Lenin was not simply analyzing the immediate conjuncture he faced and drawing conclusions from its immanent tendencies to produce practice. He was applying knowledge and practices

231

passed to him by years of prior political experience. Lenin was working with the tradition of Russian populism and its accumulated years of failure to produce a real social revolution against Czarism. Using a flawed strategy of terrorism and reliance on the spontaneous energies of the peasantry awakened by a minority of the intelligentsia, Lenin looked for solutions that at first weren't obvious fits for his conditions. He saw one in the massive success of the German Social Democratic Party, which unified under a programme based on Marxism to build a party supported by millions of workers. The German Social Democratic movement itself existed in continuity with the traditions of Chartism, radical republicanism, and Germany's own national history of labor struggle and peasant rebellion. All of these accumulated experiences of class struggle constitute the tradition of communist activity that not only Lenin was embedded in, but contemporary communists too, for better or worse. It is for this reason that I reject both Lazarus's periodization and Taylor B's use of it to argue that "we must proceed from a break to do politics under present conditions" just as "Marx broke with the utopian socialists. Lenin broke with Marx. The Cultural Revolution can be read as Mao's break with Marxism-Leninism to free politics from the party-state."

By positing history as a sequence of decisive clean breaks rather than a flux of novelty and continuity it breaks us off from the past generations of class struggle, forcing the left to completely reinvent politics for every historical sequence we encounter. Any concrete situation in history is a completely unique conjuncture while also embedded in a web of determinations that are the product of generations of social practices all corresponding with humanity's need to interface with nature. Situating ourselves in the conjuncture means looking through all of history at the accumulated lessons given to us by these social practices and building on them, throwing off the muck of the past that harms us while preserving those ideas and practices that correctly orient us, continuing the work of those before us. With this perspective, it is easy to see how it is not idealist to react to the current situation by pursuing the organization of a workers' party. Those of us who engage in such pursuits continue the work of generations of partisans before us and carry with them their lessons and methods. To build on these methods and apply them to the conditions we face is not forcing something foreign and alien upon our current circumstances. These circumstances do not exist in a vacuum completely outside of a broader historical continuity.

What *is* idealist is to assume a break in history where political actors will completely reinvent the old forms and subjectivities without building upon the historical traditions they are embedded in. We are more atomized and depoliticized than ever before, so it is easier to see ourselves as disembedded from the past and in a unique historical position where we must go back to the drawing board and completely reinvent politics in order to relate to our times. Yet this disembeddedness is an illusion, as is the accompanying notion that we can reinvent politics without regard for the traditions of the past. Any attempt to reinvent politics in such a way will inevitably be pure improvisation. Any situation requires improvisation, a "concrete analysis of a concrete situation." But improvisation in politics requires knowledge of our methods of struggle, a body of organizational and political knowledge that serves as a basis. When we disembed ourselves from the past and seek to reinvent our methods of struggle with every new phase of history (however these phases are defined) we end up losing this knowledge and having to purely improvise in the dark. And this improvisation will fall into the dominant thought patterns of bourgeois-liberal society. This is why Althusser spoke of the spontaneous ideology of scientists and it also makes sense to speak of the spontaneous ideology of activists.[4] In seeking to achieve political goals, activists come upon limitations and dead ends, just as scientists come to across moments of crisis in their fields. The activist will seek to solve these problems and limitations within the ideological framework that is dominant in society, just as the scientist turns to idealist philosophy despite the realist and materialist nature of their practice. Today, when coming across the limitations of the current moment, activists will turn towards liberal and anarchist ideas unless a coherent alternative is posed. Rather than leading to an overcoming of the dominant framework, spontaneity tends to favor it. This is why Lenin spoke of the need to "combat spontaneity." For Lenin, the role of the party was introducing a social-democratic consciousness that was not seen as possible through the accumulation of economic struggles alone. The fact that the accumulations of economic struggles would not lead to the spontaneous generation of social-democratic consciousness was what necessitated the party. Lenin saw that communist politics requires challenging the dominant worldview, and the party allowed this to be done in a conscious and systematic way.

This is the lesson of *What Is To Be Done?*, and it should be seen as a lesson that is not particular to a certain phase of history as Lazarus would have it but rather universal to politics itself. The battle for hegemony must be a protracted and systematic struggle that pushes against the dominant ideas of society while putting forward a real alternative. My argument is not that we don't need change and innovative ways of thinking and organizing, but simply that we don't fix what isn't broken. The party-form is not itself the agent of neutralization against emancipatory potentials that need to be broken with. Rather than being the cause of bureaucratism and other sources of revolutionary degeneration, the party is the precondition for solving these problems.

4 Althusser, Louis. *Philososphy and the Spontaneous Philosophy of the Scientists.* London: Verso, 1990. See chapter 3.

There is a class struggle within the party itself, between the petty-bourgeois bureaucracy and the proletarians they represent. When Taylor B speaks of the party-form as the source of neutralization, it is the victory of this petty-bourgeois stratum that is actually the source of neutralization, not the essence of the party itself. By conducting the struggle to control party bureaucracy and democratize its organizations, the proletariat itself learns how to govern society as a class. Building the workers' party allows us to constitute the proletariat into higher forms of political subjectivity by creating a collectivity that consciously and deliberately works to solve these problems. It allows us to actually become a force that can contest the class power of our enemies by out-organizing and out-strategizing them. To have any discussion about revolutionary strategy, develop an actionable plan, and put it into practice, a party is needed. Revolutionaries throughout history have realized this. Seeing the futility of endless street protests regardless of how militant, Huey Newton reacted to the challenges faced by struggling Black proletarians by helping form the Black Panther Party:

> The movement was cresting around the country. Brothers on the block in many northern cities were moving angrily in response to the problems that overwhelmed them. New York and other eastern cities had exploded in 1964, Watts went up in 1965, Cleveland in 1966, and in 1967 another long hot summer was approaching. But the brothers needed direction for their energies. The Party wanted no more spontaneous riots, because the outcome was always the same: the people might liberate their territories for a few short days or hours, but eventually the military force of the oppressor would wipe out their gains. Having neither the strength nor the organization, the people were powerless. In the final analysis, riots caused only more repression and the loss of brave men. Blacks bled and died in the riots and went to jail on petty or false charges. If the brothers could be organized into disciplined cadres, working in broadly based community programs, then the energy expended in riots could be directed toward permanent and positive changes.[5]

5 Newton, Huey P. *Revolutionary Suicide.* New York: Penguin, 2009. pp.

Newton's words are incredibly prescient today, as months of street protests in the US come up against the reality of the left's actual organizational powerlessness and incapacity to provide an alternative to the existing regime. Mass actions, riots, general strikes — these are not substitutes for having the organizational capacity to *govern*. Even if the latest wave of protest had brought the government down, the reality would have been the military enforcing a constitutionally legal transition to a replacement government, led by the same parties that were there before.

Contrary to Taylor B, I believe that Marx did have a theory of politics. While it would take figures such as Engels, Bebel, Kautsky, and Lenin to systematize it, Marx ultimately believed that politics was about classes contesting, taking, and holding power. Communism relied on the proletariat taking power on an international scale, which required a protracted struggle where the proletariat organized itself as a class that could pose as an alternative to capitalist society. To do this, the proletariat had to form a party and learn to self-govern by organizing on the national and international scales and waging a political battle for radical democratic-republicanism and the socialization of production. Unlike the socialist sectarians of today and of his own time, Marx fought for a party that would be based on unity around a political program, not a specific theoretical creed or philosophical dogma. Marx fought for the unity of all principled revolutionaries around a strategy for the proletariat to constitute itself as a class and fight for political power, not for the purity of a micro-sect. Many are wary of the project of party-building today because of the toxic attitudes of sectarians who promote disunity, and one should not mistake my argument in favor of a workers' party as an argument for a new sect. What is needed is the unity of Marxists within the existing left around a program of class independence and a strategy of building a party that will organize working-class communities and contest elections.

162-163.

Such unity will require a breakup of sectarian identities in favor of collaboration and mergers, and will not be easily won. Yet the development of arguments like those made by the comrades in Red Star DSA show a potential for such an initiative in the left. One thing is for sure — without a party, we have nothing. Because without a party, there is no 'we.'

BUILDING THE MASS PARTY: THE MERGER FORMULA IN THE AMERICAN CONTEXT

Myra Janis
December 9, 2018

What will it take to build a mass socialist party in the United States? Myra Janis argues that socialist think tanks may be a necessary first step, as well as a movement to reform electoral and labor laws through "anti-entryist" candidates.

With the buzz around the new democratic socialist congresswomen elected in the 2018 midterms and the growth of the DSA, there have been a number of different proposals on how socialists should conduct electoral campaigns and general political strategy. These proposals have ranged from the most moderate — those of Nora Belrose and other progressives — who want to work towards Michael Harrington's vision of realigning the Democratic Party through running in the party's primaries, to a more radical strategy being put forward by Neal Meyer and Ben B. of *The Call* who argue for an aggressive 'Bernie or Bust' campaign to split the left wing of the Democrats from their neoliberal masters to form a new labor/socialist party.[1] What all of

---

1 Belrose, Nora. "Put Down Your Pitchforks: Why Insurectionary Politics Doesn't Work." norabelrose.com, August 8, 2018. https://norabelrose.com/2018/08/01/put-down-your-pitchforks-why-revolutionary-politics-doesnt-work/; Meyer, Neal, B., Ben, "The Case for Bernie 2020." The Call, August 16, 2018. https://socialistcall.com/2018/08/16/bernie-2020/

these new strategies have in common is that they accept that, at the current moment, third parties are not viable.

Nora Belrose and Berniecrats represent the status quo. This makes sense given that their socialism is nothing more than a watered-down version of Social Democracy that fits within the capitalist framework, even though their 'socialism' fell out of fashion with the Democrats in the 90s with the rise of the Clintons. However, if we want to fulfill the underlying promise of socialism, of democratically empowering the lower masses and thus undermining the whole of the capitalist system, we must go well beyond being the left wing of a capitalist party.

While Neal Meyer and Ben B. halfway conceive of a successful electoral strategy based on the correct impulse of working within the system to ultimately undermine it, the strategy laid out in *The Case for Bernie 2020* has five major problems with it.

The first concerns the reason *why* third parties are not viable in the United States. This is not due to a lack of a base of potential voters. Pew Polling on third parties shows that most Americans feel there is a need for a major third party or that a vast number of American citizens refuse to vote for either party, as the 2016 election revealed.[2] These potential voters are not given any kind of choice in the matter: third-party candidates have the odds stacked against them with first-past-the-post, or winner takes all, elections being the norm at the state level. Thanks to loose campaign finance laws, corporate capital flows unendingly to the two parties. This makes the "dirty split" pointless.

Second, as Charles Post pointed out in his critique, even if causing a "dirty split" was worthwhile, it probably would not happen: most Berniecrats, like Nora Belrose, are dead set on

---

2 Saad, Lydia. "Perceived Need for Third Major Party Remains High in US" Gallup, September 27, 2017. https://news.gallup.com/poll/219953/perceived-need-third-major-party-remains-high.aspx; Shoot, Brittany. "Who Helped Trump Most in the 2016 Presidential Election? Nonvoters, Pew Study Says." Fortune, August 9, 2018. https://fortune.com/2018/08/09/nonvoters-trump-presidency-pew-study/

working within the Democratic Party, and a 'Bernie or Bust' campaign lead by socialists would most likely cause a split within the left wing of the Democratic Party rather than separating the left wing of the Democratic Party from the neoliberal center due to fears of Bernie being a "spoiler" candidate who would aid a Republican victory.[3] Third, Meyer & Ben B. do not cover how we would fund such a "campaign within a campaign," a common problem with most of these democratic socialist political strategies. Socialists need money to compete with corporate Democrats in an election. Fourth, the way politics works in the United States is by discouraging any meaningful mass participation, as both parties are hollow fundraising machines unlike the political parties of the past that had an engaged mass membership. Any kind of socialist effort would have to tackle such a problem directly, and while Meyer & Ben B. briefly bring this up, they do not have a detailed response to it.

The fifth problem is probably the most important: there is not much that separates the Socialists who would get behind a hypothetical Bernie or Bust campaign from Democrat-approved progressives like Elizabeth Warren in terms of policy. This is indicative of a much deeper problem with democratic socialists in general, as they seem to not have an independent political vision. While these flaws hold back the Bernie or Bust strategy, the impulse of working within the system in order to break it down is a good one, as the alternatives to it have consistently proven to be inadequate. Anti-union legislation has made it harder for socialists to organize a mass movement without dealing with the crooked realm of the American state. Therefore We must lay out a political strategy that will not only organize people directly, overcoming the weakness of the current labor movement but will still create a party with a distinctly socialist

3 Post, Charlie. "Debating 'The Case For Bernie 2020.'" Socialist Worker, October 16, 2018. https://socialistworker.org/2018/10/16/debating-the-case-for-bernie-2020

vision, completely independent from the two parties and under-mining the two-party system from within.

The Merger Formula in America

The need for a socialist think tank and a broader plan for build-ing the mass party must be thought of in the context of what Lenin scholar Lars T. Lih refers to as the Merger Formula. The Merger Formula posits that the success of a socialist revolution is based on the ability of the socialist movement (S) to merge with the labor movement (M) to form a mass party (S+M) through which a revolution can be carried out. The concept is implicit in Marx and Engels's *Communist Manifesto*, Karl Kautsky's *The Erfurt Programme,* and Lenin's concept of the vanguard party.[4] The role of the socialist movement, according to the Merger Formula, is to develop the concept of socialism through theory and implant it into the consciousness of the workers' movement, which acts as the mass base for socialism. In this way, the social-ist movement can be thought of as the mind of the revolution and the workers' movement its body. While some might reject such a formula as it implies that the workers are incapable of imagining socialism for themselves, this would be a simplistic misreading since — much like the literal mind and body — the socialist movement and the workers' movement are never com-pletely separated: the socialist movement is made up of the most advanced elements of the workers' movement, and the workers' movement is made up of the most advanced elements of the so-cialist movement. On theoretical grounds, the goal of the Merger Formula is to meld these two distinct-yet-connected social forc-es together to form the party and the revolution. Even during their most deformed state, transforming from revolutionary so-cialism to tepid social democracy, the mass parties of Europe

4 Lih, Lars T. "VI Lenin and the influence of Kautsky." Weekly Worker, September 2, 2009. https://weeklyworker.co.uk/worker/783/vi-lenin-and-the-influence-of-kautsky/

relied upon the strength of the labor movement to provide them with the base of support, and in the semi-industrialized world, socialist revolutions were able to substitute the M of the Merger Formula with peasants.

However, we are in a situation where the existing M in the United States has been immensely weakened by a full-on assault against the legal rights of labor to organize and an evisceration of their advantageous class position. Removing American workers from the point of production through the shipping of their jobs overseas, along with a general shift in the economy towards service work, has taken away the power that American workers traditionally had, as they once had the potential to effectively seize the means of production. This has effectively neutered the strength of the American working class, as can be seen in the long-term decline of union membership and unions in general.[5] This presents the growing socialist movement with a major problem, as it sees its long-term growth as based on traditional institutions of labor such as unions. The socialist movement is completely disconnected from such institutions, being mostly composed of declassé and/or downwardly mobile petty bourgeois. The desire to return to such traditional institutions of labor is not motivated so much by a class basis as by a desire to find a viable alternative to what is called 'identity politics,' contrasting the unity of twentieth-century workers' movements against the fragmented and easily co-opted intersectional framework of understanding oppression and struggle. Through this desire to return to traditional labor institutions of old, people like Adam Proctor (of the Dead Pundits Society podcast) hope to create a "socialism for regular-ass people," but they fail to propose a way to deal with the practical implications of workers being ripped from the point of production in the twenty-first century; they are too focused on critiquing the flaws of identity

5 N.a. "Union Members Summary." US Bureau of Labor Statistics, January 19, 2023. https://www.bls.gov/news.release/union2.nr0.htm

politics to put forward a meaningful solution beyond simply a narrow and economistic call to "organize." We must, therefore, critically evaluate what the 'M' in the Merger Formula will be in twenty-first-century America and how we connect it to the burgeoning socialist movement in a meaningful way.

We must understand that while the decline in the number of factory workers that has led to the death of the traditional labor movement is real, the proletariat is much greater than merely factory workers and, therefore, still exists. The proletariat is composed of those who are dispossessed of control over production and must therefore compete in the labor market to survive. When we start to think of the proletariat in this way, it becomes clear that everyone from permanently unemployed black people to service workers on meager wages are proletarians just as much as factory workers were in the twentieth century and that the kind of workerism which dismisses them as lumpen (or whatever other nonsensical abstraction is utilized by bigoted Marxists) must be refuted as unscientific. The modern proletariat currently does not operate primarily through traditional institutions like unions but still resists the capitalist class through various means of struggle that are scattered due to their spontaneous nature: forms of resistance like riots, wildcat strikes, and protests of various kinds, all driven by a disorganized and unconscious proletariat. This means that riots against police brutality are just as proletarian as strikes, as both the rioter and the striker are proletarians struggling against capitalist exploitation even though said exploitation comes in different shapes — one being artificially imposed unemployment and racial discrimination, the other being direct wage slavery. The goal of the socialist movement must be to study these real movements of proletarian action and deeper sentiments that are in the proletariat, which are inactive due to the suppression of resistance, and figure out how to unify these scattered forms of struggle under the banner of the proletariat and move towards a well-articulated and genuinely radical vision of socialism.

Organizing the Socialist Movement

Before we can even begin to tackle building the proletarian movement of the Merger Formula, we must first figure out how to effectively organize the burgeoning socialist movement into units that will best allow them to work as the mind of the revolution. The general tendency is to move towards the creation of "parties," which end up being pseudo-think tanks that use the brainpower of college students to put out some kind of publication filled with "Theory," Theory in this case often being a Kabbalah-like doctrine that is completely disconnected from any meaningful practice. "The Party" in this situation has no connection to any mass movement, making it ineffective as a political party, let alone as a mass party. Without this connection, "The Party" becomes a pseudo-activist NGO that has no mass appeal as it does not know how to work strategically, with all the energy of radical activists getting worked back into the Democratic Party through its network of NGOs. If the natural tendency of radical organizations in the United States is to fall into either of these two positions, then the obvious solution is to drop the pretense of our small sects being genuine vanguard parties and begin to learn from our more successful opponents in mainstream politics as to how they maintain large bases of support. While, obviously, the Democrats and Republicans only represent a minority of the nation, it is nonetheless a significantly larger minority of the nation than what the current socialist movement represents, and to learn from one's opponents does not mean one needs to copy them wholesale. Rather, it is to take specific tactics and strategies that work and take into account why the nation does not vote for the mainstream parties.

Nick Srnicek & Alex Williams's *Inventing the Future: Postcapitalism and a World Without Work* takes a step in the right direction in terms of how the socialist movement should be organized by tracking how neoliberalism developed from well-funded think tanks and proceeded to slowly but surely infiltrate the halls of power through the development of a clear and coherent alternative to the dominant Keynesian consensus of the 1950s and 60s, offering a well fleshed out policy that could be enacted by politicians and a message that could win over a large enough portion of the population to create a new hegemony of free-market dogmatism. Of course, this is all framed in a very limiting Neo-Gramscian framework that gives too much credit to the spreading of ideas in the rise of neoliberalism as opposed to the role of the evisceration of the industrial working class that served as the base of the Keynesian social democratic order that was carried out by the capitalist class. While this line of reasoning is ultimately wrong, they are correct in believing that the organization of socialist think tanks is necessary. They are also correct in wanting to study the success of mainstream political movements. The neoliberals could offer coherent policy proposals and give clear explanations for what they wanted with the authority of academic titles behind them, offering a vision of a new society, whereas socialists tend to focus on critiquing capitalism and offering nothing that isn't either something that could already be put forward by the progressive wing of the Democratic Party or is just empty nostalgia for dead regimes. It makes sense then for the socialist movement, whose natural role is to be the mind of the revolution, to organize as think tanks which, instead of having an elusive focus on critique and eulogizing over the corpse of twentieth-century communism, works out the specifics of what a revitalized socialism would look like in power, proposing a policy that is just as thorough in terms of being backed up by empirical data as something that would be put out by the Heritage Foundation or the RAND Corporation.

The think tank, as a form of an organization, has the benefit of dealing with the specifics of policy, analysis, and strategy through professionalizing such tasks. One aspect of strategy in particular that is important to the left but often overlooked is the need for funding. Leftist organizations have a major problem with funding as their ideas are fringe, and there are few mechanisms by which they can receive financial support. This often leads to leftist organizations organizing themselves in a way that is similar to a multi-level marketing scheme, having their followers (typically young student activists) buy products to sell, leaving the students in even more debt than before while only benefiting only the leaders of the organization. These sorts of pseudo-multi-level marketing schemes end up feeding into the problem of anti-democratic cult-like structures of these "parties.. Establishing a legitimate think tank gives us a way of funding ourselves that will rely less on student activist labor and more on large donations from sympathetic backers. With the popularity of "socialism" as a concept and the nice gloss professionalism that an organization like a think tank can give to a political movement, finding sympathetic backers who were willing to give a large amount of money towards socialist think tanks will not be that hard: radical chic is now in fashion with celebrities like Jim Carrey professing their support for socialism.[6] It doesn't matter how accurate these celebrities' grasp of socialism is, as radical chic and the legitimacy of the think tank form in American politics makes such a project attractive to liberal celebrities who want to flex their social justice credentials through conspicuous consumption. There is a long history of American celebrities supporting radical organizations with cash, such as Marlon Brando's support for the Black Panthers. Besides celebrities, there are probably foreign backers who are already prone to backing left-wing subversives for their own long-term goals, and again the legitimacy of a think tank will probably attract their attention. We need to find the Engels(es) for our Marx(es), and the best way to do that is through the think tank form that already exists in the United States.

6 Wang, Amy B. "Jim Carrey tells Democrats: 'We have to say yes to socialism." The Washington Post, September 10, 2018. https://www.washingtonpost.com/politics/2018/09/10/jim-carrey-tells-democrats-we-have-say-yes-socialism/?utm_term=.40c188d77c6c

Building the Proletarian Movement

With a rough outline of how to organize the socialist movement to be more effective, we can turn to the task of rebuilding the proletariat as the body of the revolutionary movement. As previously discussed, we cannot simply rely on tapping into already established unions for a base of support since they are weakened, and the proletariat is scattered in raw social movements. There are also sentiments within the dispossessed proletariat which have been described by both bourgeois political commentators and a new school of Marxists associated with the new Left Flank blog as anti-political.[7] While anti-political Marxists have a questionable theoretical framework and reading of Marx, which I have already tackled with a few friends in an article titled *To Rip Off a Band-Aid*,[8] they, along with their bourgeois liberal counterparts, are following the "widespread mood," a clear empirical trend that can be found in the patterns of low voter participation in western democracies, rising voter apathy, desire for a major third party in the United States, and populist movements that tap into this mood which is common among the proletariat.[9] All of these things point towards a general resent-

---

7 Bastasin, Carlo. "The Rise of Anti-Politics." Brookings, February 24, 2013. https://www.brookings.edu/articles/the-rise-of-anti-politics/; Humphrys, Elizabeth, Tietze, Tad. "Anti-politics: Elephant in the room." Left Flank, October 31, 2013.https://left-flank.org/2013/10/31/anti-politics-elephant-room/

8 N.a. "To Rip Off a Band-Aid." Emancipation Materials, April 13, 2018. https://emancipationmaterials.wordpress.com/2018/04/13/to-rip-off-a-band-aid/

9 Radu, Sintia. "Americans Don't Show Up at the Polls but Neither Do the Swiss." US News, November 2, 2018. https://www.usnews.com/news/best-countries/articles/2018-11-02/the-us-isnt-alone-in-low-voter-turnout; Sandel, Michael. "Right-wing populism is rising as progressive politics fails - is it too late to save democracy?" The New Statesman, May 24, 2018. https://www.newstatesman.com/long-reads/2018/05/right-wing-populism-rising-progressive-politics-fails-it-too-late-save-democracy; Saad, Lydia. "Per-

ment towards politics within the proletariat that manifests itself through the general sentiment of "anti-politics." There is also a growing trend of social alienation and antisocial tendencies developing due to the breakdown of the commons that can be seen in the media spectacle of school shootings, a thesis I argued for in my article "How Empires Die."[10]

Neatly summarized, the three main tendencies that we need to tap into to revitalize the proletarian movement are as follows:

Raw social movements that have a proletarian class character and often express themselves in disorganized forms, such as riots. Without real leadership, these movements end up being routed into the Democratic Party (e.g., Black Lives Matter).

Populism and anti-political sentiments that have been building within the class due to the inability of their voices to be heard by the clueless political elite and the capitalist class that controls them in the face of their evisceration.

The social alienation that has been growing due to the lack of community spaces in which people can be properly socialized.

How to tap into the first is relatively easy to grasp as it would involve copying the sort of organizational structures that the Democratic Party already has with activist NGOs. But, instead of seeking to route raw social movements into the Democratic Party, we would be pushing them towards the solidification of the proletarian movement and the eventual creation of a socialist party that unifies it politically. We would initially lack the resources that the Democratic Party has, but using some of the same methods of funding and leaning into the popularity of socialism among young people would allow us to gain the upper hand in terms of outflanking the Democrats when it comes to vying for control over movements like Black Lives Matter

ceived Need for third Major Party Remains High in US" Gallup. September 27, 2017. https://news.gallup.com/poll/219953/perceived-need-third-major-party-remains-high.aspx

10 Janis, Rosa. "How Empires Die." Cosmonaut, October 26, 2018. https://cosmonaut.blog/2018/10/26/how-empires-die/

and Occupy Wall Street. To tap into the second tendency, we would need to do two things: organize campaigns for electoral reform, which would focus on how awful politics currently are, and give voice to the need for popular representation that would come from the formation of a major third-party in the United States, fulfilling the promise of American democracy. Propaganda efforts would feed into the discontent with mainstream politics that already exists within the proletariat in an effort to route them into a proletarian movement along with a proletarian party. For the third tendency, we should engage in what we will call "commune building": what we mean by commune building is rebuilding the community bonding exercises and services that people used to have, such as bowling leagues and health facilities, but in a new socialist light. These will constitute the framework of the mass party. Mass parties of the past, such as the Black Panther Party and the Social Democratic Party of Germany during its heyday, were not only political organizations but also provided for social needs. The creation of socialist beer clubs, healthcare facilities, and other forms of alternative institutions will fill the gap left by bourgeois civil society in terms of creating thriving communities that will unite the class through the real social bonding that many now crave. Imagine if the young men who label themselves "incels" were taught and socialized through socialist schools instead of underfunded public schools and the dark corners of the internet. When we tap into all three of these tendencies within our society we will not only be rebuilding the proletarian movement by funneling them into a socialist mass party: we will also be bringing people together and improving their lives along the way.

The Democratic Offense

We have covered how to effectively organize the socialist movement and revitalize the proletarian movement, but before we can start to build the mass party, we need to deal with the two-party system which dominates American politics. We cannot simply run third-party candidates in the United States because the two parties which the capitalist class supports have worked together to organize elections in such a way that a third-party candidate can't be viable. In order to counter this, we would need to enact real electoral reform like getting corporate money that usually ends up keeping third-party candidates from being serious contenders in elections out of politics and replacing winner-takes-all elections with the two-round system nationwide. This last reform would eliminate the "spoiler effect" that third-party candidates have the few times they are successful. The situation is tricky. To enact the electoral reforms that are necessary for the establishment of a successful third party, and by extension, a socialist mass party, there needs to already be a successful independent electoral movement for those reforms, since they would have to be passed by elected politicians. This leaves us in an awful situation where the only way to build successful third parties is to already have a successful third party. However, avoiding electoral politics altogether is not an option either since it still manages to reach a large portion of the population and has the potential to reach an even larger portion of the population, given the mass coverage of electoral politics in the United States by the media. Having people already within the state when we move to take power will give us an advantage that simply avoiding electoral politics altogether will not give us, making the process of revolution an act of the popular will of the proletariat rather than a coup carried out by a small number of people. This means that we cannot simply avoid electoral politics as many leftists would want.

We are left with no other option than to work within the two-party system in order to undermine it. We shall not, however, simply tail the Democratic Party as DSA's right wing would want us to. Rather, we must plan out a wave of hostile campaigns at all levels of office. By running candidates in both the Republican and Democratic Party, we will be able to demonstrate that we are not progressive Democrats like the DSA candidates who are the loyal opposition to the Democratic Party but are rather an independent movement that has been forced to fight the duopoly within its den, our platforms being focused on electoral reforms that will destroy the system, popular demands like universal health care, and actual socialist positions such as nationalizing/socializing major industries. The amped-up rhetoric and openly hostile positions to both parties will separate these candidates from straightforward Democrats and Republicans, allowing said candidates to tap even further into the vital anti-political sentiment that we previously discussed. We would have to be smart and abrasive about our socialist politics to effectively appeal to the proletariat that has been betrayed one too many times by smooth-talking politicians and loud populists. The conventional party leaders would then be forced into two situations that would ultimately backfire in their faces if they were to carry them out against the socialist anti-entryist insurgencies within their parties, either forcing them out democratically in the face of public backlash that would be organized through the revitalized movements of the proletariat and socialism, or trying to compete with the mass popularity of said insurgencies with empty populism and ultimately losing out. Either way, the democratic offensive will be successful in propagandizing the movement. If and when we do win elections, we will have the means of holding our politicians accountable, unlike the DSA left of today, as we will have ways of organizing the proletariat outside of the Democratic Party with the institutions that we have built through the development of the proletarian-socialist movements. The candidates will carry out the electoral reform with popular support behind them, dragging the two parties along with them toward the establishment of a proper socialist mass party.

Through a slow build up of popular support through the development of socialist and proletarian movements and their merger in the form of the Democratic offensive, we can potentially create a clear road towards a mass socialist party and eventual revolution that works toward the emancipation of all of mankind in our revolutionary struggle.

CREATE A MASS PARTY!

Cliff Connolly
February 21, 2021

Cliff Connolly critiques CounterPower's vision of the "party of autonomy" and offers an alternative vision of the mass party.

The US left is at a critical juncture where the structure and focus of our organizations will soon be decided. On the one hand, we positively have ongoing processes of cohesion in play with DSA chapters collaborating on writing a national platform and far-flung sects coming together under the banner of Marxist Center. On the other hand, we have many comrades across ideological lines who still echo opposition to the idea of a tightly structured national organization. Central to this contradiction is the question of the party: should socialists strive to build an independent political party, and if so, what should that look like? CounterPower has put forth one possible answer in their article "Create Two, Three, Many Parties of Autonomy!" They are dedicated organizers and we should all be glad to have them in our midst. However, their strategy of eschewing the mass party model and encouraging the spontaneous formation of multiple "parties of autonomy," and counting on these disparate groups to unite into an "area of the party," is unworkable in the long term.

Their argument for the many parties strategy rests on a number of errors — historical misrepresentation (no, CPUSA was not a party of autonomy), uncritical acceptance of failed models (Autonomia Operaia gives us more negative lessons than positive ones), an over-reliance on spontaneity (movements have to be built intentionally), an aversion to leadership (no, it doesn't automatically create unaccountable bureaucracy), and a confusion of terms (putting anarchist and Marxist vocab words together does not solve the contradictions between them). We will explore each of these points in greater detail. There is also an implicit assumption of false dichotomies built into the many parties line — either we build parties of autonomy or slip into sectarianism, either parties of autonomy or dogmatism, either parties of autonomy or top-down bureaucracy. There is a kernel of truth present here; we certainly don't want a dictatorship of paid staffers. However, parties of autonomy are not a solution to this problem — in some ways, they would exacerbate the problem.

This was initially written in response to CounterPower's original essay in 2019, but has since been amended to include dialogue with the updated version published in 2020. The differences between the two are significant and raise new concerns about the many parties model. The most interesting addition in the update concerns the role of cadre — highly trained organizers dedicated full-time to party activity. While we agree wholeheartedly on the necessity of these professional revolutionaries, there is a difference of emphasis that merits debate. This issue will be explored in greater detail below.

That CounterPower started this conversation on the party question is a gift to the whole of the US left — it must be addressed for our organizations to move forward. While many of us vehemently disagree with their conclusions, we should be grateful for their company. After examining each piece of their argument for the many parties model and taking note of its shortcomings, we will investigate a viable alternative — a mass party of organizers built on the principles of struggle, pluralism, and democratic discipline.

Historical Clarification

There are a number of historical errors throughout Counter-Power's article. By this we are not referring to a difference of opinion about a certain historical figure's thought process or the motivations behind a particular decision, but rather factual inaccuracies. This in itself does not mean the thesis of the article is automatically false, but it does betray a dependency on unfounded assumptions. First, there is the assertion that the Russian soviets arose organically without being built by socialists, at which point the Bolsheviks joined them and worked harmoniously with other autonomous parties in this "area of the party" to link the soviets to other sites of struggle. Second, there is the quotation from Mao Zedong's 1957 Hundred Flowers speech, which CounterPower uses to bolster their argument for parties of autonomy. Finally, we are led to believe that both the FAI and the Alabama chapter of the Communist Party USA are exemplars of the many parties model.

We will begin with the relationship between the Bolsheviks and the soviets. Here is CounterPower's characterization:

> The organized interventions of a revolutionary party thus take place 'in the middle,' as mediations between the micropolitical and macropolitical. This has been a distinguishing feature of successful revolutionary parties, as in the example of the Russian Revolution of 1917, when clusters of Bolshevik party activists concentrated in workplaces, recognizing that the participatory councils (soviets) emerging from grassroots proletarian struggles embodied the nucleus of an alternative social system. Thus the party's organization at the point of production enabled revolutionaries first to link workplace struggles against exploitation with the struggle against imperialism, and then to link the emergent councils with the insurrectionary struggle to establish a system of territorial counterpower.

On the contrary, it is of utmost importance to recognize that the soviets, factory committees, and militias that formed the backbone of the Russian revolution were built intentionally by socialists. While different factions in the Russian Social Democratic Workers' Party eventually split into separate organizations as the Bolsheviks and Mensheviks, both groups were instrumental in the creation of these mass organizations. They did not emerge organically from economic struggles with bosses and feudal landlords like some of the trade unions and peasant associations, but instead were the product of a socialist intervention in economic struggles which emphasized the need for political organization. This strategy, commonly referred to as the "merger formula," was theorized by Marx and Engels, popularized by the German socialist party leader Karl Kautsky, and accepted by Russian socialists of all stripes (most notably Lenin).[1]

The Bolsheviks did not merely help workers build their fighting organizations. They also competed with political rivals for leadership in them. Beyond their efforts that we would call "base-building" today, the Bolsheviks also invested significant resources into propaganda efforts and electoral contests. The struggle for elected majorities in the soviets in 1917 was pursued in tandem with a strategy of running campaigns for municipal offices and the Constituent Assembly (the bourgeois parliament of the Provisional Government), and it worked. The Bolshevik candidates for the assembly were able to publicly oppose the policies of the Provisional Government, while the elected deputies in the soviets were able to win over the working class to the task of seizing political power. These electoral efforts were instrumental in establishing a democratic mandate for the October Revolution.[2] Consider these words from leading Bolshevik (and later leading opposition member purged by Stalin) Alexander Shliapnikov, in 1920:

1 Lih, Lars T. *Lenin Rediscovered: What Is to Be Done? In Context.* Chicago: Haymarket Books, 2008.
2 Nimtz, August H. *The Ballot, the Streets — or Both, From Marx and Engels to Lenin and the October Revolution.* Chicago: Haymarket Books, 2019.

The Russian Communist Party (RKP), as the history of the preceding years indicates, is the only revolutionary party of the Working Class, leading class war and civil war in the name of Communism. The R.K.P. unifying the more conscious and decisive part of the Proletariat around the Revolutionary Communist Program of action and drawing to the Communist banner the more leading elements of the rural poor, must concentrate all higher leadership of communist construction and the general direction of policy of the country.

Clearly, the Bolsheviks did not consider themselves a "party of autonomy" working side by side with the Menshevik reformists in a broad "area of the party." Nor did they simply fuse with organic economic struggles in the trade unions. The reality couldn't be further from CounterPower's insinuations: the Bolsheviks were a party of political organizers who started as a minority and slowly won over sections of the working class through diligent mass work and bitter struggle with the other parties of the day. By engaging in this process, they eventually took on a mass character and became capable of leading social revolution. The lesson to learn from the Bolsheviks is this: we must win political hegemony in whatever independent organs of proletarian power that we help build, using every available means, including running opposition candidates in bourgeois elections to expose broader sections of the class to our ideas.

Now we will consider Mao's echoing of the old Chinese proverb "Let a hundred flowers blossom, let a hundred schools of thought contend." This line of poetry is used by CounterPower to demonstrate the need for dozens of independent communist grouplets to form and collaborate on the task of social revolution. They attribute the quote to Mao, but is this how he used it? The short answer is no. It comes from a speech he gave in March 1957 at the Chinese Communist Party's National Conference on Propaganda Work. It is true that he called for a hundred schools of thought to contend, but this was in the context of winning unaligned intellectuals over to the party's socialist

257

ideals. He gave a thoughtful and nuanced analysis of how the party could accept criticism from the broader population without sacrificing their legitimacy as the ruling organization of the country:

> Ours is a great Party, a glorious Party, a correct Party. This must be affirmed as a fact. But we still have shortcomings, and this, too, must be affirmed as a fact...Will it undermine our Party's prestige if we criticize our own subjectivism, bureaucracy and sectarianism? I think not. On the contrary, it will serve to enhance the Party's prestige. This was borne out by the rectification movement during the anti-Japanese war. It enhanced the prestige of our Party, of our Party comrades and our veteran cadres, and it also enabled the new cadres to make great progress. Which of the two was afraid of criticism, the Communist Party or the Kuomintang? The Kuomintang. It prohibited criticism, but that did not save it from final defeat. The Communist Party does not fear criticism because we are Marxists, the truth is on our side, and the basic masses, the workers and peasants, are on our side.

Clearly, in March 1957 Mao was concerned with building a mass party, not opening space for a loose collaboration between multiple parties aimed at building socialism. Unfortunately, the Chinese Communist Party was underprepared for the criticism they would soon face and reversed the Hundred Flowers Campaign. By July of that same year, the Anti-Rightist Campaign brought a series of purges underway, which got so out of control that Mao had to restrain his subordinates from excess killing. Perhaps Chinese conditions in 1957 were different enough from American conditions in 2020 that this was acceptable, or perhaps Mao the statesman should not be looked to for inspiration as much as Mao the general or Mao the revolutionary. It is beyond the purview of this article to answer that question. What is certain CounterPower draws the wrong lesson out of Mao's 1957 speech.

After quoting Mao, CounterPower moves on to claim that the Iberian Anarchist Federation (FAI) is in practice a party of autonomy working within the "area of the party" of Spain's National Confederation of Labour (CNT). Although the idea of "parties of autonomy" was not formulated until forty years after FAI's founding, there may be a kernel of truth to this claim. For example, if FAI formed a loose coalition with CNT organizers and worked with them on shared projects, this argument could make sense. The reality, however, is that FAI is essentially a hard-line anarchist faction within CNT that has consistently fought for political hegemony within the broader organization and even purged ideological rivals like Ángel Pestaña. Perhaps they were right to do so; it is outside the scope of this article to pass judgment on the internal political conflicts of the CNT.

Despite CounterPower's framing of the FAI as an independent anarcho-communist organization with an "organic link" to the CNT, they are an explicitly anarchist faction struggling to dominate the politics of the Spanish labor movement. They act as a pressure group within the confederation to make CNT adhere to what they perceive as purely anarchist theory and praxis without deviation. This is not a "symbiotic relationship," it is realpolitik under a black flag. Roberto Bordiga's window dressing cannot give us a clear understanding of Spanish labor politics; historians like José Peirats and Paul Preston would be better suited to aid this investigation.

In the updated version of their essay, CounterPower cites the Alabama chapter of CPUSA as a historical example that serves to "elucidate the role and function of a party of autonomy." This could not be further from the truth. Similar to the FAI, the party of autonomy model would not even be theorized until fifty years after the Alabama chapter's founding. CPUSA was a mass party with local chapters all over the country for at least the first half of the twentieth century. The Alabama chapter in particular was the result of discussions on "the Negro question" at the Sixth World Congress of the Communist International, after which the Central Committee of CPUSA chose Birmingham as a headquarters for its foothold in the South.[3] Its success in organizing rural and urban communities in the deep south of the 1920s is proof that the mass party model can be adapted to regional conditions and accountable to local rank and file members. Describing this centralized party model as a "party of autonomy" is categorically false.

Spontaneity vs. Base-Building

Now that the historical context of CounterPower's narrative has been clarified, we should examine the contradiction between their ideological commitment to spontaneity theory on the one hand, and their practical commitment to base-building on the other. Does the working class organically form explicitly political fighting organizations, or is a socialist intervention required for this to occur? This is a never-ending debate between Marxists and anarchists, despite the pile of evidence pointing to the latter. Some would argue that this debate is pointless at the present moment, and these differences are best put aside until the workers' movement has grown. We would reply: "First, comradely debate in no way hampers unity of action. We can continue base-building efforts while disagreeing on political questions, and it is only through debate that we might one day get on the same page. Second, simply by engaging in the act of base-building with us, you are agreeing with our point in practice while denying it in theory." How is this possible?

Our comrades in CounterPower are the perfect example. They admit the masses will not come to accept communist ideas on their own:

> From strike committees to workers' councils, tenant unions to neighborhood assemblies, the disparate forms of organized autonomy that arise in the midst of a protracted revolutionary struggle will not automatically fuse with communist politics to create a cohesive system of counterpower.

3 Allen, James S. *Organizing in the Depression South.* Minneapolis: MEP Publications, 2001.

Yet they don't address where these councils and unions come from. The reader gets the sense that these organizations simply pop up during times of crisis, as workers get frustrated with bourgeois politics and independently come to the conclusion that they need to organize against their boss or landlord. This may be true in a minority of cases, but most proletarian fighting organizations come from the same source as the Russian soviets: dedicated socialist base-builders. Who built Amazonians United? Who built Autonomous Tenant Union Network? Who built UE, ILWU, and the original CIO? In every case, the answer is: workers and intellectuals who read Marx, became socialists, and decided to organize.

Our responsibilities go beyond just founding these mass organizations; we have to compete for hegemony within them as well. If we neglect this crucial aspect of organizing due to a fetishization of the autonomy of the masses, reformists and even reactionaries will gladly fill the gap. In the case of something like workers' councils, we cannot have any illusions that they provide anything beyond a means of representation for political tendencies within the movement. This is precisely why the Bolsheviks competed so vigorously with the reformist Mensheviks and populist Social Revolutionaries for elected majorities in the soviets. In fact, the Bolsheviks only adopted their famous slogan "All Power to the Soviets" after they had secured elected majorities in them.[4] We only need to look at the difference between the Soviet Republics established in Russia and the brutally crushed Soviet Republic of Bavaria to understand the limitations of the model. Without influence from committed revolutionaries, mass organizations can be rallied to the banner of class-collaboration (as the Russian soviets were before Bolshevik intervention) or adventurism (as in the case of Bavaria).[5]

4 Rabinowitch, Alexander. *The Bolsheviks Come to Power.* Chicago: Haymarket Books, 1978.
5 Gallus, Alexander. "Insurrection and Defeat in Bavaria, 1918–19 (Part 2)." Cosmonaut Magazine, 22 October 2018, https://cosmonaut.blog/2018/10/22/insurrection-and-defeat-in-bavaria-1918-19-part-2/

CounterPower's overestimation of proletarian spontaneity has practical consequences for its members. In his recent article *In Defense of Revolution and the Insurrectionary Commune*, Atlee McFellin analyzed the November 2020 election and drew parallels between it and the situation which produced the Paris Commune. Fearing that elections may never take place again, McFellin argued against any participation in electoral efforts (including, but not limited to the creation of a political party independent from the Democrats). What was proposed instead? "Self-defense forces, solidarity kitchens, and everything else that is required to repel fascist assaults." In other words, anything but a class-independent party capable of coordinating the struggle for socialism across different political, economic, and social fronts. Rather than face the reality of the radical left's current irrelevance in national politics and the labor movement, and chart a course to resolve this, comrade McFellin called for the construction of insurrectionary communes as a response to the consolidation of ruling class interests under Joe Biden. Whether the working class has the spontaneous energy necessary for this task remains to be seen; if it does, we would be ill-advised to hold our breath in anticipation but should wince at the inevitable brutal consequences if such adventurism bears fruit.

While in theory, CounterPower glosses over the role of communists in building workers' organizations, in practice they are engaged in *precisely this work*. Rather than relying on the spontaneous initiative of the masses, they actively build tenant and labor unions, political education circles, and other necessary vehicles of class struggle. In fact, they do it remarkably well. This is what makes the claim that communists must "fuse with grassroots organizations" after they appear rather than actively building them in the first place so bizarre. Ultimately, our task as communists is to build mass organizations of class struggle, and then rally the most active participants within them to a mass communist party. By uniting in one party, we can direct the efforts of thousands of organizers according to a commonly agreed upon plan, which is an absolute necessity for the workers' movement to grow.

The Role of Cadre

The discussion of cadre organizers is given new attention in CounterPower's update to their original essay. It mostly focuses on the role these committed party members play in shaping revolutionary strategy and connecting it to active proletarian struggles. As seen in my Cosmonaut article *Revolutionary Discipline and Sobriety*, those of us who favor the mass party model are in complete agreement with CounterPower on the importance of cadre:

> Any collective project, whether a revolutionary labor union or a church's food pantry, will expect a higher degree of involvement from its core organizers than from its regular members. Not everyone has the time or the technical skills needed to bottom-line such endeavors, and those who do have a responsibility to step up to the plate. These small groups, or cadre, are the powerhouse of the class. Taking direction from the masses they live and labor with, cadre members should focus their lives on facilitating the self-emancipation of the proletariat.

CounterPower rightly points out that these dedicated full-timers are a prerequisite for the development of robust internal political education, external agitation, and consistent recruitment to mass work projects. Key to the every-day functioning of these cadre groups is the organizational center to which they are accountable (and preferably subject to democratic discipline by the whole membership of the organization). While the mass party shares the party of autonomy's commitment to a common political platform and program, the main difference between the two models is one of scope. Whereas the "area of the party" is composed of diffuse autonomous organizations with separate and often contradictory programs, the local chapters of the mass party work together on a common, democratically agreed-upon plan. As the experience of the Alabama chapter of CPUSA shows, this does not mean the plan cannot be adapted to meet local concerns.

In fact, the mass party model historically proves more capable of achieving its aims than any other method of party organization, whether it is compared to the bourgeois fund-raising parties that dominate US politics or the Italian autonomist model revived by CounterPower. This will be elaborated below in our examination of the Autonomia Operaia movement. For now, suffice it to say that while we agree with our autonomist comrades on the importance of cadre, the mass party model is best suited to coordinate their efforts.

Precision of Terms

Further complicating the problems of CounterPower's revolutionary strategy is an incoherent collection of opaque and often contradictory terms. Few throughout history have tried to synthesize the theories of the Bolsheviks, Rosa Luxemburg, Bordiga, and Malatesta, mostly because it makes no sense to do so. This blend of anarchist shibboleths (affinity groups, autonomy fetishism, Bookchin references) and communist vocabulary (party cadre, collective discipline, professional revolutionaries) is neither an oversight nor the product of genuine cross-ideological left unity. CounterPower is a Marxist organization with a niche ideology informed mainly by the experience of the Italian Autonomia Operaia movement. The fact that they mask this behind an appeal to every possible leftist tendency is frankly dishonest, and makes their writing difficult to follow. Since all these ideas have been presented to us as complementary and harmonious, we must investigate the contradictions between them in order to get a clearer picture.

First, we should consider their framing of the ideas of Rosa Luxemburg:

In contrast to a bourgeois party, Rosa Luxemburg identified that a revolutionary party of autonomy 'is not a party that wants to rise to power over the mass of workers or through them.' Rather, it 'is only the most conscious, purposeful part of the proletariat, which points the entire broad mass of the working class toward its historical tasks at every step.'

The primary issue with this framing is that Rosa Luxemburg did not write or speak about "a revolutionary party of autonomy" at any point in her political career. She was a member of the Social Democratic Party of Germany (SPD) for most of her life before its left-wing split into the USPD and then Spartacist League (later renamed the Communist Party of Germany, or KPD). Both organizations were mass parties who explicitly intended to lead the working class to overthrow the existing political order and form a new proletarian government in Germany, headed by elected party officials. Her point about the party being an instrument that puts the working class in power was perfectly in line with the existing Marxist orthodoxy. Consider this quote from the SPD's leading theorist Karl Kautsky for comparison:

> The socialists no longer have the task of freely inventing a new society but rather uncovering its elements in existing society. No more do they have to bring salvation from its misery to the proletariat from above, but rather they have to support its class struggle through increasing its insight and promoting its economic and political organizations and in so doing bring about as quickly as possible the day when the proletariat will be able to save itself. The task of Social Democracy is to make the class struggle of the proletariat aware of its aim and capable of choosing the best means to attain this aim.[6]

Luxemburg and Kautsky both demonstrate the function of the mass party: cohering the most militant and forward-thinking section of the working class into one organization and giving it the tools to win political power. If the party is not "outside or

---

6 Lih, 2008.

above the revolutionary process," as CounterPower puts it, then it is coming to power through class leadership. "Providing the boldest elements in decision-making organs" is just a milder way of phrasing "winning political hegemony in the movement." While it is right to be skeptical of potential opportunists and wary of inadvertently creating an unaccountable bureaucracy, CounterPower overcorrects by trying to avoid the question of leadership altogether. No amount of out-of-context quotes from historical revolutionaries can paper over that deficiency.

After painting an anarchist portrait of Rosa Luxemburg, CounterPower then calls upon the theoretical authority of actual anarchist Errico Malatesta:

> We anarchists can all say that we are of the same party, if by the word 'party' we mean all who are on the same side, that is, who share the same general aspirations and who, in one way or another, struggle for the same ends against common adversaries and enemies. But this does not mean it is possible — or even desirable — for all of us to be gathered into one specific association. There are too many differences of environment and conditions of struggle; too many possible ways of action to choose among, and also too many differences of temperament and personal incompatibilities for a General Union, if taken seriously, not to become, instead of a means for coordinating and reviewing the efforts of all, an obstacle to individual activity and perhaps also a cause of more bitter internal strife.[7]

This is a markedly different approach to organization from the mass party model of Kautsky, Luxemburg, Lenin, et al. It is certainly more in line with the autonomists' "area of the party" theory, but are the assumptions it is based on sound? The experience of the Bolshevik party securing state power and defending the proletariat from white terror, the Communist Party of Vietnam's triumph over colonialism, the continued resistance to neoliberal imperialism in Cuba, and other achievements of

7 Malatesta, Errico. "A Project of Anarchist Organisation." Marxists Internet Archive, https://www.marxists.org/archive/malatesta/1927/10/project.htm.

the mass party model seem to indicate otherwise. Petty personal disputes and geographic distance are no excuse to abandon unified efforts to build socialism. If we take a scientific approach and compare the results of party-building trials throughout history to the results of those like Malatesta who deny the party's role, the pattern is self-evident.

Lessons of History

CounterPower's essay does an excellent job of considering the experiences of a vast number of different historical communist groups. Unfortunately, they do so without an ounce of reflection or criticism. They ask us to look at rival groups with opposing political strategies and conclude that both were right, regardless of whether either group actually achieved its aims. They mention the experience of many parties and movements — the KAPD in Germany, Autonomia Operaia in Italy, the MIR in Chile, the FMLN-FDR in El Salvador, the URNG in Guatemala, the HBDH in Turkey and Kurdistan, and more. We're given the impression that each of these groups consciously agreed with the autonomists' many parties model, and that each of these groups were successful enough to teach us mainly positive lessons to emulate. Upon closer inspection, it turns out this is not at all the case. For the sake of brevity, we will look at three examples.

Let us begin with the Communist Workers' Party of Germany (KAPD). This party could be accurately described as a sect based on its low membership, extreme sectarianism, and history of splits. Its complicated lineage is as follows — its members began in the SPD, then split into the ISD, which then joined the USPD, which then split into the KPD, and then finally split from there into the left-communist KAPD. It functionally existed for about two years before splitting again into separate factions. It was quite literally a split of a split of a split that ended up splitting. It had around 43,000 members at its height in 1921, which was minuscule compared to the hundreds of thousands of workers in the mass parties (and that number immediately declined after the factional split in 1922).

The roots of the KAPD's separation from the KPD lie in the events of the Ruhr Uprising. In 1920, a right-wing coalition of military officers and monarchists attempted to overthrow the bourgeois-democratic government of Germany. In response, the government called for a general strike, which the workers' parties heeded. In the Ruhr valley, these parties took the strike a step further by forming Red Army units and engaging right-wing forces in open combat. However, these socialist militias were divided between three different parties and could not coordinate their efforts as well as their enemies who had the benefit of a clear leadership structure. The uprising was ultimately crushed when the bourgeois government made a deal with the right-wing putsch leaders and sent their forces to slaughter the workers of the Ruhr.

What lessons did the left-communists learn from this? From their perspective, KPD leaders had given up on the struggle by agreeing to disband Red Army units after the fighting looked to be in the enemy's favor. Because of this, a split was necessary so the workers could be led by the true communist militants that would see things through to the end. In other words, the already divided proletariat needed a fourth party to further complicate the coordination of future actions. Two years later, this fourth party would then split into two factions. Lenin had this to say about the KAPD:

> Let the 'Lefts' put themselves to a practical test on a national and international scale. Let them try to prepare for (and then implement) the dictatorship of the proletariat, without a rigorously centralised party with iron discipline, without the ability to become masters of every sphere, every branch, and every variety of political and cultural work. Practical experience will soon teach them.[8]

8 Lenin, V. I. "Left Wing-Communism: An Infantile Disorder," marxist.org, 1920. https://www.marxists.org/archive/lenin/works/1920/lwc/appendix.htm

Unfortunately, Lenin was overly optimistic. Rather than having time to learn from their mistakes, the divided forces of the working class were brutally crushed by the united forces of the right. The Nazis rose to power, and fascism reigned until the Soviets took Berlin in 1945. This does not mean there is nothing we can learn from the KAPD — quite the opposite is true. There may be some diamonds in the rough, but most of the lessons we can learn from the left-communists of Germany are examples of what not to do. Fortunately, in the updated version of their essay, CounterPower scrubbed any mention of the KAPD. Whether this was due to a genuine reassessment of their example or simple editorial limitations, the new version is much stronger without the ill-fated German sectarians.

Despite their positive appraisal of the KAPD, CounterPower is not a left-communist sect. They are autonomists, and in order to understand their answer to the party question we must take stock of their movement forebears. Autonomia Operaia was a workers' movement in Italy during the period known as the "Years of Lead." This period lasted from the late 1960s to the late 1980s, and was marked by violent clashes between right and left-wing paramilitary forces. It is worth noting that much of this violence was either planned, supplied, or encouraged by the CIA and its "Operation Gladio," although that is not relevant to our discussion here. Autonomia Operaia was mainly active from '76 to '78, and was made up of many smaller socialist groups including Potere Operaio, Gruppo Gramsci, and Lotta Continua. Each group was strongly opposed to unifying into one party, preferring instead to maintain their autonomy and pursue different tactics to work towards their shared goal of social revolution.

In the end, this worked out in much the same way as it did for the sectarians in Germany decades earlier. Thousands of militants were arrested, hundreds fled the country, many were killed, and most of those who remained dissolved into terrorist groups like the Red Brigades and parliamentary parties like Democrazia

Proletaria. Neither the autonomist terrorists nor the autonomist politicians were able to move beyond the failures of the earlier autonomist movement. In retrospect, the autonomists ended up replicating the sect form (albeit with some anarchist-influenced language) and suffered the familiar consequences of this organizing technique. It is worth noting that after misappropriating numerous mass parties (the Alabama chapter of CPUSA, the Bolsheviks, Rosa Luxemburg's KPD) as successful examples of the "parties of autonomy" model, CounterPower leaves out any mention of Autonomia Operaia in the updated version of its essay. This is somewhat understandable as the movement collapsed within two years and failed to achieve its aims, but it is still dishonest. If failures are glossed over rather than rigorously examined, we are doomed to walk blindly into past mistakes. In this regard, CounterPower's update to their essay does more to obfuscate the party question than answer it.

That said, Autonomia Operaia activists had valid criticisms of the Communist Party of Italy and could have created an alternative to lead the proletariat to victory. This is the positive lesson we can learn from them: when the "official" communist party of the nation abandons its principles, it can sometimes be worthwhile to build an alternative organization. However, they chose instead to create a loose collective of semi-aligned communist clusters which failed to coordinate their actions and create meaningful change. Had they taken on the arduous task of debating long-term strategy and forging programmatic unity, things may have turned out differently. This is the primary lesson we should learn from the Italian autonomists: a proletarian victory requires structure, democratic discipline, and unity of action.

Although not directly influenced by Autonomia's answer to the party question, the FMLN-FDR of El Salvador could be theorized as an example of an "area of the party." As Counter-Power pointed out in their essay, this network was composed of five revolutionary parties and a number of mass organizations and civil society institutions who worked together in loose co-operation towards revolution. It ultimately failed, and Counter-Power makes two interesting claims about its dissolution: that the failure was due primarily to the popular front reformism of the PCS (one of the five member parties) and that its downfall does not tarnish its status as a positive example of the area of the party in action. These claims do not fare well under the spotlight of historical scrutiny, particularly when shined on the brutal internecine violence that destroyed any semblance of unity within the movement by 1983.

CounterPower's assessment of the FMLN identifies the PCS (Communist Party of El Salvador) as the weakest link in the chain, and the FPL (Farabundo Martí Liberation People's Forces) as the strongest. In many ways, this is true, as the popular front strategy of the official communist parties has consistently ended in disaster the world over and the FPL was the most powerful and trusted party in El Salvador for a time. However, this is not the whole picture. Genuine political disagreements were often buried or papered over to maintain an artificial unity, and the ensuing tension was bound to boil over. While our autonomist comrades say the FMLN established a harmonious "mechanism of communication, coordination, and cooperation among the various politico-military organizations," the reality is far grimmer. In its disagreement with other parties advocating negotiations with the Salvadoran government, the FPL resorted to gruesome assassinations to enforce its will on the rest of the FMLN. In April of 1983, FPL cadre Rogelio Bazzaglia murdered pro-negotiation leader Ana Maria with an ice pick, stabbing her 83 times. Although there was an attempt to blame the CIA or another party within FMLN, when presented concrete evidence of Bazzaglia's guilt, FPL leader Salvador Cayetano Carpio promptly wrote a suicide note and shot himself in the head. With its most trusted leaders either disgraced, dead, or both, the FMLN lost steam after many members left the network in disgust. Along with this exodus of valuable cadre went all the legitimacy of the anti-negotiation faction, and so by 1989 even successful military offensives could do nothing more than bring the Salvadoran government to the negotiation table.[9] The revolutionary potential of the FMLN died with Ana Maria, and her murder demonstrates how the "area of the party" approach only ends up recreating the problems of the sect form.

The Marxist Center

The US communist movement is essentially home to three different camps regarding the party question. Those who wish to see the movement divided into bureaucratic sects (with the belief that their particular sect is the One True Party) are on the right. Those who wish to see the movement divided into loosely aligned autonomist sects (with the beliefs outlined in Counter-Power's writing) are on the left. Those of us in the center are advocating a qualitative break with the sect form: the foundation of a mass party of organizers. This idea is often associated with a number of inaccurate claims — for instance, we are frequently lumped in with those who wish to replicate the worst aspects of the DSA model, where anyone can join the organization at any time for any reason without even committing to Marxist politics. We are also often accused of wanting to create a dogmatic bureaucracy of staunch Marxist-Leninists who will run the party as they see fit without input from membership. Neither of these claims are true.

In fact, what we desire is a party made and run by the masses themselves. Years of labor-intensive organizing will be necessary to make this happen, as the masses cannot be reached and welcomed into the socialist movement any other way. Tenant and workplace unions, unemployed councils, harm reduction

9 Jayatilleka, Dayan. *Fidel's Ethics of Violence: The Moral Dimension of the Political Thought of Fidel Castro*. London: Pluto Press, 2007.

efforts, solidarity networks, and other forms of "mass organizations" (in addition to independent electoral efforts) must be formed and rallied around a common political pole. In order for this pole to exist in the first place, the organizers engaged in mass work must debate and discuss until they articulate and agree on a comprehensive political program. In order for these debates and discussions to produce a clear program, the organizers have to see themselves as part of a common organization aimed at a shared goal. When each of these elements fall into place, something completely unique to the US left will be born: a mass party committed to praxis, programmatic unity, and democratic discipline.

By praxis, we understand a long-term commitment to building, growing, and maintaining the kinds of mass organizations detailed above. By programmatic unity, we mean collective acceptance of a comprehensive set of answers to long-term strategic questions, forged in an extended process of comradely debate and compromise. Ideally, this would take the form of a minimum-maximum program like those laid out and critiqued by Marx, Engels, and others in the first two Internationals.[10] The minimum demands are structural reforms that communicate to the working class exactly how our efforts will improve their lives and empower them at the political level. Demands like guaranteed healthcare and housing, eliminating the Electoral College, Senate, and Supreme Court, disbanding the police and forming workers' militias, ensuring union representation, and more would bring supporters into the fold and give us access to valuable comrades and organizers. They are chosen in such a way that when every demand is met, the proletariat has seized political power from the bourgeoisie and becomes the governing class of society.

10 McQueeney, Parker. "Why Have a Political Program?" *Cosmonaut Magazine*, September 3, 2018. https://cosmonaut.blog/2018/09/03/why-have-a-political-program/.

With this done, the new workers' government can focus on fulfilling the maximum demands, epitomized as communism, which would eradicate the last vestiges of capitalism and transition to a socialist mode of production. Establishing unity on long-term questions of strategy is far superior to enforcing a "party-line" on day-to-day issues and theoretical minutiae. It allows us to collaborate and exert the greatest possible combined strength of the working class in its diverse struggles without splitting over short-term tactical disagreements like "should we partner with this NGO on this tenant organizing project?" or subcultural arguments like "who was in the wrong at Kronstadt?" It also does not require agreement on "tendency" labels (such as Marxist-Leninist, anarchist, left-communist, etc). As our organizations grow, the need for a commonly accepted program will only increase. Finally, by democratic discipline, we refer to the old axiom "diversity of opinion, unity of action."

These three principles are absolutely essential for the functioning of an effective and battle-ready proletarian party. As we have seen, the organizational forms of sectarians and autonomists (like the KAPD and Autonomia Operaia respectively) crumble under pressure whereas mass parties regularly weather brutal repression. No better example of this can be found in US history than that of the Alabama chapter of the CPUSA:

> The fact is, the CP and its auxiliaries in Alabama did have a considerable following, some of whom devoured Marxist literature and dreamed of a socialist world. But to be a Communist, an ILD member, or an SCU militant was to face the possibility of imprisonment, beatings, kidnapping, and even death. And yet the Party survived, and at times thrived, in this thoroughly racist, racially divided, and repressive social world.[11]

While other cases of this phenomenon (the Russian Communist Party, the Chinese Communist Party, and others) have

11 Kelley, Robin D.G. *Hammer and Hoe: Alabama Communists During the Great Depression.* Chapel Hill: University of North Carolina Press, 1990.

274

been historically prone to corruption, preventative measures can be taken to ensure the party retains its mass character even after smashing the state and beginning socialist reconstruction. The most immediate step in this process is the collaborative drafting of and universal agreement on a party-wide Code of Conduct. This will facilitate the development of a comradely culture that balances rigorous critique and debate with an environment of pluralism and interpersonal care. In addition to understanding how to have a one-on-one organizing conversation, we should also strive to be well-versed in skills like listening, openly sharing feelings, assuming good faith in arguments, making sincere apologies, and offering support to comrades struggling with personal issues. None of these can be learned by accident in the alienated social spaces created by capitalism, so we must make a deliberate effort to establish these norms in our organization.

Another would be taking seriously the moral dimensions of Fidelismo's contribution to Marxism. In stark contrast with both Stalin's iron fist and Allende's naive pacifism, Fidel Castro's leadership of the Cuban revolution combined violent insurrection against the state with peaceful political maneuvering in the revolutionary movement. Over the course of protracted struggle on both fronts, the July 26th Movement was able to defeat the state militarily and construct a democratic mandate for political hegemony. Because Fidel and his comrades took the ethical implications of revolutionary struggle seriously, they were able to achieve victory without recourse to war crimes against the enemy or lethal violence against political competitors within the movement.[12] This commitment to moral conduct during violent struggle did not stop them from winning the war. In fact, it allowed them to win the peace. This strategy allowed Cuba to begin building socialism after national liberation without the deadly internecine conflicts that plagued other revolutionary movements (notably including the FMLN). It is crucial that we

12 Jayatilleka, 2007.

embrace this legacy by constructing an ethic of revolution for our time. More steps beyond these will of course be necessary, and their exact nature will become clear as we work towards the realization of a comradely culture together.

Perhaps the strongest indicator of the need for a mass party is the fact that the most advanced sections of the US labor movement are already calling for the establishment of a workers' party. In its recent pamphlet *Them and Us Unionism*, United Electrical, Radio and Machine Workers of America (UE) wrote:

> Throughout our history, UE has held that workers need our own political party. In the 1990s, UE worked with a number of other unions to found the Labor Party, under the slogan 'The Bosses Have Two Parties, We Need One of Our Own.' Although the Labor Party experiment was ultimately unsuccessful, UE members and locals have been active in numerous other efforts to promote independent, pro-worker alternatives to the two major parties.[13]

Other labor unions like ILWU and the Teamsters have produced leading organizers who share UE's commitment to independent worker politics. People like Clarence Thomas, who helped organize the Juneteenth port shutdown on the West Coast earlier this year in solidarity with the George Floyd uprising, Chris Silvera, who chairs the National Black Caucus in the Teamsters, and many more can be found among them. These influential voices of the labor movement have united in Labor and Community for an Independent Party, stating:

> We must build democratically run coalitions that bring together the stakeholders in labor and the communities of the oppressed, so that they have a decisive say in formulating their demands and mapping out a strategy. Most important, we need to put an end to the monopoly of political power by the Democrats and Republicans. The labor movement and the leaders of the Latino and Black struggles need to break with their reliance on the Democratic Party and build their own mass-based independent working-class political party.

13 United Electrical, Radio and Machine Workers of America. *Them and Us Unionism*. Pittsburgh. 2020.https://www.ueunion.org/ThemAndUs/

While it is certainly possible that these efforts could lead to the establishment of a reformist labor party, it is precisely this possibility that behooves us to get involved. Any union that recognizes the need for independent proletarian political action outside the shop floor can be considered "advanced" compared to business unions aligned with the Democratic Party, and relationships with them should be built as part of a communist intervention in the labor movement. As Marxists, we have a duty not only to organize our class but to bring theoretical clarity to its most active champions. If we continue building strong proletarian fighting organizations and elaborate our vision in a comprehensive program, we will be positioned to guide labor and community leaders of all stripes to the creation of a truly communist political party.

Ultimately, the disparate sects within Marxist Center and the local chapters of the DSA must form tighter bonds and consider internal reforms that would allow us to build the party our class requires. In doing so, we should seek to unite as many far-flung collectives and mass work projects as we can in order to become a true threat to bourgeois hegemony. While staying divided in a loose federation may seem like a viable model to some, history shows that it is not. The autonomists and anarchists in our ranks are dedicated organizers doing valuable work, and we should be grateful for that. However, we would be doing ourselves and them a disservice if we did not offer a comradely critique of their organizational models.

Communists will always find strength in unity.

SOCIALISM WITH AMERICAN CHARACTERISTICS

Luke Pickrell and Myra Janis
March 1, 2023

Luke Pickrell and Myra Janis critique the 2019 updated party program of the Communist Party, USA, arguing that the CPUSA's continued commitment to the Popular Front produces an unwieldy document incapable of charting a strategic path forward for socialists.

The Communist Party of the United States (CPUSA) celebrated the 100th anniversary of its founding in 2019 and signs would appear to augur well for the organization in the coming years. Recently, the party discussed running candidates for office.[1] Membership numbers are rising,[2] and the party credits itself and its allies for the "broad front" that defeated Donald Trump in the 2020 presidential election.[3] Having abandoned the Democratic Socialists of America, an orga-

---

1 Communist Party USA. "It's Time to Run Candidates: A Call for Discussion and Action." CPUSA. April 9, 2021. https://www.cpusa.org/article/its-time-to-run-candidates-a-call-for-discussion-and-action/

2 Sims, Joe. "Democracy Cannot Be Sacrificed for the Profits of the 1%." CPUSA. February 25, 2022. https://www.cpusa.org/article/democracy-cannot-be-sacrificed-for-the-profits-of-the-1/.

3 Communist Party USA Political Action Commision. "Political Action Commision's Goals for 2023." CPUSA. April 7, 2023. https://www.cpusa.org/article/political-action-commissions-goals-for-2023/

nization in a crisis of political direction, and gazed upon the desolate expanse that is revolutionary socialism in the United States, some comrades have turned away from the red rose toward the tried and true hammer, sickle, and gear. Unfortunately, these comrades will not have escaped the politics of class collaborationism by fleeing DSA and may find themselves in even hotter water.

The CPUSA marked its centenary with an updated version of the party platform: "The Road to Socialism USA."[4] Reading through the document is daunting. An astounding 61-pages long, it meanders across ten disorganized primary sections and dozens of subsections. Boundaries are porous: the introduction contains a conclusion, ideas repeat, and lists of occasionally intriguing demands are relegated to sidebars. Friedrich Engels's critique of the German Social Democratic Party's Erfurt Programme — "The fear that a short, pointed exposition would not be intelligible enough, has caused explanations to be added, which make it verbose and drawn out"[5] — applies just as accurately to the CPUSA. These comrades, hoping to attract as large an audience as possible, have thrown everything but the kitchen sink toward the proverbial wall in a desperate attempt to make something stick. Asked to accept the program, one struggles for solid footing. How can one determine agreement with such an incomprehensible document?

But determination brings rewards. Cutting through girth and clearing away the tired abstractions ("injustice," "a better world," "the 1%," "epic struggles," "the greed of the few," "fascism")[6] reveals two fundamental flaws: a commitment to the decades-old People's Front policy of alliances with anything left of the "ex-

---

4 CPUSA Party Program, https://cpusa.org/party_info/party-program/.

5 Engels, Friedrich. "A Critique of the Draft Social Democratic Program of 1891." marxist.org. June 18, 1891. https://marxists.architexturez.net/archive/marx/works/1891/06/29.htm.

6 CPUSA Party Program p. 11, 2, 60, 1, 33 https://cpusa.org/party_info/party-program/

treme right" and dedication to the Constitution and the parameters of the capitalist state. In other words, socialism with American characteristics.[7] What follows is an elaboration on these two flaws. While the comrades in the CPUSA may be motivated by a genuine desire to fight for the interests of the working class, their program provides no path forward and opens the door to opportunistic zigzags and the internal rule of bureaucrats.

Continuing the People's Front

This is far from an exhaustive chronicle of the ups and downs of the Communist Party (a job that E. J. Hobsbawm described as presenting unique difficulties).[8] Rather, reading the CPUSA program allows one to reflect on the rise and fall of American Communism and the world socialist movement more generally. At its height, the Party contributed several victories to the class struggle in the United States. It carried out exceptional work in organizing the unemployed during the Great Depression and defended the Scottsboro Boys when the NAACP refused.[9] The

---

7 Ibid. p. 3

8 E. J. Hobsbawm, *Revolutionaries*, p. 6: "The problem of those who write the history of communist parties is therefore unusually difficult. They must recapture the unique and, among secular movements, unprecedented temper of bolshevism, equally remote from the liberalism of most historians and the permissive and self-indulgent activism of most contemporary ultras. There is no understanding it without a grasp of that sense of total devotion which made the party in Auschwitz make its members pay their dues in cigarettes (inconceivably precious and almost impossible to obtain in an extermination camp), which made the cadres accept the order not merely to kill Germans in occupied Paris, but first to acquire, individually, the arms to do so, and which made it virtually unthinkable for them to refuse to return to Moscow even to certain imprisonment or death. There is no understanding either the achievements or the perversions of bolshevism without this, and both have been monumental; and certainly no understanding of the extraordinary success of communism as a system of education for political work."

9 North, Irene. "Communist Party Theory and Practice Among the Unemployed, 1930-38." marxist.org. March 1981 https://www.marxists.org/history/erol/periodicals/theoretical-review/north.html

Party's victories in states such as Alabama and New York are well-documented.[10]

The United Front strategy — how the party relates to the political institutions of the capitalist state to win members and strengthen the fighting power of the working class — began during a period of global defeat for communism.[11] Having emerged victorious from the Russian Civil War, the newly formed Third International expected a quick succession of civil wars and Communist victories across Europe. But defeats in Germany, Poland, and Hungary augured ill. The working masses had not rallied behind the banner of the Communist Parties, and the Bolsheviks were left isolated in Russia. After fending off his ultra-left detractors, Lenin oversaw the entry of the Communist Parties into alliances with non-Communist working class political forces (including Social Democratic parties) under the explicit condition of retaining organizational independence and freedom to criticize the reformist leadership. In theory, the United Front was sound.

Principled alliances with reformist parties were scrapped when Stalin came to power. The Communists had zigged right, only to zag left during the Third Period of 1928 to 1933. The Peoples' Front (America's version of the Popular Front) began a final lurch back to the right in 1935 in the context of impending war and the rise of German Nazism. Ben Rose described the People's Front as a "gradual shift towards a search for alliances and influence with the leadership of organizations believed to be instrumental in fighting domestic and international fascism, as well as those capable of pressuring the Roosevelt administra-

---

10 Kelley, Robin G.D. *Hammer and Hoe: Alabama Communists during the Great Depression*. Chapel Hill: The University of North Carolina Press, 2015; Naison, Mark D. *Communists in Harlem During the Depression*. Urbana: University of Illinois Press, 1983.

11 For a more in-depth discussion on the united front, see: Macnair, Mike. *Revolutionary Strategy*, London: November Publishing, 2009. Chapter 6. http://ouleft.org/wp-content/uploads/Macnair-Revolutionary-Strategy.pdf.

tion."[12] Tactical alliances with a section of the capitalist class subordinated working class independence to the goals of capitalists. The goal of socialism in America was abandoned, and in 1937 the Party dropped its slogan, "Toward a Soviet America." The day-to-day practice of fighting for reforms submerged the goal of a classless society, and socialism with American characteristics — socialism, after all, being just as American as baseball and apple pie — became the norm. As Mike Macnair explains:

'Official communist' and Maoist parties committed themselves to rejection of the most elementary Marxist principle — the independent political organization and representation of the working class — in favor of 'democratic' coalitions which repeat the projects Marx and Engels fought against — or, worse, in favor of coalitions for 'national independence,' which subordinate the working class to the party of order.[13]

The call for a People's Front continues today. In the name of fighting the extreme right — a nefarious entity that is "inadequate and incompetent" and "backward" one moment, and "fascist" the next — the program urges unity with all progressive forces in "defeating the extreme right's implicit and explicit drive toward fascism."[14] Divisions within the capitalist class "contain opportunities for working-class and progressive forces. On some issues, the more moderate, more realistic sections of the capitalist class and their political operatives move parallel to the people's movements, as important though partial and temporary allies. They can be pressured to adopt a more progressive stance by the strength of the people's movements and mass sentiment."[15]

12 Rose, Ben. "The Communist Party and the CIO." marxist.org. June 1981. https://www.marxists.org/history/erol/ncm-7/rose-cio.htm#fw01.
13 Macnair, Mike. "Propaganda and agitation." Weekly Worker. April 27, 2011. https://weeklyworker.co.uk/worker/863/propaganda-and-agitation/.
14 CPUSA Party Program p. 21, 3, 4, 41 https://cpusa.org/party_info/party-program/
15 Ibid. p. 41.

The program encourages alliances with the Democratic Party because it is "not identical" with the Republican Party.[16] The Democratic Party's history — the "main vehicle used by African American and Latino communities to gain representation, as well as the main mechanism used to elect labor, progressive, and even Left activists to public office..."[17] — supposedly demonstrates differences with its elephant brother. Furthermore, alleged rifts within the Party can be used to workers' advantage. One reads: "[T]here exists an internal struggle within the Democratic Party among centrist forces who collaborate with the right wing, centrist forces opposed to the right wing, and more progressive, even socialist, trends."[18] Any desire to build a mass party must bow to the existing facts of the power of the capitalist class and the Constitutional regime.

With Friends Like These...

Calls for an alliance with the Democratic Party and the NGO complex against the far right are equivalent to asking the fox to guard the hen house: the fox eats its plump ward every time. Such proposals are the equivalent of trusting the bourgeoisie of the French Third Republic to eradicate the threat of a clerical-monarchical Thermidorian reaction. During the Third Republic, the proletariat was lured away from independent politics by liberals who incessantly hollered about a grave threat to the Republic as justification for uniting under one banner. With danger knocking at the door, this was no time to wage the class struggle. Karl Kautsky explained the reality behind the facade: "...the bourgeois liberal politicians have every interest in the struggle against the Church, but by no means in triumphing over it. They can only count on an alliance of the proletariat as

16 Ibid.
17 Ibid.
18 Ibid.

long as this struggle continues."[19] Ultimately, a definitive victory is illusory. The imperative to unite against a bigger-bad never ends. How ironic that the Communist Party now advocates politics far to the right of those espoused by Second International Marxism's famous pope-turned-renegade during his period as a revolutionary thinker.

The Democratic Party is more concerned with maintaining the rule of law than prosecuting an effective campaign against an increasingly right-wing and authoritarian Republican Party and its hangers-on. See, for example, their impotent attempt to understand and resolve the events of January 6th, 2022, compared to their focus on the chauvinistic conspiracy theory of Russiagate. The state's repressive apparatus is far more concerned with countering perceived threats from the left than from the right. The bourgeois state fundamentally cannot grapple with the real social issues (poverty and economic precarity, first and foremost) upon which the seeds of far-right extremism germinate. Without class independence, the proletariat stays moored to the dock of bourgeois politics. Worse, if the working class does not create independent organizations of political power, it will be unable to stop a real fascist threat. One finds a terrifying historical specter in Chile during the Allende period when the Popular Unity government disarmed its supporters in the face of an impending coup. When the time came, the working class could not defend itself or the Allende government from Pinochet's forces.

The CPUSA program describes the all-people's-front as an "essential strategy for this historical period, not just a temporary tactic."[20] Socialism is thus always something for the distant future, a goal to pursue once the present task is complete. Yet, like Sisyphus and his boulder, the task is never concluded. An all-

---

19 For Karl Kautsky's description of the various tricks used against the working class in the French Third Republic, see: Kautsky, Karl. "The Republican and Social Democracy in France," 1905.

20 CPUSA Party Program p. 35 https://cpusa.org/party_info/party-program/

people's-front will not permanently defeat the far right. Only a socialist republic can eliminate the excrement produced by capitalism in decline, and only a socialist political party can make a new republic a reality.

Bill of Rights Socialism and Constitutional Cultism

The Constitution is an eminently undemocratic document that stands in the way of working-class political rule. It creates an entire "political playing field" that sucks in well-intentioned reformers and keeps them busy fiddling over minutia.[21] The Constitution cannot be ignored or corralled through tricks or slights of hand. Yet, the CPUSA program ducks the issue by proposing a "Peoples' Bill of Rights" and explaining that "Once the power of the corporations is broken, the vast majority of the country can use the Constitution, the Bill of Rights, a Socialist Bill of Rights, and local governments to build real democracy and equality."[22] The Party's belief that a "fundamentally new economic system" can be built on the existing Constitution is explicit; it is a hallowed document equivalent to the sacred tablets of the Ten Commandments. This devotion is apparent when they describe a speculative people's Bill of Rights as "guaranteed" upon being "enshrined" in the Constitution.[23]

The insistence on maintaining the existing state apparatus is an abdication of the necessity of the dictatorship of the proletariat. Once in power, the party must implement the minimum demands to upend and transform the existing state apparatus into a democratic republic — the state form of the dictatorship of the proletariat. From this position, the

---

21 Lazare, Daniel. "The US Constitution: Hiding in Plain Sight." Cosmonaut Magazine. September 29, 2020. https://cosmonautmag.com/2020/09/us-constitution-hiding-in-plain-sight/.
22 CPUSA Party Program p. 54 https://cpusa.org/party_info/party-program/
23 CPUSA Party Program p. 52 https://cpusa.org/party_info/party-program/

working class can *begin* the transition to communism. The CPUSA comrades are correct that the fullest expression of democracy is in the interests of the working class. Democracy is the light and air needed by the proletariat to wage an effective struggle.

However, the extension of democracy does not cease at the doors of the White House, the shrine of the Constitution, the halls of the Supreme Court, or the pentagonal grounds of the Department of Defense. The indirectly elected president holds an ever-increasing amount of power and directs the military of the world's foremost imperial power. The Constitution (designed to guard against change) enshrines the separation of powers to hedge against the boogeyman of popular will in the House of Representatives (the only body with a nominal claim to popular representation) and slows down the process of legislation by directly elected representatives. The Supreme Court is not elected by universal and direct suffrage and works primarily to defend the Constitution. The recent overturning of Roe v. Wade also led many people to question the Court's ability to take up lower court rulings. Finally, the Department of Defense provides the physical force necessary to safeguard the sanctity of private property and bourgeois law and order.

The CPUSA's loyalty to the Constitution leads them to abandon a revolutionary position. The demand for a Socialist Bill of Rights leaves the bourgeois state unscathed; in fact, it *strengthens* the state. So long as the existing constitutional order remains intact, demands for "liberty, and equality; free quality health care and education; living-wage jobs and decent housing; and a healthy environment" are just reforms. While the revolutionary party does include reforms as part of its demands, they exist as a means to create a democratic republic. A set of demands that leave the existing state intact serves only as a screen to hide bourgeois rule. The party plucks the fig leaf from absolutism only to become "oneself a screen for its nakedness."[24]

In trying to adapt Marxist-Leninism to the United States, the comrades have absorbed all the elements of the constitutional regime and dropped most of the Marxism they carried. What little remains lies mutilated beyond recognition. The program's assurance that "socialism in the United States will have distinctive characteristics because it will emerge from our unique political culture" is just another superficial justification for reformism.[25] Minimum demands must strengthen the working class while weakening the state. Such demands include a single legislative assembly elected by proportional representation; the abolition of the independent presidency and the Supreme Court's right of judicial review; the election of judges and other state officials; the expansion of jury trials and state-funded legal services; the unrestricted right of free speech; the abolition of copyright laws and monopolies of knowledge; and the abolition of police and standing army in favor of a people's militia characterized by universal training and service, with democratic rights for its members. The process could begin with organizing a nationwide election via direct, universal, and equal suffrage for an assembly tasked with writing a new Constitution for popular consideration rather than the radically minoritarian process enshrined in Article 5 of the existing Constitution.[26] Enacted in full, these demands smash the existing order and create a democratic republic.

24 Engels, Friedrich. "A Critique of the Draft Social Democratic Program of 1891." Marxist.org. June 18, 1891. https://marxists.architexturez.net/archive/marx/works/1891/06/29.htm.

25 CPUSA Party Program p. 53 https://cpusa.org/party_info/party-program/

26 For a detailed explanation of the logistics behind organizing a democratic vote for a new US Constitution, see: Grove, Ben. "Fight the Constitution! Demand a New Republic!" Cosmonaut Magazine. March 25, 2021. https://cosmonautmag.com/2021/03/fight-the-constitution-demand-a-new-republic/.

Monopolies and Stages

Like a Matryoshka doll that has gone west, the CPUSA program contains multiple programs corresponding to different stages on an imagined path to socialism. The first stage is the formation of a People's Front to defeat the extreme right. After eliminating the first threat, the People's Front will grow in strength, evolve into an anti-monopoly coalition, and turn its attention toward "the multinationals" (the nationalist assumption being that 'genuinely American' capitalists would join the fight). The defeat of the multinationals will signal the beginning of a new stage in which the anti-monopoly coalition will build proletarian consciousness and progress toward socialism. Multiple coalitions will merge with the Communist Party to create a force capable of pushing through the Socialist Bill of Rights. At some point, communism will emerge.

To the untrained eye, the discussion of monopolies is a bizarre aspect of an already strange program. Yet, references to the despotic power of monopolies — along with constant references to "the people" — have roots in older forms of American populism that pitted "the people" versus "the elites." The affinity towards populist rhetoric is explained by the reformist character of the CPUSA and its desire to create cross-class alliances in which, ultimately, workers' interests play second fiddle. In addition, the program's conception of revolution beginning only after defeating a series of foes follows the stagist theory of history often, though incorrectly, attributed to orthodox Marxism.[27] In decades past, the stagist model was used to justify the fundamental impossibility of communism in one country. Today, it appears in the CPUSA's program as a justification for continued reformism.

27 Conrad, Jack. "Memory Wars." Weekly Worker. March 11, 2023. https://weeklyworker.co.uk/worker/1417/memory-wars/#fnref5.

Road to Nowhere

The Communist Party's program contains noble sentiments. We do not doubt these comrades' desire to realize a "system in which working-class people control their own lives and destinies."[28] Socialism is the fullest extension of democracy. The social republic overcomes the division between social and political existence. The final goal remains a society in which everyone contributes what they can and receives what they need to actualize their unique potential.

The CPUSA comrades are correct in declaring the need for a revolutionary party. They correctly state that victory is not abstract: it "relies not on slogans, gimmicks, or conspiracies but rather on developing the understanding of millions cultivated in hard struggles, an understanding that grows into full class and socialist consciousness."[29] Yet, their program is brimming with slogans. Take the assertion that the revolutionary party must be "dedicated to the interests of the whole class, dedicated to the long-term vision necessary for winning fundamental change."[30] An intrepid reader finishes the program without understanding the meaning of fundamental change. After so many pages, the phrase remains a floating signifier capable of the most opportunistic interpretations. This reversion to obscurity is a long way away from the concluding paragraph of the Socialist Party of America's 1912 program: "Such measures of relief as we may be able to force from capitalism are but a preparation of the workers to seize the whole powers of government, in order that they may thereby lay hold of the whole system of socialized industry and thus come to their rightful inheritance."[31] As a party

28 CPUSA Party Program p. 2 https://cpusa.org/party_info/party-program/
29 Ibid. p. 56.
30 Ibid.
31 Socialist Party of America. "Platform 1912." Sage American History. August 14, 2014. http://sageamericanhistory.net/progressive/docs/Socialist-Plat1912.htm.

founded by the principled Left-Wing of the SPA and once ani-
mated by the fire of the Bolshevik Revolution, the CPUSA has
fallen quite a long way.

The program is the loadstone of a socialist political party. A
good program presents the demands necessary for taking power
and creating a democratic republic (the minimum program) to initiate a transition to the ultimate goal of communism (the maximum
program). Means and ends are united and never lose sight of each
other. Demands are expansive though concrete, and resonate with
the condition of all oppressed minority groups. Furthermore, a good
program is clear, concise, and memorable. It leaves elaboration to
party propagandists and trusts in the ability of the masses to decode
an unfamiliar term and infer what is left unsaid. The latest CPUSA
program is a mess. Quantity does not transform into quality; in this
case, the former works against the latter. The working class will not
find a road to power within its numerous pages. Its confusing proposals will lead only to the underwhelming and all-too-familiar dead
end of class collaboration within the existing constitutional order.

Today, the Communist Party USA rests upon a mixed historical
legacy marked by moments in which it acted as a vanguard of the
working class in the highest sense of the phrase, as well as a long
period in which it continues to be plagued by the lowest possible
opportunism. In criticizing its present class collaborationist program, we hope to provide a resource to those in the Communist
Party chafing under this orientation. As in the Democratic Socialists of America, the time has come for genuine communists to rebel
against the dominant opportunism of the largest organizations of
the working class political movement in the United States. We encourage Marxists in the Communist Party USA to begin openly
discussing the course and future of their party and the entire socialist movement. The pages of *Cosmonaut* are open to them, and re-
plies from defenders of the Communist Party's current orientation
are welcome as well — if only to train the arguments of their critics.

May the rebels prevail!

Section III
Electoral Strategy

When We Fight, We Win! For an Agitational Socialist Electoral Strategy

Jack Lundquist
May 11, 2022

Jack Lundquist draws on recent campaigns in New York City to make the case for an agitational electoral strategy.

NYC-DSA currently finds itself engaged in a number of uphill battles. We are running a series of competitive primary races for New York State legislative office, and are fighting to gain traction in Albany on a number of legislative reforms. We are also coming out of a loss: that is, New York's newly passed budget, which NYC-DSA leadership rightly asserts[1] has "fail[ed] working people, jeopardize[d] public safety, fail[ed] to take action on climate, and stall[ed] job growth."

The failure to get the funding and legislative priorities we had wanted can be attributed to many things. NYC-DSA invested fewer resources than in last year's "Tax the Rich" priority campaign. The political moment is also different: Kathy Hochul has replaced Andrew Cuomo as governor, and a

---

1 "Statement: NYC-DSA Rebukes Governor Hochul's Budget." N.a, April 8, 2022. https://docs.google.com/document/d/e/2PACX-1vSMD9JU1k-GoW23ukXBNkb0jOtkatYVp0BP3QDN6aDOJu4HqbQa7gkDULFy-0Ma0klCT597sFy_ZgJJyN/pub

tough-on-crime political bloc is ascendant. Unless we'd have preferred to shift our resources away from the work NYC-DSA we're currently doing, these are not things we have much control over. However, there is one thing we do have control over, regardless of capacity or external conditions: our voices; what stories we're telling, and the audience we're speaking to.

In my estimation, NYC-DSA's endorsed electeds (our "Socialists in Office"), alongside chapter leadership, failed to tell the public the right story about this political battle. In the face of private pressure from Democratic legislators (threats of retaliation on the one hand, quid pro quos on the other), NYC-DSA failed to publicly expose the ways that New York's establishment Democrats prevent the working class from expressing *their* democratic will, from seeing *their* priorities implemented by the state. Not only did we fail to use this private pressure to our public advantage: we caved to it. In part because of pressure from the Democratic Party establishment, not all of NYC-DSA's electeds voted no on the bill that would out more than a billion dollars[2] to the billionaire owner of the Buffalo Bills for a new football stadium. For context, this is a project that the chair of the senate's finance committee called "a terrible way to use the taxpayers' money," and a move that the Seneca Nation[3] has suggested is an attempt by Kathy Hochul to "cripple" their investment in the gaming industry in favor of their competitor: Buffalo Bills contractor Delaware North, a company that just so happens to employ Hochul's husband.

2 deMause, Neil. "Governor Hochul's Backroom Stadium Deal Happened Because New York Sucks at Democracy." Hell Gate, May 10, 2022. https://hellgatenyc.com/hochul-bills-boondoggle-democracy
3 Whalen, Ryan. "Seneca Nation speaks out against use of casino funds for new Bills stadium." Spectrum News 1, March 30, 2022. https://spectrumlocalnews.com/nys/buffalo/politics/2022/03/30/seneca-nation-criticizes-governor-for-taking-casino-funds-for-stadium

NYC-DSA's failure to effectively agitate around the 2022 budget is not just a failure on principled grounds: it is a failure of effective socialist practice. This article is an attempt to explain why that is the case.

But, before we get to the bulk of the argument, this contradiction observed by an insightful comrade makes my point succinctly: *while socialists consider moving away from overtly socialist messaging to win over a broader base, progressives and establishment Democrats alike are adopting many of the demands initially put forward by socialists.*

What are the goals for socialists when we run a campaign? There are at least three:

1. Win the race or the reform
2. Raise socialist consciousness
3. Build our organization and the organized working class

Before we continue on, it is important to note that socialists have disagreed on how to frame these political "goals" for more than a century: with the reformists (exemplified by Eduard Bernstein) on one side, and the orthodox Marxists (exemplified by Marx and Engels on the other). As outlined by Paul D'Amato,

> reformism ... argues that modern representative government affords the working class the opportunity to achieve socialism by electing a socialist majority into office. This view emphasizes the peaceful, gradual transition to socialism, and sees campaigns around elections and the work of socialist elected officials as the most important aspect of socialists' activity. The other trend, first outlined by Marx and Engels...argues for a revolutionary overthrow of the state, based upon the mass struggle of the working class, and its replacement by new organs of workers' power.[4]

In other words, there are two differing perspectives on electoral "wins." Bernsteinian reformists view electoral victory as the primary strategic objective, whereas orthodox Marxists view

4 DeMato, Paul. "Marxists and Elections." International Socialist Review, Winter 2016. https://isreview.org/issue/13/marxists-and-elections/index.html

independent working-class political power as the primary strategic objective. This article approaches strategic questions from the orthodox Marxist position on reforms: that winning reforms is an objective subordinate to the strategy of using the electoral arena as a platform for agitation and organization. From this standpoint, reforms are important. But they are important as measures of the growth of working-class consciousness and organization, and as signposts on the path towards revolutionary working-class democracy.

The fact that winning is not the primary object of socialist electoral strategy is confusing and counterintuitive, especially to those comrades who are deeply invested in the idea of winning reforms and state power through the ballot. However, we must be clear in how we frame the "goal" of winning reforms: is it the prime goal, per the reformist strategy, or is it subordinate to the goal of revolutionary working-class organization, per the orthodox Marxist strategy? If we aren't careful in examining this question, we won't be able to distinguish between the "wins" that move us towards working-class organization and the "wins" that unwittingly advance the strategic efforts of our class enemies (by disarming ourselves through the tempering of our agitation).

Now, back to the three "goals" of a campaign: "winning" in the narrow sense, raising socialist consciousness, and building working-class organization. Ideally, a campaign would accomplish all three goals. And yet, there are some on the left who seem to hold these ideas in tension. The question then becomes this: when we sacrifice raising consciousness by masking our socialist politics and holding our agitational fire, do we improve our odds of winning a race or a reform? When we promote agitation, raising consciousness and building working-class organization, do we sacrifice our ability to win races or reforms?

We can only answer these questions and assess the utility of a tactic or strategic orientation by looking at concrete conditions, historic and present. To that end, it is useful to distinguish between two different contexts: first, when there is a momentary convergence on a particular demand between the forces of socialism and a bloc of the ruling class (in this country, Democrats or a portion of Democrats are more likely to be temporarily aligned with socialists); and second, when socialist demands diverge from the demands of the ruling class writ large (Democrats and Republicans). For a moment, let's accept the premise (rejected by Marx, Engels, and Lenin, as outlined in a recent article of mine[5]) that winning reforms is the primary goal of socialists. In the first context, when there is alignment between the socialists and a bloc of Democrats, agitating against Democrats may not help win the reform.

For example, a sizeable number of Democrats (but not all!) opposed Governor Hochul's rollback of bail reform and her handouts to the billionaire oil baron owner of the Buffalo Bills. In this case, socialists joined with Democrats in opposition to these policies (although the case should loudly be made that handouts to billionaires are a bipartisan consensus in this country). However, the rest of the budget fight falls squarely into the second context: where the Democratic and Republican parties writ large oppose our demands (for example, funding for undocumented workers or for households facing eviction). Beyond that, this process, like many in the halls of power, is incredibly undemocratic and marked by the use of threats of retaliation and quid pro quos. In this case, laying off on our agitation against the Democratic Party's dirty dealings in favor of any sort of "light touch" attempt to organize them inside the halls of power is an ineffective approach at winning reforms. This is because we can't beat the party machinery at their own game: Democrats are in-

5 Lundquist, Jack, KD Isaac. "Legislative Campaigns and 'Policy Feedback': An Assessment of DSA's Orientation towards the Fight for Reforms." https://cosmonautmag.com/2022/04/legislative-campaigns-and-policy-feedback-an-assessment-of-dsas-orientation-towards-the-fight-for-reforms/

credibly well organized by the party machinery, where outliers are punished by withholding committee appointments, campaign funds and by running opposing candidates. Perhaps more fundamentally, this is ineffective because, at the end of the day, socialist demands have no meaningful bloc of support within the ruling class.

Of course, real situations are more complex than just described. Most of our fights include a bourgeois bloc in support and in opposition, and most fights use a mix of agitation, mass mobilization, and advocacy in the halls of power. However, the reason that this model is useful is that it shows us that, even if you accept that winning reforms is the central task of socialists (something I categorically reject, alongside Marx, Engels, Kautsky, Liebknecht, Luxemburg, and on and on), principled agitation is almost always a useful tool in achieving these legislative or electoral victories. After all, how often is it that our demands have the support of a meaningful bloc from the Democratic Party?

The positive case for principled agitation as a key component in socialist electoral strategy is substantial:

1. *Agitation helps build consciousness and solidarity.* This is a central goal for socialists: bringing the revolutionary message to the working masses and giving them the tools to analyze the moment and develop a plan to fight together for their interests. This is one of the primary long-term goals of socialists, for it is a key basis of our strength (the other key being our organization, our concrete forces and resources). More on this central (and under-appreciated!) point later.

2. *Agitation helps with our organizing.* Not only does exposing the injustices of our system win the working class to our side, but our work also needs a guiding political mission for it not to fall into the economist trap of dissolution after accomplishing the stated "goal" of winning a reform (both in electoral and base-building work).

3. *Agitation helps us win.* As described above, agitation *may* not help us win in all situations. But agitation does increase our outside strength (see below). And, given that the bourgeois state stands in fundamental class opposition to our working-class movement, this outside strength is a major key to the success of our campaigns.

In many ways, agitation is the language of socialism. The most successful socialist orators in history, from Eugene Debs to Martin Luther King, Jr. to Lucy Parsons, combined fiery indictments of ruling class corruption and exploitation with inspiring calls for a working-class democracy that serves the interests of the many, not the few. While this rhetoric is effective at mobilizing working people to fight for political demands, this activity all runs counter to the interests of the ruling class, who are the ones who actually have the power to grant these demands. This is the root of the contradiction highlighted earlier — it is far easier to speak as a socialist than it is to act on those politics every day, in every situation (especially those situations when the pressure to compromise is high). This is a key difference between socialists and progressives — progressives utilize socialistic rhetoric to build a constituency and the horse-trading tactics of bourgeois politics to maintain their power. Fundamentally, socialist politics differs from liberal bourgeois politics in its focus on organizing and educating the working class so that we can fight, not just for any one demand, but for a revolutionary worker's democracy. While it may seem convenient, necessary even, to play the bourgeois political game in order to win reforms, there are no shortcuts on the path towards a politically conscious mass movement capable of fighting for and winning a working-class democracy.

A concrete example of these ideas is 2019's campaign for Universal Rent Control in New York State. At the time, NYC-DSA's position was actually much weaker internally: not only did we only have one DSA member in office (State Senator Julia Salazar), but the real estate industry ruled Albany with an iron fist (demonstrated by the numerous rollbacks in rental protections since the passage of rent stabilization in the 1970s). Because of our weak internal position, our strategy relied on agitation, organization, and mass mobilization. For more than a year we knocked doors and made calls to our neighbors, organizing them to stand in support of our fight for universal rent control: a demand that didn't tinker at the margins, that captured public attention in its call for re-imagining a society that put people over profit and renters over wealthy landlords. We found out just how much money state legislators took from the real estate industry and we propagandized around this relentlessly, on social media and in the streets. Finally, we rallied our forces to go to Albany, not to *ask* for Universal Rent Control, but to *demand* that shit! While we didn't win universal rent control, we did win the first expansion to rental protections in half a century. And we did this with only one DSA state elected, relying on our ability to organize a movement and agitate around the bourgeois state's buddy-buddy relationship to the real estate industry: if that doesn't show you that agitational people power is the most important tool socialists have got, I don't know what will!

Of course, there are still some among us who feel trepidation around agitational rhetoric. Because of our relative weakness in the halls of power, they want us to tread lightly. While the above example highlights that agitation is actually a strength (especially in the context of relative weakness), these concerns are certainly valid, and deserving of consideration. In this section, I will address some of these concerns, using some choice quotes from socialists in the orthodox Marxist tradition to outline why these concerns are misguided. Here, I am indebted heavily to August Nimtz's excellent book *The Ballot, the Streets—or Both*, and his critical reappraisal of traditional Marxist political strategy around the turn of the nineteenth century, featuring the

German SPD and their correspondence with Engels as well as Lenin's early political interventions in Russia's socialist movement. I also pull on excerpts taken from another excellent work: Lars Lih's *Lenin Rediscovered*.

Concern 1: Agitation isn't what increases our power. Increasing our numbers does.

The second half of this concern is almost inarguably correct: socialists are more powerful when there are more of us. However, this concern raises two questions:

1. Is it true that agitation doesn't increase our power?
2. When we are talking about increasing our numbers, what numbers are we talking about?

The first question can only be answered after defining what we mean when we speak of "power." In an orthodox Marxist sense, socialist "power" is well defined by Lenin, in a summary of an argument by Engels:

> All that the socialists had to understand was which social force, owing to its position in contemporary society, has a deep interest in the realisation of socialism — and then communicate to that force an awareness of its interests and historical task. The proletariat is such a social force .... The political movement of the worker class inevitably leads the workers to the awareness that there is no escape outside of socialism. On the other hand, socialism only becomes a force when it becomes the aim of the political struggle of the worker class.

This is a summary of the merger formula: the idea that, in order to become a political force capable of overthrowing capitalism and instituting working-class democracy, the movement of socialists must *merge* with the movement of workers. In Engels's and Lenin's conception of the merger formula, a key role of socialists is to bring to the workers an "awareness of [their] interests and historical task." To do this, socialists must prioritize speaking to the masses about the injustices of the capitalist system and the role of the working class in transforming this unjust system. In other words, for socialists to increase their power, they must prioritize agitation that brings political consciousness and organization to the masses.

I will use Nimtz's analysis of Engel's correspondence with German SPD political leader August Bebel to answer the second question: what do we mean when we speak of increasing our "numbers?" Bolded language is my own in this quote from *The Ballot, the Streets—or Both*:

> If there is any doubt about how Engels viewed elections, read his comment to Bebel on the eve of the 1890 Reichstag elections in which the SPD was expected to make (and did make) significant gains: "[M]y only fear is that we shall obtain too many seats. Every other party in the Reichstag can have as many jackasses and allow them to perpetrate as many blunders as it can afford to pay for, and nobody gives a damn, whereas we, if we are not to be held cheap, must have nothing but heroes and men of genius." Quality and not quantity was the goal— not the demand of a bourgeois politician. It should be noted that nowhere does Engels say anything about winning a majority of the electorate through elections. The reason, as already suggested, is that he didn't expect the ruling class to allow the electoral process to go that far. Thus what was crucial for success was winning not just a simple majority in elections but rather effective supporters— that is, those who were willing to vote with their feet to resist the regime and especially those who knew how to use arms.

From this analysis, two things are clear. The first is that, for socialists in office, quality is much more important than quantity. This is because, as Engels observes (and as the history of coups in social democratic countries around the world shows us), the ruling class will not passively allow the victory of a *truly socialist* majority in the electoral process. The second is that, because winning a majority through the bourgeois electoral process is an almost certain impossibility, in terms of numbers, it is really the number of "effective supporters," or active and militant members of the worker's movement, that really matters.

This is not to say that we shouldn't try to win more races, elect more socialists to office, or even that we shouldn't attempt to win over other elected officials to our politics. The point is, more important than all these things, that a primary aim of socialists in office is to expand the ranks of our socialist movement (through the merger of socialism and the worker's movement), and that agitation is a key component in that process.

Concern 2: We could expose what's going on in Albany, but people just don't care!

We should make them care! Socialists should aim to expose the injustices of our governing institutions. Lenin's advice upon the founding of the party newspaper *Iskra* (taken from Nimtz's *The Ballot, the Streets—or Both*) makes the case well:

> [W]e wish particularly to emphasise our opposition to the view that a workers' newspaper should devote its pages exclusively to matters that immediately and directly concern the spontaneous working-class movement, and leave everything pertaining to the theory of socialism, science, politics, questions of Party organisation, etc., to a periodical for the intelligentsia. On the contrary, it is necessary to combine all the concrete facts and manifestations of the working-class movement with the indicated questions; the light of theory must be cast upon every separate fact; propaganda on questions of politics and Party organisation must be carried on among the broad masses of the working class; and these questions must be dealt with in the work of agitation.

Nimtz's assessment of Lenin's position pre-1905 is that "[n]othing could be 'more dangerous and more criminal than the demagogic speculation on the underdevelopment of the workers' and the assumption that they couldn't grasp theory." While DSA doesn't have a worker's newspaper (yet!), and while this argument may focus on theory as being outside the direct concern of the immediate working-class experience, it seems reasonable to say that Lenin's call for agitation on a wide range of questions applies in the context of the internal political dynamics within the halls of power.

There is also a less theoretical response to this concern: the idea that people "don't care" about blackmail, quid pro quos, and the dirty dealings that regularly occur in the halls of power is simply not true! Trump rode to power on a constituency united in their anger with ruling elites. And, although they commonly conceal the most heinous crimes and abuses of the state (hence the need for an independent socialist press!), there's not much the media loves more than a political scandal, almost certainly because of the scandal's ability to attract the public's attention.

Concern 3: DSA as an organization can go all-in on agitation, but our electeds need to demonstrate more restraint, especially when it comes to their colleagues in the halls of power.

While this idea of electeds as restrained political actors may seem sensible in the context of bourgeois realpolitik, it is actually counterproductive when viewed in the context of the central strategic aim of merging socialism with the worker's movement, and the central role played by agitation in achieving that aim.

Counter to this idea, because agitation is key to the merger formula, Lenin views the role of elected officials as "tribunes of the people." In Lenin's 1901 pamphlet "What Is To Be Done,"[6] he describes tribunes as:

> ...able to react to every manifestation of tyranny and oppression, no matter where it appears, no matter what stratum or class of the people it affects...to generalise all these manifestations and produce a single picture of police violence and capitalist exploitation...to take advantage of every event, however small,

6 Lenin, VI. "What is to be Done?" marxist.org, February 1902. https://www.marxists.org/archive/lenin/works/1901/witbd/iii.htm

in order to set forth before all his socialist convictions and his democratic demands, in order to clarify for all and everyone the world-historic significance of the struggle for the emancipation of the proletariat.

For Lenin:

[t]he principal thing, of course, is propaganda and agitation among all strata of the people...we are obliged for that reason to expound and emphasise general democratic tasks before the whole people, without for a moment concealing our socialist convictions. He is no Social-Democrat who forgets in practice his obligation to be ahead of all in raising, accentuating, and solving every general democratic question.

It is clear that Lenin viewed thorough, wide-ranging, principled agitation as a primary responsibility for all socialists. This is especially true for elected officials, who, in the absence of a platform for widespread public agitation, have an outsized platform to agitate.

Concern 4: DSA's electeds only have a limited amount of political capital, and it's important not to spend it all at once.

Again, we must define our terms. What is "political capital?" If we are to understand it as the capacity for an elected official to push for this or that priority, then what is the source of this political capital? How is it lost, and how is it gained? One interpretation of this concept would suggest that political capital comes from proximity to the ruling class administrators of the state: in New York, the Democratic Party establishment. A strategy following from this is that, in order to gain political capital, an elected must win the favor of the ruling class by doing favors in support of their interests; and, to avoid losing political capital, an elected must avoid angering these ruling class leaders.

German SPD political leader Wilhelm Liebknecht rejects this position in his excellent pamphlet "No Compromise — No Political Trading,"[7] writing:

...we should not sound the alarm and be misled by fear into taking steps that do not accord with the principles, the nature and the honor of our party. One does not disarm an enemy through timidity and gentleness; one simply emboldens him...No, Social Democracy must remain for itself, must seek for and generate its power within itself. Every power outside of ourselves on which we seek to lean is for us only weakness. In the consciousness of our strength, in our faith in the world-conquering mission of socialism lies the secret of our extraordinary, almost miraculous success.

Liebknecht sees the "political capital" of socialists as coming from the organized merger of the socialist and workers' movements along an agitational Marxist line (a position shared by Marx, Engels, and Lenin). This conception of socialist political power (e.g., coming from agitation and militant working-class organization) is also concretely demonstrated through the aforementioned example of the 2019 campaign for Universal Rent Control.

Ultimately, socialists in the United States are fated to hold an electoral minority in the short term. In this context, to gain "political capital" is to gain more fighting forces from among the ranks of the working class. To do that, all socialists, rank-and-file members and elected representatives alike, must join in the class struggle as tribunes capable of agitating, educating, and organizing around every manifestation of "tyranny and oppression," producing a "single picture of police violence and capitalist exploitation" in counterposition to our "democratic demands...and the world-historic significance of the struggle for the emancipation of the proletariat."

Concretely, where does this analysis lead us? I believe this leads socialists away from an electoral strategy predicated on

7 Liebknecht, Wilhelm. "No Compromise - No Political Trading." marxist. org, August 1899. https://www.marxists.org/archive/liebknecht-w/1899/ nocomp/

holding our punches, playing nice, and tailing radical move-ment demands in the name of putting "practical reforms" be-fore class-independent working-class organization imbued with revolutionary consciousness; and towards a more thor-oughly agitational political strategy, using every opportunity to ruthlessly propagandize against our class enemies and call on the masses to join our movement for working-class democ-racy. The former strategy of reformism has been tried by so-cialists around the world, and it has failed. Why continue to tread down the path roundly criticized since the debates be-tween Bernstein and his more successful, more revolutionary comrades (Marx, Engels, Kautsky, Liebknecht, Luxemburg, and on and on)?

Despite all this, there may be those who still have reserva-tions about this strategy. This is understandable: the stakes are high, after all. To those comrades, I would say this: if you still remain unpersuaded by the piles of theoretical and histor-ical evidence, at the very least let us put our differing strate-gies to the test and let contemporary empirical evidence be our guide! Let us run a more agitational race, with a candidate who does not hold back in their criticism of the oppressive and exploitative capitalist regime! Let us run a race focused on organization, using ballot registration drives to build an even larger base of militant workers and voters! Let us run in even more local races that take less of our capacity, allow-ing us to experiment with our strategic and tactical decisions even more! Let us try all these things with an eye towards an empirical assessment: can we measurably determine which is more effective at accomplishing our goals, between the more reformist and the more agitational strategies? I believe that we can make this determination, I believe that we must, and I believe that we cannot be afraid to try for fear of failure (although the evidence of agitation failing socialists is slim). After all, the project of organizing the working class to take political power for socialism is a long term one, and at the end of the day, to invoke our comrade Liebknecht, "[i]n the consciousness of our strength, in our faith in the world-conquering mission of socialism lies the secret of our extraordinary, almost miraculous success."

Debating Electoral Strategy in the Comintern, 1920: The Bulgarian Situation

Donald Parkinson
June 30, 2019

Examining the debates over electoral strategy at the Second Congress of the Comintern, Donald Parkinson reviews the strategies of the Bulgarian Communist Party and their arguments against electoral abstentionism.

The early Bulgarian Communist party is often forgotten, with little in the way of historiography. This is shocking considering that it was one of the only Comintern parties that could say it had a majority of working-class support and control over the union movement.[1] It was founded from the left-wing of a Social-Democratic movement that was far more radical than the rest of the Second International. The Bulgarian Social-Democratic Workers Party opposed World War I and supported the Bolshevik revolution. Their most Marxist faction would split from the reformists and form their own party, mirroring the Bolsheviks' split from the Mensheviks. Yet the Bulgarian Party did not take up the ultra-left position of abstention from elections; instead, they brilliantly combined electoral tactics and revolu-

---

1 Braunthal, Julius, *History of the International.* Westport, CT: Greenwood Publishing Group, 1961. p. 285.

tionary strategy without sacrificing militancy or giving into a "law and order" perspective of constitutional loyalty. A popular argument today is that participation in elections inherently leads a party toward reformist politics. Yet the experience of the Bulgarian Communist Party stands in contradiction to this claim. This reason alone calls for more attention to the early Bulgarian Communist movement.

Despite being essentially destroyed by a fascist coup in 1923 and only reemerging in the resistance to fascism during World War II, one can gather quite a bit of information on the party's early years and mass success from the proceedings of the Second Congress of the Comintern, particularly where there is a sharp debate on electoral strategy.[2] In this debate, the representative of the Bulgarian Communist Party, Nikolai Shablin, answers to the minority thesis presented by Bordiga against the notion of participation in parliament being mandatory for Comintern parties. This congress established the '21 conditions' for membership in the Comintern, so the debate on the role of elections was intensified. The Bulgarian party played a key role in defending the Comintern majority theses put together by Bukharin, which called for participation in elections to agitate for revolution, a strategy of revolutionary parliamentarism.

The minority theses put together by Bordiga for electoral abstention, or boycott, made a historicist argument about elections once being useful but now being outdated, based on the historical possibility of an imminent revolution. Bordiga concedes that "participation in elections and in parliamentary activity at a time when the thought of the conquest of power by the proletariat was still far distant and when there was not yet any question of direct preparations for the revolution and of the realization of the dictatorship of the proletariat could offer great possibilities

---

2 Riddell, John. Ed. *Workers of the World and Oppressed People's, Unite!: Proceedings and Documents of the Second Congress, Volume 1.* Cambridge: Cambridge University Press, 2017. See pp. 527-602 for the entire debate on parliamentarism.

for propaganda, agitation and criticism," but then goes on to argue that because the proletariat was now in a period of revolution, such tactics are a distraction from the central task of taking power (which cannot be done through parliament).[3] From this, it followed that parliament should be abstained from. Essentially, the argument Bordiga presented is that electoral participation was historically useful to build up the forces of the proletariat in a non-revolutionary period but in a revolutionary period the aim was to discredit bourgeois democracy, which could only be seen as hypocritical if Communists didn't boycott parliament. Bordiga added that:

> Under these historical conditions, under which the revolutionary conquest of power by the proletariat has become the main problem of the movement, every political activity of the Party must be dedicated to this goal. It is necessary to break with the bourgeois lie once and for all, with the lie that tries to make people believe that every clash of the hostile parties, every struggle for the conquest of power, must be played out in the framework of the democratic mechanism, in election campaigns and parliamentary debates. It will not be possible to achieve this goal without renouncing completely the traditional method of calling on workers to participate in the elections, where they work side by side with the bourgeois class, without putting an end to the spectacle of the delegates of the proletariat appearing on the same parliamentary ground as its exploiters.[4]

This rejection of electoral tactics based on a broad historical abstraction such as "the era of revolutions" is contrary to the dynamic revolutionary strategy of Lenin, who correctly argued against such notions exemplified by Bordiga's arguments in his *Left-Wing Communism: An Infantile Disorder.* Historically, on a grand scale, the era may have been one of revolution, but bourgeois parliaments were not discredited in the eyes of the proletariat, as reformists still maintained leadership of the labor movement. Thus the reformists had to be actively discredited

3 Ibid. p. 552.
4 Ibid. p. 554.

through political struggle, not through empty measures such as boycotts but by directly agitating and fighting for communist politics in the halls of parliament. This also meant connecting parliamentary struggles with struggles outside parliament in factories and working-class communities. The delegitimation of bourgeois parliaments would be accomplished through active political struggle, not simply declaring the nature of the historical epoch.

Another protest against electoral participation was given by a delegate from England, William Gallacher, who represented the Shop Stewards Movement. Gallacher would go as far to say that the Third International was opportunist for participating in elections and took a position further to the left than Bordiga, who still accepted the 21 Conditions of the Comintern despite his disagreements. While lacking the grand historical pronouncements of Bordiga's arguments, Gallacher's argument is essentially the same in its tactical conclusion: that electoral work is a distraction from more important work, that energy put into elections in any form offers few returns for its efforts and risks, and that this energy could instead be put into something that will truly challenge the state or more directly organize the working class. He argues that one who enters parliament can "...make speeches there and thus agitate. The result is, however, that the proletariat becomes accustomed to believing in the democratic institutions." In the end, the argument is that of "democratic mystification," that by voting in bourgeois elections and supporting workers' candidates the worker puts faith in bourgeois institutions and is "softened" by the system, compelling them to refrain from radical action. This argument is similar to Georges Sorel's critiques of electoral socialism and embrace of vitalist syndicalism, which undoubtedly captured a certain class impulse but was an openly anti-scientific and irrationalist theory that relied on a notion of myth to hold itself together. Either way these anti-electoral arguments found popularity in the Comintern due to the prominence of syndicalists entering the movement, with backgrounds similar to Gallacher's, aiming to push the Comintern into making immediate war on capitalism.[5]

Shablin answered Bordiga and Gallacher's critiques in an excellent polemic that offers insight into the tactics of the early Bulgarian Communists and their effective merging of "the ballot and the bullet." Shablin immediately attacks Bordiga's detached historicist theorizing with recognition of concrete political reality:

> Even if the Theses Comrade Bordiga proposes to us proclaim a Marxist phraseology, it must be said that they have nothing in common with the really Marxist idea according to which the Communist Party must use every opportunity offered us by the bourgeoisie to come into contact with the oppressed masses and to help communist ideas to be victorious among them.[6]

Shablin recognizes that the conditions of revolutions are not simply created by epochs of history but by the strength of the proletariat organized as a political force. To accomplish this, Communists must fight for political hegemony in all spheres of civil society and actually win the masses to their politics. The electoral sphere is one of the most publicly visible and dominant spheres in civil society underdeveloped capitalism and therefore cannot be left purely to reactionaries and reformists. For Shablin, Bordiga's theses represent the remnants of an antiquated, economist, and anti-political tendency in the labor movement that must be overcome. This tendency came from syndicalism — an anarchist school of the workers' movement that the Comintern aimed to win support from. A challenge for the Comintern was not just overcoming the limits of Social-Democracy but also the anarchism and political indifference of syndicalism which also dominated the pre-war workers' movement.

5 Ibid. pp. 556-558.
6 Ibid. p. 558.

In his rebuke to the promoters of electoral abstention, Shablin highlights the history of Bulgarian Social-Democracy. Both Bulgarian Social-Democracy and the Bolsheviks shared a record of intra-party factional struggle in which revolutionaries and revisionists, unable to reconcile, separated into distinct organizations. The starkest divide was developed between reformists who hoped to appeal to "all productive strata" (meaning a class alliance with the petty-bourgeois), and Orthodox Marxists aiming to build a class independent party. This divide led to the party split in 1903, with the "narrow socialists" vs the "broad socialists" representing the revolutionary wing and the reformist wing of the Bulgarian labor movement. The "narrow socialists" captured most of the local leadership and would go on to become the Communist Party. Unlike other sections of the Second International they opposed World War I. The Great Soviet Encyclopedia granted them the honor of being the pre-October Revolution faction of Social-Democracy closest to Bolshevism.[7] For example, their opposition to imperialism was matched only by Lenin in the Zimmerwald Left, boycotting the Stockholm Conference in 1917 because it didn't call for peace without annexations.[8] This similarity with the Bolsheviks can be seen in their mixture of revolutionary intransigence and uncompromising anti-imperialism with tactical flexibility. Yet the Bulgarian party themselves were unaware of the Bolshevik/Menshevik conflict, taking more influence from the German party.[9]

Having split from the right wing, the left Social-Democrats of Bulgaria were able to mount an opposition to imperialism. Against the notion that the rise of imperialism and revolutionary circumstances make electoral tactics obsolete, Shablin explained how the Bulgarian Revolutionary Social-Democrats

7 "Bulgarian Communist Party," The Free Dictionary, 1972. http://encyclopedia2.thefreedictionary.com/Bulgarian+Communist+Party+BCP
8 Braunthal, Julius (1961). p. 84.
9 Bell, John D. *The Bulgarian Communist Party from Blagoev to Zhivkov*. Stanford, CA: Hoover Insitution Press, 2020. p. 10.

used parliament to fight against war, citing their reaction to the Balkan wars of 1912-13 and WWI:

> The Bulgarian Communist Party fought energetically against the Balkan War of 1912-13, and, when this war ended with a defeat and a deep-going economic crisis for the country, the influence of the Party in the masses had grown so far that in the elections for the legislative bodies in 1914 it won 45,000 votes and 11 seats in parliament on the basis of a strictly principled agitation. The parliamentary group protested violently on several occasions against the decision of the Bulgarian government to participate in the European war and voted each time demonstratively against war loans. With the help of pamphlets and illegal leaflets, through zealous agitation and propaganda, the Party carried out a violent struggle against the imperialist war once it had been declared, not only inside the country but also at the front.[10]

This strategy, though bringing about a great amount of oppression from the bourgeoisie, was essentially the opposite strategy of the majority of the Second International during WWI. It combined both the ballot and mass action in a revolutionary way, and despite the repression that followed this brave anti-imperialist strategy, when the CP formed and entered elections in 1919 it was resoundingly successful:

> This bitter struggle against the war, the complete bankruptcy of the bourgeoisie's policy of conquest and the serious crisis caused by the war gave the Communist Party the opportunity to extend its field of work and its influence among the masses and to become the strongest political party in our country. In the parliamentary elections of 1919 the Communist Party received 120,000 votes and entered parliament with 47 Communist deputies. The social-patriots, the 'socialists,' could only muster 34 representatives, although the Ministry of the Interior was in the hands of one of the leaders of this party, in the hands of the Bulgarian Noske of sad memory, Pastuchov.[11]

---

10 Riddell, John. Ed. *Workers of the World and Oppressed People's, Unite!: Proceedings and Documents of the Second Congress* (2017). pp. 558-559.
11 Ibid. p. 559.

This was irrefutable proof that electoral struggle could indeed be used to further a revolutionary agenda, especially if a party is strong in its principles and has a real base among the working class. It also showed that by taking a strong anti-war stance, the Communists could gain credibility with the masses rather than conceding to chauvinism as their opponents to the right did. For the Bulgarian CP, electoral work and "mass action" were not counterposed but fed into each other. The party organized mass strikes and demonstrations, inspired by the Russian Revolution to increase the militancy of tactics. Yet this was not the end of electoral success for the Bulgarians. In 1920 their number of deputies rose to 50 even after parliament was dissolved and re-formed by the government, while the reformists dropped down to 9 deputies.

This mere electoral success terrified the bourgeois into more white terror but also showed that through electoral contestations that Communists could weaken the right wing of the labor movement that held back revolution. Communists in 1920 held a majority in parliament, so the bourgeois reacted by ejecting CP deputies. The bourgeoisie had to abandon any formality of democracy to maintain its class dictatorship in face of a parliament subverted by communists that held the backing of the masses. Shablin summarized the general strategy of the party as follows:

> The Communist Party is carrying out an unrelenting struggle in parliament against the left as against the right bourgeois parties. It subjects all the government's draft laws to strict criticism and uses every opportunity to develop its principled standpoint and its slogans. In this way the Communist Party exploits the parliamentary rostrum in order to develop its agitation on the broadest basis among the masses. It shows the toilers the necessity of fighting for workers' and peasants' soviets, destroys the authority of and belief in the importance of parliament, and calls on the masses to put the dictatorship of the proletariat in the place of the dictatorship of the bourgeoisie.[12]

---

12 Ibid. pp. 560-561

Against claims that participation in parliament would retain the stability of bourgeois democracy, the insurgent electoral strategy of the Bulgarian socialists and communists instead showed that through vigilant agitation in the halls of bourgeois power backed by a real mass movement, electoral action would break down the facade of bourgeois democracy by seeing the state resort to more dictatorial methods and creates "states of exception" in response to gains made by the working class through mechanisms of bourgeois democracy. As the Bulgarian CP "threw a wrench" into the normal "democratic" mechanisms for which the ruling class rules through the state, the bourgeois responded with white terror and dismantling of democratic structures themselves. This is what Marx called "the battle for democracy," where the proletariat shows itself to be the class that represents the true "will of the people" while the bourgeois is revealed as a class of tyranny rather than democracy. The Bulgarian CP fought this battle, but to a degree to where a heavy price in human life was paid due to the repression of the propertied classes against a rising Communist movement.

Against the argument that elections "divert energy" from direct actions or general base-building in proletarian communities, the Bulgarian CP showed how these processes could be synergistic and build each other up, not simply see electoral activities parasitic toward the on-the-ground organization of workers. This synergy is particularly described by Shablin in his speech regarding industrial actions, which at this time were seen as the true focus of organization by the "left" critics of electoral practice in many cases:

> The Bulgarian Communist Party fights simultaneously in parliament and among the masses. The parliamentary group participated in the most energetic way in the great strike of the transport workers, which lasted 53 days from December 1919 until February 1920. For this revolutionary activity the Communist deputies were robbed of their legal protection by the government, and several deputies were arrested. Comrades Stefan Dimitrov, the repre-

sentative from Dubnitza, and Temelke Nenkov, the representative from Pernik, were sentenced, the first to 12, the second to 5 years imprisonment, because they had opposed the state power arms in hand. Both comrades are today languishing in jail. A third Communist deputy, Comrade Kesta Ziporanov, is being prosecuted by the military authorities for high treason. The members of the Central Committee, three members of parliament, were prosecuted because in parliament and in the masses they carried out an energetic struggle against the government, which was supporting Russian counter-revolutionaries. They were provisionally released from custody on a bail of 300,000 Leu, which was guaranteed and paid in the course of two days by the proletariat of Sofia. All the Communist members' speeches in the chamber against the bourgeoisie are of such violence that they frequently end in a great scandal, and the government majority and the Communist group come to blows.[13]

These experiences, of course, did not prevent the rise of an anti-electoral faction in the party.

In 1919 a faction arose demanding the boycott of parliament, perhaps in reaction to the repression of Communists deputies. This was a weak faction in the words of Shablin, and was unanimously rejected when it came to a vote at the party congress. Rather seeing soviets and participating in bourgeois elections as counterposed, the Communist Party of Bulgaria worked to form soviets while running in elections at all levels of government. This was similar to the tactics of the Bolshevik party in the days leading up to October, where the Bolshevik party worked to win a majority within the Soviets around the program while also running in bourgeois elections at all possible levels. This created a synergy between the campaigns of the party to form Soviets and electoral campaigns:

> So far, in the councils in which it has possessed a majority, the Communist Party has fought for their autonomy; it calls on the workers and poorer peasants to support by mass action the budgets adopted by the Communist councils, by which the bourgeoisie is

13 Ibid. p. 561.

to be burdened with a progressive tax, which can be extended as far as the confiscation of their capital, and frees the working class from all taxes. Big sums can then be spent for public works, elementary schools, and other purposes that serve the interests solely of the working class and the poor, and the special interests of the minority of the bourgeoisie and of the capitalists go completely unheeded.[14]

This relationship saw the existence of Communists in the mass organizations of the proletariat that were counterposed to the bourgeois state as well as within the bourgeois state not contradictory but rather complementary. Winning majorities in the Soviets and demanding their authority be recognized from within the government saw a way to combine the actions of the proletariat "from below" with an electoral strategy that was "from above," to use a flawed metaphor that is nonetheless common in the left. For the Bulgarian CP, the question of power was not the ballot box or insurrection, but rather a political struggle that combined the two as necessary. When describing the workers' soviets of Bulgaria and their relation to the communist deputies, Shablin argues that the working class struggle to defend their gains or 'communes' is an educational process that will train the working class to take power. It is clear, given the level of state repression Shablin describes, that he sees the necessity and importance of working-class self-defense.

In the next session on parliamentary strategy, Shablin continued to defend his position, this time the Swiss delegate Jakob Herzog joined in to represent the "minority" anti-electoral position. Herzog begins his argument by saying that participation in democratic institutions, by giving workers an ability to increase their standard of living, deadens the revolutionary spirit of the workers is the general cause for a pro-electoral communist trend. Russia is seen as capable of revolution not because of the Bolsheviks ability to agitate legally and illegally but because of the primitive nature of its democratic institutions, making the work-

14 Ibid. p. 563.

ers more desperate to revolt. This kind of muddled, catastrophist and economist thinking shows the level of theoretical sophistication that arguments against electoral participation had in the Comintern. Herzog then goes on to mock the Communist Party of Bulgaria itself and the idea it is a "model of revolutionary parliamentarism," saying that he knows someone who saw the Bulgarian party itself and became anti-parliamentarian because of their disappointment.[15] Shablin accuses Herzog of slander, saying that parties activities are well publicized and known to all.[16] Either way, even if Herzog's story is the truth, it is not an actual indictment of electoral tactics or the CP of Bulgaria, but simply the reflection of an individual. Herzog's argument doesn't carry the day regardless, with Bukharin successfully defeating the minority thesis proposed by Bordiga. The verdict of history on anti-electoral communism isn't necessarily out yet either, but so far its track record in building long-lasting institutions of the working class is very poor.

Within the Comintern's Second Congress, the Bulgarian CP defended a line on electoral strategy close to that of the original pre-revolution Bolshevik party, while other parties argued for, essentially, syndicalist influenced notions of a party that would only put its energy into direct opposition to capitalism, the party essentially being a battalion of workers ready to go to war with capitalism. This was certainly how Bordiga saw the Italian CP when under his leadership: an organization formed during a period of international revolution to wage war on the bourgeois state. Yet this vision of the party was not able to win over the masses and can be seen as being at the root of much that was flawed with the Comintern. The notion of impending revolution may have made sense given the level of global catastrophe and class struggle, but a fatalistic understanding of this world revolution as an inevitable event that the party simply had to line up

15 Ibid. p. 567.
16 Ibid. p. 285.

319

for led to a sort of strategic sterility in many of the Comintern parties, especially earlier on. What was lacking was a long term strategy for revolution, which saw revolution not as something that would outburst at any moment, triggering the mass strikes that would lead to a Soviet Republic, but a process of which the party builds up its forces in a protracted process with tactical flexibility but programmatic clarity.

The Bulgarian CP, unlike the Bolshevik party, was not able to use their strategy to come to power. The party, despite its strength in combining electoral tactics with a revolutionary program, also had weaknesses. In 1923 a fascist coup took power in Bulgaria, triggering a spontaneous uprising. The Bulgarian CP refused to join in and take leadership, seeing the conflict as merely a squabble between two bourgeois factions. Yet spontaneous resistance without Communist leadership to fight for the dictatorship of the proletariat cannot defeat fascism. The result was that the uprising was defeated while the CP stood still. This was not an uncommon attitude in the Comintern in response to the rise of fascism, unfortunately, most famously repeated in Italy and Germany. Historian Julius Braunthal compares their attitude to that of the KPD during the Kapp putsch, where the reactionary officer caste attempted a coup and the Communist party stayed neutral to avoid "defending capitalist democracy."[17] The Comintern Executive, particularly Zinoviev and Radek, was disgusted with this failure to take the lead in resisting the putsch and ordered the Bulgarian party to organize an uprising against the new government. While the leadership of the Party rejected this, the majority voted to follow the Comintern plan and overthrow the government to work towards a Soviet Republic. The result was a fiasco, where only "small isolated groups of Communist party members did take up arms, but only in scattered villages."[18] Zinoviev and Radek, on the other hand, had hoped

17 Braunthal, Julius, *History of the International* (1961). p. 287.
18 Ibid. p. 289.

the uprising would trigger a revolution in Romania and Yugoslavia, but they were blind to the actual on the ground situation in Bulgaria. Who was to blame? Was it the Comintern Executive for forcing an uprising on the party that it wasn't prepared for, or the leadership of the Bulgarian CP for not supporting the initial mass uprising against fascism? Either way, such mistakes cannot be repeated, and mechanical uprisings engineered from abroad are unlikely to be a means success, as is refusing to take leadership in mass struggles against fascism. As for Comrade Shablin, he was murdered in 1925 by the Bulgarian police.

While the experience of the Bulgarian CP can show the use of electoral tactics, it also shows the limitations of a purely electoral approach. This is not to say the Bulgarian CP had such an approach, but rather that their success was due to the aforementioned "synergy" between electoral and mass action as well as their willingness to engage militant self-defense against the violence that the bourgeois will unleash on any attempt to throw them out of power, even if these attempts are made through legal democratic means. The Bulgarian CP faced an immense amount of repression and was only able to survive as an organization by going into illegality after 1923.

The insurgent electoral strategy of the Bulgarian CP and its predecessor Social-Democrats is far removed from the tepid reformism of much of the left, who promote an electoral strategy that tails the "left wing of the possible" and aims to compromise in every possible way, from the general notion that it is impossible to even work outside the democratic party with excuses being made for every capitulation made by a self-described social-democrats capitulation to the right. Yet on the other hand, due to the prominence of a reformist rather than insurgent electoral strategy, electoral tactics are dismissed altogether which sees the abandonment of a key weapon in the historical class struggle out of fear that such tactics can only lead to reformism. The experiences of the early Bulgarian Communist party during this period shows how electoral tactics can be a powerful tactic in the class struggle and help de-legitimate rather than legitimate the bourgeois system. The choice is not between voting and revolution, as some Maoists and anarchists like to put it. Rather, the choice is between engaging in all spheres of civil society possible where we can fight for our politics or simply leaving them as theaters for the bourgeois and their allies.

A Twelve-Step Program for Democrat Addiction

Ben Grove
December 10, 2020

Ben Grove lays out a twelve-step program for the Democratic Socialists of America to pursue a path of independent working-class politics.

Cheer up, comrades! It has been a sorrowful year for all of us, but the whole world has taken a beating — we're hardly special. We will always have choices to make, strategies to explore, and opportunities to pursue. In this piece, I will do my best to illuminate some of them.

We can transform our political prospects. But first we will have to transform ourselves. It is pointless to "keep fighting the good fight" if that means pounding on the same brick wall forever. We must rethink old assumptions and learn some new tricks. If we retreat into isolated local projects or blindly "follow the leader," we set the stage for another defeat.

Remember the Sanders campaign? Those months seem like a distant memory now. Bernie Sanders played by the rules of the Democratic Party, and those rules squashed him. Yet we have the power to write our own rulebook — not just by breaking with the Democrats, but by inventing a completely new way of doing politics. It is time to move past the obvious insights. Democrats suck; they are treating progressives unfairly; it is still a relief that Trump got fired. To do better next time, we must ask ourselves more difficult questions. The first one is very simple: who *is* "we"?

Who Are You?

Nearly every political argument invokes a "we," a common group that should mobilize around something. Although this is useful for persuasive purposes, it can also muddy the waters. In the real world, there is never just one "we" that any of us belong to — no single collective agent. Readers of this article are presumably part of many "we's."

Several examples come to mind. There is the George Floyd protest movement. There is also Bernie World: the massive network of people who supported the Sanders campaign. And many of us feel a certain kinship with all left-leaning people in America — with our friends who want some kind of welfare state, even if they lack an explicit political ideology.

Then there is a much smaller "we": the American socialist movement. People who own the word "socialism" and take it seriously, without needing a "democratic" disclaimer in front (most of us are even fine with the c-word). We clump around explicitly socialist organizations — most often the Democratic Socialists of America — and we use the dictionary definitions. We *actually* want common ownership of the means of production and a new political system to make it possible.

Socialists are a small but growing minority of the US population. How should socialists handle being in a minority? One option is to embrace it, to turn inward and form angry little echo chambers that achieve nothing. Another is to bow to outside forces, watering down our beliefs in the name of "progressive coalition-building." Both of these solutions fall short. There is nothing wrong with being in a minority, especially when your side has unique insights on how society works. What's important is to be an *outward-looking minority* — a minority with a genuine desire for growth and a clearheaded awareness of its surroundings.

Where Are We?

One tempting idea is that the American Left is finished. With Trump out of office, the masses will become complacent, apathy will reign, and there will be no more appetite for political change. In such bleak times, this pessimism is understandable, but it's also wrong.

Total nihilism about our prospects puts far too much faith in Joe Biden and the Democratic Party. The crisis in this country runs deeper than Trump. It began before Trump and will continue long after him. The public may want a return to normalcy, but that is just a short-term impulse. Biden's party will be governing in the middle of a global pandemic and an economic recession. To govern alone, they will have to pull off an extraordinary political surgery: winning a Senate majority of *one*, voting *unanimously* to reform the filibuster, adding new states, and then packing the Supreme Court to keep their legislation viable.

Judging by their track record, are the Democrats up to this task? Are they capable of such ruthless political discipline? And even if they do accomplish it, will their leadership be ready to push through major reforms to help America's struggling working class?

Perhaps Obama could make a few phone calls and threaten a drone strike on Joe Manchin. Otherwise, they will be governing at the feet of Mitch McConnell. Remember him, the Kentucky boy who looks like a turtle? *That's* the man who will be holding Joe Biden accountable, *not* progressives. The GOP controls the Senate. It now controls the Supreme Court. It has ample weapons to impose a wingnut regime on America w*ithout* Trump in office. Perhaps that is why they are refusing to wage an all-out war over Biden's victory.

There will be no "bipartisan" healing, only stagnation and decay. When discontent resurfaces, multiple forces on the Left (not to mention the Right) will pounce to take advantage of it. One force to be reckoned with is Bernie Sanders, Alexandria Ocasio-Cortez, and the rest of the left-wing Democrats in Congress. Because they will be locked out of Biden's administration, they have nowhere to go but the pulpit. Their party is already eager to marginalize them, and they know the score. The planet is burning. Millions of us have no healthcare in the middle of a pandemic. Roe v. Wade may well be overturned, making abortion illegal for millions overnight and sparking massive upheaval. Every social gain of the past fifty years stands at the mercy of the Supreme Court.

Left-wing Democrats will have to change their strategy. Will they do so effectively? No one knows, and ordinary rank and file socialists should not rely on it. They are embedded in a co-alition that prevents them from building a viable constituency. Our responsibility is to develop a more independent approach to politics, with or without their help.

To understand why, let us talk about redbaiting. It worked this year, both on the Left and the liberals (particularly in Miami). So-cialism has a powerful appeal among downwardly mobile young people who escaped their elders' Cold War indoctrination. For a majority of Americans, however, it remains a dirty word. The Democrats stoked that base when they tarred Bernie as a shill for Castro. Then Trump took up where they left off, tarring Biden as a shill for Bernie, AOC, and a communist plot to destroy Ameri-ca. He and his party made a bet that even the most ridiculous lies would send the Right marching off to Valhalla. *They bet right.*

Thanks in part to red-baiting (not to mention race-baiting, jin-goism, coddling evangelicals, and actually running an energetic campaign), Trump's coalition turned out with *millions* more than they had in 2016. The Democrats lost seats in the House and didn't win the Senate. Now the neoliberals are furiously blam-ing the Left. Representative Abigail Spanberger (D-Va.) has been particularly frustrated with her neoliberal colleagues for not re-pressing us hard enough. In a conference call shortly after Elec-tion Day, the former CIA officer had this to say:

"We have to commit to not saying the words 'defund the police' ever again," she said. "We have to not use the words 'socialist' or 'socialism' ever again."

She may well be right. Censoring those slogans would be a smart tactical move for her party (not ours). But the Representative forgets three things:

1. Socialists are here to stay and will not be shutting up.
2. Left Democrats like Bernie worked tirelessly to turn out their constituencies for Biden. Despite the Right's hatred of them, they played a crucial role in Biden's victory.
3. Red-baiting targeted *the Establishment's weaknesses* — not just ours.

That third point is counterintuitive, so it deserves some further context. Once again, the Democrats nominated an establishment candidate who set popular expectations as low as he possibly could. Why not fill the empty vessel? It made perfect sense for Trump and his allies to turn boring Joe Biden into a sinister communist puppet. The move served three basic purposes: stoke their right-wing base, pit the Democrats against their progressive wing, and avoid having to debate Biden directly because Donald Trump is an idiot.

Debating Boogeyman Bernie was easy enough, but had Real Bernie been the nominee, the dynamic would have changed in some very interesting ways. Sanders excels at something that is invaluable for all political leaders: incisive messaging. Instead of promising nothing, he would have countered Trump's red-baiting head-on by aggressively selling his ideas: "You're damn right I support Medicare for All, and let me tell you why!" Whatever the results on Election Day, his base would have emerged with hardened convictions and itching for a fight.

A moot point of course: the Bernie constituency did not harden. Instead, it was defeated, co-opted, and now discarded, left to wallow in uncertainty about its future. Bernie lost because the Establishment rigged the primary — not with mail-in ballots and computer hacks, but with *fear:* fear of losing to Trump. Fear that Bernie accepted from the outset by promising his loyalty to any nominee and justifying his entire campaign by claiming to be America's Best Trump Remover. Biden crushed that sales pitch the moment he cruised in with an orchestrated wave of big-name endorsements, signaling to all uncertain voters that the party apparatus was his. How could an open hijacker like Bernie be the Unity Candidate? The loyal crew rallied behind its captain and threw the pirate overboard.

Sold one-by-one, his policies were wildly popular, but bundling them together with a big red bow was too hard a sell for Democratic voters who feared Trump above all else. When Bernie lost the primary, he lost his podium as well. He spent the rest of the election shunted off in a corner, working quietly for Biden's coalition to "save America" from total meltdown. There was nowhere left to go on the path he had set for himself.

How did that coalition treat him? Bernie wanted Medicare for All. The DNC Platform Committee would not even accept a universal program for *children.* In 1998, Bill Clinton called for lowering the Medicare eligibility age to 55. In 2020, Biden said "lower it to 60," framing it as a generous concession to Bernie's eager young whippersnappers. When Bernie delegates pushed for a move back to Clinton's original proposal, the Committee shot that down too.

Medicare is for Seniors Only, and Biden has been quite firm on that principle. Nor was his public option a genuine concession. His campaign was happy to paste it on the website, but Biden played it down the instant Trump held his feet to the fire, claiming that it would only be a Medicaid-style program for the destitute.[1]

The American Left is being buried in coalitions that treat us like dirt. We beg them, appease them, and submit to their abuse.

---

1 Even ignoring Biden's comments, the Democrats were never actually going to pass a public option, if their congressional aides are to be believed.

Then they still fail, despite all our efforts to prevent it, and each failure deepens our dependency on them. For decades, we have been hopelessly addicted to Democrats.

Let 2020 be the final relapse. We must be our own captains and build our own ship: a self-assured, self-reliant movement with no divided loyalties. A fearless movement powered by millions who cannot be cowed or manipulated. Millions who know exactly what we stand for; who are *sold* on both our policies and the big red bow that ties them together:

An independent, socialist, working-class party.

Who Will Build the Ship?

Such tired old words! They are usually where reflection ends, because they are infinitely harder to make real.

Will the Squad build the Ship? Will Omar, Tlaib, Pressley, Ocasio-Cortez, and the rest who won their primaries this year form a Democratic Socialist Party? Before socialists rush to take orders from them, the Squad's track record deserves a partial review. They have:

- Firmly backed Medicare for All (all of them).
- Voted for a $2.7-trillion Pentagon budget (AOC, Tlaib).
- Endorsed Bernie Sanders (AOC, Omar, Tlaib).
- Endorsed Elizabeth Warren (Pressley).
- Held a sit-in at Nancy Pelosi's office (AOC).
- Called Nancy Pelosi "Mama Bear" (AOC).
- Called for defunding the police (AOC).
- Held a photo-op with the NYPD (AOC).
- Fired her chief of staff for annoying Democrats (AOC).
- Slammed the Democratic Party as incompetent (AOC).

Suspend all moral judgments. Just ask from a distance: are these the actions of a disciplined socialist movement with a clear political strategy? Or are they the actions of a loose, informal circle of left-wing Democrats?

It is the latter, of course. Just like Bernie, members of the Squad are grappling with divided loyalties, balancing their genuine desire for progress with their obligations to a party that wants none of it. There has been much talk in DSA of launching a "dirty break": having socialists run within Democratic primaries and one day splitting off to form a party of their own. But there is no evidence that anyone in the Squad has ambitions to do this. Unlike Bernie, they have spent their entire political careers working within the Democratic Party. Even if they do have secret plans, ordinary socialists are not privy to them and will have no say in how they play out.

DSA has thoroughly confused itself by viewing the Squad as its rightful leaders. A clear majority of DSA members want to chart a course away from the Democrats, but the Squad's theory of change is based on "winning the soul" of their party. This is quite different from our mission to build an independent socialist movement.

If the Squad will not build the ship, then what about organized labor? If we stay patient and work hard within the unions, could they eventually toughen up to create an American Labor Party? Perhaps — but they will have us waiting for quite a while. For over eighty years the US labor movement has functioned as an appendage of the Democratic Party. It has millions of members, but they are demoralized, dominated by stagnant leadership, and suffering from decades of decline. The Left certainly needs to rebuild labor, but trying to do so as isolated individuals is a vain abdication of responsibility. The Democrats have the labor movement in a *political stranglehold*, and to break it we must create a *political alternative*. Many times in history, it has been a left party that organizes and revitalizes the unions, rather than the other way around. Nor are labor-based parties guaranteed to be friendly to socialists — the purge of Jeremy Corbyn and the British Labour Left should give pause to would-be American Laborites. Enough waiting based on hypotheticals.

The time for independent politics is *now*.

If we need an independent party now, then what should it look like? One option is to cast the net as wide as we possibly can. Throw the s-word out and join with every left-leaning person we can find to form a broad-based progressive party. The party could appeal on just a few policies that are already highly popular, like Medicare for All, and de-emphasize other issues that "divide us."

It's a tempting idea. Ditching socialism could take the heat off our backs and make growth much easier in the short term. There is already an organization that is trying to do this: the Movement for a People's Party. Led by former Bernie staffer Nick Brana, it is determined to set up a "new nationally-viable progressive party." It has recruited tens of thousands of supporters and an impressive lineup of high-profile speakers, from Marianne Williamson to Jesse Ventura. Running on a platform loosely modeled on that of Bernie's 2016 campaign, it hopes to flip congressional seats in 2022 and win the presidency in 2024.

Although MPP's ambition is admirable, the recent track record of "left populism" does not bode well for them. Populist coalitions boom and bust; they rise to power only to implement austerity; they speak in simplistic terms of "the People" and "the Elite" that impede more sophisticated class-based analyses. Their frantic rush for the presidency is quite unwise, as is their desire to conjure up an instant majority. Socialists would do well to remember the fate of America's original Populist Party: cooptation in 1896 by a Democratic presidential candidate who adopted their demand for free coinage of silver.

Marxist political strategist Mike Macnair describes this impatient approach to politics as "conning the working class into power." Karl Marx had similar warnings to his contemporaries in 1850:

> [The faction opposing us regards] not the real conditions but a mere effort of will as the driving force of the revolution. Whereas

we say to the workers: 'You will have to go through 15, 20, 50 years of civil wars and national struggles not only to bring about a change in society but also to change yourselves, and prepare yourselves for the exercise of political power.

Socialists should be gearing up for this long-term political struggle. We see the obstacles in front of us in a way that catch-all "progressives" cannot. Progressives hold a powerless but accepted niche within the American political system. It is easy for them to cheerfully dream of "taking back our democracy" and "advancing the American experiment." Socialists have much weaker roots. Constantly derided as un-American, they are driven to question the dominant culture and the entire political system.

This political system is explicitly designed to "restrain the democratic spirit." The president is not elected by popular vote. The Senate, with total control over cabinet and judicial appointments, vastly overrepresents conservative white voters, and its members serve staggered six-year terms. This is to say nothing of the Supreme Court, whose members serve for life and claim the right to strike down any legislation as they see fit.

The add-ons are helpful as well. Ballot access laws prop up an artificial two-party system, barring all third parties from meaningfully contesting elections. Millions of felons are disenfranchised. Gerrymandering and voter suppression are rampant. Virtually all elections are in single-member districts — winner-take-all.

"But the Founding Fathers intended it this way!" the conservatives screech when pressed for any progressive reform. "You can't just change it on a whim!"

Meanwhile, they impose their own changes. They pack the courts, purge the voter rolls, and impose right-wing minority rule on the entire country. The Democratic Party will continue to submit to it for years to come because it is equally loyal to this tired Old Regime.

What is needed is not just a break with the Democrats, but a complete break in our way of conceptualizing political power.

Will socialists continue to campaign for catch-all progressives, for left Democrats and marginal third parties? Or will we introduce something completely new and unprecedented to American politics — something that challenges not just the rules but the institutions that make them?

There will be no victory for the Left within the established constitutional order. It was designed to keep uppity leftists out of power. Conservatives know this full well. We will never win if we play by their rules. Our job is to develop a coherent strategy to attack their deliberately incoherent political system. A strategy based on *incisive messaging, political independence*, and a *national struggle for power.*

Just to be clear: from this point on, when I say "we" I mean DSA. For all its flaws, it is the flagship organization for American socialists. Where its competitors have three or four-digit memberships, its rolls will soon break 100,000. It is the ideal place to hammer out some kind of future for ourselves.

No individual can do it alone. But just to get the ball rolling, I would propose the following:

A Twelve-Step Program for Socialists (To Break Our Addiction to Democrats)

1) Declare political independence.

Remember what Joe Biden said at the first debate to counter Trump's idiotic redbaiting. He said, "I am the Democratic Party." Don't hate him! It was true, and it was actually quite clever of Joe. He was leading a messy coalition and he stepped up to assert responsibility for it. With those words, he wiped out the Bernie movement and made it crystal clear what the Democratic Party is about.

Now, remember how Bernie countered his own redbaiters when his campaign was just getting started. He gave a speech about "what democratic socialism means to me." Do you see the difference here? One man is speaking assertively about an entire political coalition. The other is speaking on behalf of himself to humanize the s-word and make it less intimidating. But in doing so, he is stripping it of any standardized definition.

Is socialism an organized political movement or is it a slogan, a vague personal philosophy? Right now it is mostly the latter in the United States. Popular understandings of the term range from "equality" to "government ownership" to "talking to people, being social ... getting along with people."

If socialism is no more than a slogan, perhaps we should simply abandon it. The entire point of sloganeering is to popularize unpopular ideas. When the slogan alienates people and has no substance, it is useless.

It's not quite that simple, of course. As conservatives love to say, we can't erase our past, and picking a feel-good label for ourselves will not necessarily protect us. The Right will always be pinning the red bow on anything left of Mussolini. Just ask Podemos (and Joe Biden)!

Moreover, socialism is useful because it appeals to a critical target audience: young, downwardly mobile, working-class people who are already skeptical of American capitalism. Anyone can claim to be a progressive, from Maoists to Nancy Pelosi. Socialism is a knife that cuts us apart from the crowd; it has already captured the public's attention. We just need to make sure that we cut ourselves into an organized political constituency and not a rebellious fashion trend.

DSA should act less like Bernie and more like Joe. It should step up and say, "DSA is the Socialist Movement." When asked what socialism is, it should give a coherent definition. I will not presume to have a full answer here, but we should be clear that socialism is a mission to bring freedom and democracy to the working class — and that mission will require regime change. Moreover, because most self-professed socialists in America are also communists, perhaps we should be more straightforward about that when asked. A classless, stateless, communist society is our end goal — give or take a few generations.

That is how DSA should define itself publicly. It should also change the way it describes itself to members. It could put out a statement, even if it is completely internal, announcing that DSA considers itself an independent socialist party and expects members to conduct themselves accordingly. It will not have legal status as a party, but that doesn't matter. Many American socialists, from Seth Ackerman to Howie Hawkins, have acknowledged the need for flexibility on this question. Because state governments dictate the structure of legally recognized parties, we should simply reject their regulatory frameworks and define for ourselves what a party is. Given the public's understandable impulse to dismiss conventional third parties, we could continue to refer to ourselves officially as "DSA," "the Socialist Movement," or anything similar. Our actions will cement our political independence, not the formality of sticking the p-word in our official title.

There is nothing particularly misleading about this (if leaving out the p-word is opportunistic, then so was Rosa Luxemburg's party). From a Marxist perspective, a communist party *is* a movement — a structured, organized, revolutionary political movement.[2] Framing the party in these terms is therefore perfectly honest and acceptable. It would also subvert the shallow liberal conception of movements as flash mobs and Twitter hashtags.

All of these maneuvers may seem pretentious and overbearing, but they are *necessary*. The Right and Center have no qualms about defining socialism for the public. They define it as "misery and destitution." Nor are the Left Democrats afraid to advance vague, meandering definitions that leave the Right howling and the fence-sitters completely unconvinced.

The momentum is with DSA. Even Trotskyist sects acknowledge this by routinely imploring DSA to form a new party

2 Macnair, Mike. *Revolutionary Strategy*. London: October Press, 2008. http://ouleft.org/wp-content/uploads/Macnair-Revolutionary-Strategy.pdf

that they can "affiliate" with. We have the power to step up and assert collective responsibility for the American socialist movement. It's us, the Right, or the wavering politicians. Let there be no more talk about "What Democratic Socialism Means to Me." From now on, the phrase should be "What the Socialist Movement Demands."

2) Hold annual conventions.

This is a short point. For years DSA has held conventions on a biannual basis. Today that will not be enough. The United States has become rather unstable; conditions can change in a heartbeat and we will have to adapt to them quickly. To keep up with the pace of events, we should hold conventions every year, constantly reevaluating our platform and strategy.

3) Form statewide organizations.

What is the mourning cry of a defeated progressive? It's this: "Oh well. I'll just get involved in local politics. That's where the real change happens anyway."

A noble thought; every one of us has had it at some point. Unfortunately, it reflects an unconscious peasant mentality. Giving up on large-scale political change, the progressive returns to their village to do what little they can.

"I would never challenge His Majesty the King. Better to cultivate my little garden."

A garden is not an island. American cities have more autonomy than their counterparts in many other countries, but that is not saying much. State and federal policies shape every aspect of local government. They prohibit cities from requiring paid sick leave for workers. They require them to accept fracking within their boundaries. They force towns to base their speed limits on pre-existing traffic flows, ratcheting up car speeds and slaughtering pedestrians.

When we confine ourselves to local politics, we become functionaries of the capitalist state. We also play into the reactionary old American idea that all problems are best solved locally and that large-scale social programs can never be trusted. We must build an opposition to the capitalist state at every level, and that means creating strong regional organizations. A DSA caucus called the Collective Power Network raised this point quite effectively in 2019. What they forgot to fully address is the appropriate scale for these regional entities: the state level. The Republicans and Democrats have their state parties. So should we.

"But that's modeling ourselves on the bourgeois state!" cry the anarchists.

No, it is laying siege to the state. Our state chapters will run on simple majoritarian lines; they will not have Senates and Supreme Courts and Governors with veto power. What they will have is the capacity to run statewide campaigns and contest state policies that impact the lives of working-class people. They will also encourage local chapters to collaborate, improve outreach outside the big cities, and alleviate some of the burden on the national organization — which has been charged with the impossible task of managing 235 locals.

Admittedly, there are some sparsely populated states with very few DSA chapters, and in these areas statewide organization could be impractical, at least in the short term. A United Dakota, North and South, might make sense for DSA's purposes. Fusing states for tactical reasons is perfectly acceptable; the only inadvisable move would be creating regions that cut states into multiple pieces, preventing unified statewide campaigns.

Although a national organizing drive would be invaluable, DSA's local groups can take the initiative right now. There is already an easy, underutilized process to integrate DSA chapters. According to DSA's constitution, just two or more locals may petition to form a statewide organization, pending approval by the National Political Committee and a majority of locals within the state. A similar process is available for locals seeking to form regional organizations.

4) Nurture a committed membership base.

What does it mean to be a DSA member? One impulse is to make it an extremely demanding, prestigious title — the Navy SEALs of activism. In his classic text on Marxist strategy *What Is to Be Done?*, Vladimir Lenin called for a disciplined party of professional revolutionaries. Should American socialists aim for the same thing?

No, because for Lenin, ruthless discipline was a necessary evil, not a virtue. Russian revolutionaries operated in a Tsarist police state where the slightest misstep invited discovery, police raids, and mass arrests. The United States is in many ways shockingly repressive, but it is not a tsarist autocracy. In our context, socialists have much more to learn from socialist parties outside the Russian Empire that maintained more open membership structures. They cultivated mass movements — millions strong — to build a vibrant oppositional culture against capitalism. They offered social services, opened libraries and grocery stores, set up cycling clubs, choir societies, picnics and social outings. Germany and Austria offer intriguing historical examples. Today, Bolivian socialists are doing similar inspirational work.

But we don't just have to look abroad. There are non-socialist, all-American organizations in the United States that show us what dedicated membership looks like. In 2015 the National Rifle Association had 5 million dues-paying members, and nearly 15 million Americans identified with the organization whether they paid dues or not. It cultivates group identity with a wide array of community services — including an official magazine, concealed carry insurance, firearms training for millions, and opportunities to join its 125,000-strong army of training instructors.

Yes, the NRA is a reactionary, racist organization, riddled with corruption and now in decline. We still have much to learn from it (not to mention the churches that, for better or worse, provide millions of Americans with social services and community life). There is thrilling potential for secular left-wing institution-building, from tenant unions and worker centers to art circles and sports clubs. During the COVID-19 pandemic, hiking clubs and other outdoor activities could be a particularly powerful social service, breaking people out of their isolation and alleviating mental health burdens.

These ideas go beyond feel-good charity work. They are structured party programs, designed to build a massive support base that can be deployed for confrontational political action. They will cost quite a bit of cash.

This brings us to a crucially important, non-negotiable element of dedicated membership: *monthly dues.* Dues are the lifeblood of a mass movement; they foster group identity, incentivize recruitment, and provide the party with a steady, predictable stream of revenue.

But what about low-income, working-class people? Couldn't dues make the movement inaccessible to them?

Quite the opposite. Dues can be tapered based on income, and studies show that the poor give a greater portion of their income to charity than the rich. Asking people to pay a steady monthly fee is much more reasonable than bombarding them with fundraising emails that endlessly scream "give, give, give!" Nor is volunteer work a more accessible basis for membership than dues. Time is money, and every hour that a person spends with us is an hour that they could have spent working an extra shift or taking care of their children.

Dues allow us to make reasonable asks of others and avoid activist burnout. We don't guilt-trip the single parent working two jobs or the exhausted volunteer with mental health burdens. We say: "Don't worry. Take a break as long as you need to. Just help us stay afloat and *keep paying your dues.*" There will always be varying levels of involvement, and not all of us will be red Navy SEALs. Anyone who supports our mission, votes for our candidates, and pays their dues deserves to be called a member of the Socialist Movement.

We must still take measures to promote membership engagement. Only active members should get a vote in party affairs, and we should encourage all members to come to at least a few key events every year. All chapters need a point person to welcome newcomers and help them forge connections with other members, preventing locals from becoming insular social clubs. We will offer engaging, freewheeling education groups to introduce new members to our politics. All of this is necessary to make ourselves an "outward-looking minority."

A key task for DSA will be to reevaluate and standardize its dues structure and perhaps ask a little more of its members. DSA membership is worth more than the current 67-cent monthly minimum. Rather than dismantling dues, as some anarchist-leaning caucuses have suggested, we must embrace and *celebrate* them as the foundation of a self-reliant movement.

5) Adopt a nationwide political platform.

DSA is currently working on a platform to synthesize its political demands. This is a very exciting development and an important step to assert ourselves as a distinct force in American politics. We should develop a truly revolutionary program that, if fully implemented, would hand power to our country's working class and place society on a socialist transition out of capitalism. We must repeal every law that props up the two-party cartel and eliminate every institution that denies us an authentic majoritarian democracy. Abolish the Senate, abolish the Electoral College, and smash the Supreme Court — send Brett Kavanaugh and all his colleagues packing.

So that working people can fully participate in political life, we should also demand unimpeded labor rights, a massive reduction in working hours, and a comprehensive welfare state that would make Scandinavians blush. Create programs to reduce the power of bureaucrats and give ordinary workers administrative skills; promote worker self-management in all industries. Place the commanding heights of the economy under public ownership and rapidly phase out fossil fuel production. Dismantle the repressive arms of the state: abolish the military and policing as we know it and replace both with a democratically-accountable popular militia. This last point will be challenging yet still indispensable. We must transform the empty demand for "police abolition" into appealing slogans and substantive policy proposals.

We have our work cut out for us: we must develop a comprehensive program *and* find ways to promote it to a mass audience. Even so, we will not be working in isolation. We can learn from the history of past revolutions and from the platforms of our predecessors in socialist parties across the world.

Is this project too arrogant? Will we alienate ordinary people if we draft a comprehensive platform instead of a short list of popular demands? If we treat the platform as an inalterable holy text, then yes. If we leave it open to regular revision and use it as part of our political education process, then no. The intuitive red-meat demands are indispensable: we should certainly continue to advance Medicare for All and other programs that improve the quality of life for the working class. But we will never achieve those demands unless we attack the political order that is making them unachievable. Our platform must point towards a break with the capitalist state and fight for an authentic working-class democracy. We need to build a constituency that believes in the legitimacy of that fight. A "political revolution" will not be enough to defeat America's reactionary Old Regime. No, that will require a break of epoch-making proportions, a world-historic *social revolution.*

6) Run dedicated organizers for office.

Many "revolutionary" organizations have an impulse to steer clear of electoral politics. Stumping for office might seem to legitimize a system we want to overturn, so why do it?

The obvious answer is that the state has tremendous power and it already has legitimacy for most people. It will be here for quite a while. Retreating from the political arena does nothing to stop that. More importantly, electoral work done right can *erode* the legitimacy of the system and help us win the support of millions. Electoral campaigns can be used as a bully pulpit to attack the system and demand a new political order. Lenin did this, the German socialists did this, and so can we.

Electoral politics can also embolden and merge with the combative worker and tenant struggles that often capture leftists' attention. Bernie Sanders taught us that when he personally manned picket lines, and West Virginia teachers showed it when they drew inspiration from Bernie to go on strike.

What we need to avoid is getting sucked into another abusive coalition like Bernie. The key to this is recognizing the Democratic Party as the irredeemable zombie that it is. Bernie tried to heal the zombie and he got bitten hard. Instead of collaborating with the neoliberals, we should strive for total independence and self-sufficiency in our electoral bids. DSA could train and run gifted organizers who promise to coordinate their campaigns, accept the party platform, and vote as one bloc when elected. Candidates would be entirely free to personally disagree with elements of the platform and push for changes through internal party discussion. In the halls of power, however, they would be expected to act as one team, with accountability to the entire membership movement.

We see a preview of this approach in New York, where DSA recently ran a victorious slate of insurgent socialist candidates. If we hardened and expanded this approach nationwide, it would put us to the left of even the Squad — whose members have hesitated to endorse other primary challengers after winning office themselves.

We would not align with the Democrats. Instead, wherever they won office, our candidates would form an independent socialist caucus. Both parties would be welcome to meet with us to discuss policy — at the opposite end of a long negotiating table.

This approach would not win us much love from either side. Legislative committee appointments would be sparing or non-existent, but that is okay. Establishment politicians may hammer us as useless backbenchers, but we would simply counter by pointing out how useless they are, listing off all the ways they have betrayed their constituents in the past. We would make use of our extra free time by serving as relentless advocates for the communities that they have ignored, publicizing socialist policy proposals, providing constituent services, and assisting local organizing projects. To show their dedication, our elected officials would refuse to take more than a typical working-class salary and donate the rest to our community programs.

The value of electoral work done right cannot be understated. Many "revolutionary" leftists begrudgingly accept its necessity as a type of "propaganda," but what passes for propaganda on the Left is often just obnoxious megaphone yammering. It would be better to describe it as a form of organizing, as outreach to carve out a constituency that believes in our cause.

One popular idea in DSA is that candidates should always "run to win." It is correct that we should be running professional campaigns, with talented candidates who truly want to come out victorious. If we finish with single-digit results, that is probably a sign that we ran our campaign poorly and need to reevaluate our strategy. However, it's important to remember that the path to victory can be longer than one election cycle, and an honorable defeat can still build the movement. Cori Bush did not win her initial campaign in 2018, but now she is headed to Congress to join the Squad. Nor did Bernie Sanders win his first independent House bid in 1988 — that took a second try in 1990. If we abandon every "loser" the moment they fall short, we may end up discarding capable leaders who still have future potential.

In the long run, our goal should be to run candidates for every office possible, even where we cannot win. This boosts our visibility as a national political movement and will help us extend our presence outside the large urban centers. Like Bernie, we must eagerly engage with rural, small-town, and Republican-leaning voters. If we abstain for fear of losing, we will never be able to build a truly national constituency.

7) Stop endorsing outside the party.

Once we have a training program for this new approach to electoral work, we must wind down the faucet of endorsements. DSA should focus all of its energy, messaging, and resources on promoting its own candidates: active, committed members who promise to uphold the platform. The only exception would be strategic collaboration with candidates from other independent left parties. Electoral pacts to avoid competition in certain districts may occasionally be necessary.

Cutting off endorsements may seem like a sectarian move, but it is perfectly reasonable. AOC and other Squad members are sparing with their primary endorsements; they have not mounted a massive assault against their Democratic colleagues. They have pragmatic obligations to attend to, and so do we. We should pour all our energy into cultivating talented candidates who are embedded in our organization and committed to building an independent movement. When we endorse candidates who are not directly accountable to our membership, we muddy the waters on what DSA stands for.

None of this means that we will run around viciously denouncing left Democrats and other progressive candidates. They are not responsible for this crisis. We will sometimes criticize their political strategy, but our fiery speeches will be reserved for the ghouls who actually hold the cards: Biden, McConnell, Kavanaugh, Barrett, and so on. When our rabble-rousing socialist backbenchers take up their seats, they may want to collaborate with the major parties from time to time, and left Democrats could end up playing a valuable role as mediators. And who knows? Some of them may be impressed by our new brand of politics and join our ranks. The goal is not to be sectarian. We are just stepping up to become self-reliant, to make our own independent mark on the world.

8) Choose ballot lines at the state level.

Should we keep running our candidates in Democratic primaries, or should we rush to set up our own ballot lines?

Every state has its unique convoluted rules, so there's no easy answer to this question. That's the point. Our system is designed to encourage incoherent thinking, to fragment and divide power to make majoritarian politics impossible. When future schoolteachers describe the decline and fall of the United States, they will point to its divided political system, the fifty jurisdictions marked out on a map. The children will laugh out loud and ask how it lasted so long.

The states have had third parties running like gerbils on a wheel, focusing all their energy on petition gathering and hopeless presidential campaigns (required to secure ballot access). Even staunch third party advocates like Hawkins know that it's time to break the wheel and try something new. Perhaps we should ditch the ballot access crusades and just run nominal independents. That would allow us to stop running top-heavy presidential tickets, to be more discriminating about which elections we target.

It's clear that there are weak spots when it comes to ballot access. California, Texas, and Florida, for example, all have equitable access for independents. Why run Democrats for the House in any of those easy states?

Once we have dedicated state-level organizations, they will be able to make these judgment calls decisively. In New Jersey, where only 100 signatures are required for independent House bids and party machines brazenly rig their primaries, "clean break now" is an excellent approach.

In Georgia, the rules for independents are extremely inhospitable and primaries are open to voters from any party. There, it would make sense to antagonize the Democrats with a large slate of DSA primary insurgents. For the sake of clear messaging, ballot line choices should generally be consistent across the entire state. We would confuse primary voters if we ran an independent in one congressional district, a Democrat in the one next door, and a Republican for a county office that overlaps both districts.

Even when we run in a party primary, we should still run our candidates on the DSA platform and be committed to political independence. The line could be this: "I'm running as a Democrat. It was the only way to get on the ballot. Once I'm elected, I'll renounce my party affiliation and serve with the Socialist Independents."

Off they will go to join the rest of our rabble-rousing backbenchers. Under this framework, the "dirty break" is no longer some vague goal that we banish to the distant future. It is something that we do *every time we win an election,* enraging both capitalist parties. Call it the filthy break — perhaps we will even run Socialist Republicans in Montana! Eventually, both parties should be expected to crack down and pass laws to close up their primaries. Hopefully, we will already have a mass constituency by that point.

Right now, DSA prioritizes Democratic bids and neglects independent campaigns. That order should be reversed. Clean independent bids should always be prioritized, wherever we can realistically get a couple strong campaigns on the ballot. They establish our independence and make it clear to the public that we are *not* Democrats — that we are out to break the two-party system.

"But you'll never win as an independent!" some will protest. "I did!" Bernie Sanders would have replied in 1990. It's an uphill battle, but not an impossible one.

Vote-splitting is another valid concern. Unfortunately, it is a fact of life in *any* winner-take-all election. It happens in Democratic primaries (peace among worlds, Liz!). Even the *fear* of vote-splitting can do great damage to insurgent primary campaigns. NYC-DSA learned that the hard way when self-appointed socialist kingmaker Sean McElwee released a poll to deliberately tank Samelys López's congressional bid, claiming that she would split the vote and put a conservative Democrat in office.

Vote-splitting will happen, and we will have to find ways to reduce the public's fear of it. Establishing ourselves as a viable force *worth* splitting the vote for will be one important step. We will have to pick our campaigns carefully in the beginning to build capacity and establish a political foothold. But from the very outset, we must make it clear that we are intent on further expansion. The Socialist Movement has the right to run its candidates *across the board*, just like any other political party.

9) Target the House of Representatives.

What made the Bernie movement so powerful, so terrifying, so utterly invigorating for its participants? It was a national struggle for power.

That point deserves to be repeated: participation in the Bernie movement was participation in a *national struggle for power*. In the campaign's words, it was a mission to "defeat Donald Trump and transform America."

America alienates the US left. We are not nationalists; we are not patriots. We reject much of the dominant culture. This makes it difficult for us to conceive of politics as a nationally coordinated struggle. It is much easier to think in terms of local organizing or international solidarity. Both are crucial projects. The working class has no country; the socialist movement must be international, and our work is hopeless without effective local organizers on the ground.

But the best thing we can do for our local organizers is to integrate them into a coordinated movement for transformative change. The best thing that we can do to foster internationalism is build a real, unified revolutionary organization in America, a powerful socialist movement that can give inspiration to others around the world.

If we play our hand well, our next national struggle will be different from Bernie's in some important ways. We will be more ambitious, more independent, and less deferential to established institutions. Instead of trying to redeem the Democratic Party, we will oppose it head-on alongside the GOP. Instead of seeking a "political revolution" within the capitalist state, we will call for a world-historic revolution and a new political order: an authentic working-class democracy. How can we integrate our union work, tenant struggles, and electoral campaigns into this grand vision? Do we run another presidential campaign?

Not in 2024. Barring something completely unforeseen, we will not have the numbers, organization, and high-profile leaders necessary to mount an interesting presidential bid. We would waste precious volunteer hours collecting signatures and then come out with 1% of the vote. It would be hopping right back on the gerbil wheel. Once we have a larger base, we can contest the presidency (on a platform of abolishing the presidency by revolution).

But our main target should be the House of Representatives. It is a federal institution, elected every two years in local districts that are small enough for us to realistically target. We can run a National Slate of candidates, from Washington to Florida, from Michigan to Maine, and talk it up in our stump speeches. We can use the House as a *national soapbox* to publicize our demands. We will be speaking to America coast-to-coast, raising our public profile and giving a boost to all of our state and local candidates. The House is the most important electoral institution for us to contest in the years to come.

We can begin in the urban deep blue districts that Democrats have dominated, plus some red district bids to expand our repertoire. This will offer political choice to one-party districts that have had none for years, giving us a chance to establish viability. Then, as quickly as we can, we should strive to contest all 434 congressional seats, forcing a messy national referendum on our political demands *every two years*.

The next three points could be among the most important demands.

10) Organize for electoral reform.

We must demand an end to the two-party system. We should fight for easy ballot access for all political parties, ranked-choice voting and multi-member electoral districts, proportional representation in Congress, and anything else that gives working-class people more choice at the ballot box. In the wake of the 2020 Census and the GOP's electoral fraud witch-hunt, a new wave of gerrymandering and voter suppression will be arriving very soon. In this political climate, our campaigns for electoral reform should be connected to wider efforts to protect voting rights, such as citizen redistricting panels and automatic voter registration.

We must integrate these demands and advance them with incisive slogans, playing on popular antipathy to entrenched politicians and the two-party system. Many states have ballot initiative processes that we could use to our advantage, mobilizing voters to pass electoral reforms at the ballot box. Such campaigns have already been mounted by nonpartisan groups, successfully in Michigan, Maine, and Alaska (and unsuccessfully in Massachusetts). Although petition circulation requirements are often arduous, a volunteer-powered mass movement may well be able to blast through the obstacles.

Electoral reform campaigns are one more way to establish our political independence. They will also help us establish that socialists are champions of a richer democracy (and that the capitalist parties are not!).

11) Shoot down war budgets.

The US spends more on its military than the next ten countries combined. Trillion-dollar slush funds, poured into graft, arms manufacturers, right-wing dictatorships, and bloody imperialistic ventures all over the world. That is no secret; it is *common knowledge* to tens of millions of Americans.

We cut ourselves apart through total noncooperation. We should refuse to vote for any spending bill that pours one more penny into the bloated military, police departments, or any other repressive capitalist institution.

If we do this, will we cause endless government shutdowns? Unlikely. The Republicans and Democrats will pass their "bipartisan" budgets right over our heads. Drop a heavy boulder into a creek, and the water finds its way around it. But it gives us something to stand on to capture public attention, to erode the legitimacy of an institution that Americans are taught to view as sacrosanct.

12) Demand a new constitution.

What is a demand that would truly set us apart, that would bring the Right's worst nightmares to life?

Demand a New Union. A new constitution, developed by mass popular participation. Not an Article V convention. No state-by-state ratification. An accessible process that everyone within the borders of the United States can contribute to, combining grassroots direct democracy with a National Constituent Assembly. The final ratification would be by national referendum — a simple majority vote.

In a free society, everyone gets a say in the social contract that they live under. That is not what happened when the current constitution was written. Women had no say; black people had no say; working-class people had no say. We demand that the living, breathing people of the United States be given the right to determine its future. We demand a constitution that guarantees real democracy, majority rule, housing, healthcare — economic rights.

We will be quite clear about the additional reforms that we would advocate throughout the process: abolish the Senate, abolish the presidency, abolish the Supreme Court. All power to an expanded, improved, democratized House of Representatives.

"We demand that Congress initiate this process, but if it does not, the people have a right to do so themselves."

There is a legitimate argument to be made that the Constitution can be legally amended by referendum. This deserves an article of its own, and we should certainly invoke constitutional law as needed. Of course, none of our opponents will take our arguments too seriously. Revolutions make their own laws, and what we demand is nothing less than a *world-historic revolution* against the forces of Old America.

Let the Trumpers fume over the socialist plot to destroy the Constitution. Let the liberals lecture us about the dangers of norm erosion. Obama can start an NGO to educate young people about the beauty of our institutions and the farsighted wisdom of our Founding Fathers. We alienate most people at first, but we strike a chord with a sizable minority. And every year, we build it out, leaning into every crisis, growing, until finally something snaps.

That is the last point. To recap all twelve:

1. Declare political independence.
2. Hold annual conventions.
3. Form statewide organizations.
4. Cultivate a committed membership base.
5. Adopt a nationwide political platform.
6. Run dedicated organizers for office.
7. Stop endorsing outside the party.
8. Choose ballot lines at the state level.
9. Target the House of Representatives.
10. Agitate for electoral reform.
11. Shoot down war budgets.
12. Demand a new constitution.

Perhaps these suggestions are unrealistic. They may demand too much of a small organization like DSA; they may overestimate the potential of the era we are living in. But even if we try them and fail, at least we will fail on our own terms, in a more instructive way than ever before. Progressive reform movements rise and fall, both inside and outside the Democratic Party. For decades they have led us to defeat, cooptation, and humiliation. Many generations of the American Left have grown exhausted with this ritual, but instead of building a real alternative, the disenchanted vent their frustration with performative action. Endless rallies, megaphone chants, and radical posturing take us nowhere. Localist organizing projects "feel good," but they completely lose sight of the national struggle for power.

What we need are performative restraint and *political aggression.* Independent politics is not a distant end goal; it is not something we earn after working hard enough for the Democratic coalition. It is the heart of the socialist project, the foundation of effective revolutionary struggle, and something that we ought to start doing *right now.* The time has come to forge a new strategy that draws on the best of the Bernie campaign and everything that came before it. A fearless strategy, hardheaded yet still principled, that never loses sight of the real end goal: a world-historic, working-class revolution in the USA.

And the goal of this piece is to contribute some starting points.

SECTION IV
LABOR AND UNIONS

THE WORKER AND THE HYDRA: A REPLY TO PARTISAN MAG

Marisa Miale
July 29, 2020

The development of working-class consciousness requires more than struggles against the employer on the shopfloor, argues Marisa Miale.

The workplace is a complex system — something with too many variables to perfectly model and predict, that organizers must nonetheless try to navigate with imperfect data. To fully make sense of their surroundings, organizers need to understand the conflicting desires and influences of their co-workers, many of them hidden behind masks and contradictory premises. Every person swims in a sea of personal needs, formative experiences, and communal identities, suspended within the technical composition of production. Retail clerks exhausted with low wages but filled with hope by social movements, auto workers dabbling in both union reform and social conservatism, rideshare drivers loyal to the Democratic Party but emboldened through desire for workers control, all on winding and forked paths toward either decaying liberalism, rising fascism or a communist horizon.

The difficulty of accounting for complexity leads labor strategists to conjure practical half-truths, emphasizing specific possibilities or sites of struggle and downplaying others. Using case studies and direct experience as their sources, strategists may give primacy to the most militant or the most oppressed, to struggles against bureaucracy, liberalism or immiseration, to organic politicization or Marxist education. Strategies of this sort range from Kim Moody's rank-and-file strategy[1] to the solidarity unionism of the Industrial Workers of the World.[2] While all of these approaches can have value under certain circumstances, it is exceedingly difficult for them to account for every variable in the workplace, requiring organizers on the ground to constantly reconsider and correct their approach.

In "Class Consciousness and Communist Action,"[3] written for *Partisan Magazine*, Sean O calls for communists to examine how workers develop class consciousness through the struggle for control over the workplace, challenging the authority of the boss and asserting their humanity in the face of capitalist alienation. Sean O roots his ideas in both Marxist philosophy and his experience as a shop steward, witnessing workers awaken to their dehumanization and demand power and respect through everyday disputes with management. He then traces a thread from these mundane awakenings to the historic role of the proletariat as a revolutionary subject capable of ending capitalism.

While comrade O does an admirable job of synthesizing social practice and communist theory, he makes a number of sweeping assumptions about the development of class consciousness, and does not tie his strategy for workplace activity to a clear vision of socialist construction. This piece is both a critique of his limitations and an elaboration on his positive argument, meant to fill in some of the gaps left by his framework — namely a theory of class consciousness that can transcend conflict with individual employers and contend with the capitalist state, as well as a the-

---

1 Moody, Kim. "The Rank and File Strategy: Building a Socialist Movement in the US" Solidarity, 2006. https://solidarity-us.org/rankandfilestrategy/.

2 White, Don. "Solidarity Unionism: What It Is and What It Isn't." organizing.work, September 6, 2018. https://organizing.work/2018/09/solidarity-unionism-what-it-is-and-what-it-isnt/.

3 Sean O, "Class Consciousness and Communist Action," Partisan Magazine. https://partisanmag.com/class-consciousness-and-communist-action/

ory of socialist transition that can coordinate production across workplaces. This requires more than just workers in a given shop taking power from their own bosses. We need a communist strategy that can deal with the sheer complexity of capitalism and its interlocking aspects, which requires weaving shopfloor radicalism into something greater than itself.

Pedagogy of Revolution

Sean O asks where political struggle begins in working-class organization, versus where it is purely an economic dispute. Without communist intervention, he surmises that workers will tend toward *economism*, where their horizon is limited to negotiating over wages, benefits, and working conditions. Instead, communists should work with their coworkers to question the authority of management and assert their own control over production. We are in agreement over the limits of economism and the need for intervention, but his framework does not widen the scope of struggle *beyond* the workplace, which neither helps us develop communist consciousness or construct a socialist movement capable of transcending the worker-boss contradiction.

Comrade O ends without outlining how communists should advance forward from workplace activity, leaving the implications of his strategy up to interpretation — one could draw from him either a vision of decentralized self-management with each workforce taking over their place of work, or an unspoken political strategy building off of this shopfloor activity. He leaves open necessary strategic questions around what working-class militants should be fighting *for* — to live with dignity? To manage their own firms? To strengthen the position of workers in the nation? Or to take political power over every aspect of society, not just production?

He observes that workers have an impulse toward autonomy, leading even the most disorganized to engage in acts of protest and sabotage when they feel their humanity is being denied — for instance, a worker demanding their supervisor look them in the eye while talking to them. While he identifies this as a potential point for communists to intervene, he extends this concept further by claiming that "the worker's desire to be a free human being leads in no direction other than that of communism, whether they recognize it or not."

The phrase "whether they recognize it or not" hides a snake pit of contradictions. People of all classes are exposed to differing ideologies and formative moments, some imposed by the structure of capitalism and some incidental to their lives. These, alongside class, shape their consciousness, determining how they respond to new stimuli and adjust their ideas. While the experience of exploitation creates an opening for class consciousness, workers can draw a myriad of interpretations from each experience. These interpretations may be influenced by past experience, either their own or those they've heard secondhand, and by the conflicting interpretations of those around them, including those who speak for management and the state.

One worker may see asserting their dignity in terms of liberal egalitarianism, where everyone should learn to coexist and respect each other while maintaining the hierarchy they inhabit. Another might hold a populist outlook, with workers standing up as patriotic citizens against corporate power or foreign control. Many people will mix and match these ideas in ways that seem logical to them but incoherent to others. For instance, some Italian fascists fused revolutionary syndicalism[4] with nationalism, using class struggle as a weapon of the nation in its fight against international capital, rather than as a liberatory weapon for workers across borders. The national syndicalist Rossoni, influenced by the oppression he faced as an immigrant worker, wrote "we have seen our workers exploited and held in low regard not only by the capitalists but also by the revolutionary *comrades* of

---

4 An ideology advocating for control of production to transfer from managers to workers directly via labor unions.

other countries. We, therefore, know from experience how internationalism is nothing but fiction and hypocrisy," channeling the demand for workers to seize control of production into one for strengthening the power and prosperity of the nation.[5]

National syndicalism shares failings with reformist social democracy, in which socialists enter government in alliance with capitalists, advocating for workers to receive a larger share of profits within the capitalist system. Even when reformists themselves come from the working class and represent the workers' movement, they put themselves in a position where their power over the state can only be used to administer capitalism, disciplining the movement to the ruling class. National syndicalists achieved a similar result by radically different means, disciplining a genuinely transformative movement for self-management to the fascist state.

The gradients here are subtle, but necessary for us to incorporate into shopfloor strategy. When we assume challenging the boss can lead in no direction but communism, we leave ourselves open to cooptation. Communists play the role not just of organizer but of educator — synthesizing the direct experience of exploitation with the theory our comrades have developed through centuries of past experience. Just as we bring theory from past experience into new struggles, new struggles transform our understanding of Marxism and prepare us for those of the future. This does not mean that communists should practice didactic teaching, where the educator's role is to fill the empty heads of their students with the correct ideas. Rather, we should use what Paulo Freire calls *problem-posing* education, where educators uncover themes in the lives of the oppressed and tackle them collaboratively:

> Students, as they are increasingly posed with problems relating to themselves in the world and with the world, will feel increasingly

5 Roberts, David D. *Syndicalist Tradition and Italian Fascism*. Chapel Hill: University Of North Carolina Press, 1979. p. 108.

challenged and obliged to respond to that challenge. Because they apprehend the challenge as interrelated to other problems within a total context, not as a theoretical question, the resulting comprehension tends to be increasingly critical and thus constantly less alienated. Their response to the challenge evokes new challenges, followed by new understandings; and gradually the students come to regard themselves as committed.[6]

In this framework, communist and non-communist workers are equals in developing new theories and plans of action. Communists put our political program in conversation with the experience of other workers, transforming all of our perspectives. Our role is to uncover new and broader themes in the struggle — actively tying the problem of disrespect from an individual manager into the system of capitalist management, and then into the international rule of the employing class. This allows us to integrate the specific experience of workers with the collective experience of the movement.

Socialists often mistake militancy for class consciousness. In this conception, communist agitation is synonymous with raising the militancy of rank-and-file workers, pushing them to greater levels of escalation until they're ready to seize power from the boss and self-manage. Taken on its own, however, this approach will only lead to another form of economism — rather than petitioning management for the betterment of wages, benefits and working conditions, workers will determine their own wages, benefits and working conditions. This elides the role of struggles in the home and the neighborhood, and at the level of high politics, against oppression, imperialism, policing, and the undemocratic political order through which the capitalist class rules, and for the hegemony of the working-class in every facet of production, circulation, consumption, and political life. Trying to identify an isolated political role for shopfloor struggles is like the Greek myth of the hydra — for each head you cut off,

6 Freire, Paulo. *Pedagogy of the Oppressed*. London: Bloomsbury Press, 1970. p. 81.

another two sprout. We can only reach the communist implications of shopfloor activity through political activity that touches on every face of the ruling class, which means challenging the capitalist hydra in its heart, not just whichever head is tasked with running a given workplace.

In order to develop a fully realized communist strategy for the twenty-first century, we need to nest shopfloor strategy within a wider vision of working-class organization. Communism is not just an accumulation of single-issue campaigns and local seizures of power, but the movement of the entire working-class, capable of solving universal problems like the dictatorship of the bourgeoisie, and combining forces against particular ones like patriarchy, white supremacy and workplace management. This includes those outside stereotypic definitions of *worker*, like prisoners, unpaid domestic laborers, the unemployed, and those jumping from gig to gig. By overemphasizing the direct experience of workplace oppression, we risk ignoring those outside traditional employment, or who might see their most immediate enemy as the police, real estate developers, environmental polluters, etc.

When communists disperse into issue-based campaigns, we need to guard against the creation of separate fiefdoms of struggle. For instance, assembly line workers over production, environmentalists over nature, tenants over housing, etc. Communists must bring their specialized expertise back to the movement for universal emancipation. On the shop floor, our responsibility is to push the struggle further, beyond the workplace, challenging the entire political apparatus of the ruling class, not just those tasked with directly managing workers.

To reach the political conclusion of class struggle, communists have a responsibility to help workers synthesize ideas and push against liberal and reactionary conclusions. This can feel exceedingly difficult precisely because it doesn't always flow naturally from labor-management relations. Sometimes it will require introducing new elements that might seem unrelated, like the influence of employers on labor law, or the role of gender and race under capitalism. Chaining these themes together both strengthens the struggle and elevates it beyond the shop floor. This means communists must use the day-to-day realities of working-class life to scaffold higher levels of theory.

Other times shopfloor struggle will begin to spill out of the factory, the warehouse or the retail outlet, allowing communists in the right time and place to intervene in a struggle that, out of necessity, begins to politicize itself. For example, in the Gas Protest of 1974, where rising tensions between striking miners and state police, dovetailed with the historic memory of miner insurgency, forced the state of West Virginia to end gas rationing.[7] Another instance is the Watsonville Canning Strike of 1986, where immigrant strikers and socialist activists transformed a walkout over pay and benefits into a popular expression of the Chicano Movement.[8] In the former case, economic protest spilled out of the shopfloor and challenged the state itself. In the latter, organizers actively drew a wider movement into the strike. Both were opportunities for communists to scaffold different levels of struggle, helping striking workers develop the political acumen necessary to construct socialism.

This is not to say that power struggles within the workplace are a waste of time. However, communists who see them as naturally blossoming into a conquest of power will end up missing opportunities to uplift and expand their implications. Rather than a full curriculum in class conflict, shopfloor activity is an object-lesson that can be used to raise and discuss political

7 Ely, Mike. *Ambush at Keystone No. 1*. Kasama Project, 2009.
8 Shapiro, Peter. "The Necessity of Organization: The League of Revolutionary Struggle and the Watsonville Canning Strike." Viewpoint Magazine, August 30, 2018. https://viewpointmag.com/2018/08/30/the-necessity-of-organization-the-league-of-revolutionary-struggle-and-the-watsonville-canning-strike/.

questions from which workers can draw a variety of conclusions based on the material possibilities in front of them.

When communist militants elide these questions from our workplace strategies, we risk miseducating our comrades about the potential of shopfloor skirmishes and the necessary steps to push them further. In order to forge a new revolutionary consciousness among workers, we need to incorporate both the advantages and limitations of industrial movements and to help each other see the bigger picture.

From Labor Strategy to Revolutionary Strategy

Sean O states that the "potentiality of communism does not emerge from outside of the working class." While this is correct in a structural sense, we need to be clear that the scientific formulae workers can use to construct socialism cannot all be found through workplace action. The notion of communist theory coming from inside or outside the extant working class fails to describe the relationship between the socialist and workers' movements, simplifying our role into teasing out the inherent communism of working-class self-activity. Communist theory is drawn from the entire history of the workers' movement, meaning that what appears to be an intervention from outside can be a lesson drawn from centuries of direct experience, passed down through the socialist milieu and returned again to its home in the workers' movement. This is especially important when the consciousness of the working class is low, forcing us to look to past, more revolutionary incarnations of the movement for data.

Sean O cites the factory councils of Turin as an example of a successful challenge to managerial authority. The factory councils, however, never developed the political direction and leadership to expand beyond industrial occupation, and the socialist movement failed to intervene and empower them further, leading them to fade away in the wake of fascist reaction.[9] On the other hand, the factory committees and soviets of the Russian Revolution, which preceded the Turin movement, did succeed in effecting a revolutionary transfer of power, primarily but not exclusively under Bolshevik leadership. In the course of the revolution, they were subject to a complicated exchange between the political parties who intervened in them, the needs of different class strata, and the demands of the Russian Civil War. When committees first began to take control of production, it was primarily out of a desire to increase defense production for the First World War, combined with the democratic aspirations of the Mensheviks and Socialist-Revolutionaries. For defensists, workers' control was a means for transforming Russia into a liberal-democratic power, with the question of socialism tabled till the distant future.

After the October Revolution, some Bolsheviks in the factory committees began to argue for workers' self-management in tandem with central planning. However, the devastation of the Russian Civil War destroyed the industrial base for the committees and pushed the Bolsheviks to reintroduce labor discipline, cutting short their experiment.[10] We could speculate that under better conditions the factory committees might have found a path to both survival and workers' control, but they would have to do so in alliance with the Red Army, the peasantry, and workers outside manufacturing. The point is not that communists should put more or less emphasis on planning over autonomy, but that workers' control does not always lead to communism — and that even when it does, communists must actively win support for our program.

Setting up an inside-outside dichotomy creates an awkward model where socialist ideas must flow from organic activity in

9 Azzellini, Dario, Immanuel Ness, and Pietro Di Paola. "Factory Councils in Turin, 1919–1920." Essay. In *Ours to Master and to Own: Workers' Control from the Commune to the Present*, 130–47. Chicago: Haymarket Books, 2011.
10 Smith, S. A. Essay. In *Red Petrograd: Revolution in the Factories, 1917-1918, 258–65. Cambridge University Press*, 1983.

the present, but where we can't reapply lessons drawn from past activity. We develop richer theory and strategy when we put the different spheres of communist work in conversation. Do our coworkers see their struggle against management reflected in those against landlords, police, and politicians? Do they see these conflicts as sharing a common solution? What form will that solution take, and how should we coordinate it? Shopfloor struggle alone cannot end class society and social domination, and for masses of workers to develop a communist consciousness we need to carry out a strategy that addresses all aspects of capitalist society.

Communism is a totalizing framework, requiring us to consider the workplace as one node in a complex system that the working class needs to coordinate in its entirety. This is what political power means: governance of the whole of society. This requires being able to manage production, logistics and outputs like food, housing, and healthcare as a cohesive and interconnected project. To meet the needs of the entire populace, we need to make central decisions; a factory council in charge of producing wheat, for instance, cannot be allowed to produce too little for the supply of bread to match the needs of society. We should be clear that comrade O does not advocate explicitly for this kind of radical decentralization. However, communist strategists have a responsibility to consider these questions and incorporate them into their blueprints, or else our political opponents may channel the consciousness forged in economic struggle into avenues inimical to communism.

Science on the Shopfloor

We have opened multiple questions on revolutionary strategy and the workplace — the differing facets of class consciousness, the relationship between economic and political power, and the tension between coordination and autonomy of production. While the sections above take steps toward addressing these questions, we should not pretend to have resolved them. While we have decades of data from past movements to draw from, we should be wary of drawing from existent models uncritically. Past communists built reform caucuses, study circles, strike committees, dual unions, bureaucratic cliques, and a host of other interventions aimed at developing a revolutionary workers' movement through shopfloor activity. All of them were synthesizing political principles and the practical needs of the moment, with varying levels of success. While we can look to historical narratives for case studies and inspiration, labor strategy remains a scientific problem for us to solve.

To this end, we will conclude with an open question for study and reflection, the answers to which we may find through observation and debate: *What structures should we use to facilitate political agitation and development on the shop floor?*

Most modern socialists in the labor movement, more or less following Moody's rank-and-file strategy, operate through *transitional organizations*, bodies meant to raise the general consciousness of workers through militant but non-revolutionary *transitional demands* — for instance, Teamsters for a Democratic Union, which aims to democratize the Teamsters and put them under rank-and-file leadership, and Labor Notes, a journal which serves as a hub for union militants.[11] These organizations are usually formed by socialists toward socialist ends, but define themselves through their broader basis of unity, aiming to instill a class consciousness more amenable to socialism by virtue of its militancy and critical analysis of those in power.

Reflecting on the brief and efficient history of Labor Notes, Marxist and labor journalist Kim Moody wrote that "when choices had to be made between educating in practical strategies and actions, on the one hand, and advanced political education or mere propaganda, on the other, for better or worse we almost in-

11 Moody, Kim. "The Rank and File Strategy: Building a Socialist Movement in the US" Solidarity, 2006. https://solidarity-us.org/rankandfilestrategy/.

variably chose the former. That was the right choice and part of what made the project work as well as it did."[12] Moody's assessment highlights both the project's strength and its limits. Labor Notes promotes a pragmatic approach to workplace organizing, with its finger close to the pulse of capital. By recognizing and responding to class struggle in motion, from wildcat strikes to sophisticated union-busting schemes, Labor Notes was able to develop a base of union militants in need of down-to-earth, immediately useful analysis that could be applied to workplace activity.

Their structure for organizing conversations, for instance, is a stock training material for new labor organizers, aimed at discerning workplace issues, stoking anger around them, laying the blame on management, and finally coming to a collective solution — unionism. Organizers enter with open-ended questions and aim for the other conversant to walk away with a concrete task for the union: inviting a coworker to a meeting, composing a list of grievances, convincing their department to sign on to a demand letter, etc.

Transitional projects, however, generally measure their success via their transitional goals, not their implicit socialist purpose. This creates friction between vision and practice rather than merging the two, with trade unionism eclipsing revolutionary politics. Though the organizers behind projects like TDU and LN did initially link them with political education, their political organizations have largely faded while their transitional projects have remained resilient.[13] Explicitly socialist and communist union caucuses, study circles, and labor journals are close to nonexistent in the contemporary labor movement.

There is also the issue of whether transitional demands are effective at raising consciousness, let alone whether we can lever-

12 Moody, Kim. "The Rank and File's Paper of Record." Jacobin, November 8, 2016. https://www.jacobinmag.com/2016/08/labor-notes-rank-and-file-reform-unions-concessions-labor/

13 Moody, Kim. "The Rank & File Strategy and the New Socialist Movement." Spectre Journal, December 20, 2020. https://spectrejournal.com/the-rank-file-strategy-and-the-new-socialist-movement/

age them toward revolutionary politics. Those with direct experience of transitional organizing are best positioned to summarize and assess its success and benefit the entire movement with their findings. Unfortunately, many contemporary treatments of rank-and-file strategy, such as sociologist Barry Eidlin's *What is the Rank-and-File Strategy*, focus on the achievement of transitional demands, while downplaying the development of socialist consciousness and dismissing those who "propagandize" for socialist politics.[14] In order to fully grasp the best routes toward communist politicization, we need to evaluate the success of transitional organizations and experiment with new structures for agitation.

Sean O makes a compelling case for the role of shopfloor activity in this process, but we need to go further to generate mass communist politics and build a fighting party. We do the working-class a disservice when we develop labor strategy while leaving revolutionary strategy unspoken. Power over production can be a tool for workers to learn the willingness and expertise to govern, but only as part of a wider pedagogy of revolution. The responsibility of communists is not to simply push everyday struggles further, but to integrate them into the entire process of liberation. To accomplish this, our task is to draw the mass of workers in as co-researchers studying the construction of communism. When workers are ready to unite across sectors and movements, we will be able to strike the capitalist hydra in its heart.

---

14 Eidlin, Barry. "What Is the Rank-and-File Strategy, and Why Does It Matter?" Jacobin, March 26, 2019. https://www.jacobinmag.com/2019/03/rank-and-file-strategy-union-organizing.

COMMUNISTS AND THE UNIONS IN THE TWENTY-FIRST CENTURY

Anton Johansson
Febuary 5, 2019

Communists must take a leading role in rebuilding the labor move-
ment and fighting against anti-union laws like Taft-Hartley, argues
Anton Johannsen.

There is a continuum of left positions on unions. Syndicalism argues for very particular forms of unions as the central revolutionary organizational bodies, and often views existing unions as corrupt and useless. Trotskyists and most Stalinists see bureaucratic unions as in need of a leadership change; communists must lead them, and in turn the unions must be subordinated to the party. Anarchists, like syndicalists, often support unions of a particular anti-statist bent. With the exception of Bordigists, left communists see little to nothing of use in unions or involvement in union work. There are partial truths that all tendencies recognize across the board, yet none of these views are sufficient. In this piece, I will try to briefly outline an argument for why communists need to develop a unique strategy to help build unions and that communists must fight to strengthen workers' rights by repealing Taft-Hartley's provisions which treat US workers like indentured servants.

Unions are on the front lines of the class struggle for workers under capitalism. By "union" here I mean *some form of organi-*

zation for defense and attack at work. Note that this is an abstract definition, i.e., a simple model or category. From this abstract model, we can then bring in factors of the world or the particular form a union takes in order to concretize the discussion and clarify problems with unions.

For example, unions charge members' dues and use the money to pay staff and officers to carry out their work. We can concretize this further. Most unions pay executive national/international positions relatively fat salaries. In most unions, these positions are monopolized by bureaucrats, a form of legal corruption, and in some, outright illegal corruption.

This is beneficial to the bourgeoisie and they prefer it this way. In the 1990s, members of the Teamsters voted out the union's president, Jimmy Hoffa Jr., the notoriously employer-friendly son of the mobbed-up union boss, Hoffa Sr. Ron Carey, a reform candidate endorsed by the Teamsters for a Democratic Union, won on a platform of slashing bloated union-executive compensation and waste, democratizing the union, and supporting the drive to strike against UPS in order to bring part-timers into full-time positions, among other demands. In 1997, with Carey at the helm, 185,000 Teamsters went out on strike for 3 weeks after years of preparation through a rank-and-file organizing drive among members. The union brought UPS to its knees, and they were not happy. Carey himself recalls the negotiating meeting where UPS accede to the union's demands:

> I recall an incident which occurred in the last hours of those strike negotiations which illustrates the level of animosity the corporate community felt for me: one of the negotiators for UPS said, in the presence of then-Secretary of Labor Alexis Herman, "Okay Carey, we agree on the union's outstanding issues," and he proceeded to leave the conference room. As he was leaving, he leaned over the conference table and said to me, "You're dead, Carey, and you will pay for this, you s.o.b." I looked at Ms. Herman, and asked, "Did you hear that?" She responded, "I heard nothing."[1]

---

1 Joe Allen. "The UPS Strike, Two Decades Later." Jacobin Magazine, Au-

Over the next four years, Hoffa Jr., UPS, the corporate media, and House Republicans led a smear campaign against Carey that saw him barred from running for re-election and eventually banned from the Teamsters for life. They alleged that Carey had knowledge of a scam worked out by his campaign consultant, Jere Nash, to use union money to fund the election campaign, a significant chunk of which was kicked back to this consultant's business,

> Nash's testimony also revealed that he may have been neck-deep in a shady conflict of interest. In 1996 he received $128,000 from Martin Davis's consulting firm, which was the largest vendor for the Carey campaign. This pay was ostensibly for six months of part-time work Nash did related to the Clinton-Gore campaign. (Nash's compensation from the Carey campaign was much less: $2,500 a month.) Nash simultaneously was managing the Carey campaign and employed by its biggest creditor. The swaps occurred when Nash and Davis were looking for money to pay for a $700,000 direct-mail push for the Carey campaign — a direct-mail effort to be handled by Davis and one that would result in large profits for his firm. With Davis his main income source, Nash, then, may have had a financial incentive to go along with Davis's swap scheme and not inform Carey of it. And as Carey's attorneys noted, Nash, who is cooperating with the US Attorney, might be testifying against Carey to win a reduction in sentence.[2]

In 2001, Carey was acquitted by a jury of any knowledge of the scams. By that time, Hoffa Jr. had won a re-election campaign for President of the Teamsters. The business community was ecstatic, with the trade magazine Transport World writing in 2000:

> United Parcel Service, the nation's largest transportation company, feels that it has taken part in one of the great trades of all time

gust 4, 2017. https://www.jacobinmag.com/2017/08/ups-strike-teamsters-logistics-labor-unions-work

2 David Corn. "The Prosecution and Persecution of Ron Carey." The Nation, April 6, 1998. https://www.thenation.com/article/archive/prosecution-and-persecution-ron-carey/

in labor: James P. 'Jimmy' Hoffa for Ron Carey as president of the Teamsters union.[3]

To be clear, the bourgeoisie rule through legal corruption, and delight at the illegal corruption of workers' organizations. This helps them maintain hegemony over these organizations or crack down on them through the state. By legal corruption, I mean access and retention of office by means of money. This is legalized through restrictive pressures put on political campaigns by money: it's much easier for the wealthy to reach a broad audience. As well, access to public relations firms and resources to carry out an election campaign, even within a union, require a lot of resources.

Jere Nash, Carey's consultant, was a Democratic Party insider and campaign strategist. The set-up to Carey's downfall was also the decades of corruption fostered in the Teamsters by Hoffa Sr., which led to the standing Federal monitoring of Teamster elections through an Independent Review Board, the representatives of which also played a role in bringing Hoffa Jr. back to power.

The key here is that the anti-democratic features of the Teamsters, their corruption, led to the political intervention of the state, not in the direction of ending corruption, *but ensuring the corrupt leaders retained control.*

The other features of bureaucratic unions are liberal and anti-republican organizational rules such as meaningless referendums, powerful executive bodies, and non-representational forms of organization. Strong executives in unions and a lack of membership vote (let alone membership control over bargaining and negotiations) are preferable to the bosses because they make it easier to wring a favorable solution out of the union by buying off union bureaucrats or taking advantage of divisions between the leadership and the membership to compel agreement.

---

3 Joe Allen. "The Persecution and Vindication of Ron Carey." Jacobin Magazine. October 13, 2017. https://www.jacobinmag.com/2017/10/ron-carey-teamsters-union-labor-tdu

This dynamic toward corruption is often cited as a reason to oppose the "bureaucratic unions" by anarcho-syndicalists and for the left communists, at times a reason to abstain, forsaking any kind of struggle for influence and leadership in the unions. But there is another logical step. Left communists argue that unions are naturally prone to becoming corrupt in this way by virtue of their *form,* no matter the ideology. On the other hand, anarcho-syndicalists point out that unions are like any social organization: they reflect the choices of members and leaders in their form and their activity. Thus, unions must be anarcho-syndicalist in nature in order to succeed. So far, so good. The problem with this? The reduction of virtually every anarcho-syndicalist union in the world to national membership levels of less than 10,000 across the globe. For anarcho-syndicalists, especially in the US, the *form* of a union is in equal measure to the strategic choices of the union participants in determining the more or less effective or revolutionary aspects of the union.

Direct Unionism, a view of union organizing promoted by a tendency in the American and Canadian sections of the IWW, proposes the following as an alternative to "bureaucratic unionism":

> ... that instead of focusing on contracts, workplace elections, or legal procedures, IWW members should strive to build networks of militants in whatever industry they are employed. These militants will then agitate amongst their co-workers and lead direct actions over specific grievances in their own workplaces. The goal of such actions will not be union recognition from a single boss. Instead, the goal of the actions is to build up leadership and consciousness amongst other workers. Once a 'critical mass' of workers have experience with, and an understanding of, direct action the focus will be on large scale industrial actions that address issues of wages and conditions across entire regions or even whole countries. It will be from this base of power that the IWW will establish itself as a legitimate workers' organization.

The Direct Unionists want to build up networks of union activists, essentially. In practice, this is little different from the Labor Notes strategy. The following argument is not that this strategy is in error, just that it is incomplete. How then would the Direct Unionists proceed?

> When organizing without contracts — as direct unionist believe we should be — it is of great importance the IWW is (1) very strategic and tactical in our organizing and (2) honest with ourselves about how much power we can effectively exert in any workplace or industry.[4]

The record of the I.W.W. over the past 20 or so years has shown that regardless of how well committee organizers performed according to item 1 above, with respect to item number 2 the reality is that lasting power was never really built.

Partly this must derive from their illusion that there could be a linear growth in the number of committees in the "network" that would work together without some organizational glue to coordinate and facilitate this increasing scale. What Direct Unionism does, in fact, is ideologize a *component* of many other types of organizing pursued in industries and areas difficult for unions to get a foothold in. This is often called "minority unionism" because the committee, no matter how plugged-in and representative of the workforce, is in the position of not being recognized by the company or the state as the representative agent of the workers.[5]

Nevertheless, the Direct Unionist attempt to deal concretely with the challenges faced by organizers, given the slate of anti-union policy in the US, is admirable. But the naiveté of trying to build an industry-wide strike via *ad hoc* committee-building without any plan of centralization from the beginning reveals an underlying decentralist-anarchist ideology, whether explic-

4 "Direct unionism: A discussion paper." Libcom, May 9, 2011. https://libcom.org/library/direct-unionism-discussion-paper-09052011
5 See U.E's non-contract campaign in North Carolina, for example.

itly held by the authors or not. Again, this is made clear by the persistent failure of what end up being isolated campaigns of volunteer committees associated with the IWW in various cities.

The other component to the Direct Unionist line is anti-contractualism. This rightly identifies the pernicious way that most contract provisions which employers are able to get into contracts are contrary to the interests of the workers and that the particular strategy of unions relying on contracts works to demobilize the membership in favor of emphasizing the role of thestaff and officers of a union. The problem with anti-contractualism is that it turns this criticism of particular strategies utilized by unions under current conditions into a dogmatic opposition to contracts that holds back effective organizing that can win long-term power on the shop floor. The very existence of a contract results in the development of a staff corps in the union, marshaled by an entrenched officialdom to rotate throughout the country, servicing bargaining units as their contracts come to expire, and leaving as soon as they are negotiated.

Instead, contracts should be seen for what they are: a measure of strength. The provisions of a contract illustrate the power of the workers to compel an employer to agree to the given provisions. Ultimately, a contract is a piece of paper with rules that must be enforced. The problem to which the Direct Unionists *ought* to respond is that of the balance of power between members and officials, to the extent that the officialdom and staff enforce poor contracts against members. The other side to this is the role the state plays in limiting the actions and types of demands unions may make, as well as in regulating their internal structure.

Direct Unionists, members of the IWW that they are, are very quick to point out the importance of membership-involvement, democracy, and hold a general anti-staff position. But from here we run into a problem in the question of concrete form. To make a comparison, the UAW (United Auto Workers) and IWW both have general conventions of elected delegates as the main decision making body, with executive boards making decisions in the interim. The UAW has a presidential office, which is an anti-republican office, so that's one notch against them. The point is that every aspect of 'form' betrays a particular interpretation of the world, the structure of society, who can or ought to be able to make what decisions, and so on. Ultimately, the form gives way to the politics. The UAW has a particular form for the same reason they have lengthy provisions about collective bargaining: they have a root theory about how best to defend and help the working class and that theory is at odds with communism.

So, we have an organizational form on the one hand, and politics on the other. The organization is the means to accomplish the ends you seek, and the political ends that liberal union bureaucrats seek are collective bargaining, contracts that track in new members, land nice lump-sum payouts from profit sharing, and the like. At a minimum, through the AFL-CIO, the idea runs that collective bargaining is the best way to defend and attack for the working class. The classic line from the IWW or some leftists is that the bureaucratic unions are just a means for the bureaucrats to make money, and that the best method is committee-driven direct action; strikes and street protests are what show the workers' true power. This approach bends the stick too far.

After all, isn't collective bargaining all that unions do anyway? Even the Local 8 longshore workers in the IWW in the 1910s were engaged in a *type* of collective bargaining. They made agreements with the employers, independent of whether or not these were drawn up on paper or arbitrated by a state agency. What mattered was that *every member of the local was educated about the agreement and ready at a moment's notice to enforce it through industrial action.*

The ideology of the bureaucrats is a reformism that collapses toward liberalism. It isn't simply a question of the existence of the bureaucrats, but the nature of their grip on the organization and the ideas they offer to the members and public to justify this arrangement. These ideas are *political positions* of the bureaucrats.

The dominant ideology of the labor bureaucracy in the United States has been a form of liberal, as opposed to republican, democracy. These political positions matter because they undergird the organizational forms and strategies adopted by union leaders, distributed among members and new recruits, and lay the foundation for close links between labor and the Democratic Party. But why has this ideology persisted through generations? One interpretation is this: bureaucrats in capitalist society in general are prone to liberalism in the philosophical sense, that is, their fundamental political commitment will be to discrete individual rights, with property rights at the center, rather than democracy and equality. This is because bureaucracy is a form of private property in skillset or office. Of course, most US unions are still more 'democratic' than the US government. This is partly because they have to be, in order to mobilize enough workers to strike at least for initial recognition, but also because of the ideology of the core organizers and members. So the particular form of organization is tempered and guided by the political outlook of those who found, organize, and accompany its development. To demonstrate this point, we can briefly look at the respective constitutional preambles of the UAW and the IWW. Though they have some similarities in governing form (and many divergences) their preambles couldn't be more different. Let us first look at the preamble of the UAW:

> We hold these truths to be self-evident; expressive of the ideals and hopes of the workers who come under the jurisdiction of this INTERNATIONAL UNION, UNITED AUTOMOBILE, AEROSPACE AND AGRICULTURAL IMPLEMENT WORKERS OF AMERICA (UAW): "that all men and women are created equal, that they are endowed by their Creator with certain inalienable rights, that among these are life, liberty and the pursuit of happiness. That to secure these rights, governments

are instituted among men and women, deriving their just powers from the consent of the governed." Within the orderly processes of such government lies the hope of the worker in advancing society toward the ultimate goal of social and economic justice.

The precepts of democracy require that workers through their union participate meaningfully in making decisions affecting their welfare and that of the communities in which they live.

Managerial decisions have far-reaching impact upon the quality of life enjoyed by the workers, the family, and the community. Management must recognize that it has basic responsibilities to advance the welfare of the workers and the whole society and not alone to the stockholders. It is essential, therefore, that the concerns of workers and of society be taken into account when basic managerial decisions are made.

Note that while the UAW asserts the 'rights of workers' as individuals in a democracy to have their voices heard, they don't deny the right of management to manage, or the right of the idle rich to exploit. This is reflective of a liberal-democratic outlook, amenable to workplace reconciliation and democracy through collective bargaining. Note too that the material basis for the labor bureaucracy is this regime of collective bargaining. Their salaries are based on their success in this field.

On the other hand, the IWW's preamble asserts that *class struggle* is the governing mode of the worker-capitalist relation:

The working class and the employing class have nothing in common. There can be no peace so long as hunger and want are found among millions of the working people and the few, who make up the employing class, have all the good things of life.

Between these two classes a struggle must go on until the workers of the world organize as a class, take possession of the means of production, abolish the wage system, and live in harmony with the Earth.

...It is the historic mission of the working class to do away with capitalism. The army of production must be organized, not only for everyday struggle with capitalists, but also to carry on production when capitalism shall have been overthrown. By organizing industrially we are forming the structure of the new society within the shell of the old.

377

The world outlook of the IWW argues that class struggle shapes the relationship between worker and employer and that this will be the case until the workers get organized and overthrow the capitalist system of governing society. Unions play the role of defending the day-to-day needs of the class, educating workers about the class struggle, and drilling them into fighting shape.

The point here is that there is a limit to the 'structuralist' critique of form. At a certain point, the question becomes what the political commitments of those advocating the particular form are, and what political commitments are *implied and accomplished through* an organizational form. This needs to be viewed with respect to particular classes in society. Petit-bourgeois professionals and bureaucrats are perfectly happy with an organization investing significant powers in salaried officials and staff. Their role as lawyers, managers and the like endears them to the 'noble' applications of their skills in helping out the little guy. This is where the anarchist critique of the bureaucracy has a truth: the position of the bureaucrats does incline them to act differently.

However, this is true for the bureaucrats *as a class*. The form this self-interest takes hold ideologically or politically is through reformism. Anarchists say that reformism creates bureaucrats. While this true in the sense that particular reforms may create funding for more bureaucrats, it elides the origin of the given reform in the efforts by particular forms of bureaucracy *organic to capitalism:* the lawyer, the manager, the organization official, and so on. The development of reformism as an ideology is a cyclical process. The bureaucracy requires justification, both for the bureaucrat's own conscience, and because the bureaucrat must get *some* support in wider democratic society, especially among the workers.

The flip side of this is that *some* bureaucracy is necessary as a result of the uneven development of capitalism. That is, given the social division of labor based on property relations, bureaucrats do often possess necessary skills for the growth and survival of the organizations they serve in. The dilemma then is one of whether or not an organization is *governed by* or governed in the *interests of* bureaucrats.

Unfortunately, the IWW is also reliant on Robert's Rules of Order, as are most bureaucratic unions. While parliamentary procedure is important, it can be a tool to monopolize discrete knowledge of procedure and rules for the benefit of bureaucrats to maneuver and control the process. This can be seen in both the UAW and the IWW. Anyone who has been to an IWW convention, or has paid attention to the internal controversies in the organization, can attest to the fact that it is often the case that for a democratic decision to be taken, it has to overcome technical machinations of process. On the other hand, when faced with a seemingly obscure set of unfamiliar rules, the membership response is to simply pressure the parties involved or move the debate away from substantive disagreements and toward interpersonal conflict. The IWW lurches from one political-crisis-as-personal-dispute to the next. Effectively, by adhering haphazardly to some fundamental principles of bourgeois law, the IWW has crafted a situation where every member must be a bureaucrat in order to participate. Rather than abolish bureaucracy, it has abolished any other role for members.

New members elected to leadership positions in the IWW often find themselves in the middle of a handful of formally and informally organized cliques in the union with overlapping members based on political positions. This is to be expected in any large organization, but the goal of the structure of an organization then should be to overcome the dynamic that this fosters, frustrating any resolution of political disagreements to the effect of frustrating effective growth and successful execution of the organization's program. Instead, the mechanisms of the organization should *draw out and clarify* political distinctions in order for the membership to become openly apprised of them and to select at congresses or conventions the positions they support.

This is not to let officers off the hook. As leftists tend to point out, there are indeed problems with the leadership of unions. This leadership is exceedingly liberal-democratic in their outlook, which leads to definite problems with respect to organizational form and strategy. As anarcho-syndicalists often point out, business unions invest too much in PR campaigns, officer salaries, and staff-driven symbolic stunts. And as some left communists argue, the tendency toward the development of and coup by bureaucracy is persistent in capitalist society, both in parties and in unions.

But our response to these problems shouldn't be abstention from unions *as a principle* or the simplistic alternative of a change to a structureless organization. Instead, we should fight for changes in the governing structures and principles of unions. That means putting the maximum program of socialism in the constitution and making structural changes that allow for transparency and democracy, as well as preparing workers to govern as a class.

A central aim of communists in unions, then, is to build working class power on the shop floor. Workers without a union are barely citizens, as a result of their inability to enforce any rules in their favor at work. Mere inputs for business, workers are disposable, replaceable, and reminded of it daily. The employers exercise a dictatorship over their employees. Workers are completely at their mercy. The union offers an alternative. It offers a democratic formalization of the workers' own authority. Organized workers are prepared to act in unison. They're educated and aware of their rights on the job as a result of the work done by the union. They can stand and look their exploiters in the eye as equals, not in terms of bourgeois law, but in terms of *power*. They can begin to assert themselves as the inheritors of the fight for human emancipation.

Democratic, member-led bargaining has a history of wrenching contracts from employers that got better wages, better conditions, and restricted the grievance procedure to a short process, or, better yet, enabled workers to strike or take action to resolve grievances rather than do so through arbitration. Judith Steppan-Norris and Maurice Zeitlin have shown this in their work on left-led unions during and after WWII and the nature of their contracts and constitutional provisions. The authors write, with regard to "pro-labor" contract provisions:

> The crucial finding is that the comparative odds of the Communist camp's local contracts being prolabor, as opposed to those in the anti-Communist camp, were consistently much higher on each provision, as follows: The comparative odds that the contracts did not cede management prerogatives were 4 to 1 in favor of the Communist camp; that they did not have a total strike prohibition, 7 to 1; that they were short-term, 4.6 to 1; that they had a tradeoff, 11 to 1; that a steward had to be present at a grievance's first step, 11 to 1; that the grievance procedure had no more than three steps, 3 to 1; and that each step had a time limit, 2 to 1.[6]

That rank-and-file and socialist-led unions are more effective is also demonstrated by the aforementioned Local 8 of the Marine Transport Workers' Union in the I.W.W.'s past. They were able to wrench concessions from their employer and enforce workplace conditions through direct action. If the employer tried to bring in a work gang of non-union members, the work delegates would ensure that the workers immediately ceased work and walked off the job.[7] Communists must work to break the reliance of workers on their employers and reorient them to the institutional forms of union self-government: the shopfloor committee, the Industrial Union Local, and the International

6 Stepan-Norris, Judith, Zeitlin, Maurice. *Left-Out: Reds and America's Left-Led Unions*. Cambridge: Cambridge University Press, 2002.
7 Mouvement Communiste and Kolektivně proti Kapitálu. "100 Years Ago: The Philadelphia dockers strike and Local 8 of the IWW." Libcom, July, 2013. http://libcom.org/library/100-years-ago-philadelphia-dockers-strike-local-8-iww-mouvement-communiste-kolektivn%C4%9B-pr

Union. This means employing the known committee-building tactics, promulgated by the IWW Education committee and groups like Labor Notes, in the context of an explicitly Socialist effort to rebuild organized labor, across the country. Workers without a union rely on the mercy of their employers. They are subjected to an undue and illegitimate authority, forced to produce profit for shareholders and lavishly wealthy corporate executives in order to get crumbs with which to get by. The only way to fight back is to build up the democratic self-reliance of the working class into fighting unions where workers can make collective decisions to wage class war effectively.

Democratic organizing gets concrete results. Union workers are involved not just in voting for a union that will bargain on their behalf, but in fighting for their own demands through group effort, and will not soon forget the power that they build, nor ignore the broader political opportunity to use such power. Witness the West Virginia teachers' strike that violated the law successfully, not just for narrow demands for teachers, but for demands that would benefit teachers and the public. Union organizing prepares the working class to take part in politics, at the granular level. As Eugene Debs once argued:

> Voting for socialism is not socialism any more than a menu is a meal. Socialism must be organized, drilled, equipped and the place to begin is in the industries where the workers are employed. Their economic power has got to be developed through efficient organization, or their political power, even if it could be developed, would but react upon them, thwart their plans, blast their hopes, and all but destroy them.[8]

For these reasons, union organization raises the dignity and education of the workers themselves which opens up the possibility of workers becoming a conscious and active political constituency, fighting for their own interests. Rather than dependent wage

8 Eugene V. Debs. "Danger Ahead." Marxist.org. January 1911. https://www.marxists.org/archive/debs/works/1911/danger.htm

workers, union workers build independence by organizing to fight the employers at work. They force the boss to treat them with dignity and exert equal power in that relationship.

Building this alternative democratic authority calls forth all the intense political questions we face under capitalism. The workers' chains are money, and workers spend most of their living hours for it and end up losing it through high prices, rents, and loan scams, all the while facing disenfranchisement through corruption and bureaucracy. As the bosses, challenged by workers, call on the state to enforce their interests to the exclusion of the workers, they will be forced to ask: who does the state serve? Who ought it serve? And how do we break these chains? Bureaucratic unions often have to deal with these political questions even as their power weakens. But they retreat into the realm of lobbying bourgeois politicians in ways that are often extremely ineffective.

In stark contrast to this, communists must pose a two-pronged strategy. First, there must be a commitment to organizing workers based on democratic principles of membership, sovereignty, and transparency. This entails organizing the working class to use direct action for enforcement of every demand and contract provision as well as a bargaining strategy aiming for zero-recognition of management rights and no-strike clauses, and lengthy grievance procedures as far as possible. Second, communists must augment this work with political work mobilizing votes to repeal Taft-Hartley. Taft-Hartley is a federal law which requires advanced notice for strike action wherever workers hold a contract with an employer. This severely limits workers' abilities to enforce their contracts through direct action and attain the robust and fighting labor movement we aim for, outlined above.

Prioritizing the repeal of Taft-Hartley means making it a litmus test for any candidate for office. This further requires that there be a broad enough base of support in elections, but ultimately in the streets and at work, as the French Yellow Jackets and West Virginia teachers have shown. Politicians are important to help spread our ideas and eventually pass reforms, but street protests and industrial actions are key to winning and keeping them. This is why the need to begin organizing now is so important. Communists must combine the day-to-day fight to rebuild the labor movement with a national political campaign to repeal Taft-Hartley. In turn, Taft-Hartley's repeal will bolster union organizing and help strengthen the fight for a communist movement based on democracy.

OF COURSE LABOR LAW ADVANCES THE CLASS STRUGGLE

Anton Johansson

July 29, 2020

Anton Johannsen argues that labor law is a terrain of class struggle that can only be ignored at our own peril.

Nick Walter, labor organizer, IWW member, and writer at Organizing.Work recently published an article titled "Labor Law Doesn't Advance Class Struggle, The End." As the pithy title indicates, the argument is that labor law isn't the answer for developing and pushing forward the class struggle. Walter's solution? *Direct action.*

But Walter's piece suffers from a simple error — a *reification*. To reify is to mistake an abstract category for something concrete. In Walter's case, he mistakes the particular or concrete labor laws which he dislikes for the abstract category "labor law" as a whole. This mistake is a function of ideology. Walter's outlook is straightforwardly in line with that of Organizing.Work (OW from now on) more broadly, which is a kind of mass strike anarchism. This outlook views the law, and thus politics and the state, in a reified way — as nothing more than a distraction from direct action militancy. Unfortunately, this position is ahistorical and ends up contradicting itself in practice. As a result, either the theory or the practice must change.

The error is simple: If I claim all sandwiches are bad because they have mayonnaise, I'll be hard-pressed to justify any future obsession with paninis. Even if I drag out the point that the paninis I eat don't have mayonnaise, I've contradicted my initial claim: how can paninis be good if all sandwiches are bad? This silly illustration highlights the logical problem of Walter's position. What he's really after is *better* labor law, not the abolition of labor law. He even says as much: "I was arguing for concerted activity protections like exist in the United States and the people from a few of the unions were uneasy about that."

This is also the clearest sign that not all labor law is the same. Walter *likes* Section 7 of the Wagner Act. This section protects the right of workers — *union or not* — to engage in certain protected, concerted activity while at work. But then is this too a mere snare? How does this hold back militancy? If anything, it appears to *protect* it. So does all labor law hold back militancy or not? Walter's position reveals itself to be a contradictory one.

I suspect that such a frank contradiction of the essay's central argument is a result of Walter's practical focus. He's less concerned with abstract consistency than with what works in practice. That's not a completely unreasonable position to have as a labor organizer, but unfortunately that approach will *lead to* contradictions in practice. In order to describe the contradictions that Walter's pragmatic unionism runs into with the law, it will help to establish the outlook of OW more clearly.

OW is a blog edited by organizers in the IWW. It is not an official publication of the union, but is instead an effort by organizers to share stories about organizing and discuss strategy. OW's outlook is basically that of the anarcho-syndicalists and left-wing of the Second International, which dedicated its efforts to organizing for mass strikes:

> Many of us — the contributors and editor — are members of the
> Industrial Workers of the World. As a model, we favor "solidarity

unionism": a committee of workers in the workplace democratically running the union effort, and taking direct action "on the shop floor" to get what they want.

This is to be expected, as the IWW was firmly in this camp from its founding throughout its peak.

The outline of the mass strike strategy is that any sort of revolutionary movement of workers for a new society requires the development of the working class's ability to carry out mass, militant direct actions to force their demands. This much united the Left-Wing and Center of the Second International.[1] Where the Left goes one step further than the center is its claim that direct action and direct action alone *is* the class struggle, and everything else a mere reaction to or distraction from this activity.

Walter and other authors at OW have argued that unions ought to exist primarily to develop this direct action capability. Where unions don't develop direct action, they fail, no matter the bread and butter gains, changes in working dynamics, and power at work. In contrast, where unions develop militancy, they are winning, no matter their size, their reach, and barring only outright manifestations of backward political development (racism, misogyny, etc.). For example, Walter writes:

> CUPW won pay equity in the 1970s through massively disruptive strikes that were less than legal. The Employment Insurance we have in Canada is as much due to a riot in the 1930s in Regina, Saskatchewan than any other single factor. Class struggle is how we turn around the current state of things. We certainly don't win every time. But if you count up all the wins over a long period you notice that you make a staggering amount of progress that way, far more than you would from all of the best legal minds and an infinite budget for arbitrations and board hearings.

Here, Walter is equating mass direct action to class struggle. Indeed, this position has been put forward in multiple OW pieces.

---

1 Indeed, it united the IWW left-wingers like Big Bill Haywood with IWW and SPA Centrists like Eugene Debs.

In "Canvassing is not Organizing," Ray Valentine argues that political organizing isn't the same as union organizing. But this isn't what the title says. The title argues that a tactic which even unions have used to success is somehow not organizing at all. The author's *real* point is that "The techniques of political campaigns are designed for a particular purpose, and that purpose is not organizing the working class to wrest control of social institutions and emancipate itself." This outlook appears to suggest that because capitalists use the "technique" of drafting organizational rules, any working-class movement must avoid drafting rules. After all, we're told that because a *capitalist* might organize a political party and campaign for support, the very practice is therefore off-limits. This is absurd on its face. The state is the *preeminent* social institution in capitalism, and politics is a struggle between classes over which controls the state. Valentine's claim that politics is *not* a struggle over which class controls social institutions falls on its face.

Walter's own review of Jane McAlevy's "No Shortcuts" argues that electoral politics are a snare for union members and leaders. Elections distract union members and leaders from the use of their "subversive" and most effective element — *direct action*:

> This subversion of the existing economic logic of society is why the right wing and business interests hate unions so much. But when unions break from this logic and enter conventional politics they find themselves drawn onto a terrain where they have no power. It allows union leaders (and high-profile union staff) to believe there is something other than economic disruption that gives them a bargaining chip. It's not that union leaders can never have political influence inside the halls of power; it's that the only influence they can have comes from laying down the source of their power.

The essay at hand provides other evidence of this outlook. Walter is critical of card check, first contract arbitration, and imposing certification where the employer's illegal anti-union conduct tainted the election process. Why? Because these laws: "exist ... to condition a certain kind of union into existence." What kind of union? A union that *dampens* militancy rather than developing it. The unstated premise is that developing workers' capacity to carry out militant direct action should be the primary focus of unions.

I want to note that I agree with Walter's criticisms of the limits to card check and first contract arbitration. They pose the danger of conferring the responsibility of being a union without having developed local leaders and organizing capacity. But what are we developing militancy and direct action capacities for? To *change social relations*. As noted above, the purpose of politics is to *contest* sovereign power. I'm using the concept of sovereign power here because I share anarchists' reasonable skepticism of the capitalist state. But politics doesn't have to be solely about winning control in the extant state. Politics can also be about reshaping that state, or even fighting for a new form of state, or sovereign power, altogether. Ultimately it is the *form* of state power that determines which class is sovereign. This need to contest the sovereign power in society — the need to engage in *politics* as such is connected to Walter's aversion to legal issues: the law is, after all, what the state enforces.

In contrast to the Left, the Center of the Second International saw mass direct action as a necessary but insufficient component of class struggle.[2] One purpose of the political realm of the class struggle is to *shape the legal terrain* upon which direct action can take place. Viewed in this light, questions of law lose their mystification — no law vs. some law becomes a debate about

---

2 See, for example, E. Debs: "Socialism must be organized, drilled, equipped and the place to begin is in the industries where the workers are employed. Their economic power has got to be developed through efficient organization, or their political power, even if it could be developed, would but react upon them, thwart their plans, blast their hopes, and all but destroy them." "Danger Ahead," marxist.org, 1912. https://www.marxists.org/archive/debs/works/1911/0100-debs-dangerahead.pdf

what kinds of laws and *why?* Though the state form determines which class is sovereign, the nature of *class* sovereignty is such that it must permit some degree of freedom, even for members of the oppressed and exploited classes. This is a key feature in the distinction between slave societies and class societies — the exploited in a slave society aren't juridical persons, but instead, property. In contrast, workers are, constitutionally speaking, afforded the same rights in the state as professionals, small business owners, landlords, bankers, and capitalists. However, in the regulation of *private affairs,* the state may reach out and accommodate landlords here, or tip the scale against workers there. Thus, the state's structure — its working rules, the limitations it puts on the actions of workers on the one hand, and capitalists on the other — determines which class is sovereign *in and through* its regulation of 'civil society' or contracts, agreements, and disputes between supposedly 'non-state' individuals.

Here is where the contradictions come in for Walter. It is illusory to fight for a *purely* state-independent labor movement in the US and it always has been. The first reason this is true is that it isn't *practical.* The second reason is that there is no historical basis for doing so.

In theory, Walter wants to develop the independent power of the working class to take militant direct action to force demands. But in practice, almost every I.W.W. campaign touted on OW has availed itself of the National Labor Relations Board and filing Unfair Labor Practices (ULPs) in order to pressure employers to cave. When we file a ULP we're asking a well-salaried government official to investigate the illegal conduct of the employer. We're asking that they bring the weight of the government to bear on employers, that eventually this weight either leads to a decision and enforcement against the employer or, more likely, ends up pressuring the employer to settle.

This isn't a marginal question if you argue that working-class power comes from direct action and self-organization *alone.* It's a straightforward contradiction. According to this logic, if we really want to develop mass working-class militancy, then we need to eschew ULPs, the NLRB and everything related. We would also be expected to eschew even the rare federal injunctions by courts *against* employers and many other court-ordered judgments. But why? What business does a *class struggle (read "direct action") union* have relying on the bourgeois state?

After all, any reliance on the state and its force against the bourgeoisie supposedly *legitimates* the state as an institution that executes law on behalf of workers. Even if it is merely a court injunction, it deludes the workers into thinking that they can expect the state to go to bat for them again in the future.

However, Walter and OW *clearly do not* advocate for a pure anti-state position. And the reason they don't do this is the same reason Walter doesn't actually believe all labor law holds back class struggle: it wouldn't be *practical*. Indeed, beyond his praise for Section 7 rights, Walter admits to even minor benefits from contracts: "A union contract can represent a more favorable legal terrain for certain disputes but more often than not it's also about writing down a series of trade-offs." It is indisputable that *all law* is just words on paper or in the mouths of lawyers and judges without *enforcement*. But when we assume an anti-legal political posture, we cut off opportunities to utilize court-ordered enforcement of the law and any discussion and development of a strategy to do so. Walter's position foments the type of disengagement that leads to less favorable enforcement of the law and as such, it is a retreat from a theater of class war.

The second contradiction is that labor history provides us with legal reforms that have allowed or encouraged the development of class struggle. It is common for leftists, especially mass strikists and anarchists to point to the 1933-34 strike wave as a spontaneous or at least purely *direct action* affair. The strike wave was an explosion of working-class militancy and organizing which then led to the emergence of legal reforms that certified in law the rights won in practice. But this is a convenient fiction. The 1933-34 strikewave wasn't spontaneous. The central flaw of this claim is that it assumes what it needs to explain. Why did workers decide to engage in strikes across the country in 1933?

It wasn't just prior organizing. Yes, for years prior to the passage of the Norris LaGuardia Act, Socialists, Anarchists and Communists were involved in every type of organizing — boring from within and forming independent unions.[3] This organizing developed the radicals as militants within the labor movement, earned them respect, and set them up to take advantage of the economic crisis that would emerge at the turn of the decade. But most of their organizing attempts were rolled back and crushed. The historical reality is that it was a set of *political-legal* reforms that triggered the strike wave. The passage of the Norris-LaGuardia and the National Industrial Recovery Act was the 1-2 punch that opened up space for workers to lead the 1933-34 strike wave.

The first punch was the Norris LaGuardia Act, which restricted the power of federal courts to issue injunctions in labor disputes. For decades, US courts had granted and enforced injunctions against striking workers. Anytime an employer was faced with mass direct action of workers, they would go to the courts and argue that this action violated the rights of the employer.[4] Senator George Norris and Representative Fiorello LaGuardia were two progressive Republican politicians that pushed their bill through Congress in 1932. The act laid out 9

---

3 Zeitlin and Steppan Norris, p. 33-39.

4 "Injunctions are orders issued by courts to prevent unlawful interference or threatened interference with the rights of the plaintiff, who relies on one or more of the following principles of equity — that the damage would be irreparable, that the remedy at law through criminal prosecution is inadequate, that the interference threatens to continue, or that a multiplicity of actions would be involved" https://library.cqpress.com/cqresearcher/document.php?id=cqresrre1950032500

things Federal courts could no longer enjoin, including striking, joining a union, supporting striking, and publicizing about an ongoing strike or labor dispute. This restraining of federal district and appellate courts helped tie up the hands of the judiciary for the 1933 strike wave.

The second punch was the National Industrial Recovery Act. Passed in 1933, the NIRA included this language:

> ...employees shall have the right to organize and bargain collectively through representatives of their own choosing, and shall be free from the interference restraint, or coercion of employers of labor, or their agents, in the designation of such representatives or in self-organization or in other concerted activities for the purpose of collective bargaining or other mutual aid or protection[.][5]

This is Section 7(a) of the National Industrial Recovery Act. It would go on to form the basis for the same Section 7 of the Wagner Act which Walter finds so appealing. This second blow pushed the capitalist class off-balance enough that millions of workers began streaming into unions — liberal, communist, anarchist — whichever, in the wider context of the depression. These two pieces of legislation opened up space for workers across the country to assume an offensive posture against employers. In other words, they *advanced the class struggle*.[6]

These contradictions suggest two things. First, it suggests that the position of OW and Walter is untenable because it is contradictory *in practice*. This in turn calls for the OW types to reconcile their outlook, either going for the deeply impractical position of being 'purely anti-state' or merely adjusting their ideology to reflect their practice — admit that the law *can* at

5 Section 7(a) of the NIRA. https://www.ourdocuments.gov/doc.php?-flash=false&doc=66&page=transcript

6 See Davis, Mike. *Prisoners of the American Dream: Politics and Economy in the History of the US Working Class*. London: Verso Book, 1986. pp. 55-69. Davis rightly describes 1933-37 as the "highwater mark of the class struggle in modern American history[,]" and notes that it "start[ed] with the 1933 'NRA' [National Recovery Administration, set up by the NIRA] strikes...."

times "advance" class struggle. That is, law can be useful for workers and unions to use because it can allow us to leverage power to limit *some* conduct of the employers. OW accepts this in practice but rejects it in theory.

Second, if it is true that the state can be leveraged to help worker organizing, then it suggests that *class struggle is not exclusively limited to direct action by workers.* Then we should develop a clearer theory of the law and a better strategy for using it *in practice.* We should ask what ways of using the legal arena comport with our principles.

I suspect this will be a hard pill to swallow. I have a great deal of respect for Walter and the writers and editors of OW, but by reducing the class struggle to direct action, they risk painting themselves into a corner. The argument goes like this: We need a revolution in our political system. Political change happens with class struggle. Class struggle is the mass direct action of the working class. Then, either *true* politics is limited to direct action *or* if politics is defined to go beyond direct action (voting in elections, running campaigns for legal reforms) then politics is merely a distraction from class struggle. The result is that as long as this outlook is hegemonic, we will continue to organize on legal terrain laid down by our class enemies, instead of winning reforms that shape the terrain in ways advantageous to the working class. If we don't start thinking politically and legally, we'll remain cornered in our defensive posture indefinitely — and labor's last fifty years of body blow after body blow will continue, unabated.

Trust the Bridge That Carried Us Over: The Failure of Operation Dixie, 1946-53

Veronica Darby
August 12, 2022

Veronica Darby presents a history of the Congress of Industrial Organizations' (CIO) failed seven-year-long attempt to organize the Southern United States.

On March 3rd, 1946, the Congress of Industrial Organizations (CIO) announced that they were starting Operation Dixie, an ambitious new plan to organize unions in the South. The headline story boasted that the CIO's leaders were making "plans for one of the greatest organizing drives in labor history," organizing "millions of unorganized workers in Southern states" placing "special interest" on the region's booming textile industry.[1]

This ambitious vision to bring unions to the anti-labor South would not succeed. Starting in 1947, barely a year into the organizing drive, the CIO began to narrow the scope of the project, reducing the number of states it included, as well as the resources they devoted to it. It would carry on in limited capacity for a few years, until the CIO formally ended Operation Dixie in 1953, as they prepared to merge with their former rivals in the American Federation of Labor (AFL). At that time, the CIO had won just

---

1 "CIO Launches New Organizing Drive" in *The CIO News*, vol. 9, no. 10; March 4th, 1946; pg 7. https://archive.org/details/mdu-labor-057493/page/n113/mode/2up.

64 of the 232 union elections they contested through Operation Dixie, less than 30%, and had actually lost members in the coveted textile industry.[2]

The failure of such an ambitious and necessary project should worry those of us building the labor movement today. It raises a number of difficult questions, including: Can you organize on a mass scale in an area hostile to labor? What does it take? In this article, I will lay out a history of the project and discuss a number of its structural failures, while contrasting it to successful labor organizing taking place in the same time and region. From this, I intend to draw out some key understandings for contemporary labor organizers, and provide a nuanced look at an often forgotten part of US labor history.

King Cotton

To understand Operation Dixie, we must begin with the context of the Southern textile industry. The textile industry was the engine of growth for the post-Civil War Southern economy. When Northern troops left the South at the end of Radical Reconstruction in 1877, politicians and businessmen sought to regain the power that they had lost during Reconstruction. Big landholders began to consolidate their holdings, accumulating the capital necessary to open textile mills. At the same time, tenant farmers and small land holders faced decreasing agricultural profitability. For example, from 1880 to 1920, in Durham County, North Carolina both the average size of a farm and the percent of farmers owning their own land shrank by a third.[3] In response to this agricultural crisis, families began looking for ways to supplement their income. Many families began sending members of the family, typically women or children, to earn money in factories during the off-season for the farm. This only exacerbated the instability of small farms, and gradually fami-

---

2 Minchin, 32, 1.
3 Janiewski, 25.

lies abandoned farming entirely, with all members of a family taking jobs in textile factories and moving into company owned housing adjacent to the mills. Employment grew nearly 10 percent per year from 1870 to 1900, as textile mills and surrounding mill villages sprung up across the South in a crescent-shape across the Southern piedmont from Virginia to Alabama.[4] Most mill jobs and mill villages were exclusively white. Black workers were confined to poorly-paid non-production jobs, such as cleaning, and resided in segregated neighborhoods.

Starting in 1929, the Communist Party of the United States (CPUSA) began to send organizers to these Southern textile mills. Many of these CPUSA organizers were labor movement veterans, including many who had organized in the textile industry in the North. This effort was part of the larger CPUSA labor strategy. At their 1929 convention, CPUSA rejected their previous strategy of boring from within the established trade unions of the American Federation of Labor (AFL). Instead they developed a three-pronged labor strategy: organizing their own unions through the Trade Union Unity League (TUUL), while also maintaining opposition movements within certain AFL unions, and creating looser industrial leagues where they were not strong enough to launch full-fledged, national industrial unions.[5]

The reasons for this new CPUSA strategy were twofold: first, it reflected their own experiences working within the AFL and the establishment American labor movement, which was often hostile to their political aims. Secondly, this labor strategy was influenced by Communist International (Comintern) policy. During this time, known as the Third Period, the Comintern saw worsening economic conditions globally as leading to an imminent world revolution. To the Comintern, this necessitated

4 Salmond, 2.
5 Victor G. Devinatz, "The CPUSA's Trade Unionism during Third Period Communism, 1929–1934," *American Communist History*, vol. 18 no. 3-4 (2019), 251-268, DOI: 10.1080/14743892.2019.1608710.

a decisive break with Trotskyism, reformist socialism, and liberalism to build independent Communist bodies, including labor unions.

In the textile industry, the CPUSA established the National Textile Workers Union (NTWU), an independent, Communist alternative to the AFL's United Textile Workers of America (UTW) which did not have a large presence in the South. Many of the NTWU organizers had experience in the Northern textile industry, but conditions in the South were more difficult than those in the North. Southern textile workers made 30-50% less than their Northern counterparts, and many many Southern textile workers lived in mill villages, which were tightly surveilled by management. Furthermore mill owners were often very well connected, and had influence over local police and politicians, leaving many workers rightfully afraid of retaliation.[6] Despite the challenging conditions, NTWU organizers encountered agitated workers, due to deteriorating working conditions, including the "stretch out," a speed up of work with no raise in pay. This allowed NTWU to have some success in organizing unions and collective actions. Most famously, NTWU organizers and rank and file leaders organized a strike at the Gastonia Mill in North Carolina in 1929 that garnered national attention. Although the Gastonia strikers lost, it was a great display of worker power and solidarity, with one young striker describing it as "the first time I'd ever thought things could be better."[7]

As mass strikes in the AFL and the rise of industrial unionism in the CIO began to achieve success in depression-era America, many TUUL members and organizers rejoined the mainstream labor movement. At the same time, the Comintern began to prioritize coalition work in response to the rise of fascism. Combined, these two trends spelled the end of the TUUL, and by extension the end of NTWU, along with other Communist-led

6 Salmond, p. 2.
7 Salmond, p. 33.

unions in the South, some of which were having great success organizing black workers.[8]

A Whole New Atmosphere

At the start of WWII, union density was very low in the textile industry, as the CIO's Textile Workers Union of America (TWUA) had made very limited gains in the South. Mill owners took advantage of this, and expanded their textile operations, which were booming from wartime demand in the non-union South. Here, mill owners were able to offer raises to textile workers while still keeping labor costs lower than in the union North.

This rapid growth caused an increase in living standards along with a rise in wages for textile workers. Where a generation earlier a Southern textile worker lived in a company owned shotgun shack, by the end of WWII, textile workers were renting or buying homes and modern consumer goods, such as refrigerators and cars. Junius Scales, a North Carolina Communist, described these post-war mill towns as "a whole new atmosphere."[9]

Thus, when the CIO launched Operation Dixie in 1946, they were up against a rapidly changing industry which presented a number of new challenges. Many TWUA organizers struggled to make inroads with textile workers, who remembered the harsh union-busting of the 1920s and 1930s and feared retaliation from mill owners. The small, rural towns where textile mills were located were functionally company towns, and mill owners were often tightly connected to politicians and police, making many workers afraid to get on management's bad side. Furthermore, there was often limited outside employment in these towns, particularly for women, which further heightened workers fears of retaliatory firing. Another issue in the post-war

---

8 For a more comprehensive study of the third period and popular front amongst Black workers in Alabama, see Robin D.G. Kelly's classic *Hammer and Hoe*.

9 Minchin, p. 22.

landscape was that many of the luxuries creating this "new atmosphere" were purchased on consumer debt, leaving workers both more prosperous and precarious than their counterparts a generation earlier.

These issues would be in conflict with the strategy laid out for TWUA organizers by the CIO under Operation Dixie. The CIO pursued an aggressive, strike-heavy strategy, which required significant resources and buy-in from workers. These strikes were typically over recognition or refusal to bargain a first contract, rather than unfair labor practices or subsequent contracts in established unions. Strikes on these issues are more risky, as losing the strike means losing union recognition. Many of these strikes did fail, in part because of the strength of the textile industry and power of mill owners. During a 1948 strike in Siler City, North Carolina, a TWUA organizer reported that "none of our people broke ranks" but that the company "had been advertising [for scabs] all throughout the state, South Carolina, and Virginia" and "company representatives spent everyday after work, and every weekend, scouring the countryside for scabs."[10] Furthermore, "manufacturers often supported each other in their efforts to oust unions."[11] Thus, TWUA was pushing strikes against well-resourced bosses willing to do whatever it took to keep unions out, which would have been challenging for even the most skilled organizers and passionate rank-and-file. The negative results of this strategy were twofold. Firstly, it drained both human and financial resources to pursue frequent strikes, limiting TWUA's organizing capacity. Secondly, most of these strikes occurred before reaching a first contract, leaving workers without union representation.

The CIO also placed great emphasis on winning as many elections as possible, and then moving on to the next shop, rather than staying to continue to organize for a first contract.

10 Minchin, p. 76.
11 Ibid, p. 75.

According to a report in *Textile Labor*, one year into Operation Dixie, there were 30 textile mills where an election was held but no contract had been reached.[12] As one TWUA organizer put it, "winning an election is not enough."[13] Bargaining a first contract is a slow and arduous process that typically takes months, if not years. Without support, many union campaigns fall to management pressure or lose momentum during this process. Furthermore, if a contract is not reached in the first year, a decertification vote can be held, ending the union entirely.

These challenges of rising wages and living costs, and the limitations of a strike-heavy strategy can clearly be seen in the 1951 Danville, Virginia textile strike. Dan River Mills had been a long time leader in textile worker organizing, and had set industry standard pay patterns throughout the region. Two weeks into the 1951 strike, more than half of the mill's white workers had crossed the picket line. A week later, two-thirds of white workers had crossed the picket line, weakening the union's position to the point that management successfully decertified the union later that summer.[14] Many workers cited high living costs as the reason they had to cross the picket line, a strain that only increases with the length of the strike. For this reason, long strikes require significant worker buy-in and union infrastructure, both of which were vulnerabilities for the TWUA.

The failure of the strike also demonstrated how such a strike-heavy strategy was not suited to the conditions of the Southern textile industry. Norris Tibbetts, a business agent involved in running the strike said that "we made our first mistake in trying to make noises like an industry-wide union, which we are not. We have about 15% organization in the South. A solid strike among what we have organized would affect only 10% of the cotton industry."[15] Strikes in low-density industries makes it easier

12 Ibid, p. 69.
13 Ibid.
14 Ibid, p. 134.
15 Ibid, p. 117.

for management to hire replacement workers, and causes less of an impact to the overall industry. For these reasons, the TWUA strategy was ill-suited to the conditions of the post-war South. The CIO's strategy borrowed fully from their Northern experience, where union density was much higher and the textile industry did not exert as much control on the economy, rather than a strategic response to the Southern industry. As Tibbetts put it, "Who the hell are we to act like the UAW and GM?"[16]

The Dan Mill strike reveals another trend: differences between the response of white and Black workers. When a majority of white workers at Daville Mills crossed the picket line, 95% of Black workers remained on strike.[17] While the textile industry was still significantly white by 1946, labor shortages during the war led to more Black workers entering the industry. Roles within the textile industry were still typically segregated, and Black workers still received lower pay.

Union locals, including the Danville TWUA, were also segregated. For Black workers, segregated union locals provided a strong opportunity to represent themselves, and in Danville led to the election of an interracial board of union officers and convention delegates, and no doubt contributed to their strength on the picket line.[18] However, these gains in some segregated locals did not extend to the whole of TWUA activity in the South. Integrated TWUA locals did not offer equal treatment for Black workers with many locals across the South limiting the voice of Black workers in the union, while others barred them from attending altogether.[19] While some TWUA locals did provide advancement for Black workers and improve race relations, TWUA, or even the CIO, does not appear to have had a strategic effort to address the racial question in their organizing, or to advance racial equity through their work.

16 Ibid.
17 Ibid.
18 Ibid, p. 137.
19 Ibid, pp. 140-1.

Given the challenges of the textile industry, it is necessary to consider why the CIO continued to focus on this industry specifically. During WWII, the CIO grew in membership thanks to the expansion of their key Northern industries as a result of defense demand, including steel and automotives. As the defense industry expanded they entered into an agreement with AFL and CIO leaders to adopt a higher wage scale across the board, in exchange for the union leaders signing a national no-strike deal during the war. However, this "labor peace" did not extend to non-union shops, creating a "Southern differential" in wages. CIO leaders began to fear that manufacturers would move South to circumvent the unions, undercutting the membership and dues of the CIO and weakening the union.

Organizing textile factories was thus a strategy selected by the CIO based on numbers: as the largest industry in the South it had the potential to shore up CIO membership. By 1945, 80% of the textile industry was located in the South, but only 20% of workers were under a union contract, proving a potential for massive CIO membership growth.[20] A series of articles in *The CIO News* in February 1947, the one-year anniversary of Operation Dixie, demonstrated the CIO's focus on membership growth, highlighting 64 union elections and 14,500 new members in Texas, 22,000 new members in North Carolina and 18 election wins, and 40 New Locals In Tennessee.[21] This membership focused choice not only overlooked the challenges of the textile industry outlined above, but also failed to examine what industries in the South were seeing organizing success.

---

20 Ibid, p. 1.

21 "Texas Leads in CIO's Southern Campaign" in *The CIO News*, vol 10, no. 6, February 10th, 1947, 10. https://archive.org/details/mdu-labor-057494/page/n93/mode/2up; "22,000 Join CIO in North Carolina" in *The CIO News*, vol 10, no. 8, February 24th, 1947, 19. https://archive.org/details/mdu-labor-057494/page/n125/mode/2up; "40 New Locals in Tennessee" in The CIO News, vol 10, no. 5, February 3rd, 1947, 6. https://archive.org/details/mdu-labor-057494/page/n77/mode/2up.

Civil Rights Unionism

Many of the industries seeing organizing success in the post-war period were those with a large concentration of Black workers. Wartime industry growth had opened up more industrial jobs to Black workers, which were typically segregated, with management giving Black workers the most dirty and dangerous positions first. Although as the war went on, the labor shortage would open up more positions to Black workers. Regardless of their position, Black workers faced harassment, lower wages, and lower job security. In response, they began staging numerous wildcat labor stoppages, such as sit downs and walkouts, for better treatment. White workers responded with "hate strikes" or labor action to reject what they saw as a challenge to their working conditions in the form of Black labor militancy. Combined, this led to an average of over 10 strikes a day in both 1944 and 1945.[22]

These shop floor tensions between Black and white workers remained high after the end of the war, as management sought to return to the pre-war labor status quo. Evelyn Bates, a Black worker in the Memphis Firestone Tire plant, summed this up, saying that "When the men started coming home from the war, they started giving the men their jobs back, 'cause it was a man's job... A lot of the Black womens they laid off. They didn't lay you off according to seniority,' cause you didn't have no seniority over white womens."[23]

Management used racism to turn white workers against union campaigns. A 1949 strike at Memphis Furniture, one of the largest employers of Black women in Memphis, failed as a result of this anti-union tactic. One Black striker did not "remember seeing any white people [on strike or] at the union hall" during the events of 1949, and said that the almost entirely white up-

22 Lipsitz, p. 87.
23 Honey, p. 192.

holstery department "kept on working as long as they could."[24] With white workers continuing to work and refusing to join the union, Memphis Furniture was able to successfully break the strike, despite the fact that "five times, maybe ten times" more Black people worked for the company than whites.[25]

Similarly, an early effort by the CIO's URW (United Rubber Workers) to organize Firestone workers in Memphis failed because "all of the back voted for the CIO" but "the whites didn't buy it."[26] One Black Firestone worker, George Holloway, states that only about 10% of white workers, who made up roughly 65% of the plant, attended a CIO action at this time.[27] After the failure of the CIO to organize a wall to wall union in the plant, the AFL organized white tradesmen which according to fellow Black Firestone worker Clarence Coe "was good for them," but left unorganized Black workers vulnerable.[28] However, "the CIO promised us [Black workers] justice" and so Black workers continued to organize, with renewed determination inspired by the loss. Holloway recalls that Black workers would "slow down work so the whites couldn't make any money" until "the whites needed the Blacks to cooperate to make changes in the plant."[29] URW succeeded in winning recognition at Firestone in 1942, only because they were able to agitate amongst Black workers and refuse to capitulate to white workers' racism, instead showing them how the management exploited the racial division to harm all workers. URW would go on to be an engine for integration in the plant post-War, while many CIO efforts at that time would stall after being unable to organize interracially.

After the end of the TUUL in 1935, when CPUSA reoriented towards working within the CIO, CIO unions with a Com-

---

24 Ibid. p. 117.
25 Ibid.
26 Ibid. p. 71.
27 Ibid. p. 69.
28 Ibid. p. 79.
29 Ibid. 71.

munist presence were the most successful in organizing Black workers. The Food, Tobacco, and Agricultural Workers (FTA) are a particularly notable example, as they articulated a Communist-influenced strategy and a political vision including the role of race in worker exploitation. As one tobacco worker in Winston-Salem, North Carolina put it: "They are using the poor whites to whip the [Blacks] and the [Blacks] to whip the poor whites. If the poor whites sort of get out of line, they fire them and put [Blacks] in their jobs and they do [Blacks] the same way."[30] Communist organizers in FTA understood this relationship between race and exploitation, and used it to successfully organize amongst Black workers, connecting with their experiences of discrimination in the workplace.

Roger Korstad refers to this as "civil rights unionism," where Black workers used union organizing as a vehicle to fight racial oppression. The Communists offered a program that resonated with Black workers because it "had an explanation of events locally, nationally, and worldwide which substantiated everything they had felt instinctively from their experience. It was right in their guts."[31] By showing that the union "meant business on racism," FTA was able to effectively recruit and mobilize Black workers for political action.[32] The Communist approach saw shop floor grievances as one aspect of a larger issue of racial capital, and sought to organize in the community as well. In Winston-Salem, this included participation in local elections and fighting for better housing, through FTA's strong political action arm. The FTA also began to organize tobacco leaf workers in the Eastern part of the state, who were impoverished, rural, seasonally-employed and overwhelmingly Black. The FTA success with tobacco leaf workers is particularly remarkable, as agricultural workers are excluded from the National Labor Relations Act, which led the TUUL to

30 Korstad, 97.
31 Ibid. p. 275.
32 Ibid.

focus on other sectors of workers.[33] The strategy of the Communist-led FTA contrasts strongly with that of the CIO, who targeted industries based on their ability to provide new members, rather than a political analysis of worker exploitation that extended beyond the workplace.

The Communist-led Farm Equipment Union (FE) was also able to break into the South in the post-War era, organizing the International Harvester (IH) plant in Louisville, Kentucky. FE's organizing materials clarified their political vision: one FE pamphlet read "the southern bosses have for generations played Negro against white, and white against Negro" and "there was a direct connection between this and the fact that Southern workers were the lowest paid in the country."[34] This analysis that connected low wages to larger conditions of inequality resonated with the IH workers in Louisville, Kentucky. There, the Southern differential was particularly poignant, as International Harvester workers in Indiana, just across the Ohio river from Louisville, were making substantially more. FE remained committed to industrial organizing and integration, and was able to win recognition for a interracial, wall to wall union in 1947.[35] Like FTA, FE would take these struggles beyond the shop floor, challenging segregation throughout Louisville, both in sanctioned union activities and via rank-and-file action.[36] Through their militant shop floor organizing, FE demonstrated to their members that advancement could only be made when all workers acted in solidarity, which they took beyond the gates of International Harvester.

An End To Wildcatting the Year 'Round

FE, however, faced another challenger beyond the bosses: the United Auto Workers (UAW), who made a national effort to take

33 Devinatz, 17.
34 Gilpin, p. 165.
35 Ibid. p. 162.
36 Ibid. p. 219.

over FE's shops, stretching the FE's resources thinner, which would prevent them from expanding further into the South. FE would lose the Memphis International Harvester plant to UAW. At the time, FE had only three organizers in the city, and their successes and headquarters were far away in Chicago.[37] UAW rejected the militant, Communist vision of FE and instead promised an era of cooperation between management and labor, known as "labor peace." Walter Reuther, the architect of this strategy, promised "the end of wildcatting the year 'round," referring to the unrest of the 1940s.[38] Despite this vision of cooperation, and a large staff and resources, UAW struggled to win the Memphis Harvester plant. International Harvester refused to recognize the union by acclamation for two years, forcing a vote, and continued to exert pressure, resulting in a first contract that included limited gains.[39] The Communist strategy that UAW attacked was producing wins that UAW could not get on their own, leaving them to snatch up members through takeovers.

Of course, UAW was not alone in aggressively attacking Communist-led unions. Following the declaration of the Popular Front in 1935, and the end of the TUUL, Communists began to bore from within the CIO, and maintained a strong leadership presence in a number of unions. In addition to the aforementioned UFW, FE, and FTA, this included the United Electrical Workers (UE), International Longshore and Warehouse Union (ILWU), and the Mine, Mill, and Smelter's Union (Mine Mill). Communists in these unions continued to organize with a theory of class struggle, understanding that "only through solid unity of all workers can people hope to meet with the large companies on even terms. Anything to disrupt this unity, be it color prejudice, religious prejudice, or what have you, is a crime against all working people."[40] Rank and file leaders in these unions became

37 Honey, 157.
38 Gilpin, p. 218.
39 Honey, p. 157.
40 Gilpin, p. 212.

"fellow travelers," adopting this organizing outlook without officially joining the Party.

Reuther, by contrast, envisioned a post-War America that "represented an attempt to expand labor's involvement in helping to administer production in the name of industrial peace and the general welfare."[41] This vision of shared prosperity, built on cooperation and high production levels, required a reduction in work-stoppages and quelling labor-management hostilities. Thus, in 1945, Reuther tried to channel striking GM workers "toward the pursuit of demands that the company could easily afford to grant, while diverting attention away from more complex local grievances concerning working conditions."[42] This conciliatory attitude and effort to reduce strike activity led *The FE News* to claim that "an anti-union corporation yells for help and Walter Reuther comes running to the rescue."[43]

Of course, fears about Communists in the labor movement, and the expansion of union membership during WWII went far beyond Reuther. When workers launched a series of strikes across a variety of industries in 1945 and 1946 to demand that wartime gains in employment and wages remain, anti-labor and anti-Communist politicians seized the opportunity, and amended the National Labor Relations Act (NLRA) to rollback workplace protections. This law came to be known as the Taft-Hartley Act, and among its provisions was a requirement that all union leaders sign affidavits stating that they were not members of CPUSA.

This resulted in a large campaign of redbaiting during the years of Operation Dixie, as anti-Communist politicians, union leaders, and bosses used alleged involvement in the Communist Party to oust radical leaders and turn workers against their unions. The CIO seized on Taft-Hartley's limitations on Communist involvement in the labor movement to purge the radical

---

41 Lipsitz, p. 109.
42 Ibid. p. 110.
43 Gilpin, p. 179.

unions from the CIO, including FE. The expulsions would set the stage for a series of raids that took place over the next couple of years as the AFL and CIO sought to take over shops previously held by Communist unions.

Anti-Communist Consolidation

In the South, this became particularly tense, as politicians proclaimed that all unions were Communist, and that Communists were on a path toward integration, which would lead to the subjugation of the white race. Mississippi Senator James Eastland went as far as to warn of the "harlemization" of the country. Statements like this were clearly meant to stoke fears about race, which were used to divide the labor movement.[44]

This would have disastrous consequences for radical unions in the South. In 1946, the business friendly *Winston-Salem Journal* ran a front page story entitled "Communist-Union Collusion Is Exposed in City; Appeal is Made to [CIO President Phillip] Murray for Labor Leadership." This story appeared three weeks into a pivotal strike by the FTA at R. J. Reynolds, just four days after the passage of Taft-Hartley. The author clearly sought to vilify the Black-led union by warning that communists were "creating class hatred as a preliminary to violence, and finally chaos," and further alleged that this influence went all the way to CIO president Phillip Murray, ironically an active anti-Communist.[45] The fearmongering about unions was so great that when FTA sought out donations to support the strike, the Fellowship of Southern Churchmen refused to do so without

44 Woods, Jeff. *Black Struggle, Red Scare: Segregation and Anti-Communism in the South, 1948-68.* Baton Rouge: Louisiana State University Press, 2004. p. 43.
45 Leon S. Dure Jr., "Communist-Union Collusion Is Exposed in City; Appeal is Made to Murray for Labor Leadership." *Winston-Salem Journal*, May 19th, 1947. Courtesy of North Carolina Special Collection, Forsyth County Library, Winston-Salem, NC.

first going on a "fact-finding" trip to determine the nature of Communist activity in the union.[46]

With business owners, the liberal establishment, and the mainstream labor movement, all agitating white workers against the union, the FTA was in danger. In 1949, the AFL and CIO contested the FTA's representation at the Reynolds plant, part of a series of raids across industries. FTA retained a high level of loyalty amongst Black workers, adopting the slogan "trust the bridge that carried us over," highlighting the level of trust that their militant organizing on and off the shopfloor fostered amongst Black workers. However, the AFL and CIO divided the white vote, paving the way for "no union" to win a plurality. The final count: No union 3,426; FTA (independent) 3,323; Tobacco Workers International Union (TWIU-AFL) 1,514; United Transportation Service Employees (UTSE-CIO) 541.[47] Despite the CIO's stated goal of promoting unionism in the South through Operation Dixie, their anti-union campaigning cost workers their union.

Of course, business owners were not content with the defeat of the Communist unions, but continued to attack all organized labor as Communist. During the UAW campaign at the Memphis International Harvester plant, a local paper accused Walter Reuther of being a socialist.[48] Such public attacks were clearly meant to both deter union membership and ostracize those associated with the union.

While themselves being decried as Communists, anti-communist CIO leaders continued to use anti-Communism to consolidate their power. In Memphis, local CIO officials attacked UFWA leaders after the 1949 Memphis Furniture Strike, while national leaders purged Communists from the union nation-wide. This left the majority-Black local without officials

---

46 Korstad, p. 330.
47 Ibid. p. 407.
48 Honey, p. 157.

dedicated to organizing and building an interracial movement.[49] Thus the CIO's attacks on Communist unions not only weakened the position of the left-wing unions, but of the entire labor movement in the South.

"A Body Without Spirit"

Given the role of redbaiting in attacks on Operation Dixie and other post-war labor organizing, it is worth examining the big picture consequences of the hunt for Communists in the labor movement, in order to put the decline of Operation Dixie into context.

Following the end of WWII, the US government turned against their wartime ally the USSR, and escalated their pursuit of domestic radicals. At the same time, CPUSA did not return to a TUUL-style strategy of pursuing independent union work. Instead, party members continued to work within the CIO. For many CPUSA members, this meant remaining in unions like the FTA or FE, which were part of the CIO but were widely known and regarded as Communist. However, these unions lacked the support from the Party that the early CIO and TUUL had during the third period, such as the Labor Defense Fund (ILD). Without the institutional support of the Party, members were vulnerable to both the government and the CIO's attacks on Communists. Radicals who remained in the labor movement at this time often took steps to distance themselves from the Party and refused to disclose their membership status, primarily remaining active as independents and individuals, not as Party members.

By the late 1940s, many Communists had successfully "bored from within" to bureaucratic leadership positions within the CIO. After the 1947 purge of Communist unions from the CIO, Communist labor leaders were either in the left-wing unions that were both underfunded and under attack, or subservient to the anti-Communist leadership that had expelled their

49 Ibid. p. 181.

comrades. In only a decade, the radical element within the CIO went from a prominent force to fighting for its life.

This had, of course, come at great expense to the CIO as well. Purging Communist unions removed a million members from the CIO, and weakened the position of the remaining unions. This would leave a CIO that was, as one former member put it, "a body without spirit."[50] To consolidate power and out-maneuver the radical unions, the CIO merged with the AFL in 1953, ending nearly two decades of rivalry. The AFL-CIO would continue to raid shops of the now expelled Communist unions, and all the independent, Communist unions but UE and ILWU would fall in the coming years. Neither of these remaining Communist unions had a strong presence in the South, and the Communist unions who did fell quickly: FE would fold in 1955, FTA in 1954, Mine Mill in 1967. Only UFWA would hold on past 1970, albeit in less radical form, lasting until 1987. It is unsurprising then that union density in the United States peaked in 1953, as the CIO failed to mount an organizing strategy to compensate for the losses in the Communist-controlled unions, and limitations imposed by Taft-Hartley.

The CIO also quietly ended Operation Dixie in 1953, leaving an extremely weak track record. If the CIO hoped to defeat the Southern differential, they failed. If the CIO undertook the project out of a commitment to building a long lasting workers' movement, they failed. If the CIO wanted to consolidate membership and power, they won, but because they had joined forces with their historic rival to defeat many of the very organizations that propelled their initial rise to power, not because they defeated the Goliath of the Southern textile industry.

Conclusion

By any measure, members added, union votes, strikes, or contracts, Operation Dixie did not succeed in taking on King Cot-

50 Boyer and Morias, p. 361.

ton. What are we to make of such a failure?

Historian Barbara Griffiths, in the only monograph on Operation Dixie, called the project "the legacy of a Northern encounter."[51] In other words, the CIO did not develop an organizing strategy for the South, and was unprepared for the hostile labor and race relations there. Without a larger political analysis motivating their actions, the CIO was unable and unwilling to engage in the long term struggle needed to make inroads in the South. Instead, they left TWUA organizers with a half formed strategy that could not support the needs of workers, even when they were agitated and in favor of the union. The focus on union elections and recognition strikes stretched resources thin, and meant that every loss on the picket line set the campaign back.

At the same time that the TWUA was struggling, Communist labor organizers in the post-war South developed a strategy and accumulated some victories, both on the shop floor and against segregation. Their success reveals a fundamentally different approach to the purpose of a union. For the Communists, a union was an inherently adversarial tool to improve the lives of workers and change society. Communist unions were committed to interracial unionism and organizing Black workers, which gave them an agitated base for their campaigns, while advancing a progressive agenda of "civil rights unionism."

But as the Cold War took off and turned its attention towards domestic radicals, Communist organizers received the ire of business, government, and mainstream CIO leadership. This left them with dwindling resources with which to fight against fierce raids and decertification campaigns, on top of their usual labor struggles. In summary, we can identify four key failures in Operation Dixie: the strength of the textile industry in the South, an overemphasis on recognition strikes and union elections, a weak stance on integration and the race issue, and the rise of anti-Communism.

51 Griffith, Barbara. *The Crisis of American Labor: Operation Dixie and the Defeat of the CIO*. Philadelphia: Temple University Press, 1988, p. 169.

All of these decisive issues remain for labor organizers to grapple with today. As organizers take on Target, Amazon, and Starbucks, they are facing business owners just as politically powerful and connected as the mill owners of the New South, and just as ready to bend and break the law. Organizers must keep these conditions in mind as they develop their strategy. Similarly, they must be prepared to take on the long fight; bargaining a first contract can take just as long, if not longer, than organizing for a recognition vote. It is our duty as organizers to inoculate against the idea that the campaign ends at an NLRB vote, and to encourage our coworkers and comrades to build patience. Finally, we as socialists need to articulate a political vision for the power of the workers' movement, not only to address issues in the workplace, but throughout the system. This vision and our organizing must be dedicated to fighting inequality, or else risk both alienating our allies and fueling our enemies' attacks.

Milton Keynes UK
Ingram Content Group UK Ltd.
UKHW020741190124
436321UK00015B/685